Leading Philosophers and Educators

1500AD	1900AD

Descartes (1596-1650) Berkeley (1685-1753) Royce (1855-1916) Butler

Kant (1724-1804)

Harris (1835-1909) Ger (187

Ho (18

Hegel (1770-1831) Horne (1874-1946)

Bacon (1561-1626) Locke (1632-1704) Herbart (1776-1841) Whitehead (1861-1947)

Rousseau (1712-1778) Spencer (1820-1903) Russell (1872-1970)

Pestalozzi (1746-1827) Froebel (1782-1852) Montessori (1870-1952)

Bacon (1561-1626) **Rousseau (1712-1778)** Pierce (1839-1914)

Locke (1632-1704) Darwin (1809-1882) Hall (1844-1924)

Comenius (1592-1670) James (1842-1910) Dewey (1859-1952)

Comte (1798-1857) Parker (1837-1902) Kilpatrick (1871-1965)

More (1478-1535) St. Simon (1760-1825) Marx (1818-1883) Counts (1889-1974) Illich (1926-   )

Fourier (1772-1835) Freire (1921-   )

Owen (1771-1859) **Dewey (1859-1952)** Brameld (1904-   )

Buber (1878-1965) Sartre (1905-1980)

Jaspers (1883-1969)

Heidegger (1899-1976)

Kierkegaard (1813-1855) Marcel (1889-1973)

Hobbes (1588-1679) Comte (1798-1857) Pavlov (1849-1936)

Watson (1878-1958) **Skinner (1904-   )**

Moore (1873-1958) Ayer (1910-   )

Russell (1872-1970) Peters (1919-   )

Wittgenstein (1889-1951) Ryle (1900-1976)

PHILOSOPHICAL FOUNDATIONS OF EDUCATION

SECOND EDITION

Howard A. Ozmon

Samuel M. Craver

Charles E. Merrill Publishing Company
A Bell & Howell Company
Columbus Toronto London Sydney

Published by Charles E. Merrill Publishing Company
A Bell & Howell Company
Columbus, Ohio 43216

This book was set in Souvenir.
Production Editor: Kathy Vance Gillis
Cover Design Coordination: Will Chenoweth

*The authors wish to thank Dr. William Friedman for his help in preparing the
chart used in this book, as well as Mrs. Patti Aignor for typing the manuscript.*

Library of Congress Catalog Card Number: 80–83169

International Standard Book Number: 0–675–08049–5

Printed in the United States of America

1 2 3 4 5 6 7 8 9 10—86 85 84 83 82 81

CONTENTS

FOREWORD

This book is a revision of *Philosophical Foundations of Education* and was written to be used as a text in a beginning course on educational philosophy. The term, *foundation,* implies a base or structure on which something is to be built. The implication fits this text. The content of the book is sturdy enough to help support the beginning student who is developing a point of view about schools and their role as a societal institution. The text explains different philosophical positions according to the best-known schools of thought and the individuals who advocate the tenets of these schools.

An important question to raise about a text on the philosophy of education is whether or not it also provides help for the student to engage in reflective and personal thought in addition to learning about existing philosophies and philosophers. The reader should be able to engage in logical thought and discourse if the text provides appropriate information and background, and the test of whether or not this role is fulfilled lies in the content of the text with respect to the following: clear explanations of philosophical viewpoints, articulate language that is technically precise, identification of important issues, and an opportunity for the reader to cultivate knowledge from which straightforward and systematic thinking will emerge. An effective text should clarify rather than confuse, enlighten rather than perplex, expand alternatives rather than shrink options, and supply the reader with more confidence to discuss contemporary questions through familiarity with the past. The first edition of *Philosophical Foundations of Education* was successful in large measure because the authors provided these essentials. In this revised edition, Ozmon and Craver have surpassed their initial effort by editing for more clarity, sharpening explanations, and adding topics that strengthen their first text immeasurably. Despite the temptation to revise a text with only a few cosmetic changes, particularly a text that has been welcomed by the profession, the authors have made noteworthy and substantial additions or revisions. A few examples illustrate these improvements.

The discussion of Plato has been expanded, and excerpts from his *Republic* have been added to make this primary source readily available to the reader. The position of the realists has been keyed to more of the contemporary concerns such as the alleged moral decay of modern societies and the questions of pupil achievement in basic learnings and teacher accountability. The chapter on pragmatism has added selections from "My Pedagogic Creed" by Dewey, and *Democracy and Education* has been more heavily quoted to give the student firsthand information to study and analyze. The concern of the reconstructionists for the future is expanded by additional references to Alvin Toffler, Ivan Illich, and the enduring position of George Counts. A careful selection has been made of these ubiquitous, nontraditional, and crusading views for changing the status quo of schools (or eliminating them altogether). The chapter on existentialism has additional writings from Sartre's *Existentialism and Human Emotions* and Van Cleve Morris's concerns about subjectivity, paradox, and anxiety. More content is included in the chapter on behaviorism from Skinner's *Beyond Freedom and Dignity*. In the chapter on analytic philosophy, the writings of Jane Martin on the distinction between "knowing that" and "knowing how" are provided. Though the first edition contained much of the information in the present text, these additions have added more depth and examples to the narrative. The revisions have been blended smoothly into the text without disrupting the previous narrative and organization.

The changes listed are only representative and alone would constitute a marked strengthening of the text. However, a new chapter (Chapter 8) has been provided that will be a welcome part of this current edition. Chapter 8 ties the previous chapters together and stimulates the reader with useful and provocative questions and comments that help to focus on the essence of the text. One major part of this chapter includes synoptic statements about each philosophical position and offers an extended discussion on the relationships among theory, philosophy, and practice. Some view the relationships among these three as symbiotic, yet others find little relationship between any two of them. The reader will have an opportunity to relate individual and personal viewpoints to those of others and examine different positions about theory, philosophy, and practice. Chapter 8, an excellent capstone to the book, serves as a bridge to the Epilogue, an overview of the role of philosophy from the past to the present.

The current edition, as was true of the first edition, is neither doctrinaire nor manipulative. The student who wants to learn about different philosophical positions through writings that are neutral and objective will profit from this edition. Ozmon and Craver rendered a service to the field by writing their first edition. They have made another major contribution through their careful and responsive rendition of this revision.

Donald E. Orlosky
Professor of Education
University of South Florida

PROLOGUE

It could be said that philosophy of education began when people first became conscious of education as a distinct human activity. While primitive societies did not have long-range goals and the complex insights we find in modern times, and while they did not have the analytical tools that modern philosophers have, even primitive education involved a philosophical attitude about life. Man had a "philosophy" of education long before he knew what it was or what it could mean in terms of educational development.

In earlier times, education was primarily a means for survival. Children were taught the necessary skills for living. Gradually, however, people came to use education for a variety of purposes. Today, education may be used not only for purposes of survival (though recent ecological studies show that it may still be used for such purposes) but also for better use of leisure time and refinements in social and cultural life. As the practice of education has developed, so also have theories about education, but it has become easy for us to overlook the connection between theory and practice and to deal with practice apart from theory. We may be in a dilemma today because we seem to be more involved with the "practical" aspects of education than we are with an analysis of educational theory and its connection with practice. What we need is not only better theorizing about education, and better methods, but also a concerted effort to join the two. Thinking about education without consideration for the "practical" world means that philosophers of education become web spinners of thought engaged in mere academic exercises. On the other hand, tinkering with educational methods without serious thought results in practices that have little substance or meaning.

A study of philosophy of education seems imperative today, for we are in a critical era of transition. There has always been change, but seldom at our present accelerated rate, creating in many individuals what Alvin Toffler has called the sickness of "future shock." In such an age, it is easy for people either to embrace more and more change with little thought to eventual consequences or to resist change and keep old values no matter what. Educational philosophers, regardless of the particular theory they embrace, suggest that the solutions to our problems can best be achieved through critical and reflective thought.

In one basic sense, we can say that philosophy of education is the application of philosophical ideas to educational problems. We can also say with equal force that the practice of education leads to a refinement of philosophical ideas. From this viewpoint, educational philosophy is not only a way of looking at ideas but also of learning how to use them in the best way. No intelligent philosophy of education is involved when educators do things simply because they were done in the past. A philosophy of education becomes significant at the point where educators recognize the need to think clearly about what they are doing and to see what they are doing in the larger context of individual and social development.

It is interesting to note that many major philosophers have written about education. Probably this occurs because education is such an integral part of life that it is difficult to think about not having it. The human is not only a tool-making being but also an education-making being. For in human history, education has been closely connected with the development of civilized beings. Thinking about life in general has often been related to education in particular, and education has often been viewed as a way of bringing a better life into existence. Someone once remarked that the purpose of philosophy is to get people thinking about what they are doing. If this state of affairs had a wide application, we might not need philosophy as a separate discipline at all. We need to think about what we are doing, whether it be in engineering, science, or anything else. It is only to repeat a truism to say that many of the world's problems result from poor thinking.

The study of philosophy does not guarantee that individuals will be better thinkers or educators, but is does provide a valuable base to help us think more clearly. Traditionally, the word *philosophy* has meant the pursuit of wisdom. This is not to imply that philosophy provides answers; rather, it offers an avenue for serious inquiry into ideas and traditions. Philosophers have been acute observers of the human condition and have articulated their observations in ways that are instructive. Educators are not only aided by a careful and systematic approach to ideas that philosophers have fostered, but also they can gain inspiration from philosophy and develop new insights into educational problems. While educators may choose to disregard the philosophical approach to problems, in doing so, they ignore a vital and important body of knowledge or thought.

One of the roles of philosophy has been to analyze critically the intellectual tools of any given era. Another role has been to suggest alternative methods of thinking. Still another has been to develop sensitivity to the logic and language we use in constructing solutions to problems in education and society. It is possible to trace the history of ideas by tracing the development of philosophical thought. Philosophy is descriptive of some of humanity's best thinking, our collective wisdom so to speak. It could be said that to think philosophically is to reflect upon who we are, what we are doing, why we are doing it, and how we justify all these things.

Education is involved with both the world of ideas and the world of practical activity; good ideas can lead to good practices, and good practices can lead to good ideas. In order to behave intelligently in the educational process, the educator needs the things philosophy can provide; that is, understanding of thinking processes and the nature of ideas, the language we use to describe education, and how these may interact with practical affairs. For the educator, philosophy is not simply a professional tool but a way of improving the quality of life because it helps us gain a wider and deeper perspective on human existence and the world around us.

One of the problems that seems to disturb many people about the study of philosophy is the fact that philosophers disagree. However, it is often from such disagreement that the search for new social, political, economic, religious, and educational systems has developed. One can find philosophical disagreements on practically every issue. It may be that those who look upon disagreement as a negative factor and prefer clear-cut answers overlook basic concerns about the development of civilization; that is, if there had been no disagreement about ideas, purposes, and methods, we probably would still be back in the Stone Age. Disagreement has often brought about change, and it still continues to do so.

Many differences in educational viewpoints have arisen because of the changes that have occurred in society. We know that personal and social development often necessitate changes of both viewpoint and behavior. As societies have developed, there has been the need to change working ideas or methods. Of course, this will probably always go on. It would be gratifying if all the educational changes we have today resulted from people reflectively examining issues and clarifying direction, but we know that this is not particularly true. Many past events that affected social and cultural developments were largely out of human control, and although people often tried to study them, they had little control over the developments events would take. Even more to the point, all too many social and cultural changes that man could have controlled have wreaked havoc in history. Consequently, much philosophizing in the historical context was done after the fact — and events ran their own capricious course. However, as people sought to develop more control over such forces through education, they were faced with the problem of dealing with control in some direction. This has led to questions of whether or not the controls do more harm than good. For example, today we can systematically control individuals and groups to some extent through psychological conditioning in the educational process, but whether such control is good or bad is debatable. Thus, the need arises for philosophical activity and debate to examine the value of controls to uncover the basic assumptions of those advocating or rejecting these controls, and to analyze the meanings and concepts involved and what they hold for human life.

One of the problems in dealing with philosophy of education is that people often come to it looking for *the* answer to debatable issues, and when they fail to find it, they reject philosophy in the same way a spoiled child might reject a parent who does not have all the answers. A tragic error is made in rejecting philosophies because they are old or because they are difficult to understand. There are those who question the validity of studying philosophy at all, saying it has no "relevance"; but many of the problems philosophers have dealt with — the roles of individual and society, the purposes of education, the meanings of terms and concepts, and so on — are very relevant today.

Practically everything we do in education reflects some point of view. That view may not be readily apparent to the pupil, the parent, or the educator. It may be that the point of view is unclear, disjointed, and a loose collection of ideas, all lumped together without much logic or coherence. What is needed in such cases is a clarification and sorting out, but because many educators lack skill with the tools that promote clarification, they continue to drift aimlessly in a sea of rhetoric and patchwork panaceas. Indeed, there does seem to be some deep-seated feeling of drift today, and much of the drift of modern education attests to this aimlessness and helplessness. Attempts to solve these problems usually end up in a chaotic jumble of programs and superficial bickering among ideological camps. "Practical" educators assume we should throw out philosophy and get on with the task at hand. The problem with this "practical" outlook is that its advocates approach educational problems with the same old attitudes and remedies. They assume they can read the face of an intelligible universe unencumbered by "ivory tower" intellectual schemes. That outlook itself is a "theory," a set of assumptions for which the last word has yet to be said.

It seems that the educator, like everyone else, is caught up in his own humanity. There is no certainty with regard to all facets of life in *any* known approach to education, for the perfect approach has not yet been invented. We are left with the necessity to *think* about what we do, to attempt to reason out and justify our actions so that they are coherent, meaningful, and directed toward desirable educational results.

This book is designed as an introductory text, one that assumes the reader has had little or no formal study of philosophy of education. The approach taken in the following pages is meant to develop understanding of the varied philosophical nature of educational issues rather than encourage mere acceptance or imitation of philosophical schools of thought. The intent of the book is to show how philosophical thought — even thought contained in ancient philosophies — has influenced education and still continues to do so. There are those who maintain that no logical connections can be made between formal philosophical systems and the practical world of education; that is, what some philosopher says has no necessary logical connection with what ought to be done in a practical educational context. This may be true, but it has not kept both philosophers and educators from making the attempt. There may well be no logical connection between, for example, Plato's view of the good society and his construction of educational means to achieve this society. Many people have made such connections (whether logical or otherwise), however, and educational programs have been developed and instituted, drawing heavily upon Plato and other philosophers in the process. This can be seen in recommendations put forward concerning the aims and purposes of education, curriculum content, teaching methods, and in many other areas of educational endeavor. Although Plato lived over 2000 years ago, what he and his contemporaries said and thought about life and education still influence us, even if we are unaware of it. Part of the task of the student of education, then, is to become familiar with leading philosophical ideas about education and to understand the impact they have had and continue to have on our thinking.

Certain ideas and recommendations about education have a great deal of influence today, particularly in shaping public attitudes about "back to the basics" and "moral values" education. People who advocate such things may lack any philosophical sophistication or knowlege of the origin of these notions, but philosophers have often recommended certain "basics" and "values" that figure in these recommendations. Philosophical systems and recommendations are part of many of the "working ideas" and traditions of our society today. Many of us assume these things to be true and obvious without any clear idea of why. Thus, we may blindly accept a large number of educational recommendations without knowing whether they are justified or not. The student who seeks to become an educator needs to be informed about these ideas and traditions in order to sift through rhetoric and argument and to reach a more intelligent understanding of the current scene.

This book is organized in a way that enables the student to develop a coherent grasp of various philosophies of education. Chapters 1 through 7 give the historical development of a given philosophy, its current status, how it has influenced education, and a critique of its leading ideas. Taken together, these chapters provide a chronological development of the philosophy of education. In addition, each chapter is followed by short selected readings from major philosophers who have been identified with that philosophy, The selections have been carefully chosen to illustrate leading themes in each chapter. They have also been selected to furnish students with primary source materials of sufficient length and depth to provide some firsthand acquaintance with leading works in the field. These selections are meant to give insight without overwhelming students and to whet their appetite to do further reading in philosophy of education.

The last two chapters vary from this format. Chapter 8 examines the nature of theory, leading ideas derived from philosophy, and the interrelationships of theory and practicality in today's world. The Epiloque investigates the contemporary scene in philosophy of education and attempts to shed light on the so-called hiatus that exists between some contemporary philosophical positions. A Selected Bibliography and Index are included at the end of the book. In the authors' opinion, the format is organized in such a way to allow the student to attain a comprehensive and critical view of the philosophical foundations of education.

Many contemporary philosophers of education maintain that an "ism" or "school-of-thought" approach is unsuitable. Others insist that it is one of the best ways to help students come to some comprehension of the broad scope of the educator's task. Still others prefer a school-of-thought approach because they believe there is one philosophy superior to all the others, and the best way to show this is by way of comparison. The authors embrace none of these, although we show some sympathy for the comprehension argument. We think the school-of-thought approach is useful for several reasons, although we clearly recognize that it is not the only way. Our intent is to encourge students to explore a number of philosophical points of view about education for the purposes of becoming informed about what has been done before, what is going on now, and what possibilities they may pursue in their further development as professional educators. First, an examination of schools of thought is helpful in introducing students to the variety of philosophical thought on education. The quest must not stop here however, for to do so makes philosophy of education simply a matter of "receiving" ideas from the past and gives the impression that all worthwhile thinking on education has already occurred. At the same time, it is both good and helpful for students to understand how the field has developed, both past and present.

Second, the present approach helps students to establish foundations for future growth, for there are many sound and useful ideas from the past upon which to build. Students who attempt to understand education in the philosophical sense are certainly handicapped if they have no knowledge of what has been done and perforce try to reinvent old educational "wheels." Third, the approach involves more than just schools of thought but includes critiques of each school and a general exploration of the contemporary division that exists between traditional and contemporary philosophy of education.

Finally, it should be noted that the text is intended as an introduction to the philosophical foundations of education and does not pretend to invite converts to any particular philosophy. It is designed for the student of education and is not written for the advanced student in philosophy. The book attempts to be comprehensive in an introductory way and lays no claims to advanced specialization in philosophy of education. Numerous and excellent works are readily available for that purpose, many of which are cited in the chapter bibliographies and the Selected Bibliography.

The study of philosophy of education can be an exciting and challenging venture. It allows us to encounter some of the great and enduring ideas of human thought. It enables us not only to understand what has gone on in the past in education but also to develop the kind of perspective and intellectual tools that will help us deal with the educational problems of today and the years ahead.

Socrates
(469-399)

Plato
(427-347)

Plotinus
(205-270)

St. Augustine
(354-430)

IDEALISM

Idealism is perhaps the oldest systematic philosophy in Western culture, dating back at least as early as Plato in ancient Greece. Of course, there was philosophy and there were philosophers before Plato, but it was Plato who developed one of the most influential philosophies dealing with education.

Generally, idealists believe that ideas are the only true reality. It is not that all idealists reject matter (the material world), but rather they hold that the material world is characterized by change, instability, and uncertainty, while some ideas are enduring. Thus, idea-ism might be a more correct descriptive term for this philosophy than idealism. However, we must guard against over-simplification and attempt to get at a fuller and more wide-ranging understanding of this complex philosophy

In order to achieve a more adequate understanding of idealism, it is necessary to examine the works of selected outstanding philosophers who are usually associated with this philosophy. No two philosophers ever agree on every point, so to understand idealism or any other school of thought properly, it is wise to examine the various approaches of individual philosophers. This will be accomplished by an exploration of three areas: Platonic idealism, religious idealism, and modern idealism and its characteristics.

Descartes	Berkeley		Royce	Butler
(1596-1650)	(1685-1753)		(1855-1916)	(1908-)
	Kant		Gentile	
	(1724-1804)		(1875-1944)	
		Harris	Hocking	
		(1835-1909)	(1873-1966)	
	Hegel			
	(1770-1831)	Horne		
		(1874-1946)		

1

IDEALISM AND EDUCATION

The Development of Idealism

Platonic Idealism

Plato (427–347 B.C.). Plato was a Greek philosopher who became a disciple of Socrates and remained an ardent admirer throughout his life. Plato is largely known for his writings in which Socrates is the leading protagonist in a series of dialogues dealing with almost every conceivable topic. Two of his most famous works are the *Republic* and the *Laws*. After Socrates' death in 399 B.C., Plato opened up his own school, the Academy, where students and professors engaged in a dialectic approach to problems.

According to Plato, men should concern themselves primarily with the search for truth. Since truth is perfect and eternal, it cannot therefore be found in the world of matter that is both imperfect and constantly changing. Mathematics demonstrated that eternal truths were possible. Concepts such as 2 + 2 = 4 or

3

the definition that a perfect circle is one where all points on the circumference are equidistant from the center are ideas that always have been true (even before man discovered them), are true, and always will be true. Mathematics shows that universal truths with which all men can agree can be found, but mathematics only comprises one field of knowledge. Plato believed that we must search for other universal truths in areas such as politics, religion, and education; hence, the search for absolute truth should be the quest of the true philosopher.

In the *Republic*, Plato wrote about the separation of the world of ideas from the world of matter. The world of ideas (or forms) has the Good as its highest point—the source of all true knowledge. The world of matter, the ever-changing world of sensory data, is not to be trusted. Man needs, as much as possible, to free himself from a concern with matter so that he can advance toward the Good. This can be done by transcending matter through the use of the dialectic (or critical discussion) in which one moves from mere opinion to true knowledge.

We might describe the dialectic as follows. All thinking begins with a thesis or point of view such as "War is evil." We might support this view by pointing out that war causes people to be killed, disrupts families, destroys cities, and has adverse moral effects. As long as we only encounter people of similar persuasion we are not likely to alter our point of view. However, when we encounter the antithesis (or opposite point of view) that "War is good," we are forced both to reexamine and to defend our position. Arguments advanced to support the notion that war is good may include the belief that war promotes bravery, helps keep down population, and produces many technical benefits for man through war research. Simply put, the dialectic looks at both sides of an issue. Assuming that our antagonists are philosophers seriously interested in getting to the truth of the problem of whether war is good or evil, they will engage in a dialogue in which both advancement and retrenchment may occur. If given ample time to argue their positions, Plato believed the two discussants would come closer to agreement, or synthesis, and therefore closer to truth (which may be that there are both good and bad aspects of war). This kind of dialectical discussion could not be accomplished by those who simply argued to win or who would not maintain a critical perspective. It is for this reason that Plato thought preparation in the dialectic should involve a lengthy period of education beginning with studies in mathematics. He was particularly critical of inexperienced people who used the dialectic, for he believed that they were not mature enough for training in the dialectic until age thirty.

Plato saw the dialectic as a vehicle for assisting man in moving from a concern with the material world to a concern with the world of ideas. Supposedly, the dialectic crosses the "divided line" between matter and idea. The process begins in the world of matter with the use of the brain, the tongue, gestures, and so forth, but it ends in the world of ideas with the discovery of truth. In the "Allegory of the Cave," Plato depicted prisoners chained in a world of darkness, seeing only shadows on a far cave wall that they took for reality. Imagine one of these prisoners freed from his chains, advancing up a steep slope and into the sunlight, and eventually able to see the sun, realizing it as the true source of heat and light. He would be happy in his true knowledge and would wish to contemplate it even more. Yet, when he remembers his friends in the cave and returns to tell them of the real world outside, they will not listen to someone who cannot now compete with them in their knowledge of shadows. If the fortunate one insists upon freeing the prisoners, they may even kill him. The meaning of the allegory is this: we ourselves are living in a cave of shadows and illusions, chained by our ignorance and apathy. When we begin to loosen ourselves from our chains it is the beginning of our education, and the steep ascent represents the dialectic that will carry us from the world of matter to the world of ideas—even to a contemplation of the Good represented by the sun. Note Plato's admonition that the man, now the philosopher, who has advanced into the realm of true knowledge must return to the cave to bring enlightenment to his fellowmen. This points to Plato's strong belief that philosophizing should not only be an intellectual affair, but that the philosopher also has a duty to share his learning with other men, doing this even in the face of adversity or death.

Plato did not think that man creates knowledge; rather, man discovers it. In another interesting myth, he conjectured that man's soul once had true knowledge but lost it by being placed in a material body that distorted and corrupted that knowledge. Thus, man has the arduous task of trying to remember what he once knew. This "Doctrine of Reminiscence" is illustrated by Socrates, who spoke of himself as a midwife who found men pregnant with knowledge, but knowledge that had not been born or realized. Through his discussions with people, Socrates sought to aid them in giving birth to ideas that in some cases they never knew they had. Plato described Socrates' meeting with a slave boy in the *Meno*, where through skillful questioning, the philosopher shows the boy that he knows the Pythagorean theorem even though he does not know that he knows it.

In the *Republic*, Plato proposed the kind of education that would help bring about a world in which man and society are moved as far as they are capable of moving toward the Good. He understood fully that most people do believe in matter as an objective reality, that there are individual differences, and that injustice and inhumanity are ways of life. He wished to create a world in which outstanding people such as Socrates could serve as models and would be rewarded instead of punished. In essence, Plato suggested that the state must take a very active role in educational matters, and that it must offer a curriculum leading bright students from a concern with concrete data toward abstract thinking. It is interesting to note that Plato thought both girls and boys should be given an equal opportunity to develop themselves to the fullest in this respect, but those who showed little ability for abstractions should go into pursuits that would assist in the practical realities of running a society (such as industry, business, military affairs, and so forth). Those who demonstrated proficiency in the dialectic would continue their education and become philosophers in positions of power to lead the state toward the highest good. Plato believed that until philosophers were the rulers, states would never pursue the highest ideals of truth and justice.

Plato's idea was that the philosopher-king must not only be a thinker but a doer. He must supervise the affairs of the state, and like the philosopher who made his way out of the cave and yet returned to teach other men, he must see that his wisdom pervades every aspect of state life. Needless to say, such a ruler would have no interest in materialism nor even in ruling itself, but he would rule out of a sense of duty and obligation because he is the most fit to rule. Such a ruler could be either a male or a female, and Plato seriously championed the position that women should occupy equal positions in the state, including all levels of military life. Plato's philosopher-king would not only be a person of wisdom but also a good person, since evil stems more from ignorance than from anything else.

Even though Plato's theories about society have never been fully implemented, he did attempt to establish such a society under the patronage of Dionysius II of Syracuse that failed when the tyrant finally realized what Plato was doing. The value of Plato's ideas is that they have stimulated a great deal of thinking about the meaning and purpose of man, society, and education and have even entered into modern thinking and practice in many subtle ways. Who would not, for example, want the best person to lead our state, assuming we knew what "best" really means. Today, we provide an educational system with great state involvement that has much to say about what occupation a person will eventually pursue as a result of the education he or she receives; and we recognize the tremendous influence of social class in education, as in Plato's utopian society, where he separated people into the three classes of workers, military personnel, and rulers.

Plato influenced almost all philosophers who came after him, whether they supported or rejected his basic ideas. Indeed, there is a great deal of merit in the observation by Alfred North Whitehead that modern philosophy is but a series of footnotes to Plato.

Religious Idealism

Idealism has exerted a great amount of influence on Christianity. For one thing, Judaism, a precursor of Christianity, contained many beliefs compatible with idealism. The idea of one God as pure Spirit and the Universal Good can be readily recognized as compatible with idealism. For another, Greek culture was spread across the Mediterranean world by Alexander the Great. Wherever there was a solid Greek influence, there were also Greek schools; consequently, many of the writers of the New Testament had been at least partially influenced by Greek culture and philosophy. Paul, who wrote a considerable portion of the New Testament, was born Saul of Tarsus, and Tarsus was a city heavily influenced by Greek (or Hellenistic) culture and thought. One can find a heavy tinge of idealism in Paul's writings, stemming from both the Jewish and Greek traditions.

Augustine (354–430). The founders of the Roman Catholic Church were also heavily influenced by idealism. Augustine was born into, and reared under, the influence of Hellenistic culture. In the *Confessions*, he described his early life of paganism and the debauchery of his youth until his conversion to Christianity. Although Augustine thought his conversion was a movement away from Greek paganism, one can find allusions to Greek philosophy and literature, specifically to Plato, interspersed throughout his Christian writings.

Augustine was very much concerned with the concept of evil and believed that since man inherited the sin of Adam, he was continuously engaged in a struggle to regain the kind of purity he had before the fall. This idea is akin to Plato's myth about the star where souls that lived near the Good were exiled to the world of matter to suffer pain and death and struggle to return to the spiritual existence they once had.

He readily accepted Plato's notion of the "divided line" between ideas and matter, but he referred to the two worlds as the World of God and the World of Man. The World of God is the world of Spirit and the Good. The World of Man is the material world of darkness, sin, ignorance, and suffering. Needless to say, Augustine believed one should, as much as possible, release oneself from the World of Man and enter into the World of God. Although no one was able to do this in any final sense until after death, a person could transcend this world by concentration on God, through meditation and faith. Augustine, like Plato, felt that people do not create knowledge: God has already created it, but people can discover it through trying to find God. Since humans have souls, they are the closest things people have to divinity, and Augustine believed that we should look within our souls for the true knowledge that exists there. He thus promoted an intuitive approach to education and agreed with Plato that concentration on physical phenomena could lead us astray from the path of true knowledge. Like Plato, Augustine was a strong supporter of the dialectical method of learning, and there are a number of written dialogues between Augustine and his illegitimate son Adeodatus whereby the dialectic is used to facilitate discovering true ideas about God and man. Augustine's ideas about the nature of the true Christian found more acceptance among those who leaned toward a monastic conception of Christianity. Such monastics believed that the Christian should cut himself off from worldly concerns and meditate. There is a monastic order of Augustinians still in existence today.

It is not surprising that idealism and religion have been closely intertwined. Christianity, in particular, promotes the idea of God as transcendent and pure Spirit or Idea. Furthermore, there is the Christian concept that God created the world out of Himself or out of Spirit or Idea. This is very similar to the Platonic concept that true reality is, after all, basically idea.

Augustine's position was influenced by Plotinus, a philosopher of the third century, who believed that the primary purpose of teaching was to lead men back to an awareness of a union with the source from which all things come—the One or the Good. To achieve such a union requires perfect moral purity and intellectual effort. Plotinus believed that the Good (or God) is so great that it cannot contain itself and overflows into various levels, the highest level being pure spirit and the lowest level what we call matter. Such a view indicates very clearly how the ideas of Plato might be applied to Christian thought, and

Plotinus had a considerable influence on Christian philosophers as well as on the philosophy of Islam.

It is not surprising that religious idealism exerted tremendous influence on education and schooling. Early Christians were quick to realize that Christianity would fare better if its adherents were given some kind of systematic teaching. When they established schools, they established them in patterns with which they were familiar. Thus, many Jewish and Greek ideas about the nature of man, society, and God went into the Christian schools along with the distinctly Christian ideas. For centuries, the Christian church was the creator and protector of schooling, and the generations educated in those schools were indoctrinated with the idealist point of view.

The mutuality of idealism and Judeo-Christian religion was brought together in a unity of European culture by the Middle Ages and afterward. This may help explain several characteristics of modern thought. To Plato, ultimate reality is idea, and our bridge to it is the mind. To the Judeo-Christian, ultimate reality is God and our bridge to it is the soul. It is a logical step to connect Idea and God on the one hand, and mind and soul on the other. Thus, man's contact with ultimate reality is by means of mind and soul (or their congeners, self, consciousness, and subjectivity).

The Development of Modern Idealism

By the beginning of the modern period (here arbitrarily set with the rise of the "scientific revolution" in the fifteenth and sixteenth centuries), idealism had come to be largely identified with systematization and subjectivism; and this was encouraged by the writings of René Descartes, George Berkeley, Immanuel Kant, Georg W. F. Hegel, and Josiah Royce.

René Descartes (1596–1650). Born in the small town of La Haze, France, Descartes was educated by the Jesuits, for whom he retained admiration but with whom he developed dissatisfaction because of their doctrinaire teachings. Although his philosophical thinking challenged Catholic doctrine on many points, it seems that he remained sincere in his Catholicism.

It is difficult and misleading strictly to classify an original thinker such as Descartes by a philosophical school. Certainly, much of his philosophy may be characterized as idealism, but he also contributed a great deal to philosophical realism and other thought systems. For present purposes, the significant works of Descartes to be considered are his celebrated *Discourse on Method* and *Meditations on the First Philosophy*.

It was principally in the *Discourse* that Descartes explored his "methodical doubt," whereby he sought to doubt all things, including his own existence. He was searching for an idea or ideas that are indubitable, and he thought that if he could discover ideas that are "clear and distinct," then he would have a solid foundation upon which to build other true ideas. He found he could throw all things into doubt except one—that he himself was doubting or thinking.

Although he could doubt that he was doubting, and although this factor was a mirrorlike infinite regression, Descartes could still not doubt that he was thinking. In this manner, he arrived at the famous Cartesian first principle: *Cogito, ergo sum,* "I think, therefore I am."

The Cartesian *cogito* has served to stimulate quite a bit of philosophical thought since Descartes's time. Traces of it may be found in many modern philosophies. However, the *cogito* is solidly in the tradition of idealism, for it reaffirms the centrality of mind in the relation of man and the world.

Descartes realized that even though the *cogito* was indubitable, he could not easily move from that stage to other indubitables. Objects outside the *cogito* are grasped by the senses, and the senses are notoriously subject to error. Furthermore, any particular idea or thought depends upon other ideas. One cannot think of a triangle, say, without considering angles, degrees, lines, and so forth. Thus, Descartes encountered the necessity of one idea referring to another. He wanted to arrive at the idea at which further reference stopped. He found it impossible to arrive at any idea—even the indubitable *cogito*—that did not refer to something other than itself, except the idea of Perfect Being. Descartes thought he had, by arriving at Perfect Being, encountered God, the infinite and timeless Creator, the source of all things.

Thus, Descartes arrived at the two principles upon which he based his system: the *cogito* and the Deity. He had the indubitability of human thought in the *cogito*, and the foundation for all the objects of thought in the Deity. From these principles, he proceeded to build a philosophy that has, in one way or another, influenced practically all philosophy since. That some of these principles are within the tradition of idealism can be readily seen: there is finite mind contemplating objects of thought founded in God, or we may say in Platonic terms, human mind contemplating the ultimate reality of Ideas. For Descartes, it was the manner in which he arrived at his principles, the method of his analysis, that brought new life into philosophy. The Cartesian method was extended into numerous fields of inquiry, including the natural sciences.

George Berkeley (1685–1753). Berkeley was born in Ireland, educated there, and spent most of his professional life as a minister in the Episcopal Church of Ireland. While still a young man, he developed most of his innovative ideas, writing a number of treatises on philosophy, including *The Principles of Human Knowledge.* Basically, Berkeley's position was that all existence is dependent on some mind to know it, and if there are no minds, then for all intents and purposes nothing would exist unless it is perceived by the mind of God. Berkeley was attacking the view of philosophical realism that there is a material world existing independent of mind. According to Sir Isaac Newton, the universe is composed of material bodies moving in space and controlled by mathematical laws such as the law of gravity.

Berkeley held that no one had experienced such matter firsthand, and further, such a theory is really a conception of mind. Berkeley thought people made a common error in assuming that objects such as trees, houses, and dogs exist where there is no mind to perceive them. Instead, to say that a thing exists means that it is perceived by some mind, or *esse est percipi* (to be is to be perceived). To the classic question, "Does a falling tree in the middle of a forest make some sound if there is no one around to hear it?", Berkeley would answer no, if we rule out the idea of it being perceived by God. There is no existence without perception, but things may exist in the sense that they are perceived by God.

Berkeley's philosophical views were strongly conditioned by his religious views. He held that immaterial substance (ideas or spirit) has been profaned by science, and science has brought on "the monstrous systems of atheists." What exists or has being is not matter: it is Spirit, Idea, or God. Berkeley's efforts may be viewed as a kind of "last-ditch" stand against the encroachments of science and scientific realism that holds to the materialistic thesis.

Berkeley refuted matter by showing that matter cannot exist except as a form of mind. We can only know things as we consciously conceive them, and when we think of the universe existing before finite minds can conceive it, we are led to assume the existence of an Omnipresent Mind lasting through all time and eternity. Thus, we might say that although people may not be conscious of the trees falling throughout eternity, God is. Berkeley was a champion of ideal realities and values whose main purpose is to make evident the existence of God and to prove that God is the true cause of all things.

It was the Scottish-born philosopher David Hume, however, who proved to be the greatest antagonist to the ideas of Berkeley. Hume was born at Edinburgh, studied law, and later served in France as a member of the English embassy. His writings were not widely received at their inception and according to his own accounts "fell deadborn from the press." His major work, *Treatise upon Human Nature*, written when he was only twenty-six, was one of the strongest attacks on idealism ever written. While Hume began with an acceptance of the Berkeleyan principle that *esse = percipi*, he drew the conclusion that since all we can know are our own impressions and ideas, we have no real basis for asserting the reality of either material or spiritual substances; and we cannot discover anything that justifies necessary connection or causation. To connect one occurrence with another, Hume pointed out, is merely the habit of expecting one event to follow another based upon an indefinite series of such happenings. All we can really know is that we have ideas and impressions, one following another in a kind of chaotic heap. While Berkeley believed his philosophy had adequately dealt with atheism, Hume felt that there was no more justification for the existence of a deity than for the existence of matter. Thus, just as Berkeley thought he had destroyed atheism and materialism, so Hume believed he had also destroyed the concept of mind and God. Hume recognized that his theories resulted in skepticism that affected both religion and science, but he was unable to reconcile the paradox of a seemingly sensible world with the logic of human thought.

Today, Berkeley's ideas may appear strange to us, but the concepts he developed have influenced scholars in many fields. His notion of the centrality of subjective mind, and that the existence of anything is dependent upon a perceiving mind, has helped influence scholars to study the nature of perception and the objects of thought further.

   Immanuel Kant (1724–1804). Kant was born in humble conditions, the son of a saddler. Educated in the schools of his hometown, Königsberg, he eventually rose to become perhaps the most famous professor that the University of Königsberg ever had. Without a doubt, Kant is generally recognized as one of the world's great philosophers.

   Among other things, Kant's work was basically a critique of past systems in which he sought to pull off a "Copernican revolution" in the field of philosophy. Two important works he accomplished in this effort were *Critique of Pure Reason* and *Critique of Practical Reason*, in which he sought to bring order to the divergent and warring philosophic camps of rationalism and empiricism.

   The rationalists sought universal truths or ideas by which a coherent system and structure of knowledge could be deduced. They distrusted sense perception because its results are so individualized and erratic. On the other hand, the empiricists held to the immediate perceptions of experience because these are practical and connected with everyday life. They rejected rationalism because it is so abstract and disconnected from the practical. Kant saw that the skirmishes between these divergent philosophic views were getting nowhere. Basically, he accepted the validity and reliability of modern science and believed that the constant bickering between the two positions was doing nothing to further science through the development of a compatible philosophic view of knowledge. This set the stage for Kant's philosophical task.

   Kant's idealism basically comes from his concentration on human thought processes. The rationalist, he held, thinks analytically while the empiricist thinks synthetically. He worked out a system based on *a posteriori* (synthetic) and *a priori* (analytic) logical judgments that he called synthetic *a priori* judgments.

   He thought he had arrived at a new system whereby we could have a valid knowledge of human experience established upon the scientific laws of nature. In short, we would have the best of both rationalist and empiricist insights gathered together in a unified system. This would give science the underpinnings it needed, for Kant recognized the scientific need for an empirical approach while at the same time acknowledging science's claim to discover universal laws. He recognized the importance of the human self or mind and its thought processes as a prime organizing agent in accomplishing this system.

   Kant had to face the problem of the thinking subject and the object of thought. He rejected Berkeley's position that things are totally dependent on mind, for this notion would reject the possibility of scientific law. He was also caught by the problem of how subjective mind could know objective reality. He concluded that nature, objective reality, is a causal continuum, a world connected in space and time with its own internal order. Subjective mind cannot perceive this order in itself or in totality, for when subjective mind is conscious of something, it is not the thing-in-itself (*das Ding an sich*). Mind is conscious of the experience of the *phenomenon* of the thing-in-itself. The thing-in-itself is the *noumenon*. Each experience of a thing (phenomenon) is one small additional piece of knowledge about the total thing (noumenon). Thus, all we know is the content of experience. When we go beyond this, we have entered into the rationalist argument and into speculation on the ultimate or noumenal reality of things-in-themselves, or else we have become engaged in moral and ethical considerations.

Kant explored the moral and ethical realm primarily in *Critique of Practical Reason*. His effort was to arrive at universal postulations concerning what we may call moral ideals, moral imperatives, or moral laws. This aspect of Kant's thinking was not tied to nature, so we might call this his "spiritual" side.

Much of Kant's efforts were directed toward refuting the skepticism of David Hume, for Kant wanted to show that real knowledge is possible. His efforts to do this were clouded by the uneasy manner in which he united apparently opposing themes, such as phenomenon and noumenon, the pure and the practical, and subjectivity and objectivity. The two *Critiques* illustrate this conflict, for one speaks to the logic of thought, and the other to its "practical" applications. In the *Critique of Pure Reason*, the result ends up very close to Hume's skepticism, since Kant found it impossible to make absolutely universal and necessary judgments about human experience purely on rational and scientific grounds. In essence, he had to "switch gears" and go to the "practical" side, the moral and ethical side, in *Critique of Practical Reason* where, he thought, universal judgments could and should be made. Thus, his moral or "practical" philosophy consists of moral laws that he held to be universally valid, laws that he called "categorical imperatives" such as, "act always so that you can will the maxim or the determining principle of your action to become a universal law."

This line of thinking permeates Kant's writings on education, a matter he considered to be of primary moral concern. He held that " . . . the greatest and most difficult problem to which man can devote himself is the problem of education." One of the categorical imperatives he established in his moral philosophy was to treat each person as an end and never as a mere means. This imperative has greatly influenced subsequent thought about the importance of character development in education.

Most of his educational statements are maxims derived from his categorical imperatives. He held that humans are the only beings who need education and that discipline is a primary ingredient of education that leads people to think and seek out "the good." Children should not simply be educated for the present, but for the possibility of an improved future condition that Kant called the "idea of humanity and the whole destiny of mankind." For the most part, he thought education should consist of discipline, culture, discretion, and moral training. The essence of education should not be simply training, however, for to Kant the important thing was "enlightenment" or teaching a child to think according to principles as opposed to mere random behavior. This is closely associated to his notion of will. The education of will does not mean acting according to the duties flowing from the categorical imperatives. In fact, Kant thought that an important part of the child's education was performing his duties toward himself and others.

We can readily see Kant's idealism in his concentration on thought processes and the nature of the relation between mind and its objects on the one hand, and universal moral ideals on the other. Even though his attempts to bring about a "Copernican revolution" in philosophy failed, his systematic thought has been greatly influential on all subsequent Western philosophy, idealistic and otherwise.

Georg Wilhelm Friedrich Hegel (1770–1831). Hegel is perhaps the capstone of idealistic philosophy in the modern era. He was born in Stuttgart, Germany, and led a rather normal and uneventful life as a youth, receiving his education until the age of eighteen in his native city. He then went to the University of Tubingen and majored in theology, graduating in 1793. He showed no particular promise as a budding philosopher, according to his professors, and for the next several years he worked as a tutor with little economic success. He continued to study, and after receiving a small inheritance from his father, his efforts became more successful. For a while he was a lecturer at the University of Jena, then rector of a secondary school until 1816. He was a professor at the University of Heidelberg for two years, and in 1818 became a professor of philosophy at the University of Berlin, remaining there until his death. Although practically all his major works were written before he went to Berlin, it was there that he became a prominent and overriding figure in philosophy. One can find elements of his thought in such disparate recent philosophies as Marxism, existentialism, and American pragmatism. In examining Hegel, we will look at three major aspects of his system: logic, nature, and spirit. Some of his important books are *Phenomenology of Mind*, *Logic*, and *Philosophy of Right*.

One of the striking characteristics of Hegel's philosophy is his logic. He thought he had developed a perfect logical system that supposedly corrected the inadequacies of Aristotelian logic. The word "dialectic" best fits Hegel's logic, and it has often been portrayed as a rather mechanical warring between thesis and antithesis, with the result being a synthesis. Yet, his logic was not quite that inflexible, for it included many variations and shadings of the triadic categories. Even more to the point, Hegel conceived of thought as a continuum, not a series of mechanical synthetic unions. We could say that the continuum is characterized by a moving constant "synthesizing," a moving, growing, ever-changing thought process.

Hegel maintained that his logical system, if applied rigorously and accurately, would arrive at Absolute Idea. This is similar to the notion of unchanging ideas. The difference is that Hegel was sensitive to change (even though some of his critics charge that his explanation of change is a failure). Change, development, and movement are all central and necessary in Hegel's logic. Even Absolute Idea is really the final stage only as it concerns thought process, for Absolute Ideas have an antithesis—Nature.

To Hegel, Nature is the "otherness" of Idea, its opposite, or we may say, the difference between value and fact. He did not view Idea and Nature as finally separate, a dualism at which Descartes arrived, for to Hegel, dualisms are intolerable as any final stage: there must be a final synthesis. In holding this view, Hegel was not denying the ordinary facts, stones, and sticks of everyday life; rather, these are a lower order of reality, and not the final synthesis.

The final stage of the synthesis of Idea and Nature is Spirit, and this is where the final Absolute is encountered. Absolute Spirit is manifested by the historical development of a people and by the finest works of art, religion, and philosophy. Yet, these manifestations are not Absolute Spirit—they are *only* its manifestations. Hegel did not think this final and perfect end had been reached, but he did think of it as a final end toward which we move, however slowly and tortuously, and however many backslides we might make. It is in this view that Hegel's idealism is most apparent—the search for final Absolute Spirit.

One of the major features of the Hegelian system is movement toward richer, more complex, and more complete syntheses. To Hegel, history showed this movement just as much as logical thought processes did. It is as if all the universe, in Hegel's view, is moving toward completion and wholeness. Thus, in Hegel's system, if we examine any one thing, we are always referred to something else connected to it. Such was the case with the development of civilization; that is, history moved in a dialectical, rational process. Those who are familiar with the thought of Karl Marx will note similarities with Hegel, for Marx was very much indebted to him.

Hegel's thought no longer holds the preeminent position it once held. One reason for this is that his system led to a glorification of the state at the expense of individuals. It led some of his followers to believe in a mystical, foreordained destiny in the face of which individuals are powerless. In this view, individuals are mere parts or aspects of the greater, more complete and unified whole, the state.

Hegel has had considerable influence on the philosophy and theory of education. Ivan Soll has attempted to show some of Hegel's contributions to philosophy of education, contributions that must be viewed against the grand manner in which Hegel saw philosophical problems. Basically, Hegel seemed to think that in order to be truly educated, an individual must pass through the various stages of the cultural evolution of mankind. This idea is not as preposterous as it may seem at first glance, for he held that individuals benefit from all that has gone before them. We can illustrate this by referring to the development of science and technology: to an individual who lived three hundred years ago, electricity was an unknown thing except perhaps as a raw natural occurrence such as lightning. Today, practically every person depends on electrical power for everyday usage and has a working, practical knowledge of it entirely outside the experience of a person three hundred years ago. A contemporary person can easily learn elementary facts about electricity in a relatively short time; that is, he can "pass through" or learn an extremely important phase of our cultural evolution. Hegel thought it was possible (if not always probable in every case) for at least some individuals to know everything essential in the history of man's collective consciousness. Today, because of the "knowledge explosion" and the increasing complexity and extent of human knowledge, such an encompassing educational ideal is naive. Yet Hegel's position still retains some credibility, for there is still the need to pass on the cultural heritage and develop an understanding of people's paths to the present. Even to Hegel, the attainment of such a universal and encyclopedic knowledge was an ideal, possible only to the elite.

One of the most influential spokesmen for Hegelian idealism at the turn of the century in America was Josiah Royce. Royce maintained that the external meaning of a thing depends entirely on its internal meaning, that is, its "embodiment of purpose." He argued that "embodiment of purpose" is the criterion of "mentality," and thus the internal essence of anything is mental. It might be added here that Royce, like most idealists, saw his philosophical views as having great correspondence with religious teachings (the Christian religion in his case), and he spent much effort in demonstrating their compatibility.

Royce believed that ideas are essentially purposes or plans of action, and the ideas' fulfillment are plans that have been put into action. Thus, purposes are incomplete without an external world in which they are idealized, and the external world is meaningless unless it is the fulfillment of such purposes. Whose purposes are fulfilled? Royce answered in very Hegelian terms that it is the Absolute's purposes. He believed that one of the most important things for man to develop is a sense of loyalty to moral principles and causes. This implies a spiritual overtone in which one achieves the highest good by becoming a part of the universal design. One can see the influence of this kind of thinking in the educational enterprise in terms of teaching people not only about the purposes of life but also about how they can become an active ingredient in such purposes.

Following Kant and Hegel, there was a continuing interest in idealism in a number of countries. German idealism influenced an important movement in England, seen in the writings of Coleridge, Wordsworth, Carlyle, and Ruskin. The English school of idealism included such philosophers as Thomas Hill Green whose writings included suggestions for ethical, political, and economic reforms; and Francis Herbert Bradley who argued strongly against empiricism, utilitarianism, and naturalism.

In the United States, in addition to the work of Royce, there was much in the writings of Ralph Waldo Emerson that reflected idealist philosophy as did the transcendentalism movement in general. William T. Harris was another American philosopher and educator involved with idealism in the United States. Harris later became the director of the Concord School of Philosophy where he was very active in an attempt to merge New England transcendentalism with Hegelian idealism.

Idealism as a Philosophy of Education

In general, idealists have shown a great concern for education, and many have written extensively about it. Plato made education the central core of his utopian state, the Republic. Augustine gave extensive attention to the need for Christians to become aware of the importance of education. Kant and Hegel wrote about education or referred to it a great deal in their writings, and both made their living by being teachers. In more recent times, there have been idealists such as William Torey Harris, Herman Horne, William Hocking, Giovanni Gentile, and J. Donald Butler, who have tried systematically to apply idealist principles to the theory and practice of education.

Aims of Idealist Education

Idealists generally agree that education should not only stress development of the mind but should also encourage students to focus on all things that are of more lasting value. Along with Plato, they believe that the aim of education should be directed toward the search for true ideas. Another important idealist aim is character development, as the search for truth demands personal discipline and steadfast character. This aim is prevalent in the writings of Kant, Harris, Horne, Gentile, and others. What they want in society is not just the literate, knowledgeable man, but the *good* man.

The Search for Truth. One of the major emphases of idealist philosophy is the search for truth. Plato thought that truth cannot be found in the world of matter because it is an impermanent world that is ever changing. At the Academy, students were encouraged to reach out toward the conceptual world of ideas rather than the perceptual one of sense data. The material world is not a real world anyway but is analogous to the shadows and illusions with which the prisoners in the cave contented themselves. Plato believed that one must break away from the chains of ignorance, greed, or apathy. Such a person would then be on the road to enlightenment and might become a philosopher. In Plato's view, philosophic wisdom or the conception of true ideas is the highest aim of education and one toward which all people should strive.

Idealists have always stressed the importance of mind over matter. Some idealists, such as Berkeley, reject the idea that matter exists by itself, whereas others, like Augustine, take the position that matter may exist in a generally detrimental way. Platonic idealists maintain that a proper education will include examining such areas as art and science, which should lead the student to the more speculative and abstract subjects of mathematics and philosophy. In any event, idealists place less stress on the study of physical and concrete areas than they do on the nonphysical and the abstract. The important thing for the idealist is to arrive at truth, and truth cannot be ever shifting.

There are some idealists, who while not adhering strictly to the Platonic idea that truth is eternal and perfect, do believe that it is substantial and relatively permanent. Thus, for such idealists there may be many truths, even conflicting ones, but they are truths of a more lasting nature; consequently, many idealists favor studies in religion and the classics, two areas that contain enduring ideas.

Augustine, who was himself a neo-Platonist, agreed with Plato that the highest aim is a search for the truth, but he believed even more strongly than Plato that truth has overwhelming spiritual implications. The search for Truth is a search for God. A true education leads one to God. Since God is pure idea, then God can only be reached through contemplation of ideas; therefore, a true education is one that is concerned with ideas rather than matter.

Other idealists have maintained that there may be levels of truth. Kant, for example, maintained the truths of both pure reason and practical reason. Hegel thought that truth is in development, moving from the simple to richer and more complex ideas. A great number of religions in the world claim that their ideas are true, even though they are in conflict with each other. This is why many idealists feel that it is not truth per se that is important, but the search for truth. Even Socrates seemed to imply this position by stating that all ideas are open to challenge, and a literal reading of the term philosopher is not that one is a discoverer of truth but a searcher for it.

Some modern educators, who share many things in common with idealist philosophy, have compiled lists of "Great Books" that contain disparate points of view ranging from the Bible to Marx's *Das Kapital*, and from Augustine's *Confessions* to Voltaire's *Candide*. The idea behind using such books is not that any or all of them contain the final truth, but rather that they contain some of the best and most lasting ideas conceived by man. Even though the books are different, many of the selections complement each other. What is most noticeable, however, even with the books on science, is that they extol thinking and ideas rather than mere sense data, and they concentrate on great concerns rather than on mere particulars. One of the books often found on such lists is Herman Melville's *Moby Dick*. The idealist would go awry if he found the book to be only a sea story or only concentrated on such things as the kinds of ships used or the number of fish caught. *Moby Dick* is a work containing great ideas about life, justice, evil, and courage, truths that one needs to ponder. The aim is not to see this or any other such book as a literal rendering of events, but as something that provides insight into ourselves and the universe of which we are a part. The value of any major work in art or science lies in its carrying us to a higher point in our thinking. We should not use literature and art only as vehicles for moving us into the world of ideas, but into the realm of *great* ideas, ideas of substantial value to us in understanding truth.

Needless to say, idealists conceive of people as thinking beings, having minds capable of attaining truth. They see them as beings who breathe, eat, and sleep, but above all are thinking beings whose thoughts can range from the ridiculous to the sublime. For example, Plato believed that the lowest kind of thinking should be called mere opinion. On this level, people's ideas are not well thought out and are usually contradictory. People can aspire to wisdom, meaning they can improve not only the way they think, but also the quality of their ideas. They can obtain ideas that are of substantial value and endurance, if not perfect and eternal. People can come closer to this ideal by using the thinking of others or with the assistance of their writings. The important point is to direct our thinking toward more universal concepts than those employed in the perfunctory matters of day-to-day living. Reading the daily newspaper, for example, may be useful in learning what is happening in the world, but the newspaper is not of great assistance in understanding why it is happening. This not only demands thought on our part, but the ability to relate the thinking of others to a critical understanding of the problem. Some have contended that the Bible, *Moby Dick*, and the *Republic* do not speak to our present concerns about pollution, the armaments race, and racial bigotry, but the idealist would reply that although individuals may not find any particular answers to a particular problem in such works, they can find issues dealt with in a general way that is more conducive to an understanding of specific problems and their solutions.

The Bible, for example, deals with the problems of war and bigotry, and a book such as *Das Kapital* speaks at length about many economic problems that still have contemporary significance. Our failure to deal adequately with our present problems is not from a lack of facts, but from not using the facts in relationship to great and encompassing ideas.

Self-realization. The idealist emphasis on the mental and spiritual qualities of human beings has led many idealist philosophers to concentrate quite heavily on the concept of individuals and their place in education. This flavor of idealism gives it a considerable subjectivistic orientation as opposed to its more objective aspects. The subjectivistic side is held by many to be one of idealism's most redeeming features, especially in regard to education.

J. Donald Butler, a contemporary educator, holds that the concern for the individual is one of the primary characteristics that makes idealism still viable for modern man. His analysis of the problem, in *Idealism in Education*, indicates that self lies at the center of idealist metaphysics, and we may conclude, at the center of idealist education. Accordingly, he finds that the self is the prime reality of individual experience; that ultimate reality may be conceived as a self and that it may be one self, a community of selves, or a Universal Self; and hence, education becomes primarily concerned with self-realization. He quotes Giovanni Gentile that self-realization is the ultimate aim of education.

Such a theme has its roots deeply embedded in the idealist tradition. Descartes placed the thinking self at the very base of his metaphysical schema and his methodological search with his famous *cogito*: "I think, therefore I am." Some scholars date modern subjectivism from this development. Thinkers such as Berkeley further developed the notion of subjective reality that led to solipsism on the one hand, or skepticism on the other. Berkeley's notion that things do not even exist unless perceived by the subjective individual mind, or the mind of God, gave quite a bit of impetus to the subjectivistic trend of idealist educational thought. Since thinking and knowing are central in educational concerns, it is little wonder that idealism has exerted so much influence on educational views about individual mind and self.

Even though subjectivism is a major wing of idealism, we must not forget another equally powerful idealist notion—the relation of the part to the whole or the symbiotic relationship of the self to society. Plato could not even conceive of the individual apart from a specific place and role in society. This same theme, although enunciated differently, can be seen in Augustine's view of the connection of finite man to infinite God. In the modern era, perhaps this theme was most fully developed by Hegel. He held that the individual must be related to the whole, for it is only in the setting of the total relationship that the real significance of a single individual can be found. This led Hegel to assert that an individual finds his true meaning in serving the state, a statement very close to Plato's idea. Hegel would even go so far as to say that one must relate himself to the total of existence, the cosmos, in order to gain true understanding of himself.

The impact of these ideas on education is readily apparent in the writings of Horne, Gentile, and Harris, all of whom have influenced modern education.

Horne, an American idealist in the early twentieth century, maintained that education is an account of man finding himself as an integral part of a universe of mind. The learner is a finite personality growing into the likeness of an infinite ideal. Because of his immaturity, it is the role of the teacher to guide the learner along the correct paths toward the infinite. This calls for the teacher to be a well-informed person, for he must possess the knowledge and personal qualities necessary to accomplish this feat. The education of willpower becomes central here, for it is easy for the learner to wander away from the desired path by the siren calls of corruption and untruth, a dilemma often referred to by Augustine and other religious thinkers. For Horne, education should encourage the "will to perfection" for the pupil, and it is an activity whereby one shapes oneself into the likeness of God—a task that requires eternal life for its fulfillment.

Gentile, the Italian idealist, thought that the individual is not only a part of a community of minds but connected with the mind of God; hence, all education is religious education. He maintained that one of the primary functions of education is to open the soul to God.

Harris, an American educator and philosopher, proposed that education should lead people to what he called "a third level of enlightenment." This involves the individual becoming aware of the spiritual nature of all things, including union with God and personal immortality. The influence of Hegel's thought is very prominent in Harris's educational philosophy, particularly where he recommends taking the student up through insight into the personal nature of the Absolute. For Harris, human development and education are a series of dialectical experiences.

Consequently, we may conclude that self-realization is a central aim of idealist education, but this does not imply that the self is realized in isolation. The individual self is a part and can only have meaning in the larger context.

Character Development. Idealists have given considerable attention not only to the search for truth, but also to the persons who are involved in it. The teacher that idealists favor is the more philosophically oriented person, one who can assist students in choosing important material and infuse them with a desire to improve their thinking in the deepest possible way. Perhaps the best way to understand this is by looking at Socrates as a prototype of the kind of teacher the idealist would like to have. Socrates spent a great deal of time analyzing and discussing ideas with others, and he was deeply committed to action based on reflection. The idealist-oriented teacher would seek to have these Socratic characteristics and would encourage students to better their thinking, and to better their lives based upon such thinking. Idealists are, in general, greatly concerned with character development, and they believe that a good education would make this one of its foremost goals.

Idealist philosophy is also very much concerned with the student as one who has enormous potential for growth, both morally and cognitively. The idealist tends to see the individual as a person whose moral values need to be considered and developed by the school. While the idealist may not always be willing to give "evil" an objective existence, yet it is there in the sense that students may choose things that are harmful. Therefore, the idealist maintains that the school has an obligation to present students with models for develop-ment, and he would agree with Plato that religious ideas should be presented in ways so that students can use them for guidance. It could be said that the teacher, from the perspective of the idealist, is in a unique and important position. It is the duty of the teacher to encourage students to ask questions and to provide a suitable environment for learning. The teacher exercises judgment about the kinds of materials that are the most important and encourages diligent study of material that is of more ultimate worth.

The idealist position has ramifications for the way we look at the individ-ual. Rather than seeing a person simply as a biological organism in nature, idealists see him as the possessor of an "inner light," a mind or soul. For religious idealists, the student is important as a creation of God and carries within him some of the godliness that the school should seek to develop. Most idealists, whether religious or not, have a deep feeling about the inner powers of an individual, such as intuition, that must be accounted for in any true education. Too much of what passes for education deals with filling the person with something, rather than bringing out what is there, the truths that already exist. As discussed earlier, Plato speaks of the "Doctrine of Reminiscence," whereby the soul regains the true knowledge it lost by being placed in the "prison house" of the body. The dialectic is the tool for regaining this lost wisdom.

Augustine thought that truth was inherent in the soul of the individual. Education is the process of bringing these truths to the surface, and since many of these truths are directly related to God, education is the process of salvation. Education can be conceived as not only consisting of the dialectic, but also the technique of meditation to bring out truths already possessed by the soul. This outlook on education was characteristic of monastic education in the Middle Ages where salvation was to be achieved not by direct action but by meditation. Even today, many religious institutions practice such an approach as a part of the students' formal training. Some church schools still set aside a portion of time for pupils to meditate upon the ultimate meaning of things.

Many idealists are concerned with moral character as an outgrowth of thinking and thoughtful actions. The movement toward wisdom itself, the ideal-ist would argue, results from a moral conviction. Augustine thought of God as the highest wisdom, and the movement toward wisdom (or God) the highest moral principle. This concept is probably best expressed by Hegel who de-scribed the dialectic as a movement going from the simple to the complex in terms of Spirit trying to understand itself. Hegel believed that man can know God, and he argued against theologians who say that God is unknowable. One achieves his fullest stature when one understands the movement toward wis-dom and fully participates in it.

One of the more prominent advocates of character development as a proper aim of education was Immanuel Kant. He made reason, not God, the source of moral law; consequently, the only thing morally valuable is a good will. Accordingly, a person who has a good will knows what his duty is and conscien-tiously seeks to do that duty. Kant promoted what he called the "categorical imperative"; that is, one should never act in any manner other than he would have all other people act. The proper function of education, then, is to educate people to know and to do their duty in ways that respect the "categorical imperative." This is character education, and idealists generally agree, as J. Donald Butler has pointed out, that any education worthy of the name *is* character education. The education of character includes not only the sense of duty, but also the development of willpower and loyalty.

Herman Horne put emphasis on the education of the will. By this he meant that students should be educated to resist temptations and to apply themselves to useful tasks. The education of the will involves effort, for Horne believed that education is directly proportional to the effort expended. While some educators maintain that a child should only follow his interests, Horne held that the development of willpower enables a child to do things that may not be particularly interesting but are extremely valuable. Even though a person may not be particularly intelligent, Horne maintained that effort would enable one to achieve far beyond the point mere interest would have taken him.

Idealists such as Giovanni Gentile, who supported the Facist regime of Benito Mussolini, have emphasized the development of loyalty as an important aspect of character education. Along with Hegel, Gentile thought that the destiny of the individual is tied to the destiny of the state; consequently, it is necessary for the individual to have a strong sense of loyalty to the state. Proper character education would thus have the attribute of loyalty, for an individual without loyalty would be incomplete. When the teacher acts according to the interest of the state, the true interests of the student are being met. By the same token, a student's proper role is to abide by the authority of the teacher.

Methods of Education

Most idealists who look at our schools today are greatly dismayed at what they find. They see students regimented into studying facts, later becoming specialists of some kind, and using those specialities with little humane concern for their fellowman. Modern students seem like robots surveying bits and scraps of everything, thereby obtaining an "education" with little depth, operating on the basis of rules rather than on inner conviction. Idealists lean toward studies that provide depth, and they would strongly suggest a modification of the view that things should be studied simply because they are "new" or "relevant." They find that much of the great literature of the past has more pertinence to contemporary problems than what is considered "new" and "relevant." Almost any contemporary problem, idealists would argue, has its roots in the past. Problems such as the relation of the individual and society have been debated extensively by great philosophers and thinkers. To ignore what great minds have to say in these areas is to ignore the most relevant writings about them.

As has been indicated in the aims of education, idealists do not favor specialized learning as much as learning that is holistic. They ask us to see the whole rather than a disjointed collection of parts. The holistic approach leads to a more liberal attitude toward learning. Although subjects like the natural sciences are useful, they are only of maximum value when they help us to see the whole picture.

Plato believed that the best method of learning was the dialectic. Through this critical method of thinking, he believed man could see things *en toto*. The *Republic*, which is essentially the fruit of dialectical thinking, attempted to integrate a wide range of learning into a meaningful whole. Essentially, Plato believed that we can develop our ideas in ways that achieve syntheses and universal concepts. This method is one that can be learned, but it requires a critical attitude, a background in mathematics, and extended study. The dialectic is a winnowing-out process in which ideas are put into battle against each other with the more substantial ideas enduring the fray.

Although one does not see a great use of this method in schools today, the dialectic was widely used as an educational technique throughout the Middle Ages. It came to be a matter of disputation where ideas were to be placed in the arena of battle and only if they emerged victorious would there be some reason for believing in them. Churchmen such as Peter Abelard used it in vindicating the truths of Christian doctrine. Abelard's famous *Sic et Non* was a way of looking at both sides of the question and allowing the truth to emerge.

In addition to dialectical method, some idealists maintain that truth is also received through intuition and revelation. Augustine practiced the dialectic, but he also put great stress upon the intuitive approach to knowledge. His argument was that God, the inner light of human beings, could speak to us if we made ourselves receptive. Augustine believed that we need to reject any materialistic concerns as much as possible so we can attune ourselves with God. One still finds this approach used in monasteries or in religious orders that are basically contemplative in nature. Even outside strictly religious schools, most idealists advocate a conceptual method that includes both the dialectic and the intuitive approach to learning. Plato held that one does not learn as much from nature as from dialogues with other people. Augustine believed that though a man be blind and deaf, incapable of any feeling in his senses, he can still learn all the important truths and reach God.

Many modern idealists champion in spirit the idea of learning through the dialectic or contemplation, but these methods are not as widely used in practice as they once were. Today, idealists lean more toward the study of ideas through the use of classical works or writings and art that express great ideas. The Great Books of the Western World, a program that began at the University of Chicago in the 1950s, achieved wide attention and is advocated by many idealist educators as a vehicle for encouraging students toward learning of a more conceptual nature. Idealists do believe, however, that any study of the Great Books should be undertaken with experienced leadership, using a seminar type of education to insure thinking on the highest possible plane. Saint John's College at Annapolis has such a program in operation and is a good example of the kind of education that many idealists favor. At Saint John's, students read the classics, analyze them, and then apply them to an understanding of current problems. Although no book less than fifty years old has been added to the official list of great books, students are encouraged to read Hemingway, Faulkner, and others as supplementary reading. The emphasis in modern writings, however, as well as classical ones, is upon those containing universal concepts that are germane to people in all places and times.

Although one might easily see how this idealist approach can be applied to college-level education, it may not be so apparent how it could be used in elementary and secondary schools. To begin with, one must be clear on the purpose of learning. The idealist is not primarily concerned in turning out students with specific technical skills but in giving them a broad understanding of the world in which they live. The curriculum revolves around broad concepts rather than specific skills. In elementary and preschool education, students are encouraged to develop habits of understanding, patience, tolerance, and hard work that will be of assistance to them later when they undertake studies of a more substantial nature. This is not to say that students cannot learn some important ideas at any age, but the earliest years are basically preparatory in acquiring the skills to undertake more in-depth work at a later stage.

The idealist believes that the teacher is an important ingredient in the instruction of the young. The teacher should not only understand the stages of learning but also should maintain constant concern about the ultimate purposes of learning. Some idealists stress the importance of emulation in learning, for they feel that the teacher should be the kind of person we want our children to become. Socrates has been used by idealists, not only as a prototype of learning but also as a model for emulation.

Butler maintains that modern idealist educators like to think of themselves as creators of methods rather than as mere imitators. They prefer alternative ways of approaching learning, but they still like to see at least an informal dialectic in operation. In questioning and discussing sessions where the dialectic really operates, the teacher should help students see alternatives they might have otherwise missed. Thus, while it may be an informal dialectical process, it should not become a mere pooling of the ignorance of immature students, for the teacher should participate to maintain the integrity of the process.

The lecture method still has a place in the idealist's methodological tool kit, but lecture is viewed more as a means of stimulating thought than merely passing on information. In fact, some idealist teachers discourage note taking so that students will concentrate on the basic ideas. To the idealist, the chief purpose for giving a lecture is to help students comprehend truths. Idealists also use such methods as projects, supplemental activities, library research, and art work. The importance of such diverse methods must be, however, that they grow out of the topic of study at hand. This illustrates the idealist's desire to show the unity of knowledge and his dislike for random and isolated activity.

One of the cardinal objectives of idealism and idealistic education is the ancient Greek notion to "know thyself." Self-realization is, as noted above, an important aim of education; hence, idealists stress the importance of self-activity in education. In essence, they believe a true education occurs only within the individual self. While the teacher cannot get inside a child's mind, he can provide materials and activities that influence learning. It is the response of the learner to these materials and activities that constitutes education. The sources of this action are personal and private, therefore, for in idealism all education is self-education. The teacher must recognize that he or she cannot always be present when learning occurs and should attempt to stimulate the student so that learning continues even when the teacher is not present. The project method might be one concrete example of self-activity. The idealist only insists that the nature of any such activity be on a high plane of thought.

Curriculum

While not underemphasizing the development of a curriculum, idealists stress that the most important factor in education at any level is to teach students to think. The psychologist, Jean Piaget, and others have shown that it is not unreasonable to expect students to demonstrate some critical regard for the material they are exposed to at various stages of development, even with nursery tales that are read to them.

Idealists are generally in agreement, however, that many of the educational materials used by children are inadequate. Although the materials may help teach skills such as reading, idealists do not understand why such skills cannot be taught in ways that develop conceptual ability as well. One might argue that the McGuffey readers that were widely used in schools seventy years ago taught the child something in addition to reading. They fostered ideas about parental relationships, God, morality, and patriotism. A counterargument might be that these are the wrong kinds of concepts, but are the more current sterilized readers portrayed by the Dick and Jane types an improvement? While most idealists claim that they are opposed to the use of reading material for indoctrination, they do not see why reading material cannot, while it is helping a child learn to read, encourage thinking about ideas involving brotherhood, truth, and fair play. Although there is a dearth of books and materials that express such ideas for children, idealists still believe that the teacher should encourage a consideration of ideas in the classroom. Even with a Dick and Jane type of book, for example, a teacher should help a child to explore the materials for meanings such as the purpose of family, the nature of peer pressures, and the problems of growing up.

With older children, one can use materials that are more appropriate to this kind of learning. *Treasure Island*, *The Adventures of Tom Sawyer*, *Peter Pan*, all contain material that is well written and lends itself admirably to a discussion of ideas. With high school students, there is even more material at one's disposal that is idea engendering: *The Iliad*; *Hamlet*; *Twice-Told Tales*; and *Wind, Sand, and Stars*. Since these materials are already widely used, one might wonder what is so special about the way idealists would use them. Idealists charge that teachers are not always equipped to use such materials for the ideas contained in them. Such books may become, in the eyes of teachers and students, another hurdle to get over, another benchmark or list of books to be read.

Idealists believe that ideas can change lives. Christianity was once merely an idea, and so was Marxism, but such ideas have transformed whole societies.

Idealists think that humans can become more noble and rational by developing the ability to think. The use of the classics for humanizing learning experiences has been encouraged by idealists. Whatever factors are involved in man's evolutionary past, the idealist holds that the most important part of man's being is his mind. It is to be nourished and developed. It has a potentiality for an accumulation of facts, and it has the ability to conceptualize and to create.

Idealists charge that the schools neglect this important consideration of mind. Even when the classics are taught, students are often required to memorize dates and names without due attention to the creative aspects of the mind. Creativity will be encouraged when students are immersed in the creative thinking of others, and when they are stimulated to think reflectively. This can only come about in an environment that promotes the use of the mind.

While idealist educators stress classical studies, this does not mean that such studies are all that they stress. Indeed, some idealists recommend studies that are distinctly modern in tone. For example, William T. Harris developed a curriculum plan centered around five studies: (1) mathematics and physics, (2) biology, (3) literature and art, (4) grammar, and (5) history. Herman Horne suggested seven major studies: physics, biology, psychology, mathematics, grammar, literature, and history. Both Harris and Horne felt that these areas were important enough to be considered on every curriculum level and broad enough to contain even elective studies. It should be noted that the sciences are heavily represented in both of these recommendations. This points to the fact that idealists such as Harris and Horne did not disregard the development of new knowledge or the needs of twentieth-century man. Neither Harris nor Horne saw any incompatibility between studies in the liberal arts and the natural sciences. In fact, they maintained that a more complete understanding of the universe necessitates studies in both the arts and the sciences.

Critique of Idealism in Education

Idealism is often considered a conservative philosophy of education because much of its thrust is to preserve cultural traditions. This is borne out by examination of the idealists' concern for perennial and ultimate truths and their notion that education is largely a matter of passing on the cultural heritage. Many adherents point to the strengths of idealism, such as (1) the high cognitive level of education idealists promote, (2) their concern for safeguarding and promoting cultural learning, (3) their great concern for morality and character development, (4) their view of the teacher as a person of respect central to the educational process, (5) their stress on the importance of self-realization, (6) their stress upon the human and personal side of life, and (7) their comprehensive, systematic, and holistic approach.

Historically, the influence of idealism on education has been of such proportions that even today it is hard to find schools that do not in some way reflect idealist principles. While idealism's influence has suffered in recent decades, probably no other single philosophy has affected education for as great a period of time as idealism. Beginning with Plato in the fourth century B.C., through scholasticism in the Middle Ages, to Kant and Hegel, and up to the twentieth century, idealism has been a dominant force with which to reckon. Several factors have contributed to a weakening of idealism in contemporary affairs: industrialization and technological advances have taken their toll, developments in the field of science have brought about fundamental challenges to idealistic principles, the renewed vigor of realism and naturalistic philosophies has put more emphasis on the material as opposed to ideal aspects of life, and the contemporary emphasis on newness as opposed to cultural heritage and lasting values has eroded the idealist position.

Many idealists counter that certain ideas contained in traditional writings, some written over two thousand years ago, are as relevant today as ever. They maintain, with Ecclesiastes, that "There is nothing [really] new under the sun," for many contemporary problems we face today are problems philosophers and others faced long ago. Plato, for example, dealt extensively with the problems of democracy, individuality, and language. The Bible discusses topics such as human suffering, greed, wealth, and human purpose. When Herman Melville wrote *Moby Dick*, he drew upon central Biblical themes of good and evil that still provide human guidance. There are a number of seminars, based on the Great Books program, conducted today that deal with such themes, and from the point of view of some idealists, provide more insight than do most books on the best-seller list. Such seminars have found their way into schools, libraries, reading circles, and even into adult education programs in many prisons. Many of the people who attended the Great Books program in the 1950s, when it began, still look back on their experience with a sense of nostalgia. Today, the Encyclopaedia Britannica publishes the Great Books for home use, and the accompanying Synopticon provides a key to help the reader locate and understand the central ideas of the books. Many people are amazed that so many issues we think are new, such as euthanasia and abortion, are treated extensively by even the ancient authors. Students of the Great Books often find flashes of insight from their readings that stimulate their thinking along new paths.

Opponents of idealism have looked to the onslaught with joy, for they have long searched for ways to get around what to them is the lethargic nature of idealism. What they object to primarily are its fundamental premises. For example, the idealist notion of a finished and absolute universe waiting to be discovered has hindered progress in science and the creation of new ideas and processes. If one accepts the concept of absolute ideas, it is not possible for him to go beyond those ideas without questioning or doubting their absoluteness. This was one of the chief problems modern science had in gaining acceptance, for science is premised on tentativeness and hypotheses rather than on stability and axioms. Indeed, contemporary science is largely characterized by Heisenberg's "principle of indeterminacy" that says, in effect, we cannot be certain about anything. Einstein's theory of relativity has been used to challenge the idealist assertion of a fixed universe. Still another cause of the weakening of idealism is the historical decline of traditional religious influence in contemporary affairs. Because idealism has been intimately linked with traditional religion, the weakening of the one has in turn led to the weakening of the other.

However, there are signs that the decline in religion may be changing. While the influence of traditional organized religion has decreased, there has been a recent renewal of interest in mysticism, eastern religious thought, and various forms of meditation that take new directions from the more traditional religious views. In addition, there has been a resurgence in evangelical Christianity in recent years with a great deal of emphasis on education of the young. These developments usually have idealistic underpinnings, especially in their views on the proper aims and content of schooling.

From the standpoint of education, it seems there are several issues that need further scrutiny. The idealist influence on education has been of great magnitude, but there are serious reservations about whether that influence has always been beneficial. While idealist education has emphasized the cognitive side of man, it has tended toward intellectualism to the detriment of the affective and physical side. Not only has it often ignored the affective and physical side, but it has ignored the large number of people who find its cognitive emphasis narrow and pedantic. This has made idealism tend toward developing an intellectual elite.

The problem of elitism goes deep into idealism's roots. Plato advocated an intellectual elite of philosopher-kings. Augustine argued for the superiority of the monastic life over the secular because of the higher quality of mind and intelligence to be found there. Monks were a select group set aside for special treatment. Idealists have tended to view formal education not for the masses but for a chosen few who could understand and appreciate it properly; consequently, they have concentrated on education for the upper classes of society, particularly for those going into leadership positions in government or the church. This factor has often helped formal education to be viewed as a luxury, available only to the privileged few. To the extent that idealist regimes have tried to extend at least some formal schooling to the public, the view has been that vocational and technical studies are sufficient for the masses, while liberal studies are fit only for the elite. While not all idealists have felt this way, the tendency toward elitism has been generally recognized.

In spite of its generalist approach to studies, idealism is susceptible to the charge of shortsightedness with regard to the affective and physical side of man. If we include in our definition of "affective," not only the aesthetic but also the emotional and personal-social side of life, then such a charge gains credence. The idealist curriculum is overly bookish, and while attending to books is not bad in itself, if we fail to recognize emotional and social needs, then we are not really attending to the complete person. Idealists claim to be holistic and universal, yet in their extreme cognitive and bookish approach, they seem to fail to take their own advice in this regard. For example, it is one thing to learn about human nature from reading enduring scholarly treatises on the subject, but it is quite another to engage purposefully in social relationships with fellow human beings in the everyday world. Consequently, idealist knowledge is often only "arm-chair" knowledge rather than the deep insight that comes from interaction with other people.

In recent years, the idealist curriculum has increasingly come under attack for lacking relevance. Idealists have offered some rather compelling defenses, but there is still an element of truth in the charge that will not go away. To the extent that idealists only concentrate on works of the past, the charge gains credibility. Certainly, there are insights in the great writings of the past, but often they are too general to aid in dealing with specific contemporary problems. It is true that we should study great ideas from the past, but this does not mean that we should ignore contemporary ideas and writings. One of the criticisms leveled at educational institutions such as Saint John's of Annapolis is that they deal too much with the past and too little with the present and the future. Although defenders of these programs maintain that there is allowance for more recent literature, it still remains true that most of the reading is hundreds or thousands of years old. This approach tends to ignore or downgrade a large body of contemporary materials in many areas such as art, science, philosophy, literature, and the mass media.

One of the claims made by idealists is that they give more attention to the development of character than do advocates of other philosophies. This is probably true, but there are serious questions to be raised as to why idealists are so concerned with character development and what kind of character they want to develop. Often what parades for character development in idealist philosophy is conformity and subservience on the part of the learner. Harris, for example, said the first rule to be taught to students is order; pupils should be taught to conform to the general standards and to repress everything that interferes with the function of the school. More explicitly, pupils should have their lessons ready on time, rise at the tap of the bell, and learn habits of silence and cleanliness. One might well question whether this is character development or training for docil-ity. This kind of character training may assist in educational and social stability, but it is often at the expense of creativity and self-direction. The kind of character training idealists promote may also result in the gullibility of students to accept ready-made ideas without serious examination. Many of the so-called great ideas, for example, rest on premises or assumptions that are questionable, and in the final analysis, may be socially harmful. Giovanni Gentile and Josiah Royce, for example, spent a great deal of time dealing with the concept of loyalty as central to the development of character. While loyalty may be socially useful in some cases, it can also be harmful when it encourages the learner to submerge all questioning and intellectual independence with regard to concepts involving church, state, or school.

Some idealists, such as Butler, emphasize the self-realization aspect of character education, yet such self-realization is often seen as a derivative of a universal self; hence, even under a softer idealist approach, the individual self is subsumed under a larger and more important concern, that is, the universal self or God. This line of reasoning can be traced back to Hegel who saw the individual person achieving meaning by serving the state.

Another aspect of idealist philosophy that deserves attention is the contention that the primary function of philosophy is to search for and disseminate truths. One finds this view elaborated by Plato, for example, who believed that truth is both perfect and eternal. Even today, idealists point out that the search for wisdom is really a search for truth, an ongoing pursuit each new generation of students must do, although the final answers may always be the same. This viewpoint leads to a type of staticism. The assumption is that we have the truth already at hand in great works of the past. The danger in this belief is that it discourages a search for new ideas and develops a kind of dogmatism and false sense of security. While idealists maintain that modern man is too relative and tentative in his thinking, the absoluteness of many idealists may be a more serious weakness.

While this attitude may characterize a number of idealists, some have a more pluralistic conception of truth, maintaining that there may be not one but many truths that people should ponder, not only for the sake of knowledge but for the intellectual stimulation provided. Idealism, of course, like all other philosophies, has many shades and meanings, and it would be grossly unfair to lump all idealists together. Each writer describes or reinterprets ideas in the light of his experiences, and thus no two are the same. However, there are certain tendencies toward areas such as character development and education in general that idealists share, and the purpose of this chapter has been to point out these general trends.

Plato

The Republic

The Republic *has often been considered one of the greatest expressions of idealist philosophy and Plato's most thorough statement on education.* Writing in the fourth century, B.C., Plato described his utopian view of human society. It was not unusual for him to depict central ideas in allegorical format. In this selection, he shows Socrates attempting to explain how achieving higher levels of thought (i.e., thinking philosophically), is akin to prisoners escaping from their shadowy prison in a cave. Plato demonstrates both the painful difficulty of the ascent toward wisdom and its potentially dangerous consequences. Many scholars believe the story parallels Socrates' own life and death.*

And now, I said, let me show in a figure how far our nature is enlightened or unenlightened:—Behold! human beings living in an underground den, which has a mouth open towards the light and reaching all along the den; here they have been from their childhood, and have their legs and necks chained so that they can not move, and can only see before them, being prevented by the chains from turning round their heads. Above and behind them a fire is blazing at a distance, and between the fire and the prisoners there is a raised way; and you will see, if you look, a low wall built along the way, like the screen which marionette players have in front of them, over which they show the puppets.

I see.

And do you see, I said, men passing along the wall carrying all sorts of vessels, and statues and figures of animals made of wood and stone and various materials, which appear over the wall? Some of them are talking, others silent.

You have shown me a strange image, and they are strange prisoners.

Like ourselves, I replied; and they see only their own shadows, or the shadows of one another, which the fire throws on the opposite wall of the cave?

True, he said; how could they see anything but the shadows if they were never allowed to move their heads?

And of the objects which are being carried in like manner they would only see the shadows?

Yes, he said.

And if they were able to converse with one another, would they not suppose that they were naming what was actually before them?

Very true.

And suppose further that the prison had an echo which came from the other side, would they not be sure to fancy when one of the passers-by spoke that the voice which they heard came from the passing shadow?

No question, he replied.

To them, I said, the truth would be literally nothing but the shadows of the images.

That is certain.

And now look again, and see what will naturally follow if the prisoners are

---

*Selection from Plato, *The Republic*, trans. B. Jowett (New York: Dolphin Books, 1960), pp. 205–8.

released and disabused of their error. At first, when any of them is liberated and compelled suddenly to stand up and turn his neck round and walk and look towards the light, he will suffer sharp pains; the glare will distress him, and he will be unable to see the realities of which in his former state he had seen the shadows; and then conceive some one saying to him, that what he saw before was an illusion, but that now, when he is approaching nearer to being and his eye is turned towards more real existence, he has a clearer vision,—what will be his reply? And you may further imagine that his instructor is pointing to the objects as they pass and requiring him to name them,—will he not be perplexed? Will he not fancy that the shadows which he formerly saw are truer than the objects which are now shown to him?

Far truer.

And if he is compelled to look straight at the light, will he not have a pain in his eyes which will make him turn away to take refuge in the objects of vision which he can see, and which he will conceive to be in reality clearer than the things which are now being shown to him?

True, he said.

And suppose once more, that he is reluctantly dragged up a steep and rugged ascent, and held fast until he is forced into the presence of the sun himself, is he not likely to be pained and irritated? When he approaches the light his eyes will be dazzled, and he will not be able to see anything at all of what are now called realities.

Not all in a moment, he said.

He will require to grow accustomed to the sight of the upper world. And first he will see the shadows best, next the reflections of men and other objects in the water, and then the objects themselves; then he will gaze upon the light of the moon and the stars and the spangled heaven; and he will see the sky and the stars by night better than the sun or the light of the sun by day?

Certainly.

Last of all he will be able to see the sun, and not mere reflections of him in the water, but he will see him in his own proper place, and not in another; and he will contemplate him as he is.

Certainly.

He will then proceed to argue that this is he who gives the season and the years, and is the guardian of all that is in the visible world, and in a certain way the cause of all things which he and his fellows have been accustomed to behold?

Clearly, he said, he would first see the sun and then reason about him.

And when he remembered his old habitation, and the wisdom of the den and his fellow-prisoners, do you not suppose that he would felicitate himself on the change, and pity them?

Certainly, he would.

And if they were in the habit of conferring honors among themselves on those who were quickest to observe the passing shadows and to remark which of them went before, and which followed after, and which were together; and who were therefore best able to draw conclusions as to the future, do you think that he would care for such honors and glories, or envy the possessors of them? Would he not say with Homer,

> *"Better to be the poor servant of a poor master,"*

and to endure anything, rather than think as they do and live after their manner?

Yes, he said, I think that he would rather suffer anything than entertain these false notions and live in this miserable manner.

Imagine once more, I said, such a one coming suddenly out of the sun to be replaced in his old situation; would he not be certain to have his eyes full of darkness?

To be sure, he said.

And if there were a contest, and he had to compete in measuring the shadows with the prisoners who had never moved out of the den, while his sight was still weak, and before his eyes had become steady (and the time which would be needed to acquire this new habit of sight might be very considerable), would he not be ridiculous? Men would say of him that up he went and down he came without his eyes; and that it was better not even to think of ascending; and if any one tried to loose another and lead him up to the light, let them only catch the offender, and they would put him to death.

No question, he said.

This entire allegory, I said, you may now append, dear Glaucon, to the previous argument; the prison-house is the world of sight, the light of the fire is the sun, and you will not misapprehend me if you interpret the journey upwards to be the ascent of the soul into the intellectual world according to my poor belief, which, at your desire, I have expressed—whether rightly or wrongly God knows. But, whether true or false, my opinion is that in the world of knowledge the idea of good appears last of all, and is seen only with an effort; and, when seen, is also inferred to be the universal author of all things beautiful and right, parent of light and of the lord of light in this visible world, and the immediate source of reason and truth in

the intellectual; and that this is the power upon which he who would act rationally either in public or private life must have his eye fixed.

I agree, he said, as far as I am able to understand you.

Moreover, I said, you must not wonder that those who attain to this beatific vision are unwilling to descend to human affairs; for their souls are ever hastening into the upper world where they desire to dwell; which desire of theirs is very natural, if our allegory may be trusted.

Yes, very natural.

And is there anything surprising in one who passes from divine contemplations to the evil state of man, misbehaving himself in a ridiculous manner; if, while his eyes are blinking and before he has become accustomed to the surrounding darkness, he is compelled to fight in courts of law, or in other places, about the images or the shadows of images of justice, and is endeavoring to meet the conceptions of those who have never yet seen absolute justice?

Anything but surprising, he replied.

Any one who has common sense will remember that the bewilderments of the eyes are of two kinds, and arise from two causes, either from coming out of the light or from going into the light, which is true of the mind's eye, quite as much as of the bodily eye; and he who remembers this when he sees any one whose vision is perplexed and weak, will not be too ready to laugh; he will first ask whether that soul of man has come out of the brighter life, and is unable to see because unaccustomed to the dark, or having turned from darkness to the day is dazzled by excess of light. And he will count the one happy in his condition and state of being, and he will pity the other; or, if he have a mind to laugh at the soul which comes from below into the light, there will be more reason in this than in the laugh which greets him who returns from above out of the light into the den.

That, he said, is a very just distinction.

But then, if I am right, certain professors of education must be wrong when they say that they can put a knowledge into the soul which was not there before, like sight into blind eyes.

They undoubtedly say this, he replied.

Whereas, our argument shows that the power and capacity of learning exists in the soul already; and that just as the eye was unable to turn from darkness to light without the whole body, so too the instrument of knowledge can only by the movement of the whole soul be turned from the world of becoming into that of being, and learn by degrees to endure the sight of being, and of the brightest and best of being, or in other words, of the good.

Kant

Education

Kant believed that education is "the greatest and most difficult problem to which man can devote himself," and in the following selection, he shows how education can be used to shape human character through maxims, or enduring principles for human activity.* Although written in the eighteenth century, this essay shows a decidedly contemporary concern for child development and learning through activities. Kant stressed character development and a commitment to duty. This concern is illustrated in his descriptions of various maxims and how they should give certain results.

Moral culture must be based upon "maxims," not upon discipline; the one prevents evil habits, the other trains the mind to think. We must see, then, that the child should accustom himself to act in accordance with "maxims," and not from certain ever-changing springs of action. Through discipline we form certain habits, moreover, the force of which becomes lessened in the course of years. The child should learn to act according to "maxims," the reasonableness of which he is able to see for himself. One can easily see that there is some difficulty in carrying out this principle with young children, and that moral culture demands a great deal of insight on the part of parents and teachers.

Supposing a child tells a lie, for instance, he ought not to be punished, but treated with contempt, and told that he will not be believed in the future, and the like. If you punish a child for being naughty, and reward him for being good, he will do right merely for the sake of the reward; and when he goes out into the world and finds that goodness is not always rewarded, nor wickedness always punished, he will grow into a man who only thinks about how he may get on in the world, and does right or wrong according as he finds either of advantage to himself.

"*Maxims*" ought to originate in the human being as such. In moral training we should seek early to infuse into children ideas as to what is right and wrong. If we wish to establish morality, we must abolish punishment. Morality is something so sacred and sublime that we must not degrade it by placing it in the same rank as discipline. The first endeavour in moral education is the formation of character. Character consists in readiness to act in accordance with "maxims." At first they are school "maxims," and later "maxims" of mankind. At first the child obeys rules. "Maxims" are also rules, but subjective rules. They proceed from the understanding of man. No infringement of school discipline must be allowed to go unpunished, although the punishment must always fit the offence.

If we wish to *form the characters* of children, it is of the greatest importance to point out to them a certain plan, and certain rules, in everything; and these must be strictly adhered to. For instance, they must have set times for

---

*Selection from Immanuel Kant, *Education*, trans. Annette Charton (Ann Arbor: Ann Arbor Paperbacks, The University of Michigan Press, 1960), pp. 83–94.

sleep, for work, and for pleasure; and these times must be neither shortened nor lengthened. With indifferent matters children might be allowed to choose for themselves, but having once made a rule they must always follow it. We must, however, form in children the character of a child, and not the character of a citizen. . . .

Above all things, obedience is an essential feature in the character of a child, especially of a school boy or girl. This obedience is twofold, including absolute obedience to his master's commands, and obedience to what he feels to be a good and reasonable will. Obedience may be the result of compulsion; it is then *absolute*: or it may arise out of confidence; it is then obedience of the second kind. This *voluntary* obedience is very important, but the former is also very necessary, for it prepares the child for the fulfilment of laws that he will have to obey later, as a citizen, even though he may not like them.

Children, then, must be subject to a certain law of *necessity*. This law, however, must be a general one—a rule which has to be kept constantly in view, especially in schools. The master must not show any predilection or preference for one child above others; for thus the law would cease to be general. As soon as a child sees that the other children are not all placed under the same rules as himself, he will at once become refractory.

One often hears it said that we should put everything before children in such a way that they shall do it from *inclination*. In some cases, it is true, this is all very well, but there is much besides which we must place before them as *duty*. And this will be of great use to them throughout their life. For in the paying of rates and taxes, in the work of the office, and in many other cases, we must be led, not by inclination, but by duty. Even though a child should not be able to see the reason of a duty, it is nevertheless better that certain things should be prescribed to him in this way; for, after all, a child will always be able to see that he has certain duties as a child, while it will be more difficult for him to see that he has certain duties as a human being. Were he able to understand this also— which, however, will only be possible in the course of years—his obedience would be still more perfect.

Every transgression of a command in a child is a want of obedience, and this brings *punishment* with it. Also, should a command be disobeyed through inattention, punishment is still necessary. This punishment is either *physical* or *moral*. It is *moral* when we do something derogatory to the child's longing to be honoured and loved (a longing which is an aid to moral training); for instance, when we humiliate the child by treating him coldly and distantly. This longing of children should, however, be cultivated as much as possible. Hence this kind of punishment is the best, since it is an aid to moral training—for instance, if a child tells a lie, a look of contempt is punishment enough, and punishment of a most appropriate kind.

Physical punishment consists either in refusing a child's requests or in the infliction of pain. The first is akin to moral punishment, and is of a negative kind. The second form must be used with caution, lest an *indoles servilis* should be the result. It is of no use to give children rewards; this makes them selfish, and gives rise to an *indoles mercenaria*.

Further, obedience is either that of the child or that of the *youth*. Disobedience is always followed by punishment. This is either a really *natural* punishment, which a man brings upon himself by his own behaviour—for instance, when a child gets ill from overeating—and this kind of punishment is the best, since a man is subject to it throughout his life, and not merely during his childhood; or, on the other hand, the punishment is artificial. By taking into consideration the child's desire to be loved and respected, such punishments may be chosen as will have a lasting effect upon its character. Physical punishments must merely supplement the insufficiency of moral punishment. If moral punishment have no effect at all, and we have at last to resort to physical punishment, we shall find after all that no good character is formed in this way. At the beginning, however, physical restraint may serve to take the place of reflection.

Punishments inflicted with signs of *anger* are useless. Children then look upon the punishment simply as the result of anger, and upon themselves merely as the victims of that anger; and as a general rule punishment must be inflicted on children with great caution, that they may understand that its one aim is their improvement. It is foolish to cause children, when they are punished, to return thanks for the punishment by kissing hands, and only turns the child into a slave. If physical punishment is often repeated, it makes a child stubborn; and if parents punish their children for obstinacy, they often become all the more obstinate. Besides, it is not always the worst men who are obstinate, and they will often yield easily to kind remonstrance.

The obedience of the growing *youth* must be distinguished from the obedience of the *child*. The former consists in submission to rules of duty. To do

something for the sake of duty means obeying reason. It is in vain to speak to children of duty. They look upon it in the end as something which if not fulfilled will be followed by the rod. A child may be guided by mere instinct. As he grows up, however, the idea of duty must come in. Also the idea of shame should not be made use of with children, but only with those who have left childhood for youth. For it cannot exist with them till the idea of honour has first taken root.

The second principal feature in the formation of a child's character is *truthfulness*. This is the foundation and very essence of character. A man who tells lies has no character, and if he has any good in him it is merely the result of a certain kind of temperament. Some children have an inclination towards lying, and this frequently for no other reason than that they have a lively imagination. It is the father's business to see that they are broken of this habit, for mothers generally look upon it as a matter of little or no importance, even finding in it a flattering proof of the cleverness and ability of their children. This is the time to make use of the sense of shame, for the child in this case will understand it well. The blush of shame betrays us when we lie, but it is not always a proof of it, for we often blush at the shamelessness of others who accuse us of guilt. On no condition must we punish children to force the truth from them, unless their telling a lie immediately results in some mischief; *then* they may be punished for that mischief. The withdrawal of respect is the only fit punishment for lying.

Punishments may be divided into *negative* and *positive* punishments. The first may be applied to laziness or viciousness; for instance, lying, disobedience. Positive punishment may be applied to acts of spitefulness. But above all things we must take care never to bear children a grudge.

A third feature in the child's character is *sociableness*. He must form friendships with other children, and not be always by himself. Some teachers, it is true, are opposed to these friendships in schools, but this is a great mistake. Children ought to prepare themselves for the sweetest enjoyment of life.

If a teacher allows himself to prefer one child to another, it must be on account of its character, and not for the sake of any talents the child may possess; otherwise jealousy will arise, which is opposed to friendship.

Children ought to be open-hearted and cheerful in their looks as the sun. A joyful heart alone is able to find its happiness in the good. A religion which makes people gloomy is a false religion; for we should serve God with a joyful heart, and not of constraint.

Children should sometimes be released from the narrow constraint of school, otherwise their natural joyousness will soon be quenched. When the child is set free he soon recovers his natural elasticity. Those games in which children, enjoying perfect freedom, are ever trying to outdo one another, will serve this purpose best, and they will soon make their minds bright and cheerful again. . . .

Children should only be taught those things which are suited to their age.

Many parents are pleased with the precocity of their offspring; but as a rule, nothing will come of such children. A child should be clever, but only as a child. He should not ape the manners of his elders. For a child to provide himself with moral sentences proper to manhood is to go quite beyond his province and to become merely an imitator. He ought to have merely the understanding of a child, and not seek to display it too early. A precocious child will never become a man of insight and clear understanding. It is just as much out of place for a child to follow all the fashions of the time, to curl his hair, wear ruffles, and even carry a snuff-box. He will thus acquire affected manners not becoming to a child. Polite society is a burden to him, and he entirely lacks a man's heart. For that very reason we must set ourselves early to fight against all signs of vanity in a child; or, rather, we must give him no occasion to become vain. This easily happens by people prattling before children, telling them how beautiful they are, and how well this or that dress becomes them, and promising them some finery or other as a reward. Finery is not suitable for children. They must accept their neat and simple clothes as necessaries merely.

At the same time the parents must not set great store by their own clothes, nor admire themselves; for here, as everywhere, example is all-powerful, and either strengthens or destroys good precepts.

Selected Readings

Butler, J. Donald. *Idealism in Education*. New York: Harper and Row, 1966.
    A compact and insightful treatment of philosophical idealism in contemporary educa-

tion. A good starting point for examining idealism in education.

Horne, Herman H. *The Democratic Philosophy of Education*. New York: Macmillan, 1935.

This book was written as a challenge to the growing strength of pragmatic philosophy in educational circles. It makes a case for returning to basic ideals and educational practices as the best way to achieve and maintain democracy.

Kant, Immanuel. *Education*. Annette Charton, ed. Ann Arbor: University of Michigan Press, 1960.

A historically influential work that examines education as both a theoretical and practical endeavor, this book introduces the Kantian influence into many aspects of education from discipline to curriculum.

Plato. *Republic*. New York: Oxford University Press, 1945.

One of the most famous treatises on education ever written, this work has influenced countless people across the centuries. It is a highly speculative and utopian approach to education as the basis of the good society.

Strain, John Paul. "Idealism: A Clarification of an Educational Philosophy." *Educational Theory* 25 (1975): 263–71.

This article is a recent survey of the contributions of philosophical idealism to education in the twentieth century. Although the author recognizes the declining popularity of the idealist approach to philosophy, he points out that many people still hold an idealist philosophy of education that reveals itself in continuing traditions and practices.

**Aristotle
(384-322)**

**Aquinas
(1225-1274)**

REALISM

Like idealism, realism is one of the oldest philosophies in Western culture and dates back at least as early as ancient Greece. Because of its respectable age, realism has had a variety of spokesmen and interpretations. Consequently, there are several varieties of realism ranging from classical and religious realism to scientific, natural, and rational realism. Because of this confusing array of variations, it seems most reasonable to approach this philosophy from common threads that are interwoven throughout its long history.

Perhaps the most central thread of realism is what may be called the principle or thesis of independence. In essence, this thesis holds that reality, knowledge, and value exist independent of the human mind. In other words, realism rejects the idealist notion that only ideas are real. The realist asserts, as fact, that the actual sticks, stones, and trees of the universe exist whether or not there is a human mind to perceive them. In one sense we may say that for the realist, matter is real; however, this does not mean that all realists are rampant materialists. What is of importance is that matter is an obvious example of an independent reality. In order to understand this complex philosophy, we need to examine its development from classical times, how it was transformed by the scientific revolution, and what it is today.

Bacon	Locke	Herbart	Whitehead
(1561-1626)	(1632-1704)	(1776-1841)	(1861-1947)
	Rousseau	Spencer	Russell
	(1712-1778)	(1820-1903)	(1872-1970)
	Pestalozzi	Froebel	Montessori
	(1746-1827)	(1782-1852)	(1870-1952)

2

REALISM AND EDUCATION

Classical Tradition

Aristotelian Realism

Aristotle (384–322 B.C.). Plato believed that matter had no lasting reality and that we should concern ourselves with ideas. It was Plato's pupil Aristotle, however, who developed the view that while ideas may be important in themselves, a proper study of matter could lead us to better and more distinct ideas. Aristotle studied and taught at Plato's Academy for about twenty years and later opened his own school, the Lyceum. His differences with Plato were developed gradually, and in many respects he never got out from under Plato's influence.

According to Aristotle, ideas (or forms), such as the idea of God or the idea of a tree, can exist without matter, but there can be no matter without form. Each piece of matter has both a universal and particular property. The particular properties of an acorn, for example, are those things that are peculiar to it and that differentiate it from all other acorns. These properties include its size, shape, weight, and color. There are no two acorns exactly alike, so we can talk about some particular properties of any acorn as essentially different from those of all other acorns. However, each acorn shares in a universal property with all other acorns. This can be called its "acornness," and it is what is universal with all other acorns. Perhaps this can be understood better by referring to humans at this point. People, too, differ in their particular properties. They have different shapes and sizes, and there are no two exactly alike. Yet all people do share in something universal, and this could be called their "humanness." Both human-ness and acornness are realities, and they exist independently and regardless of any one particular human or acorn. Thus, we may say that forms (universals, ideas, or essences) are the nonmaterial aspects of each particular material object that relate to all other particular objects of that class. Nonmaterial though form may be, we arrive at it by examining material objects that exist in them-selves, independent of us. Aristotle believed we should be very much involved in studying and understanding the reality of all things. Indeed, he agreed with Plato on this position. They differed, however, in that Aristotle felt one could get to form by studying particular material things, and Plato believed form could be reached only through some kind of reasoning such as the dialectic.

Aristotle argued that the form of things, the universal properties of objects, remain constant and never change whereas particular components do change. The shell of an acorn may disintegrate and an acorn may be destroyed, but the form of all acorns, or acornness, remains. In terms of people again, though individual persons die, humanness remains. Even if all men should die, humanness would remain, just as the concept of circularity would remain even if all existing material circles were destroyed. If we look at this in terms of the development of a person, we can see that as a child an individual has the particular characteristics of a child. As he grows, however, his body changes and he enters the phase of growth called adolescence; later he becomes an adult. Humanness remains even though the developmental process of the individual changes several times. Thus, form remains constant while particular matter changes. Aristotle and Plato agreed on the point that form is constant and matter is always changing, but Aristotle believed form was within particular matter and was even the motivating force of that matter. By the same token, the modern philosopher Henri Bergson spoke about an *élan vital*, or vital principle that each object has and that directs it in terms of fulfilling its purpose. This can be seen in the actual growth process of an acorn fulfilling its purpose in becoming an oak tree. It must take in the proper amount of sun and water, it must set its roots just so deep, and it must receive nourishment in the proper way. Each object, Aristotle thought, has a tiny "soul" that directs it in the right way.

Aristotle was both a scientist and a philosopher, and he believed that although we may separate science and philosophy artificially, there is a relation-ship between them in which the study of one aids us in the study of the other. For example, by studying the material aspects of an acorn, its shell, its color, and so forth, we should be led deeper into a contemplation of what the acorn really is, that is, its essence or form. Of course, a great deal depends upon asking the right questions. There are scientific questions and there are philosophical questions, and they can overlap. If we went to the seashore and picked up a shell, we could ask ourselves many scientific questions about that shell. What is it composed of? How long has it been here? What lived in it? How much does it weigh? There are many such questions and answering them would tell us quite a bit about the shell, but we would only be asking about its particular physical aspects. We could also ask other kinds of questions. What is its meaning? Who or what created it? What is its purpose? These kinds of questions are basically philosophical, though they can be brought out by scientific investigation. It has been pointed out, for example, that *The Bulletin of Atomic Physicists* is becoming a more philosophically oriented journal each year. This would support Aristotle's claim that the deeper we go into matter the more we are led to philosophy.

The most important questions we can ask about things relate to their purposes. Aristotle felt that each thing has a purpose or function. What is the purpose of a fish? If we examine it carefully, we might say that its purpose is to swim. The purpose of a bird is to fly. What, though, is man's purpose? Aristotle believed that since humans are the only creatures endowed with the ability to think, their purpose is to use this ability. Thus, we achieve our true purpose when we think, and we go against this end when we do not think or when we do not think intelligently.

According to Aristotle, there is design and order in the universe, for things happen in an orderly way. An acorn becomes an oak tree and not a sycamore. A kitten becomes a cat and not a dog. We can understand the universe by studying it in terms of its purposes. Thus, whatever happens can be explained according to purpose: the acorn follows its destiny and the kitten its destiny. With regard to humans, we have already seen that our purpose is to think, but we admitted that we can refuse to think or think poorly. We can avoid thinking by not paying attention, by misdirecting our thinking, or by otherwise subverting thinking. Aristotle believed that we can refuse to think and therefore go against the design of the universe and the reason for our creation; hence, we have free will. When we go against this purpose, however, we suffer the consequences of erroneous ideas, poor health, and an unhappy life, among other things.

For Aristotle, the man who follows his true purpose leads a rational life of moderation, avoiding extremes. There are two Aristotelian extremes: the extreme of too little and the extreme of too much. In terms of eating, if a man eats too much, he will gorge himself and suffer from obesity, lack of energy, poor health in general, or death. The moderate man or woman, the thinking person, avoids such excesses. For Aristotle, the proper perspective is the Golden Mean, a path between extremes.

Aristotle's concept of the Golden Mean is illustrated by his notion of the soul as an entity to be kept in balance. He spoke of the three aspects of the soul being vegetative, animal, and rational. We might say that when a man vegetates he is following the extreme of too little, when he is angry and hostile the extreme of too much; but when he uses his reason to keep his vegetative and animal aspects in harmony, he is following the path for which he was designed and is fulfilling his purpose. We might also relate this idea to Plato's concept of the ideal state where the good state is one where all of its classes, that is, brass (vegetative), silver (animal), and gold (rational) are in balance and harmony. Aristotle believed that a good education helps to achieve the Golden Mean and thereby promotes the harmony and balance of both soul and body.

Balance is central to Aristotle's view. He saw all the universe in some balanced and orderly fashion. As far as humans were concerned, he did not view body and mind in opposition as Plato did; rather, body is the means by which data come to us through sense perception. The raw data of sense perception are organized by the reasoning of mind. Universal principles are derived by mind from an examination of the particulars by sense perception. Thus, body and mind operate together in a balanced whole with their own internal consistencies.

Aristotle did not separate a particular thing from its universal being. Matter and form are not two different kinds of being, but fundamental aspects of the same thing. Form is in matter, for formless matter is a false notion, not a reality. The important thing to see is that all matter is in some stage of actualization. Whereas Plato was primarily interested in the realm of forms or ideas, Aristotle tried to unite the world of matter with the world of forms. An example of this is his view of actuality and potentiality. Actuality is that which is complete and perfect—the form. Potentiality refers to the capability of being actualized or gaining perfection and form. It is the union of form and matter that gives concrete reality to things. In other words, an individual acorn contains both form and matter that make up the "real" acorn we experience in the common sense world of every day.

This is further illustrated by Aristotle's conception of the four Causes: (1) the Material Cause, the matter from which something is made; (2) the Formal Cause, the design that shapes the material object; (3) the Efficient Cause, the agent that produces the object; and (4) the Final Cause, the direction toward which the object is tending. In common sense language, when we talk about a house, the material it is made of (the wood, bricks, and nails) is its Material Cause; the sketch or blueprint followed in constructing it is its Formal Cause; the carpenter who builds it is its Efficient Cause; and its Final Cause is that it is a place in which to live, a house. Matter is in process, moving to some end. In this respect, Aristotle's thought is very similar to the modern view of evolution and the notion of an open-ended universe. The difference between Aristotle and this modern view is that Aristotle saw this movement headed toward a final end, so for him the universe is open-ended only so much. The power that holds all creation and process together is God, by which Aristotle meant the power or source to which matter points beyond itself, an Ultimate Reality; hence, God is the First Cause, the Final End, the Unmoved Mover, beyond all matter and form. In this respect, we may observe that Aristotle's philosophy is as esoteric as Plato's. Yet, for Aristotle, God is a logical explanation for the order of the universe, its organizational and operational principle.

Indeed, organization is essential to Aristotle's philosophy. Everything can be organized into a hierarchy. For example, man is biologically based and rooted in nature. However, man strives for something beyond himself. If man is characterized by body, he is also characterized by soul, or his rational aspect, the capacity to move from within. If body and soul are balanced they are also organized, and soul is of a higher order than body, more characteristically human than anything else. For Aristotle man is the *rational* animal, most completely fulfilling his purpose when he thinks, for thinking is the highest characteristic of man. So it is, with Aristotle, that everything is capable of being ordered, for reality, knowledge, and value exist independent of mind, with their own internal consistency and balance capable of being comprehended by mind.

In order to search out the structure of independent reality, Aristotle worked on logical processes. Plato used dialectic to synthesize opposing notions about truth. Aristotle was concerned with truth, too, and he sought access to it through attempting to refine the dialectic. The logical method he developed was the syllogism. Basically, the syllogism is a method for testing the logic of statements. A famous but simplistic version of it goes as follows:

> All men are mortal.
> Socrates is a man;
> therefore, Socrates is mortal.

The syllogism is composed of a major premise, minor premise, and conclusion. Aristotle used the syllogism to help us think more accurately by ordering statements about reality in a logical, systematic form that would correspond to the facts of the situation under study.

Basically, Aristotle's logical method is deductive; that is, it derives its truth from generalizations, such as "all men are mortal." One problem with this method is that if the major premise is false, the conclusion will be false. A catch comes in determining the truth of the major premise: by what method do we test its accuracy? If we continue to use the syllogism, we also must continue to rely on unproven general premises. Aristotle's logical method runs contrary to his insistence that we can better understand form (general principle) by studying specific material objects. In this latter instance, Aristotle's thrust is inductive; that is, we come to truth by way of specifics, or the process goes from specifics to the general. His syllogism, however, goes from generalizations (all men are mortal) to specific conclusions (Socrates is mortal). This problem of logical method was a stumbling block to thinkers for centuries. The syllogistic approach led to many false or untenable positions. It was not until the sixteenth century that Francis Bacon devised a more suitable inductive approach.

The chief good for Aristotle is happiness; however, happiness is dependent upon a virtuous and well-ordered soul. This can only come about as we develop habits of virtue that are shaped through the proper kind of education. Education necessitates the development of our reasoning capacity so that we can make the right kinds of choices. As already indicated, this means the path of moderation. An acceptance and following of such a principle becomes the core of Aristotle's educational proposals. Although Aristotle did not go into specific detail about his educational ideas, he felt that the proper character would be formed by following the Golden Mean. This would result in proper social development and would assist the state in producing and nurturing good citizens. In the *Politics*, Aristotle further developed his view that there is a reciprocal relationship between the properly educated person and the properly educated citizen.

The Aristotelian influence has been one of immense importance and includes such things as recognizing the need to study nature systematically, using logical processes in thought, deriving general truths through a rigorous study of particulars, and emphasizing the rational aspects of human nature.

Religious Realism

Thomas Aquinas (1225-1274). Aristotle's ideas had a great impact upon the Christian religion, and in many respects they have tended to encourage the secularization of the church, as opposed to the monasticism engendered by the writings of Augustine. Gradually, the ideas of Aristotle were incorporated into Christianity and provided it with a philosophical base. Thomas Aquinas became the leading authority on Aristotle in the Middle Ages and found no great conflict between the ideas of the pagan philosopher and the ideas of Christian revelation. He argued that since God is pure reason, then the universe is reason, and by using our reason, as Aristotle suggested, we could know the truth of things. Aquinas also put emphasis on using our senses in order to obtain knowledge about the world, and his proofs of God's existence, for example, depend heavily upon sensory observation.

Aquinas believed God created matter out of nothing, and God was, as Aristotle stated, the Unmoved Mover who gave meaning and purpose to the universe. In his monumental work, *Summa Theologica*, he summed up the arguments dealing with Christianity. He used the rational approach suggested by Aristotle in analyzing and dealing with various religious questions. As a matter of fact, many of the supporting arguments in Christian religion are heavily derived from Thomas Aquinas, regardless of what branch of Christianity is considered. Roman Catholicism considers Thomism its leading philosophy.

Thomas Aquinas was first of all a churchman. For him all truths were eternally in God. Truth was passed from God to man by divine revelation, but God had also endowed man with the reasoning ability to seek out truth. Being the churchman that he was, Aquinas would not subordinate revelation to reason, but he did want to give reason a proper place. Essentially, he viewed theology as the primary concern and philosophy as the "handmaiden of theology." Thus, by recognizing the supremacy of theology, he was able to explore the philosophical development of religious thought more fully.

Aquinas agreed with Aristotle that we come to universals by a study of particulars. He accepted the thesis of independence and "form" as the principle characteristic of all being. He upheld the "principle of immanence" that is akin to Aristotle's view of each existence moving toward perfection in form. While he agreed that soul is the form of body, he held that soul is not derived from man's biological roots; rather, soul is a creation, immortal and from God.

Aquinas' views on education are consistent with his philosophical position. Accordingly, knowledge can be gained from sense data, and it can lead one to God provided the learner views it in the proper perspective. In essence, his views are that one should proceed from the study of matter to the study of form. He disagreed with Augustine that we could only know God through faith or some intuitive process; rather, Aquinas maintained that man can use his reason to reach God through a study of the material world. Thus, he saw no inconsistency between the truths of revelation accepted on faith and the truths arrived at through careful rational observation and study.

Aquinas believed the proper education is one that fully recognizes both the spiritual and material natures of man. Since he thought the spiritual side was the higher and more important, Aquinas was strongly in favor of primary emphasis on the education of man's soul.

Both Aristotle and Aquinas held to a dualistic doctrine of reality. This can be seen in Aristotle's view of matter and form, and in Aquinas's view of the material and spiritual sides of man. This dualism was later carried on in the great conflict between a scientific and religious view of reality.

Development of Modern Realism

One of the chief problems of classical realism was its failure to develop an adequate method of inductive thinking. While the classicists had developed the thesis that reality, knowledge, and value may be ascertained by studying particulars, they were still caught in an essentially deductive style of thinking. They often had their truths in hand at the start, never really doubting that there was a First Cause or an Unmoved Mover. Modern realism developed out of attempts to correct such errors, and it may be said, these corrective attempts were at the heart of what we today call the "scientific revolution" that swept Western culture. Of all the philosophers engaged in this effort, perhaps the two most outstanding realist thinkers were Francis Bacon and John Locke. They were involved in developing systematic methods of thinking and ways to increase human understanding.

Francis Bacon (1561–1626). Francis Bacon was not only a philosopher but a politician in the courts of Elizabeth I and James I. History shows that Bacon was not very successful in his political efforts (he was removed from office in disgrace), while his record in philosophical development is much more impressive. Bacon's philosophical task was ambitious if not pretentious in its scope. He claimed to take all knowledge as his field of investigation. That he nearly accomplished this is testimony to his genius. Perhaps his most famous work is *Novum Organum*, in which he challenged Aristotelian logic.

Bacon attacked the Aristotelians for contributing to the lethargic development of science by their adoption of theological methods of thought. The problem with theology was that it started with dogmatisms and *a priori* assumptions and then deduced conclusions. However, Bacon charged that science could not proceed this way, for science must be concerned with inquiry pure and simple, inquiry not burdened with preconceived notions. Bacon held that science must begin in this fashion and must develop reliable methods of inquiry. By developing a reliable method of inquiry, we could be freed from dependence on the occurrence of infrequent geniuses and could develop knowledge through the use of the method. Bacon believed "knowledge is power," and it was through the acquisition of knowledge that we could more effectively deal with the problems and forces that beset us on every side. In order to accomplish these things, he devised what he called the inductive method.

Bacon opposed Aristotelian logic primarily because he thought it yielded many errors, particularly concerning material phenomena. For example, religious thinkers such as Thomas Aquinas and the Scholastics accepted certain axiomatic beliefs about God—that He exists, is just, all powerful, and so forth—and then they deduced all sorts of things about the use of God's power, His intervention in human affairs, and so on. Bacon's inductive approach, which asked that we begin with observable instances and then reason to general statements or laws, counteracted the Scholastic approach, for it demanded verification of specific instances before a judgment was made. For example, after observing instances of water freezing at 32° Fahrenheit, we might then state as a general law that water freezes at 32° Fahrenheit. This law is only valid, however, so long as water continues to freeze at this temperature. If, because of a change in atmospheric or terrestrial conditions, water no longer freezes at 32° Fahrenheit, then we would be obliged to change our law. Through deduction one might also alter beliefs, but when one begins with absolute truths he is less likely to change them than when he begins with neutral data.

A historical example of this involved the dispute between Galileo and the Catholic Church concerning the position of the earth in the solar system. The church defended the Ptolemaic theory that the earth was the center of the universe, while the other planets, including the sun, rotated around it. This position was supported by a number of deductions. To begin with, since God created the earth, it was reasonable to assume He would place it in the center. Also, since God chose to place man on earth, the earth must have had an important place in the plan of creation, and this gives added weight to the importance of the earth being centrally located. The story in the Bible about Joshua fighting a difficult battle and asking God to make the sun stand still seemed to give even more support to this position. But Galileo argued for the Copernican theory, that the sun and not the earth is the center of the universe, for the earth moves and rotates about the sun. The position of Nicolaus Copernicus (as set forth in *The Revolutions of the Heavenly Bodies*) was disputed by the church because it belittled the earth and God's plan, and it challenged the veracity of revelation. Galileo used a telescope to give empirical proof to the Copernican position, and this increased the wrath of the church. It is reported that a Jesuit, who had been invited into Galileo's study to look through the telescope for proof, claimed that the devil was putting those things there for him to see. Church officials demanded that Galileo refute his position, yet his work was later substantiated in whole or in part by scientists such as Johann Kepler, Tycho Brahe, and Sir Isaac Newton.

Since the scientific or inductive approach uncovered many errors in propositions that had originally been taken for granted, Bacon urged that we reexamine all our previously accepted knowledge. At the very least, we should attempt to rid our minds of various "idols" before which we bow down and cloud our thinking. These idols, said Bacon, are primarily four in number. There is the Idol of the Den, whereby we believe things because of our own limited experiences. If, for example, an individual had several bad experiences with men with moustaches, he might conclude that all men with moustaches are bad, a clear case of faulty generalization. Another idol is the Idol of the Tribe, whereby we tend to believe things because most people believe them. There are numerous studies to show that many people will change their opinions to match those of the majority. Another idol that Bacon believed interfered with our thinking is what he called the Idol of the Marketplace. This idol deals with language, for Bacon believed that words are often used in ways that prevent understanding. For instance, words such as "liberal" and "conservative" might have little meaning when applied to people because one could be liberal on one issue; conservative on another. Bacon referred to the final idol as the Idol of the Theatre. This is the idol of our religions and philosophies that may prevent us from seeing the world objectively. He called for a housekeeping of the mind where we break away from the dead ideas of the past and begin again by using the method of induction.

Essentially, induction is the logic of arriving at generalizations on the basis of systematic observations of particulars. The general thrust of this view can be found in Aristotle, but Aristotle never developed it into a complete system. According to Bacon, induction involves the collection of data about particulars, but it is not merely a cataloging and enumeration of data. The data must be examined, and where contradictions are found, some must be discarded. In addition, facts must be processed or interpreted at the same time. If the inductive method were well developed and rigorously applied, it would benefit us to the extent that it would give us more control over the external world by unlocking the secrets of nature.

John Locke (1632–1704). Following somewhat in Bacon's footsteps, John Locke sought to explain how we develop knowledge. He attempted a rather modest philosophical task, to "clear the ground of some of the rubbish" that hindered man's gaining knowledge. In this respect, he was attempting to rid thought of what Bacon referred to as "idols."

Locke was born in England, the son of a country lawyer. He was educated at Westminister School and at Christ Church College at Oxford, where he was later a fellow. His education was classical and scholastic. He later turned on this tradition, attacking its Aristotelian roots and its scholastic penchant for disputations, which he thought were mere wrangling and ostentation.

Locke's contributions to realism were his investigations into the extent and certainty of human knowledge. He traced the origin of ideas to the object of thought, or whatever the mind entertains. For Locke, there are no such things as innate ideas. At birth the mind is like a blank sheet of paper, a *tabula rasa*, upon which ideas are imprinted. Thus, all knowledge is acquired from sources independent of the mind or acquired as a result of reflection on data from independent sources. In other words, all ideas are derived from experience by way of sensation and reflection.

Locke did not overly concern himself with the nature of mind itself but concentrated on how ideas or knowledge are gained by mind. External objects exist, he argued, and they are characterized by two kinds of qualities: primary qualities such as solidity, size, and motion; and secondary qualities such as color, taste, smell, sound, and other "sense" qualities. We may call primary qualities *objective* (adhering or directly connected with the object) and secondary qualities *subjective* (dependent upon our experiencing them).

Locke was an empiricist. He respected the concrete and practical while he distrusted abstract idealisms; consequently, what we know is what we experience. We experience the qualities of objects, whether these are material or ideational qualities. The data with which the mind operates are *experienced* data, and while they come from without, mind *can* combine and order experience and can become aware of its operations. Thus, knowledge is dependent upon sensation *and* reflection.

Concerning the nature of the external objective world, Locke had little to say. He basically assumed its existence, and he explained this existence with the "doctrine of substance"; that is, substance or external reality is a necessary support for experience. Thus, he assumed an independent reality but did not try to prove it. His major contribution to philosophy was the development of an acute awareness of experience. Rather than speculation about innate ideas or essences, or an independent material reality, his field of investigation was human experience and human knowledge.

Locke's views on education, as expressed in *Some Thoughts Concerning Education*, are not as theoretical as his speculations on epistemology. They are practical ideas about conduct, laziness, rewards and punishments, and other generalities in the educational process. Locke's ideas lead to the kind of "gentlemanly" education for which English education is strongly noted. One might argue that despite Locke's philosophical penchant for democracy, his educational ideas lend themselves to an aristocratic elitism.

Contemporary Realism

For the most part, contemporary realism has tended to develop most strongly around concerns with science and scientific problems of a philosophical nature. This movement has occurred mostly in the twentieth century and has been associated with the development of such new schools of thought as logical positivism and linguistic analysis. Yet, within this development, there has been a continuance of the basic thesis of independence.

Two of the most outstanding figures in contemporary realism were Alfred North Whitehead and Bertrand Russell. These men had much in common, including the fact that both were English, and collaborated on mathematical writings. Eventually, they both came to teach in some of the outstanding universities in the United States, and were interested in and wrote about education. With all this commonality, they went in philosophical directions unique to each man. Whitehead's direction was almost Platonic in his search for universal patterns; Russell's went toward mathematical quantification and verification as the basis of philosophical generalization.

Alfred North Whitehead (1861–1947). Perhaps one of the most fruitful things creative philosophers do is to bring about reconciliation between contending systems of thought. Aquinas did this when he reconciled Aristotelianism with Christianity. Kant did this in trying to reconcile science and traditional values. Alfred North Whitehead sought to do this by attempting to reconcile some aspects of idealism with realism, thereby reconstructing the philosophical bases of modern science.

Whitehead came to philosophy through mathematics. He coauthored with Bertrand Russell a work titled *Principia Mathematica*. He was past sixty when he turned to philosophy on a full-time basis as a professor of philosophy at Harvard. One of his outstanding philosophical treatises is *Science and the Modern World*, and some of his major statements on education may be found in *The Aims of Education and Other Essays*. Basically, *process* is central to Whitehead's philosophy, for he held that reality *is* process. What man encounters in this process are actual entities or "occasions" (the real "things" or objects), "prehensions" (relational processes between the experiencing person and experienced objects), and "nexus" (extended time sequences in which "occasions" and "prehensions" fit together in ongoing existence).

In many respects, Whitehead sought to unite philosophical oppositions such as subjective perception and objective entities, and he believed that we must recognize both aspects. He rejected a bifurcated reality, yet recognized the individuality of a thing in itself and the relational or universal aspects of things. What he objected to was going too far in one direction to the detriment of the other. He rejected the separation of the mental into a realm by itself, for mental activity had to be viewed in the context of experience. He preferred realism as a philosophy because he thought it helped man correct the excesses of subjective thought.

It may appear that Whitehead rejected the thesis of independence. This is true to the degree that he did not see objective reality and subjective mind as absolutely separate. They are together in an organized unity or pattern. Yet, at the same time, this organic unity itself can be seen as an active system, an ultimate reality so to speak, that operates according to its own principles in process. Philosophy is simply a search for pattern in the universe. Man can never grasp pattern in any complete sense, although he may get aspects of it. Ultimately, the universe does have rationality to it and is not mere arbitrariness.

We may say that Whitehead was following solidly in the footsteps of Aristotle, for it is apparent that pattern in Whitehead's terms is similar to form. He also followed Aristotle in going to particulars to discern pattern, yet he deviated because he held that particulars are *events* that have to be viewed in terms of open-ended process. Thus, his events are not inert particulars but organic to, and moving with, process and according to pattern.

This brings us to a consideration of Whitehead's view of education. To him, the important things to be learned are ideas. In this sense, we may say he was Platonic. However, he was adamant in urging that education be concerned with "living ideas," ideas connected with the experience of learners, ideas that are useful and capable of being articulated. He warned against learning inert ideas simply because it had been done in the past. This shows his organic orientation, that education should enable us to get into the flow of existence, the process-patterns of reality.

Bertrand Russell (1872–1970). Bertrand Russell was born in Wales in rather comfortable economic circumstances. He received his degree at Cambridge University in philosophy and mathematics. One of the first-rate minds of the twentieth century, Russell exerted quite a bit of influence as both a writer and teacher. Some of his books are *Our Knowledge of the External World*, *Religion and Science*, and the famous work he coauthored with Whitehead, *Principia Mathematica* (1910–1913). In education, he wrote *Education and the Social Order* and *Education and the Modern World* among other books. He taught at Cambridge, the University of Chicago, and the University of California.

Russell was a controversial figure. In World War I, he was imprisoned for his pacifist activities. His distaste for Victorian morality, especially his views on sex and marriage, often led him into conflict with his English peers. In the 1960s, he was at the center of "Ban the Bomb" movements and anti-Vietnam war protests in England and Europe.

Russell was a maverick realist in some respects. Where Whitehead concluded that the universe is characterized by pattern, so did Russell, but Russell felt that these patterns can be verified with precision and analyzed mathematically. There is a need, he held, to merge the logical and mathematical so that pattern can be discerned both verbally and mathematically.

Basically, he held that the role of philosophy is both analytic and synthetic; that is, it should be critical in its analytic phase by showing the logical fallacies and errors in past systems, and it should be constructive in its synthetic phase by offering hypotheses about the nature of the universe that science has not yet determined. However, Russell felt that philosophy should be mainly analytical. It should base itself upon science, since only science has any genuine claim to knowledge. From the standpoint of science, we can see Russell's adherence to realism and what we have called the thesis of independence. It was not so much the results of science as the methods that he accepted. By using these methods, he hoped to arrive at valid philosophical constructions, not constructions of large generalization, but rather piecemeal, detailed, verifiable constructions.

One could get two sorts of particular data on independent reality: hard data and soft data. Hard data refer to the facts of the situation, facts that can withstand the scrutiny of reflection and remain intact. Soft data are such things as beliefs, things that can neither be verified nor denied with any degree of certainty. Russell's stated purpose was to base his philosophical constructions as much as possible on the hard and verifiable side, the side of science, but he also recognized the soft side. This, he held, should make us more sensitive to overgeneralizing and its accompanying dangers of arriving at false certainties.

By using a cautious or more temperate approach to science, Russell hoped we could begin to solve such perplexing problems as poverty and ill health. He thought of education as the key to a better world. If we would use existing knowledge and apply tested methods, then through education we could eradicate such problems as poverty and thus transform the world. Russell even speculated that if this were done on a wide scale, the transformation could conceivably be accomplished in one generation.

For a time, Russell tried to put some of his educational ideas to work at the school he founded called Beacon Hill. However, his radicalism met resistance, and his own driving inquisitiveness soon led him to other causes and reforms. Although his efforts in education at Beacon Hill met with limited success, Russell continued to the end of his life to try to bring about changes through education that he deemed beneficial to the good of humanity.

Realism as a Philosophy of Education

Realism is a confusing philosophy because there are so many varieties: classical realism, religious realism, scientific realism, and others. This confusion stems back to Aristotle, for although his prominence in philosophy was primarily derived from his differences with Platonic philosophy, yet there are probably more similarities overall than differences between Plato and Aristotle. The primary confusion over realism may be between a religious realism and a secular or scientific realism. Religious realism would show the similarities of Aristotle's philosophy to Plato and Thomas Aquinas; secular realism would relate Aristotle's work more to the development of scientific philosophy through the works of Bacon, Locke, and Russell. Whitehead may be said to incorporate aspects of each in his interpretation of realism.

Aims of Realism

Plato, as an idealist, believed that such abstractions as truth, goodness, and beauty could only be reached through the study of ideas, primarily through the use of the dialectic. Aristotle, on the other hand, thought that ideas (forms) are also found by studying the world of matter. Essentially, Plato and Aristotle end up at the same place, but the method of getting there is different. Plato believed that one acquires knowledge of ideas through contemplation of ideas; Aristotle believed that one could acquire knowledge of ideas or forms through a study of matter. Whereas Plato rejected matter as an object of study or as a real entity,. Aristotle used matter as an object of study to reach something further.

For the religious realist, matter is not so important in itself as when it leads to something beyond itself. Aristotle recognized that one may look at any object simply as a scientific study, but this would only be dealing with one aspect of matter. A scientist finding a shell on the seashore may examine it descriptively in terms of size, shape, weight, and so on. Such concerns, however, should also lead to questions of a philosophical nature relating to the beginnings and purpose of the shell. This is illustrated by contemporary scientific efforts to study the moon. Specimens brought back by the astronauts are studied intensively. Many photographs and television compositions have been made on the natural makeup of the moon, but these have not been made simply to catalog its shape, size, and weight; rather, the purpose has been much deeper. Scientists and thinkers of various disciplines are interested in discovering knowledge about the very origins of our universe. This shows that scientific inquiry can lead to the most profound ultimate kinds of philosophical questions. Thus, one can transcend nature and use it to venture into the realm of ideas.

The use of a study of nature for transcending matter is for the religious realist the prime reason for its being. The argument might run thus: God, who is pure spirit, created the world. He created it out of nothing, but He put himself into the world, giving it order, regularity, and design. By studying the world carefully, and by discovering its order and regularity, we can come to know about God. Religious realists, such as Thomas Aquinas, would say this is our prime purpose—God created the world to provide a vehicle through which people could come to know Him.

There have been many thinkers (not necessarily philosophical realists) who have believed that nature could provide us with something greater than itself. William Wordsworth, Ralph Waldo Emerson, and Henry David Thoreau, all nineteenth-century romanticists, used the theme that nature could be transcended by thinking and that individuals could venture into higher realms of thought. Religious realists believe this kind of transcending should be the principal aim of education.

On the other hand, secular realists emphasize the sensory material world and its processes and patterns rather than the transcendent spiritual world to which sensory data might lead. This approach is basically scientific in nature. The scientific movement beginning with Francis Bacon ushered in an era of thought that stressed not only an understanding of the material world but control of it as well. It was Aristotle who pointed out the order and regularity of the material world, and by this same process, scientists came to talk about the "laws of nature."

Secular realism stresses an understanding of the material world through the development of methods of rigorous inquiry. Bacon first suggested that men should clear their minds of the idols of generalization, language, and philosophy. Deduction, which was the prevailing method of thought prior to Bacon, was based primarily on rational thought. Reason alone, however, had led to many errors not only in Aristotle's thinking but to the metaphysical extravagancies of the Scholastics. It was reason that produced such imaginings as mermaids, devils, centaurs, and the like. For the secular realist, the way out of this dilemma, that is, deciding which ideas are true, is to verify them in the world of experience. John Locke gave great support to Bacon's empiricism by showing that no ideas are innate, but through reflection or reason we may create ideas, such as the idea of a purple cow, which does not exist in the world of experience. The empirical movement that Bacon and Locke encouraged requires that ideas must be subject to public verification. This means that ideas that cannot be proven through scientific experiment must be considered only as hypotheses.

The secular realist promotes a study of science and the scientific method. He believes that man needs to know the world in order to use it to insure his own survival. This idea of survival is an important one. For example, Herbert Spencer, the nineteenth century British philosopher and social scientist, placed self-preservation as a primary and fundamental aim of education. In other words, the things a child most needs to know are those things which maintain his existence as an individual, as a member of a family, and as a citizen. The secular realist sees our control over nature as a vast improvement from our early beginnings when we were at the mercy of nature. Our misunderstanding of nature, such as the superstitious explanations for typhoons and floods, led to many false beliefs. Today, our continued advancement depends upon even greater understanding and control of nature. We might say that our technical skill has gotten us into the ecological mess, but the secular realist would add, it can also get us out of it.

Secular realism maintains that there are essential ideas and facts to know that can only be learned by a study of the material world. It places great stress on a study of basic facts, both for the purpose of survival and the advancement of technology and science. One could say that technical schools such as the Massachusetts Institute of Technology are "realist" in their approach to education. The Soviet Union seems to prefer this approach to education for both technical and political purposes. In the United States, there has been strong support for a more technical and scientific education since the launching of Sputnik in 1957. Many education critics such as Admiral Hyman Rickover have argued that American education has become too "soft," dealing with "fads and frills," and that education needs to return to "basic" studies like mathematics and science.

Realism as an educational philosophy has long been with us in one way or another, but it tends to assert itself most in times of turmoil. It is almost as if we have other educational philosophies when we can afford them, but realism is a necessity. The claim is that we will always have some need for basic factual data and subjects like reading, writing, and arithmetic. This tendency seemed to be pointed up particularly when the Soviets launched the first satellite. Many people believed our second-place technical position in this respect was due in large measure to the schools, which were not teaching enough basic subject matter, particularly in the areas of science and mathematics. Rickover pointed to the dearth of competent scientists in this country as compared with the Soviet Union. He also praised Swiss education for its adherence to basics and believed that the American system should do likewise. He laid much of the blame for our lack of technical know-how and creativity at the door of John Dewey and the progressives who were promoting an education that Rickover thought was not only superficial but actually dangerous in terms of our survival. An even more caustic critic was Max Rafferty, whose *Suffer Little Children* was an extremely popular book, and who believed that basic subject matter and other staples of American education, such as a concern for religion, patriotism, and capitalism were being neglected.

A group of educators who were greatly concerned with the decline of basic subject matter in American schools formed an organization called the Council for Basic Education. This organization has fought strenuously to keep and add basic subject matter in schools, not only the three Rs, but subjects such as science and history. One of the leading spokesmen for the council, James Koerner, believes that part of the problem lies in the training of teachers who are given survey courses instead of more basic data and who come to the classroom intellectually impoverished.

A major problem, according to the realists, is a general cultural malaise caused by a lack of commitment to fundamental values. This is shown in the breakdown of discipline and disregard for basic traditions. Perhaps the best illustration of this is the fact that schools have drifted away from a concentration on the essentials of reading, writing, arithmetic, and character development. The "open education" movement is a recent example of this drift. Rather than having children study essential but not always exciting subjects, a "do your own thing" ethic was instituted where children were encouraged to "explore" and "discover" things that interested them personally. This creates a problem, many realists charge, because children seldom have clearly identified interests with enough focus to direct their needed educational development. In addition, they do not always know what is best for them or what they need, and this is confirmed by adults in later life who claim such educational approaches failed to prepare them for the real world. Perhaps the crowning evidence of the failure of "discovery" and "open" approaches, realists argue, is the embarrassing number of high school graduates who are functionally illiterate.

The breakdown of commitment to basic cultural values is not just limited to education but is reflected in the larger society. The confusion surrounding the Vietnam war and the United States' role in it is but one major example. Democracy depends on public debate of issues, but many realists feel that the willingness of organized society to allow young adults to rebel against authority when the country was engaged in military conflict reflects the extent of the breakdown and the failure of education to secure allegiance to basic values.

Perhaps the best illustration of the realist charge is the Watergate scandal, where government officials, including the president, were involved in a cover-up of illegal and unethical political activities. Critics point to the fact that all of the people involved in this scandal went through American schools. Yet, the schools apparently failed to instill those character traits and basic values necessary for ethical leadership. One wonders, even in the wake of Watergate, whether the schools have yet risen to meet the challenge. Despite all the talk about "back to the basics" and "accountability" in education, many observers of realist orientation question what is actually being done.

The failure can be seen at the local and national levels but is also present in international affairs. Many critics point to the erosion of America's political, economic, and military power. Americans have been held hostage by militarily weak foreign powers, and the United States has been virtually powerless to act. Other nations have been invaded by powerful neighbors, and the United States has been unable to reassert its once potent political leadership. Probably most frustrating of all is the decline in economic power, a much-vaunted strength in the past, so that American industrial might is at the mercy of small nations who control energy resources. Many nations have viewed education as a weapon to achieve economic, political, and military power and critics wonder why Americans do not use this source now by showing a commitment to education through expansion of funding and programs rather than the budgetary restraints currently fashionable.

One of the most tragic consequences of all of this, as frequently pointed out by such figures as Admiral Hyman G. Rickover, is that the talent of our most precious resource—the intellectually gifted—is being squandered. "Watered down" courses and "fads and frills" have limited the development of superior students by bringing them down to the level of the common denominator. Textbooks reflect this by simplified reading material and content geared to the mythical "average" student. Instead of pulling students up to their academic capabilities, such practices only pull them down to the "accepted" average.

Critics of the advocates of "basic education" consider them alarmists crying wolf and say that their approach to education looks backward to the American schools of a bygone era. They assert it is a conservative approach, a realism more interested in facts than in brotherhood, creativity, and human relations. Many educators maintain that facts can be taught in a pleasant atmosphere without the rote-style education associated with realism. Realists respond by saying this argument is often a cover-up for the schools' neglecting the hard tasks of education.

When we look back over the long history of education, we are reminded of the story about the archeologist who found an ancient clay tablet on which was written, "Why aren't they teaching them anything in schools anymore?" One of the functions of education from the earliest times has been to teach pupils the kinds of things society needs to know in order to survive. In ancient Egypt, students were expected to know the religious and political demands and how to prepare for an afterlife. In Greece and Rome, young men were taught oratory as a way of improving their stations in life. In the Middle Ages, a few were prepared for the priesthood while others were taught the code of chivalry. In the early history of our own country, the American Indian had elaborate ceremonies in which to educate the young into the ways of the tribe. Education has always been used as a way of teaching essential things to people, and in this respect it has served a very valuable function. The need for knowing these essentials is no less today, argues the realist; in fact, it is probably greater, since there are more things to learn than ever before. When we fail to teach a child how to read and write, we doom that child to difficulty in finding a job, in knowing how to vote, or in developing socially. It is possible that because of this limitation the child will become a liability rather than an asset to society. In the same way, when we fail to teach children the kind of preparation and skills needed for our technological maintenance and development, we are not using the schools to their fullest capacity. This may damage our status as a nation of power and influence in the world.

Although the realist argues that education should develop technical skill and turn out specialists and scientists, he is not opposed to education in the humanities. However, he finds that the schools are not teaching the humanities in ways conducive to cognitive development. It seems that teachers are more interested in turning out critics of literature than in teaching the literature itself.

Educators such as Harry Broudy would like teachers to take a critical look at what they are doing. After seeing the negative effects the trend in contemporary education is having, it is hoped that they will reverse this trend by returning to more basic subject matter. Realists complain that they have been equated with such caricatures as Dickens's Mr. Gradgind, and Irving's Ichabod Crane. They say they are not for mere memorization and rote learning of facts, nor do they dismiss problem solving, projects, and enjoyable experiences in learning activities. They do feel, however, that such experiences should be fruitful in terms of producing students with needed knowledge and skills. They would very much like to see our institutions of higher education turn out teaching specialists who are capable, and who would serve as models for the future development of students. In today's world, when we are producing a generation of children first to witness man's flight to the moon, and certainly soon to other planets, we should equip them with information to understand such events and to assist in the advancement of knowledge in the future. The realists argue we can only do this by providing students with basic and essential knowledge.

It must be kept in mind that while realists share many concerns, there are also variations. If they agree schools should promote the essentials, they each reach the meaning of "essential" from individual perspectives. For instance, Whitehead was almost idealistic in his recommendation that education be primarily concerned with ideas, but he condemned what he referred to as "scraps of information" and "inert ideas," for ideas should be learned in a practical and useful context. What makes his thought realistic is his view that man learns most truly from the material world in which he actually lives. He defended both classical and specialized studies if these studies have important applications now. Inertness, he held, is a central hazard in all education; consequently, Whitehead's view of the essentials might be very different from what someone else views as necessary, for he had a distinct notion of what education should contain.

Realists put great emphasis on the "practical" side of education, and their concept of practical includes education for moral and character development. John Locke, Johann F. Herbart, and Herbert Spencer all held that the chief aim of education should be moral education. Whitehead was close to this position when he said, " . . . the essence of education is that it be religious." Spencer, in his essay "What Knowledge Is of Most Worth?", held that science provides for both moral and intellectual education because the pursuit of science demand integrity, self-sacrifice, and courage. For Locke, good character is superior to intellectual training; however, Locke's views on character education seem to have been directed primarily at the English gentry of his day who were supposed to set examples for the rest of society. Herbart thought that moral education is founded on knowledge, and Spencer agreed with this theory.

Thus, we can see different approaches to a common thrust. Realists agree education should be based on the essentials and the practical, but they vary in their individual approaches to these things. Regardless of these individual approaches, however, there is an underlying common element. The essentials and the practicalities of education lead to something beyond themselves, an element that is distinctly Aristotelian; that is, it proceeds from matter to form, from imperfection to perfection. Realists are Aristotelian in viewing education as the process of developing our rational powers to their fullest so that we can achieve the good life.

Methods of Realism

The secular realist maintains that a proper understanding of the world necessitates an understanding of facts and ways of ordering and classifying knowledge. The establishment of scientific laws, for example, depends on verification of factual data that are up to date. The schools should teach such fundamental facts about the universe, and a good school program will present material in interesting and enjoyable ways. Not only facts, but the method of arriving at facts must also be taught. The realist places enormous emphasis upon critical reason aided by observation and experimentation.

Secular realism has had more recent impact upon philosophy of education than has religious realism. It is not surprising, for example, that critics like Hyman Rickover and James Bryant Conant are also scientists. The kind of education they promote is primarily technical and leads to specialization. The idea of specialization, which is so repugnant to the idealist, arose out of the efforts to refine and establish definitive scientific knowledge. Secular realists charge that the generalist is prone to wide flights of fantasy, very little of which is capable of verification. It is very important to establish what we know, and this can only be accomplished by many people, each one working on a small component of knowledge. The realists believe less in the personality of the teacher than in the effectiveness of the teacher to impart knowledge about the world that students can use.

Realists support the lecture method and other formal ways of teaching. While such objectives as self-realization are valuable, realists maintain that self-realization best occurs when students are knowledgeable about the external world; consequently, they must be exposed to facts, and the lecture method can be an efficient, organized, and orderly way to accomplish this objective. The lecture method is not the only one realists promote, for they insist that whatever the method used, it should be characterized by the integrity that comes from systematic, organized, and dependable knowledge. Reflect for a moment on our chaotic history and how we have suffered because of ignorance of facts about such things as a balanced diet, diseases and their causes, and the causes of natural disasters—knowledge we take for granted today. Our grasp of knowledge and the enjoyment of a better life have come as a result of a slow but steady accumulation of facts. Man could not exist for long without knowledge of at least some basic facts. Realists think that education dealing with the factual side of learning need not necessarily be presented in ways that are painful or boring; in fact, they hold that learning should be enjoyable as well as useful. John Locke thought that play is a distinct aid to learning. He seems to have had a feel for child psychology, and he advocated methods that appear to be very modern and contemporary. In addition to the usefulness of play, he urged that a child should not be vexed by boring lessons, that he should not be pushed beyond his level of readiness (even if this means a year's delay in learning to read), that a child should be given positive rewards to encourage further learning, and that the teacher should never push a child beyond his natural inclinations. In many respects, Locke stands as a forerunner of much in modern educational theory. His recognition that a child should not be pushed beyond his ability and readiness sounds very contemporary, and his sensitivity to a child's "natural inclinations" has a strong resemblance to the major tenets of contemporary child growth and development theories.

While some realists such as Locke were systematic and organized from the standpoint of specific aspects of the child or the environment, others such as Whitehead looked to more general patterns in human activity. Whitehead spoke of the "rhythmic" flow of education that can be discerned in three primary stages. First, there is the stage of romance, up to about the age of fourteen, in which the child's educational activity should be mainly characterized by discovering broad themes, shaping questions, and devising new experiences. The second stage, from the age of fourteen to eighteen, is the stage of precision characterized by the disciplined study of specific and particular knowledge. Stage three is the stage of generalization, from eighteen to around twenty-two. It focuses on the student becoming an effective individual capable of dealing with immediate experiences whereby he or she applies the principles of knowledge to life.

In spite of the attention given to the nature of the child and the flow of experience by realist thinkers like Locke and Whitehead, critics of realism point out that in practice, realism is rigid. They charge that, in fact, realist theory results in practices such as Herbart's "five formal steps of learning": preparation, presentation, association, systematization-generalization, and application. Russell Hamm charges that such an approach leads mechanically to reviewing homework, presenting new material, having a question-and-answer period, doing desk work, and receiving new homework assignments. Herbart, for example, also recommended that children be kept occupied as much as possible and that corporal punishment be used when necessary. His recommendations could be due to the realist affinity for precision and order. The desire for order and precision is found in such contemporary school practices as ringing bells, set time periods for study, departmentalization, daily lesson plans, course scheduling, increasing specialization in curriculum, prepackaged curriculum materials, and line-staff forms of administrative organization.

Although all realists promote the importance of knowledge about the physical universe, there is a difference in the ends to which such knowledge is put. The religious realist believes that knowledge should ultimately lead to things beyond itself such as God or Truth. One of the fundamental obligations of the teacher is to help the student know about the world and see the use of this knowledge as a way of reaching ultimates. In some parochial schools, for example, students study areas such as geography, history, and science, but these subjects are presented in ways that put an emphasis on the religious character or morality they entail. The secular realist, however, tends to see knowledge about the physical world primarily in its use-value in improving technology and advancing civilization. Although realists may study the same things, these things may be viewed for different purposes.

Many realists support competency, accountability, and performance-based teaching. They assume that educational growth in terms of competency, performance, and knowledge of the facts can be achieved and is measurable to a considerable extent. Furthermore, while it may be difficult to measure a student's growth in such areas as values, ethical considerations, and social relations, realists generally maintain that anything which exists, exists in some form capable of measurement. The best way to approach and deal with such problems as ethics is through our knowledge about the facts of ethics. It may be, for example, that the best ethics is one that shows us how to put ourselves in tune with the laws of the universe.

Realists place considerable importance on the role of the teacher in the educational process. He should be a person who presents material in a systematic and organized way and should promote the idea that there are clearly defined criteria one can use in making judgments about art, economics, politics, and education. For example, realists would assert that a work of art, such as a painting, can be evaluated in terms of objective criteria like the kind of brush stroke used, the shading of colors, the balance and quality of the subject matter, and the message involved. The same thing applies to the activity of education; there are certain objective criteria one can use to judge whether particular activities are worthwhile—for example, the type of material presented, how it is organized, whether or not it suits the psychological makeup of the child, whether the delivery system is suitable, and whether it achieves the desired results.

Contemporary realists emphasize the importance of scientific research and development. The "Scientific Movement in Education" has been accomplished primarily since 1900 and has brought about the advancement of knowledge in the psychology and physiology of education, and developmental approaches to education. This movement has also been largely responsible for the extensive use of IQ tests, standardized achievement tests, diagnostic tests, and competency tests. Curriculum has reflected the impact of the movement in the appearance of standard work lists, homogeneous grouping of students on the basis of intelligence, and standardized and serialized reading textbooks. The movement has also spawned the application of more precise and empirically based administrative techniques. Perhaps a more recent development is the growing extent to which computer technology is used in the schools. While these developments have often met with sharp resistance and counterattacks, it seems that this aspect of realism in education has also met with increasing acceptance on the part of many professional educators. Contemporary critics of American education often strike at the widespread use of scientific technology as one of the prime evils in the schools. Others, while less acid in their criticism of technology and science itself, quarrel with the underlying realist theory as being the culprit behind the misuse of science and technology, largely because they think realists are too accepting and uncritical of things labeled "scientific." Whatever the position one wishes to take on the issue, the existence of such an issue is witness to the vitality realist ideas still have.

Curriculum

Although realists have different views about what subjects should comprise the curriculum, they are in agreement that studies be practical and useful. Locke, in *Some Thoughts Concerning Education*, approved of such practical studies as reading, writing, drawing, geography, astronomy, arithmetic, history, ethics, and law, with supplementary studies in dancing, fencing, and riding. Locke, as did Froebel, emphasized the educational value of play and physical activity. Locke believed that children should spend much time in the open air and accustom themselves to "heat and cold, shine and rain." He focused his attention upon the complete person and included not only intellectual concerns, but also diet, exercise, and recreation. He believed instruction in reading should begin as soon as a child is able to talk. Writing should begin soon afterward. He promoted studies in languages, particularly French and Latin. He favored gardening and carpentry as useful educational experiences, as well as the idea of "a grand tour" with one's tutor. However, when one carefully peruses Locke's writings, one finds that there are really two curricula in his system: one for the rich and one for the poor. He proposed that all children, between ages three and fourteen, whose parents were on relief, should be sent to a work school for as long as they resided with their parents. They should earn their way at this school so as not to burden the local government financially. While there, they should have a "belly-full of bread daily" and in cold weather "a little warm water gruel." They were to be taught the manual skills of spinning, knitting, and "some other part of woolen manufacturing," and "some sense of religion."

One of the historical features of the realist curriculum has been the great attention given to the use of didactic and object studies in education. For example, Comenius, a theologian and educator in the sixteenth century, was the first to introduce an extensive use of pictures in the educational process. He believed that it was possible for an individual to obtain all knowledge provided he had the proper kind of education. This proper kind of education should be based on a curriculum to perfect one's natural powers by training the senses. He stressed the importance of studying nature, and his curriculum included such subjects as physics, optics, astronomy, geography, and mechanics. In stressing this "pansophic" goal of achieving all knowledge, Comenius felt that schools should be enjoyable places with sympathetic teachers.

This idea of developing the senses in education was also adopted by Jean-Jacques Rousseau, Johann Pestalozzi, and Friedrich Froebel, among others. Pestalozzi held that "sense impression of Nature is the only true foundation of human instruction, because it is the only true foundation of human knowledge." All that follows, he believed, is a result of this sense impression. Pestalozzi promoted such skills as spinning and gardening, with subjects such as arithmetic to be correlated with nature by having children apply numbers to objects. Froebel, the founder of the kindergarten, who studied at the Pestalozzian Institute of Frankfort, also believed in "object studies," and his primary educational methods focused on "gifts," songs, and games. Although Froebel's educational techniques began in the material world with material objects, he saw all things unified in God, who expresses Himself both in physical nature and in the human spirit.

Johann F. Herbart was another realist educator strongly influenced by Pestalozzi. Herbart criticized what he characterized as the atomistic curriculum of his day. He felt that there should be a system of "correlation and concentration" whereby each subject would bear upon, and be integrated with, other related subjects. Teaching, he believed, should be multilateral. Geography, economics, and history should be taught so that the student can see relationships that provide the basis for new knowledge. Herbart felt that ideas are kept alive through interest, and one function of education is to see that ideas are retained in the mind through books, lectures, and other teaching devices.

A more recent educator who promoted both interest and the use of objects in the educational process was Maria Montessori. In the Montessori method, there are all sorts of experiences with blocks, cylinders, and geometric patterns. These objects not only assist in the cognitive development of the child, but in his physical development as well.

Although her approach was originally designed for so-called mentally defective children, she later expanded it to include all children. Montessori believed that we can know a child by observing him, and she felt too many educators interfere with his "spontaneous activity." In The Secret of Childhood, she maintained that children have a secret world of their own that the educator can learn if he or she makes the effort. Basically, education means removing barriers from the path a child takes to discover the world. Education should therefore consist of a "prepared environment" with materials children can use that teach them how to learn. This method is solidly in keeping with the realist educational advocacy of sense perception and object lessons.

When we look at an overview of what realist educators propose for a curriculum, we see that it tends to be one that is both mental and physical, places an emphasis on subject matter, and is highly organized and systematic in its approach.

Critique of Realism in Education

Realism has steadily gained ground in American education. To say that this began with Sputnik and the accompanying clamor in 1957 and 1958 would not be true, although this event certainly accelerated the movement. Realism received its major thrust from the industrial and technological age that has characterized American society from the late nineteenth century to the present. It is little wonder that our schools would see as their major task the training and preparation of professionals and technicians in a society where professionalism and technical skill are so highly prized. Yet many critics decry this state of affairs as shortsighted and dehumanizing, pandering primarily to material concerns. Although classical and religious realists still recognize the higher ends of moral and spiritual values, critics charge that scientific realists generally maintain a materialistic conception of human nature biased toward social control and social order.

While the problems of order and control are often laid at the door of secular and scientific realism, there is evidence that the bias toward order and control goes back to Aristotle and Thomas Aquinas. These thinkers tended to see the universe in terms of an independent reality with its own internal and systematic order. Thus, there is the necessity for us to adapt and adjust to this reality; our dreams and desires have to be subsumed under its demand. The contemporary outcome of this is the pressure for us to adjust ourselves to the needs of the corporate industrial state, or totalitarian regimes, religious systems, and other overriding and apparently enduring world views. John Dewey tried to counteract what he considered to be the negative aspects of both realism and idealism by showing that what we know as real is neither totally in the mind nor totally objective and external; rather, he argued that human reality is comprised of both individuality and environment. Instead of adjustment to environmental and social conditions as a one-way movement, Dewey advocated the use of intelligence to transform the world more in line with human values. Dewey's detractors have accused him of promoting the "life adjustment" movement in education, but this movement is more characteristic of realism than of Dewey's philosophy.

Perhaps the most vocal critics of realism are those who have an existentialist orientation. They attack realism because it has advocated the idea of a fixed, intelligible universe, capable of being perceived objectively by the observing intellect. This view, they charge, has been promoted down through the centuries, through the Age of Reason and the Enlightenment, and into the contemporary scene of the technological society. It has deified reason to the detriment of the total human by ignoring passion, emotion, feeling, and irrationality. If we want truly to understand the human being in the world, we must consider the totality or entirety of man, a totality that realism tends to ignore or hide. Realists claim that they do view man in his entirety, and his entirety is one of dependence on a universe much larger than himself. The critics reply that the realist view of the totality of man in the world is conditioned by preconceived notions about the universe.

These preconceived notions often lead realists to conclusions about humanity that create difficulties in the field of education. For instance, Whitehead disparages "the dull average student." Although such "average" students may comprise a majority of our school-age population, realists seem more concerned with the necessity of the students measuring up to the standard curriculum than seeing them as individuals. Russell believed in the love of knowledge for its own sake, despite all of his talk about individuality, subjectivity, and humanistic concerns. He spoke of "excellencies" as the desirable things to achieve in education, a view that would probably meet with little resistance except that the underlying assumption is that achievement of these "excellencies" has to be measured against external criteria. The net result of views expressed by both Whitehead and Russell is that students come to be seen in terms of subservience to a superior entity such as the curriculum or standards of excellence. This problem lies central to the criticism directed against realism about its dehumanizing effects.

This point of contention can be illustrated further by reference to the controversy over liberal and vocational education. While many realists support the need for both, they seem to view liberal education as intensive studies in the arts and sciences for superior students and feel that slower students should be given a more narrow technical-vocational training. James Bryant Conant, for example, studied the social conditions of our inner cities and concluded that the conditions of the urban poor, particularly the black poor, were breeding grounds for "social dynamite." Critics point out that while Conant could have devised uplifting, sensitive, and humanitarian reform proposals, he recommended that poor people be provided with vocational education. The outcome of such outlooks all too often results in one kind of education for the "superior" people and another kind of education for everybody else.

Despite the historical insistence of realists on holism, they have for good or bad encouraged a movement in education toward specialism. This may be a corollary of the knowledge explosion we are all facing, and realists like others, are caught up in this problem. Their tendency to concentrate on specialized, piecemeal modules of knowledge does little to cure the problem. Comenius advocated a "pansophist" approach in education to enable individuals to use reason to gain all knowledge. This idea has been promoted historically by many realists, but their proclivity for the piecemeal approach does not lend itself to holistic and unified conclusions. Today, the realist ideal of the scientist and technician shows very little recognition of the unity of knowledge, for scientists often work on one small component of a larger entity without understanding that larger entity or appreciating its implications for humanity. Thus, it is possible for a scientist to work on a project that may have antisocial or antihuman implications without being aware of it. The highly trained technician working on expensive space technology at Cape Canaveral may ignore the fact that his expensive gadgetry takes up resources that could be used to alleviate human misery in other places.

Realism displays a bias in favor of a fact-based approach to knowledge. While this has its laudable aspects, it is also susceptible to various errors. What was once thought to be indisputable fact in so many cases is now considered to be interesting myth and outright ignorance, for example, the Ptolemaic conception of the universe that was once supported by religious realism. Even the "laws" of modern physics, which have tremendous research and experimentation behind them, may fall to new ideas in the future. There is also confusion over what is meant by "fact," for there are "facts of reason" and "facts of empirical research." Aristotle thought it was self-evident that objects of different weights fall at different speeds. It was not until Galileo that this "fact of reason" was overturned by empirical research; he reportedly tested the proposition and found it false. Keeping these problems in mind, it is understandable that a "factual" approach may lead to closed-mindedness and narrowness. If one already has the truth in hand (whether religious or scientific), he is hardly motivated to search further. This point of view is antiphilosophical to the extent it discourages an open mind and the unshackled search for wisdom.

One of the current controversies in education that has its roots in the realist tradition is the problem of testing. A realist assumption, as expressed by E. L. Thorndike, that anything which exists, exists in some quantity and is capable of being measured, has led to a plethora of standardized tests ranging from the IQ tests of young children to college board and national teachers' examinations. The testing movement has been touted as "scientific" and "fact based," and it has gained an almost uncritical acceptance in some quarters. The same kind of criticism can be directed toward statistical research studies such as opinion surveys and other kinds of data sampling. The assumption is that what one finds by statistical research is "scientific" and "factual," and this, in turn, leads the researcher to believe that his findings really reveal some truth. What can happen is the "pygmalion effect"; that is, the data influence the way a teacher views the members of the classroom. The dangers of such a faith in "factual data" have received widespread attention in various professional journals, but it seems that testing is hardly abating and may even be growing. It is almost as if educators were caught in the clutches of a blind faith in anything labeled a "scientific fact."

It is often claimed that the testing movement is one of the areas where science has had its greatest impact. This movement has accelerated in recent years in conjunction with the clamor for "cost-effectiveness" and a "systems approach" to education. The movement has been directed toward finding some way to gauge teacher-effectiveness and student performance more efficiently. Many states already require students to pass competency tests before they can graduate. Some school systems also make competency tests mandatory for prospective teachers seeking employment in an attempt to achieve adequate teaching standards. The National Teachers Examination is another kind of test designed to assure that teachers have a grasp of the basic fundamentals of the profession before being licensed. Such a trend can provide valuable objective support to those concerned with educational quality, but some critics argue that such tests are culturally biased and operate in a punitive way against various social groups. Perhaps, in light of this, we should consider the other extreme presented by the Russian educator Makarenko, who said that whenever he received a file on a student, he threw it into the fire lest it color his objective opinion of that person.

Finally, the realist advocacy of discipline and hard work can be criticized for various internal difficulties. Religious realism has supported the notion of the doctrine of original sin, a view that has led to a belief that man is by nature basically corrupt, lazy, and prone to wrongdoing. While modern secular realists may reject this view, there are still remnants of it in education, for hard work and discipline are considered "good" for us, and a student's head should be filled with "factual truth" so that he does not come to a bad end. The "hard work and discipline" syndrome and the emphasis on "factual truth" have been vigorously attacked and disputed by thinkers from Rousseau to contemporary proponents of "open education." These advocates maintain that it makes just as much sense to take an opposite view: that people are basically good, energetic, and naturally inquisitive. Education should not be forced upon people; rather, it should be made available in a palatable and enjoyable fashion recognizing our basic makeup. Both of these positions are probably extreme, and it could be said that they are both susceptible to the same basic error; that is, they are too sure that man's nature can be determined or that it is basically oriented toward good or bad behavior. The point is that realism has been criticized for the weakness of a narrow, restrictive view of human nature that has had a debilitating effect on schooling and educational theory.

Despite the shortcomings, a realist philosophy of education often finds strong support from many educators, parents, business and religious institutions, and grass-roots America. Apparently this occurs because a realist approach appears to be a "no non-sense" education that concentrates on things most people believe to be important. Numerous polls show that a great percentage of the public believes that lack of discipline is the number one problem found in schools today, and the emphasis on discipline in realist philosophies of education appeal to this sector of the public. The emphasis on discipline includes not only behavior, but a disciplined approach to subject matter, learning, and life activities. When one seriously examines existing school practices both here and abroad, he may find that more schools are following realist educational principles than those of any other single philosophy.

Aristotle

The Politics of Aristotle

Aristotle thought that a primary aim of education is to produce a virtuous person. He believed education should not be limited to the schoolroom but is a function of the state as well.* His approach to wisdom was "practical," using the method of science as well as philosophy. A major concern of his was to shape understanding and "correctness of thinking." Aristotle's educational writings have had a significant impact on the development of Western education. His thought has greatly influenced our conceptions of education in both the humanities and the sciences, and his ideas have found favor with both secular and religious thinkers in education.

No one will doubt that the legislator should direct his attention above all to the education of youth, or that the neglect of education does harm to States. The citizen should be moulded to suit the form of government under which he lives. For each government has a peculiar character which originally formed and which continues to preserve it. The character of democracy creates democracy, and the character of oligarchy creates oligarchy; and always the better the character, the better the government.

Now for the exercise of any faculty or art a previous training and habituation are required; clearly therefore for the practice of virtue. And since the whole city has one end, it is manifest that education should be one and the same for all, and that it should be public, and not private—not as at present, when everyone looks after his own children separately, and gives them separate instruction of the sort which he thinks best; the training in things which are of common interest should be the same for all. Neither must we suppose that anyone of the citizens belongs to himself, for

they all belong to the State, and are each of them a part of the State, and the care of each part is inseparable from the care of the whole. In this particular the Lacedæmonians are to be praised, for they take the greatest pains about their children, and make education the business of the State.

That education should be regulated by law and should be an affair of state is not to be denied, but what should be the character of this public education, and how young persons should be educated, are questions which remain to be considered. For mankind are by no means agreed about the things to be taught, whether we look to virtue or the best life. Neither is it clear whether education is more concerned with intellectual or with moral virtue. The existing practice is perplexing; no one knows on what principle we should proceed—should the useful in life, or should virtue, or should the higher knowledge, be the aim of our training; all three opinions have been entertained. Again, about the means there is no agreement; for different persons, starting with different ideas about the

---

*Selection from Aristotle, *The World's Great Classics: The Politics of Aristotle*, trans. Benjamin Jowett (New York: The Colonial Press, 1899), pp. 196–208.

nature of virtue, naturally disagree about the practice of it. There can be no doubt that children should be taught those useful things which are really necessary, but not all things; for occupations are divided into liberal and illiberal; and to young children should be imparted only such kinds of knowledge as will be useful to them without vulgarizing them. And any occupation, art, or science, which makes the body or soul or mind of the freeman less fit for the practice or exercise of virtue, is vulgar; wherefore we call those arts vulgar which tend to deform the body, and likewise all paid employments, for they absorb and degrade the mind. There are also some liberal arts quite proper for a freeman to acquire, but only in a certain degree, and if he attend to them too closely, in order to attain perfection in them, the same evil effects will follow. The object also which a man sets before him makes a great difference; if he does or learns anything for his own sake or for the sake of his friends, or with a view to excellence, the action will not appear illiberal; but if done for the sake of others, the very same action will be thought menial and servile. The received subjects of instruction, as I have already remarked, are partly of a liberal and partly of an illiberal character.

The customary branches of education are in number four; they are—(1) reading and writing, (2) gymnastic exercises, (3) music, to which is sometimes added (4) drawing. Of these, reading and writing and drawing are regarded as useful for the purposes of life in a variety of ways, and gymnastic exercises are thought to infuse courage. Concerning music a doubt may be raised—in our own day most men cultivate it for the sake of pleasure, but originally it was included in education, because nature herself, as has been often said, requires that we should be able, not only to work well, but to use leisure well; for, as I must repeat once and again, the first principle of all action is leisure. Both are required, but leisure is better than occupation; and therefore the question must be asked in good earnest, what ought we to do when at leisure? Clearly we ought not to be amusing ourselves, for then amusement would be the end of life. But if this is inconceivable, and yet amid serious occupations amusement is needed more than at other times (for he who is hard at work has need of relaxation, and amusement gives relaxation, whereas occupation is always accompanied with exertion and effort), at suitable times we should introduce amusements, and they should be our medicines, for the emotion which they create in the soul is a relaxation, and from the pleasure we obtain rest. Leisure of itself gives pleasure and happiness and enjoyment of life, which are experienced, not by the busy man, but by those who have leisure. For he who is occupied has in view some end which he has not attained; but happiness is an end which all men deem to be accompanied with pleasure and not with pain. This pleasure, however, is regarded differently by different persons, and varies according to the habit of individuals; the pleasure of the best man is the best, and springs from the noblest sources. It is clear then that there are branches of learning and education which we must study with a view to the enjoyment of leisure, and these are to be valued for their own sake; whereas those kinds of knowledge which are useful in business are to be deemed necessary, and exist for the sake of other things. And therefore our fathers admitted music into education, not on the ground either of

its necessity or utility, for it is not necessary, nor indeed useful in the same
manner as reading and writing, which
are useful in money-making, in the man-
agement of a household, in the acquisition of knowledge and in political life,
nor like drawing, useful for a more correct judgment of the works of artists,
nor again like gymnastic, which gives
health and strength; for neither of these
is to be gained from music. There
remains, then, the use of music for intellectual enjoyment in leisure; which appears to have been the reason of its
introduction, this being one of the ways
in which it is thought that a freeman
should pass his leisure; as Homer says—

> "How good is it to invite men
> to the pleasant feast,"

and afterwards he speaks of others
whom he describes as inviting

"The bard who would delight them all."

And in another place Odysseus says
there is no better way of passing life
than when "Men's hearts are merry and
the banqueters in the hall, sitting in
order, hear the voice of the minstrel." It
is evident, then, that there is a sort of
education in which parents should train
their sons, not as being useful or necessary, but because it is liberal or noble.
Whether this is of one kind only, or of
more than one, and if so, what they are,
and how they are to be imparted, must
hereafter be determined. Thus much
we are now in a position to say that the
ancients witness to us; for their opinion
may be gathered from the fact that
music is one of the received and traditional branches of education. Further, it
is clear that children should be instructed in some useful things—for example, in reading and writing—not only
for their usefulness, but also because

many other sorts of knowledge are
required through them. With a like view
they may be taught drawing, not to prevent their making mistakes in their own
purchases, or in order that they may not
be imposed upon in the buying or selling
of articles, but rather because it makes
them judges of the beauty of the human
form. To be always seeking after the
useful does not become free and exalted souls. Now it is clear that in education habit must go before reason, and
the body before the mind; and therefore boys should be handed over to
the trainer, who creates in them the
proper habit of body, and to the
wrestling-master, who teaches them
their exercises. . . .

It is an admitted principle, that gymnastic exercises should be employed in
education, and that for children they
should be of a lighter kind, avoiding
severe regimen or painful toil, lest the
growth of the body be impaired. The evil
of excessive training in early years is
strikingly proved by the example of the
Olympic victors; for not more than two
or three of them have gained a prize
both as boys and as men; their early
training and severe gymnastic exercises
exhausted their constitutions. When
boyhood is over, three years should be
spent in other studies; the period of life
which follows may then be devoted to
hard exercise and strict regimen. Men
ought not to labor at the same time with
their minds and with their bodies; for
the two kinds of labor are opposed to
one another, the labor of the body
impedes the mind, and the labor of the
mind the body.

Concerning music there are some
questions which we have already raised;
these we may now resume and carry
further; and our remarks will serve as a
prelude to this or any other discussion

of the subject. It is not easy to determine the nature of music, or why anyone should have a knowledge of it. Shall we say, for the sake of amusement and relaxation, like sleep or drinking, which are not good in themselves, but are pleasant, and at the same time "make care to cease," as Euripides says? And therefore men rank them with music, and make use of all three—sleep, drinking, music—to which some add dancing. Or shall we argue that music conduces to virtue, on the ground that it can form our minds and habituate us to true pleasures as our bodies are made by gymnastic to be of a certain character? Or shall we say that it contributes to the enjoyment of leisure and mental cultivation, which is a third alternative? Now obviously youth are not to be instructed with a view to their amusement, for learning is no pleasure, but is accompanied with pain. Neither is intellectual enjoyment suitable to boys of that age, for it is the end, and that which is imperfect cannot attain the perfect or end. But perhaps it may be said that boys learn music for the sake of the amusement which they will have when they are grown up. . . . .

The first question is whether music is or is not to be a part of education. Of the three things mentioned in our discussion, which is it?—Education or amusement or intellectual enjoyment, for it may be reckoned under all three, and seems to share in the nature of all of them. Amusement is for the sake of relaxation, and relaxation is of necessity sweet, for it is the remedy of pain caused by toil, and intellectual enjoyment is universally acknowledged to contain an element not only of the noble but of the pleasant, for happiness is made up of both. All men agree that music is one of the pleasantest things, whether with or without song; as Musæus says,

"Song is to mortals of all things
the sweetest."

Hence and with good reason it is introduced into social gatherings and entertainments, because it makes the hearts of men glad: so that on this ground alone we may assume that the young ought to be trained in it. For innocent pleasures are not only in harmony with the perfect end of life, but they also provide relaxation. And whereas men rarely attain the end, but often rest by the way and amuse themselves, not only with a view to some good, but also for the pleasure's sake, it may be well for them at times to find a refreshment in music. It sometimes happens that men make amusement the end, for the end probably contains some element of pleasure, though not any ordinary or lower pleasure; but they mistake the lower for the higher, and in seeking for the one find the other, since every pleasure has a likeness to the end of action. For the end is not eligible, nor do the pleasures which we have described exist, for the sake of any future good but of the past, that is to say, they are the alleviation of past toils and pains. And we may infer this to be the reason why men seek happiness from common pleasures. But music is pursued, not only as an alleviation of past toil, but also as providing recreation. And who can say whether, having this use, it may not also have a nobler one? In addition to this common pleasure, felt and shared in by all (for the pleasure given by music is natural, and therefore adapted to all ages and characters), may it not have also some influence over the character and the soul? It must have such an influence if characters are affected by it. And that they are so affected is proved by the power which the songs of Olympus and of many others exercise; for beyond question they inspire enthusiasm, and enthusiasm is an emotion of the ethical part of the soul. Besides, when men hear imitations, even unaccompanied by melody or rhythm, their feelings move in sympathy. Since then music is a pleasure, and virtue consists in rejoicing and loving and hating aright, there is clearly nothing which we are so much concerned to acquire and to cultivate as the power of forming right judgments, and of taking delight in good dispositions and noble actions. Rhythm and melody supply imitations of anger and gentleness, and also of courage and temperance and of virtues and vices in general, which hardly fall short of the actual affections, as we know from our own experience, for in listening to such strains our souls undergo a change. The habit of feeling pleasure or pain at mere representations is not far removed from the same feeling about realities; for example, if anyone delights in the sight of a statue for its beauty only, it necessarily follows that the sight of the original will be pleasant to him. No other sense, such as taste or touch, has any resemblance to moral qualities; in sight only there is a little, for figures are to some extent of a moral character, and [so far] all participate in the feeling about them. Again, figures and colors are not imitations, but signs of moral habits, indications which the body gives of states of feeling. The connection of them with morals is slight, but in so far as there is any, young men should be taught to look, not at the works of Pauson, but at those of Polygnotus, or any other painter or statuary who expresses moral ideas. On the other hand, even in mere melodies there is an imitation of

character, for the musical modes differ essentially from one another, and those who hear them are differently affected by each. Some of them make men sad and grave, like the so-called Mixolydian, others enfeeble the mind, like the relaxed harmonies, others, again, produce a moderate and settled temper, which appears to be the peculiar effect of the Dorian; the Phrygian inspires enthusiasm. The whole subject has been well treated by philosophical writers on this branch of education, and they confirm their arguments by facts. The same principles apply to rhythms: some have a character of rest, others of motion, and of these latter again, some have a more vulgar, others a nobler movement. Enough has been said to show that music has a power of forming the character, and should therefore be introduced into the education of the young. The study is suited to the stage of youth, for young persons will not, if they can help, endure anything which is not sweetened by pleasure, and music has a natural sweetness. There seems to be in us a sort of affinity to harmonies and rhythms, which makes some philosophers say that the soul is a harmony, others, that she possesses harmony. . . .

Two principles have to be kept in view, what is possible, what is becoming: at these every man ought to aim. But even these are relative to age; the old who have lost their powers, cannot very well sing the severe melodies, and nature herself seems to suggest that their songs should be of the more relaxed kind. Wherefore the musicians likewise blame Socrates, and with justice, for rejecting the relaxed harmonies in education under the idea that they are intoxicating, not in the ordinary sense of intoxication (for wine rather tends to excite men), but because they have no strength in them. And so with a view to a time of life when men begin to grow old, they ought to practise the gentler harmonies and melodies as well as the others. And if there be any harmony, such as the Lydian above all others appears to be, which is suited to children of tender age, and possesses the elements both of order and of education, clearly [we ought to use it, for] education should be based upon three principles—the mean, the possible, the becoming, these three.

Locke

Some Thoughts Concerning Education

*Locke's educational writings are classics of pedagogy that dominated the eigh-
teenth century and still influence us today.* Basing his observations on experience, Locke's educational proposals were aimed at producing the well-
mannered, well-informed English gentleman. In addition to being a philosopher,
Locke was also a physician, and it is not surprising that he included, in addition to
intellectual concerns, health, exercise, and physical growth and development. He
presented a liberal and humane view of education, especially as compared with
what existed in his day, but while he advocated democracy, his educational
recommendations were aimed primarily at the children of the upper classes. He
emphasized individuality, self-discipline, the importance of reasoning with the
child, and development of character as well as intellect.*

A sound mind in a sound body, is a short, but full description of a happy state in this world; he that has these two, has little more to wish for; and he that wants either of them, will be but little the better for any thing else. Men's happiness, or misery, is most part of their own making. He whose mind directs not wisely, will never take the right way; and he whose body is crazy and feeble, will never be able to advance in it. I confess, there are some men's constitutions of body and mind so vigorous, and well framed by nature, that they need not much assistance from others; but, by the strength of their natural genius, they are, from their cradles, carried towards what is excellent; and, by the privilege of their happy constitutions, are able to do wonders. But examples of this kind are but few; and I think I may say, that, of all the men we meet with, nine parts of ten are what they are, good or evil, useful or not, by their education. It is that which makes the great difference in mankind. The little, or almost insensible, impressions on our tender infancies, have very important and lasting consequences: and there it is, as in the fountains of some rivers, where a gentle application of the hand turns the flexible waters into channels, that make them take quite contrary courses; and by this little direction, given them at first, in the source, they receive different tendencies, and arrive at last at very remote and distant places.

I imagine the minds of children, as easily turned, this or that way, as water itself; and though this be the principal part, and our main care should be about the inside, yet the clay cottage is not to be neglected. I shall therefore begin with the case, and consider first the health of the body, as that which perhaps you may rather expect, from that study I have been thought more peculiarly to have applied myself to; and that also which will be soonest dispatched, as lying, if I guess not amiss, in a very little compass.

How necessary health is to our business and happiness; and how requisite a

---

*Selection from John Locke, *Some Thoughts Concerning Education*, in *The Works of John Locke*, vol. X (London: printed for W. Otridge and Son et al., 1812), pp. 6–7, 35, 50, 128, 143–44, 147–48, 150, 152, 172–73, 175–76, 186–87, 204–5.

strong constitution, able to endure hardships and fatigue, is, to one that will make any figure in the world; is too obvious to need any proof. . . .

This being laid down in general, as the course ought to be taken, it is fit we come now to consider the parts of the discipline to be used a little more particularly. I have spoken so much of carrying a strict hand over children, that perhaps I shall be suspected of not considering enough what is due to their tender age and constitutions. But that opinion will vanish, when you have heard me a little farther. For I am very apt to think, that great severity of punishment does but very little good; nay, great harm in education: and I believe it will be found, that, cæteris paribus, those children who have been most chastised, seldom make the best men. All that I have hitherto contended for, is, that whatsoever rigour is necessary, it is more to be used, the younger children are; and, having by a due application wrought its effect, it is to be relaxed, and changed into a milder sort of government. . . .

Manners, as they call it, about which children are so often perplexed, and have so many goodly exhortations made them, by their wise maids and governesses, I think, are rather to be learned by example than rules; and then children, if kept out of ill company, will take a pride to behave themselves prettily, after the fashion of others, perceiving themselves esteemed and commended for it. But, if by a little negligence in this part, the boy should not put off his hat, nor make legs very gracefully, a dancing-master will cure that defect, and wipe off all that plainness of nature, which the à-la-mode people call clownishness. And since nothing appears to me to give children so much becoming confidence and behaviour, and so to raise them to

the conversation of those above their age, as dancing; I think they should be taught to dance, as soon as they are capable of learning it. For, though this consist only in outward gracefulness of motion, yet, I know not how, it gives children manly thoughts and carriage, more than any thing. But otherwise I would not have little children much tormented about punctilios, or niceties of breeding.

Never trouble yourself about those faults in them, which you know age will cure. . . .

I place virtue as the first and most necessary of those endowments that belong to a man or a gentleman, as absolutely requisite to make him valued and beloved by others, acceptable or tolerable to himself. Without that, I think, he will be happy neither in this nor the other world. . . .

When he can talk, it is time he should begin to learn to read. But as to this, give me leave here to inculcate again what is very apt to be forgotten, viz. that great care is to be taken, that it be never made as a business to him, nor he look on it as a task. We naturally, as I said, even from our cradles, love liberty, and have therefore an aversion to many things, for no other reason, but because they are injoined us. I have always had a fancy, that learning might be made a play and recreation to children; and that they might be brought to desire to be taught, if it were proposed to them as a thing of honour, credit, delight, and recreation, or as a reward for doing something else, and if they were never chid or corrected for the neglect of it. . . .

Thus children may be cozened into a knowledge of the letters; be taught to read, without perceiving it to be any thing but a sport, and play themselves into that which others are whipped for. Children should not have any thing like work, or serious, laid on them; neither their minds nor bodies will bear it. It injures their healths; and their being forced and tied down to their books, in an age at enmity with all such restraint, has, I doubt not, been the reason why a great many have hated books and learning all their lives after: it is like a surfeit, that leaves an aversion behind, not to be removed. . . .

The Lord's prayer, the creed, and ten commandments, it is necessary he should learn perfectly by heart; but, I think, not by reading them himself in his primer, but by somebody's repeating them to him, even before he can read. But learning by heart, and learning to read, should not, I think be mixed, and so one made to clog the other. But his learning to read should be made as little trouble or business to him as might be. . . .

When he can read English well, it will be seasonable to enter him in writing. And here the first thing should be taught him, is to hold his pen right; and this he should be perfect in, before he should be suffered to put it to paper: for not only children, but any body else, that would do any thing well, should never be put upon too much of it at once, or be set to perfect themselves in two parts of an action at the same time, if they can possibly be separated. . . .

As soon as he can speak English, it is time for him to learn some other language: this nobody doubts of, when French is proposed. And the reason is, because people are accustomed to the right way of teaching that language, which is by talking it into children in constant conversation, and not by grammatical rules. The Latin tongue would easily be taught the same way, if his tutor, being constantly with him, would talk nothing else to him, and make him answer still in the same language. But because French is a living language, and to be used more in speaking, that should be first learned, that the yet pliant organs of speech might be accustomed to a due formation of those sounds, and he get the habit of pronouncing French well, which is the harder to be done, the longer it is delayed.

When he can speak and read French well, which in this method is usually in a year or two, he should proceed to Latin, which it is a wonder parents, when they have had the experiment in French, should not think ought to be learned the same way, by talking and reading. Only care is to be taken, whilst he is learning those foreign languages, by speaking and reading nothing else with his tutor, that he do not forget to read English, which may be preserved by his mother, or some body else, hearing him read some chosen parts of the scripture or other English book, every day. . . .

At the same time that he is learning French and Latin, a child, as has been said, may also be entered in arithmetic, geography, chronology, history, and geometry too. For if these be taught him in French or Latin, when he begins once to understand either of these tongues, he will get a knowledge in these sciences, and the language to-boot.

Geography, I think, should be begun with; for the learning of the figure of the globe, the situation and boundaries of the four parts of the world, and that of particular kingdoms and countries, being only an exercise of the eyes and memory, a child with pleasure will learn and retain them: and this is so certain, that I now live in the house with a child, whom his mother has so well instructed this way in geography, that he knew the limits of the four parts of the world, could readily point, being asked, to any country upon the globe, or any county in the map of England; knew all the great rivers, promontories, straits, and bays in the world, and could find the longitude and latitude of any place before he was six years old. These things, that he will thus learn by sight, and have by rote in his memory, are not all, I confess, that he is to learn upon the globes. But yet it is a good step and preparation to it, and will make the remainder much easier, when his judgment is grown ripe enough for it: besides that, it gets so much time now, and by the pleasure of knowing things, leads him on insensibly to the gaining of languages.

When he has the natural parts of the globe well fixed in his memory, it may then be time to begin arithmetic. By the natural parts of the globe, I mean several positions of the parts of the earth and sea, under different names and distinctions of countries; not coming yet to those artificial and imaginary lines, which have been invented, and are only supposed, for the better improvement of that science.

Arithmetic is the easiest, and consequently the first sort of abstract reasoning, which the mind commonly bears, or accustoms itself to: and is of so general use in all parts of life and business, that scarce any thing is to be done without it. This is certain, a man cannot have too much of it, nor too perfectly. . . .

As nothing teaches, so nothing delights, more than history. The first of these recommends it to the study of grown men; the latter makes me think it the fittest for a young lad, who, as soon as he is instructed in chronology, and acquainted with the several epochs in use in this part of the world, and can reduce them to the Julian period, should then have some Latin history put into his hand. The choice should be directed by the easiness of the style; for wherever he begins, chronology will keep it from confusion; and the pleasantness of the subject inviting him to read, the language will insensibly be got, without that terrible vexation and uneasiness which children suffer where they are put into books beyond their capacity, such as are the Roman orators and poets, only to learn the Roman language. When he has by reading mastered the easier, such perhaps as Justin, Eutropius, Quintus Curtius, &c. the next degree to these will give him no great trouble: and thus, by a gradual progress from the plainest and easiest historians, he may at last come to read the most difficult and sublime of the Latin authors, such as are Tully, Virgil, and Horace. . . .

Though the systems of physics, that I have met with, afford little encouragement to look for certainty, or science, in any treatise, which shall pretend to give us a body of natural philosophy from the first principles of bodies in general; yet the incomparable Mr. Newton has shown, how far mathematics, applied to some parts of nature, may, upon principles that matter of fact justify, carry us in the knowledge of some, as I may so call them, particular provinces of the incomprehensible universe. And if others could give us so good and clear an account of other parts of nature, as he has of this our planetary world, and the most considerable phænomena observable in it, in his admirable book "Philosophiæ naturalis principia mathematica," we might in time hope to be furnished with more true and certain knowledge in several parts of this stupendous machine, than hitherto we could have expected. And though there are very few that have mathematics enough to understand his demonstrations; yet the most accurate mathematicians, who have examined them, allowing them to be such, his book will deserve to be read, and give no small light and pleasure to those, who, willing to understand the motions, properties, and operations of the great masses of matter in this our solar system, will but carefully mind his conclusions, which may be depended on as propositions well proved. . . .

Though I am now come to a conclusion of what obvious remarks have suggested to me concerning education, I would not have it thought, that I look on it as a just treatise on this subject. There are a thousand other things that may need consideration; especially if one should take in the various tempers, different inclinations, and particular defaults, that are to be found in children; and prescribe proper remedies. The variety is so great, that it would require a volume; nor would that reach it. Each man's mind has some peculiarity, as well as his face, that distinguishes him from all others; and there are possibly scarce two children, who can be conducted by exactly the same method. Besides that, I think a prince, a nobleman, and an ordinary gentleman's son, should have different ways of breeding. But having had here only some general views in reference to the main end and aims in education, and those designed for a gentleman's son, who being then very little, I considered only as white paper, or wax, to be moulded and fashioned as one pleases; I have touched little more than those heads, which I judged necessary for the breeding of a young gentleman of his condition in general; and have now published these my occasional thoughts, with this hope, that, though this be far from being a complete treatise on this subject, or such as that every one may find what will just fit his child in it; yet it may give some small light to those, whose concern for their dear little ones makes them so irregularly bold, that they dare venture to consult their own reason, in the education of their children, rather than wholly to rely upon old custom.

Selected Readings

Aristotle. *Politics.* New York: Modern Library, 1943.

   A well-developed and classic statement of the realist approach to education. The author relates educational reform to social and political aims.

Broudy, Harry S. *Building a Philosophy of Education.* Englewood Cliffs, N.J.: Prentice-Hall, 1961.

   This book presents a strong case for realism in modern education, and an appeal for more fundamental and basic approaches and studies in the schools. It is regarded as one of the better, more recent statements of realism in education.

Broudy, Harry S. *The Real World of the Public Schools.* New York: Harcourt Brace Jovanovich, 1972.

   The author provides a critical analysis of the public schools at a time when public dissatisfaction of them is mounting. He argues for more discipline, rigor, and respect in schools, and a recovery of their central mission of providing a knowledge base for a mature society.

Locke, John. *John Locke on Education*. Edited by Peter Gay. New York: Teachers College Bureau of Publications, 1964.

This work contains some of Locke's best-known thoughts on education. It deals with educational problems ranging from individual learning experiences to the importance of environment. It is an empirical approach to education and is representative of early modern realism.

Russell, Bertrand. *Education and the Good Life*. New York: Boni and Liverright, 1926.

This is the leading educational statement of one of the foremost spokesmen for modern realist philosophy. The book is somewhat polemical in its urgings for social reform. It shows Russell's reformist tendencies and demonstrates his view of the importance of education.

Whitehead, Alfred N. *The Aims of Education and Other Essays*. New York: Free Press, 1957.

A collection of wide-ranging essays on education, this volume shows Whitehead's approach to philosophical patterns of thought. It is particularly incisive in its critique of inertness in education and attention to the creative process.

PRAGMATISM

The root of the word pragmatism is a Greek word meaning "work." Pragmatism is a philosophy that encourages us to seek out the processes and do the things that work best to help us achieve desirable ends. Since this idea is so sensible, one might wonder why people insist on doing things and using processes that do not work. Of course, there are any number of reasons why such impracticality exists, and among these are the weight of custom and tradition, as well as fear and apathy. Habitual ways of behaving developed in the past worked very well in their own time but have often lost their practicality in today's world. Pragmatism seeks to examine traditional ways of thinking and doing, and where possible and desirable, to reconstruct our approach to life more in line with the human needs of today.

While pragmatism is primarily viewed as a twentieth-century philosophy developed by Americans for the most part, its roots can be traced backward in time to British, European, and ancient Greek philosophic traditions. One important element of this tradition is the developing world view brought upon modern man by the "scientific revolution." The questioning attitudes fostered by the Enlightenment and the development of a more naturalistic humanism have been outgrowths of this movement. The background of pragmatism can be found in the works of such figures as Francis Bacon, John Locke, Jean-Jacques Rousseau, and Charles Darwin. But the philosophical elements that give pragmatism a consistency and system as a philosophy in its own right are primarily the contributions of Charles Sanders Peirce, William James, and John Dewey.

Bacon
(1561-1626)

Locke
(1632-1704)

Comenius
(1592-1670)

Comte
(1798-1857)

Rousseau
(1712-1778)

Pierce
(1839-1914)

Darwin   Hall
(1809-1882)   (1844-1924)

James   Dewey
(1842-1910)   (1859-1952)

Parker   Kilpatrick
(1837-1902)   (1871-1965)

3

PRAGMATISM AND EDUCATION

Roots of the Pragmatic World View

The antecedents of the philosophy of pragmatism are many and varied, but there are some basic elements that are vitally important. These are induction, the importance of human experience, naturalistic humanism, and the relations between science and the culture of man.

Induction: A New Way of Thinking

Francis Bacon (1561-1626). Sir Francis Bacon's chief concern was with the ways by which we think. He believed that the method used before his time—deduction—was primarily the method of religion and speculative philosophy, and yielded many errors, particularly with material phenomena. Deduction began with certain axiomatic statements or premises and other statements or conclusions were deduced from them. Aristotle's syllogism is a good example

81

of the method of deduction. An instance of the problems generated by a purely deductive approach can be seen in Aristotle's belief that if objects of different weights are dropped from a given height they fall at different speeds. Instead, Bacon tried to get people to cease putting their faith in old beliefs, generalizations from the past that may or may not have validity and reliability. He urged us to think, to develop valid knowledge. Induction would allow people to be experimental in their approach to the world. In essence, Bacon's ideas put a premium on human experience of and within the world of everyday life.

Bacon's influence on pragmatism has been significant. The method of induction that he suggested has served as the basis for the "scientific method," which in turn has been of fundamental importance to pragmatism. While Bacon thought science should be concerned primarily with material things, the pragmatists extended its range to include problems in economics, politics, psychology, education, and even ethics. For instance, in *How We Think*, John Dewey set forth the process of scientific thinking as central to the method of education. Indeed, according to Dewey, when we think in an orderly and coherent fashion, we are really thinking along the lines of scientific method, although we may not be conscious of it as such. If the nature of the thinking process were made conscious—if we were all educated in it—then our thinking would more likely be characterized by orderliness, coherence, and desirable consequences.

In broad terms, the general thrust of pragmatic method is toward a heightened sensitivity to consequences as the final test for thought. Hence, pragmatic results are not always "practical" in the ordinary sense. First, pragmatists hold that there can be no artificial separation of means from ends; that is, the means used always dictate to some degree the actual ends achieved. In this case, sensitivity to consequences calls for an increased vigilance over the means used. Second, the consequences of thinking are not always "practical" in the ordinary sense, for the consequences may be aesthetic, or moral, or even religious in quality. Thus, the pragmatist, while an enthusiastic advocate of scientific method, is no recluse in a sterile laboratory; rather, he wishes to apply his version of the scientific method to the problems of mankind in order to secure a more satisfying life for all.

The inductive approach that is so characteristic of pragmatism is illustrated by the thought of George Herbert Mead. Mead applied induction to social and psychological behavior in a more thoroughgoing manner than had been accomplished previously. His view of the self as social particularly influenced Dewey and other pragmatic thinkers in education. Mead himself thought that if we viewed the child from the standpoint of induction, we would see that a child did not learn to be social; rather, he had to be social even to learn. In other words, for Mead the self is by nature social and not some mentalistic, inner thing hidden from view.

William James applied inductive method to moral and religious questions. For him, the consequences that follow the application of a moral belief determine the truth or falsity, the rightness or wrongness of that belief. This view shows James extending the inductive method far beyond previous attempts, since to him the method was capable of extension to human experiences not included in ordinary empiricism. James was inductive to the extent that he rejected old assumptions about the nature of things and built his ideas on the basis of experience. In matters of religion, he held that religious beliefs had value if they provided suitable consequences. Belief in God, for example, could not be rejected if that belief provided personal meaning and value.

Thus, we can see that some pragmatists did not narrowly construe the meaning of induction so as to restrict it only to physical and material studies. Mead applied it to social and psychological areas, James used it in explaining religious and moral beliefs, while Dewey, learning from his predecessors, applied it to education and society in broad terms. There is a complicating factor involved in the pragmatic use of induction, and this refers to pragmatism's "hard" and "soft" sides. James represents the "soft" side by such things as his investigations in religion. The "hard" side of pragmatism is seen where it insists on a rigorous application of induction that yields objective and verifiable data. Both the "soft" and the "hard" sides can be seen in Dewey as he applied the pragmatic method to a wide range of problems.

The Centrality of Experience

Human experience is an important ingredient of pragmatic philosophy. This ingredient and the central emphasis it receives has helped give pragmatism a decidedly environmental orientation. The emphasis on experience, however, had its precedent in British and European philosophic traditions.

John Locke (1632–1704). John Locke investigated how man experiences and comes to know things, and his examination led him to the view that man's mind at birth is blank, a *tabula rasa*. Ideas are not innate as Plato maintained; rather, they come from experience, that is, sensation and reflection. As people are exposed to experiences, they are impressed on the mind; thus, a baby soon has the idea of milk acquired through the sense of taste, perfume through the sense of smell, velvet through the sense of touch, green through the sense of sight. These experiences are all imprinted on the mind through one or more of the five senses. Once they are in the mind they can be related in a variety of ways through the use of reflection. Therefore, one can create the idea of green milk or perfumed velvet. Locke believed that as people have more experiences they have more ideas imprinted on the mind and more to relate. He argued, however, that man can have in his mind false ideas as well as true ones. A person can have a true idea of an apple or of a horse, but he can also have the idea of a mermaid created by erroneously relating the idea of a woman and a fish, both obtained from the sensory world. The only way we can be sure our ideas are correct is by verifying them in the world of experience. We can find physical proof for a horse or an apple, but we cannot do the same for a mermaid.

One might think of the human mind as a kind of computer, and until something is programmed in, one cannot get anything out; consequently, Locke emphasized the idea of placing children in the most desired environment for their education and pointed to the importance of environment in making people what they are. His book, *Some Thoughts Concerning Education*, described the ideal education of a gentleman who is to be exposed to many varied experiences, including extensive travel among people of different cultures. Locke's heightened sensitivity to the importance of experience and its relation to thought processes and personal development served as a stimulus to many thinkers who came after him.

Locke's notion of experience, however, contained internal flaws and caused difficulties. His insistence that mind is a *tabula rasa* established mind as a passive, malleable instrument buffeted by a weltering conflict of impressions received through the senses. When carried to its logical conclusion, Locke's notion leads to the separation of mind from body with the result being that one can only know ideas. This lay at the base of George Berkeley's conclusion that "to be is to be perceived," or the existence of anything is dependent upon mind. David Hume took Locke's view and developed it to the point of skepticism regarding the existence and meaning of both ideas and matter. Thus, we arrive at the philosophical problems generated by the notion of a passive mind and uncertainty regarding the nature of reality.

According to John Dewey, it was Charles Peirce who opened the road leading out of the impasse generated by Locke. Ideas are not to be perceived as only isolated impressions on a blank tablet, but as interrelated parts of experience. Dewey took this to mean that ideas have to be defined functionally in reference to a particular problem, rather than as mere mental constructs. Locke's view of mind was too passive for Dewey, for it meant that one's ideas were formed primarily by external sources.

Dewey, like Kant, pointed to the importance of mind as an active agent in the formulation of ideas as well as an instrument to effect changes in the environment that in turn affect us. Dewey constantly stressed the transactional nature of the relations between the organism and the environment. Empirically, we experience things as beautiful, ugly, and so forth, but we do not experience such things as projections of a subjective mind on objective reality; rather, they are the result of the connection and the continuity of experience and nature.

Not only did Dewey reject Lockeian epistemology but also Locke's social theories that led to a philosophy of liberalism in the classic sense. Locke's notion of freedom was the *power to act* in accordance with choice. This freedom, combined with his concern for economic factors, led to a theory of laissez-faire with regard to property, industry, and trade that encouraged the limitation of government and police functions. Dewey held that this view of Locke resulted in so-called popular philosophies of "self-expression" where the "self-expression" of a few may impede the self-expression of the many. Classic Lockeian liberals believed that individuals were endowed with ready-made capacities that if unobstructed would lead to freedom. Dewey maintained, however, that such a movement only assisted the emancipation of those having a privileged antecedent status, while it provided no general liberation of the masses.

Dewey also challenged the notion advanced by Baruch Spinoza that real freedom can only be achieved when each man gains power as he acts in accord with the whole, "being reinforced by its structure and momentum." This idea of the individual acting in accordance with "the whole" leads to a kind of Hegelian subservience to the state or other such external agencies. Dewey argued, however, that we should act intelligently in terms of the practical world in which we find ourselves; that is, we cannot act in isolation from others, nature, or institutions. Because of Dewey's cognizance of such social forces, many interpreters have believed that this gives support to a social-adjustment or "life-adjustment" view of education; that is, that one should be taught to adjust to the way things are. It is true that Dewey did promote an awareness of contemporary conditions as well as interaction with them, but this did not preclude one's working constantly to improve existing institutions or to abolish them and establish new ones. Indeed, rather than advocating the kind of conservatism identified with Spinoza, Locke, and classical liberals, Dewey's views reflect a kind of underlying radicalism with regard to individuality and social action.

Jean-Jacques Rousseau (1712–1778). Another figure whose philosophical views had great import for pragmatic theory was Jean-Jacques Rousseau. Along with Locke, Rousseau wrote extensively about the relation of education and politics. His *Social Contract* and *Emile*, both of which appeared in 1762, antagonized so many of those in power that Rousseau had to leave Paris and seek refuge in Bern, Switzerland.

Rousseau was born in Geneva, Switzerland, but lived most of his life in France. His first philosophical work was a prize-winning essay on a subject proposed by the Academy of Dijon in 1749: "Has the Restoration of the Sciences and the Arts Contributed to Purify Morals?" Rousseau's answer was an emphatic *no*, for he followed Locke's insistence on the importance of environment in shaping human experience and thought. He maintained that civilization in its present form (that is, art and science) was harmful because it had led us away from nature.

Rousseau thought that individuals were basically good but corrupted by civilization. He did not believe that people would give up all of their artistic and technological developments, but he did think these should be controlled, particularly where they prevented us from being natural. Simply put, Rousseau argued for those aspects of civilization that are not corrupting to a natural life. He chose Daniel Defoe's story of Robinson Crusoe as representative of the kind of "Noble Savage" he envisioned and used it as the basis for *Emile*. According to the story, Robinson Crusoe visited his shipwrecked vessel many times and took off such civilized implements as he needed for survival. Yet, these things did not interfere with his natural life: he built his own house, killed his own food, and devised his own means of transportation. Other similar Noble Savage types from literature would include the Swiss Family Robinson, Natty Bumpo in the James Fenimore Cooper stories, and Thoreau at Walden Pond.

Rousseau's proposals for education are found in *Emile*, where he removes a child from civilization and brings him up in the country. Once in the country, Emile has a private tutor who sees to it that he lives naturally, and the tutor tries to arrange things so that Emile learns from nature. Rousseau did not think highly of books, which he felt only reinforced the artificialities of civilization, and in *Emile*, he ignores books altogether until Emile reaches age twelve. He gave little attention to the education of women but did have one or two chapters dealing with Sophy, who is Emile's counterpart. As Rousseau viewed it, Sophy is to be Emile's helpmate; consequently, she is to have the kind of education that would complement Emile's. Rousseau's suggestion that her education should consist of serving, cooking, and the development of charm is out of favor today, but he did not consider this demeaning; rather, it was a consequence of sex.

One of Rousseau's major contributions is the manner in which he saw a connection between nature and experience. It is upon this intimate connection that he largely built his theory of education. While many modern observers may tend to dismiss Rousseau as a romantic because of his views on the Noble Savage, there is something distinctly refreshing about his opinions in light of the ever-increasing complexity of modern technological society. Certainly, his connection of nature and experience has influenced many educational theorists, including Johann H. Pestalozzi, Friederich Froebel, Francis W. Parker, G. Stanley Hall, and John Dewey.

Rousseau's emphasis on the place of naturalism in education has affected the way pragmatic educators view the child. Children are no longer seen as miniature adults, but as organisms going through various stages of development. This conception of the child as a developing person particularly influenced psychologists such as G. Stanley Hall who is regarded as the founder of scientific child psychology. Rousseau's views helped educators to pose questions concerning what is natural for children. In other words, it is not natural for children to sit still for long periods of time, to concentrate on abstractions, to remain quiet, or to exhibit refined muscular control. Rousseau helped educators to become more sensitive to the physiological, psychological, and social developmental stages of childhood. His attention to the physiological aspects of learning directly influenced the theories of such people as Maria Montessori.

Rousseau's attention to the nature of child development and his belief in the inherent goodness of people set the stage for contemporary "child-centered" education. Although this theme is found in pragmatic theory and practice, there are those who object to the sentimental romanticism that has grown up around Rousseau's works—a romanticism that has often been identified as uninhibited permissiveness. While this sentiment has often been attributed to Rousseau, not even Rousseau believed in the kind of license this permissiveness suggests. One hears the same charge leveled against modern pragmatic educational practices, but the charge is unfounded when one carefully examines the writings of leading pragmatic thinkers, particularly John Dewey or Sidney Hook.

What Rousseau really believed was that education should be guided by the child's interests. An interest is not the same thing as a whim, and by "interest" Rousseau meant the child's native tendency to find out about the world in which he lives. He believed in the child's autonomy but regarded it as a natural autonomy where the child has to suffer the natural consequences of his behavior. Even contemporary writers such as A. S. Neill, whose Summerhill

School has strongly reflected a Rousseauian bias, advocates freedom but not license. Rousseau's impact on pragmatism is his sensitivity to the part of nature in education and the natural developmental process involved in one's learning experiences.

Science and Society

Modern science has dramatically changed our views of human destiny. That there has truly been a scientific revolution is not to be denied, for old metaphysical views, religious views, even social and political philosophies, have either been altered or have fallen before the juggernaut of the scientific revolution. The advance of science has not only affected theoretical views of society, but the practical area of social structures and social relations as well. The social problems resulting from this scientific advance have been of central concern to pragmatism, for its social philosophy has not developed in a vacuum. In this regard, pragmatism has been influenced by persons such as Bacon, Locke, and Descartes. While science has helped bring about many contemporary social problems, pragmatists believe that it can also help alleviate these problems.

Auguste Comte (1798–1857). Perhaps one of the most intensive philosophical efforts to apply science to society was made by Auguste Comte. Although not a pragmatist, Comte, like Bacon, influenced the early development of pragmatic thought by helping pragmatic thinkers become sensitive to the possibilities of using science to help solve social problems. For example, Dewey told how he was attracted to Comte's notion that Western civilization is disorganized due to a rampant "individualism" where only a few are truly individuals while the many are submerged. From Comte, he drew the idea that science can be a regulative method in social life. Comte's philosophical dream was to reform society by the application of science. Accordingly, science deals with both the organic and inorganic. Inorganic matter is handled by such sciences as physics and chemistry, while organic considerations are dealt with by physiology and sociology; thus, all matter is the province of science. While theology and metaphysics once served as a useful function in helping explain things, the rise and perfection of scientific thinking has surpassed them. The secrets of man and nature can now be unlocked, and we can live in harmony with ourselves and all other matter.

Today we might say that Comte was too optimistic, for we have discovered that scientific and positivistic thought often produces results that threaten to destroy us. Comte did help establish the application of science more directly to society rather than to just physical matter. Indeed, Comte was one of the fathers of modern sociology. His willingness to view social structures and relationships as capable of systematic study and control helped usher in elements of social theory that are distinctly pragmatic.

Charles Darwin (1809–1882). Perhaps the single most important influence on pragmatism from the standpoint of science, however, was the work of Charles Darwin. Darwin first went into the field of medicine as his life's calling.

However, he was given the opportunity to go on a scientific expedition to the southern hemisphere. He spent five years aboard the H.M.S. *Beagle* and returned home in 1838. Thereafter, he devoted his life to developing his scientific theories that were based to a large extent on the data he collected while on the voyage.

His major work, *On the Origin of Species* (1859), rocked the intellectual and religious communities of the Western world. Religionists attacked Darwin's theory because it brought Biblical creation into question. Intellectuals were stunned by it because it challenged old cosmological beliefs.

The underlying cosmological theory Darwin used was that nature operated by means of a process of development. This theory was not new with Darwin, for elements of it had been expressed by predecessors, but it was Darwin who gathered quantities of evidence and who painstakingly put it together in a most revealing way. Although his research was highly scientific, he wrote his findings in such a way that practically any literate person could understand them. He argued that a species evolves naturally through what he called a universal struggle for existence. This evolution occurs in an interplay between organism and environment. Food supply, geographical conditions, presence or absence of predators, all these set the stage whereby natural selection occurs. Favorable characteristics are maintained, and unfavorable characteristics die out. It is through this process that some species (such as dinosaurs) rise for a time and then disappear as conditions alter, and this selection process operates over a considerable time span.

Darwin's theory caught the popular imagination because he enunciated something every livestock farmer who practices selective breeding knows. It is not a high-blown philosophical utopia, but something connected with ordinary experience. These conditions have helped foster an examination of many areas of intellectual inquiry, and the cosmology of development, spurred by Darwin's efforts, has become more widely applied in fields that even Darwin himself never envisioned.

In philosophy, the cosmology of development directly attacked the Platonic notion of essences and universals. This helped foster philosophical views that the universe itself is in process of development. Reality is not to be found in Being, but in Becoming. Gradually, such ideas have led to the rejection of a block universe and to notions that see reality as fixed or capable of being comprehended in its entirety by intellect. For the pragmatists, this came to mean that reality is open-ended, in process, with no fixed end. These views of open-endedness have further encouraged the view in pragmatism that man's education is directly tied to his biological and social development. From this standpoint, both William James and John Dewey attempted to weld humanism together with naturalism in a systematic and integrated manner.

The American Pragmatists

It has been said that the philosophy of pragmatism is "as American as apple pie." This is true in part, but as we have just seen, pragmatism had its roots in

European philosophical traditions. In addition, F. C. S. Schiller developed a British version of pragmatism. By and large, however, pragmatism received its fullest treatment from three Americans: Charles Sanders Peirce, William James, and John Dewey.

Charles Sanders Peirce (1839-1914). In many respects, Peirce was never given the recognition in his own day that he deserved. Although he was friends with such leading American intellectuals as William James, he never received a permanent post at any university, and his major ideas never won public acclaim. For most of his life he was a lonely and reclusive man, and he died in straitened economic circumstances.

What he achieved philosophically was primarily in his influence on later figures. His works got an eventual posthumous publication, but probably his most influential work was in an article titled "How to Make Our Ideas Clear" that appeared in *Popular Science Monthly* in January 1878. In the article, he attempted to attack head-on the problem of the dualism of mind and matter, or the subjective and the objective. For the most part, he accepted the proposition that mind is different from material reality. In this respect he agreed with Aristotle's view, but he also maintained that what we know about objective reality resides in the idea we have of any given object. The important thing, consequently, is to make sure our ideas are as clear and precise as possible. He argued that we should always remain extremely sensitive to the consequences of conceiving an idea in any particular fashion. In fact, Peirce maintained that it is the concept of practical effects that make up the whole of our concept of an object. We might say that our mental grasp of any object is nothing more than the meaning we apply to that object in terms of consequences. As Peirce put it, "Our idea of anything is our idea of its sensible effects." Thus, ideas or concepts cannot be separated from human conduct, for to have an idea is to be aware of its effects and consequences or their probability in the arena of human affairs.

Peirce concluded that true knowledge of anything depends upon verification of our ideas in actual experience. In and of themselves, ideas are little more than hypotheses until tried upon the anvil of experience. Although Peirce's complete thought system was very complex, even going into speculations about the nature of God, immortality, and the self, it was his work on the nature of ideas and the necessity for verification in experience that most influenced pragmatism.

William James (1842-1910). Although Peirce was largely ignored during his lifetime, there was another figure who brought pragmatic thought to a wide public audience, and this was William James. The son of a prominent family, James rather leisurely tried his hand at several vocations, including medicine, but he made his mark in the fields of psychology and philosophy. He was not a particularly systematic thinker; rather, his contribution to philosophy lay in the power of his ideas that ranged from psychology to the nature of religious experience.

James took Peirce's admonition about the practical consequences of ideas seriously, for this lay at the heart of James's theory of truth. He viewed the truth of an idea in terms of that idea's "workability." Truth is not absolute and immutable; rather, it is *made* in actual, real-life events. Truth does not belong to an idea as some property adhering to it, for it is found in acting on ideas, in the consequences of ideas. Truth is not always objective and verifiable; it is also found in concrete individuality. For James, there is the "inexpugnable reality" of individual existence. In the life of an individual, experiences occur that have meaning and truth to that individual but that cannot necessarily be verified objectively to someone else. This view of truth—verifiability or "workability" and inexpugnable reality—is what James called "radical empiricism." In effect, he held that truth is inseparable from *experience*, and in order to get at truth we must study experience itself, not some immutable, otherworldly Absolute, extraneous to experience.

Thus, for James the primary datum is human experience. He concentrated on what he called the "stream" of experience, the sequential, serial course of events. Experience, he cautioned, is a "double-barrelled" word, for there is experiencing, the actual lived, undergoing aspect; and there is the experienced, the things of experience. Thus, experience, as the primary datum, is capable of being studied cross-sectionally (the experiencing), and longitudinally (the experienced). James called upon thinkers to concentrate on experience in lieu of essences, abstractions, and universals. There is no Truth, Reality, or Absolute, but as his study of experience revealed to him, the universe is open-ended, pluralistic, and in process.

John Dewey (1859–1952). James popularized pragmatic thought, and John Dewey "systematized" it and carried its leading ideas to far-reaching development. It is of interest to note that Dewey was born in 1859, the same year that Darwin's *Origin of Species* was published. Darwin's thought was to play an important part in Dewey's philosophy, for the cosmology of development was central to his beliefs. Like James, he believed that there were no absolutes or universals, and his primary datum was experience; and like Peirce, he sought to clarify ideas in terms of their consequences in experience. Dewey's contributions were not ignored as in the case of Peirce, and while his ideas certainly had power and impact, as did James's, Dewey had the additional virtue of being able to pursue the most intricate problems doggedly and to search out their practical implications.

Dewey owed a great deal to Darwin, Peirce, and James but made his serious beginnings in philosophy primarily through the Hegelian tradition. The most influential part of Hegel was, for Dewey, the Hegel who pursued process and development, and not the Hegel who arrived at Absolute Spirit. Dewey once remarked, " . . . that acquaintance with Hegel has left a permanent deposit in my thinking." If Dewey was taken with anything, it was the growing, developing, dynamic nature of life, not its speculative ultimates. He accepted James's notion of experience as a stream, and from this basis Dewey was launched upon a wide-ranging philosophical career that spanned from horse and buggy days to post-World War II and the atomic age.

The Nature of Experience. For Dewey, experience is not just an isolated happenstance—it has depth and reaches into nature. Experience and nature are not two different things separated from each other, but rather experience itself is *of* nature. Experience could, in the reflective sense, be divided into the experiencing being and the experienced things, but in the primary sense of the word, experience is of nature. Man does not experience "experience" but the world in which he lives, a world of things, ideas, hopes, fears, and aspirations, all rooted in nature. What had misled previous philosophy, he claimed, was the confusion over experience itself and our thoughts about it. Too many thinkers had concentrated on the reflective products of experience and had held these to be the ultimate reality. Unfortunately, philosophers settled upon abstractions and not genuine experience.

The centrality of experience and the extent to which Dewey used it is revealed by the titles of some of his major books: *Essays in Experimental Logic*, *Experience and Nature*, *Art as Experience*, *Experience and Education*. His investigations into experience were not just speculative adventures, for he primarily directed his efforts toward real-life problems. Dewey took Peirce to heart and looked at the practical consequences of ideas. He held that genuine thought begins with a "problematic situation," a block or hitch to the ongoing stream of experience. In encountering these blocks, consciousness is brought to focus, and one is made more acutely aware of the situation. It is in dealing with these real problems, Dewey argued, that creative intelligence is capable of development. Older philosophies had taken "problematic situations" and attempted to fit them to a preexisting set of abstractions. He urged that each situation be looked upon as unique and dealt with experimentally by investigating the probable consequences of behaving in particular ways. This approach shows Dewey's position that the world—experience and nature—cannot be understood in a monolithic way. The consequences of this state of affairs are that we must be sensitive to novelty and variation, and we must seek to be creative in dealing with our problems. Dewey headed in the direction of developing an experimental methodology and believed that method takes precedence over explanatory metaphysical schemes.

According to Dewey, experience is of and *in* nature. Nature consists of stones, plants, diseases, social conditions, enjoyments, and sufferings. In short, Dewey maintained we cannot separate experience and nature. Nature is what we experience, and we must view our experience in terms of its natural connections. In this respect, Dewey viewed nature as both precarious and stable, problematic and determinate; that is, there are some things that change slowly. Some experiences are stable, while others are in fluctuating confusion.

For example, natural changes in many plant and animal species take place over long stretches of time, and often it takes centuries for the physical contours of land masses to change. However, some forms of life, for example, certain kinds of bacteria, are capable of fairly rapid evolution, and land masses may be rapidly altered by volcanic action. Nature, therefore, has certain characteristics that are fairly stable and others that fluctuate, and the same can be said for human affairs, which Dewey considered to be a part of nature. Some types of human behavior relating to family life seem to be enduring across the ages, while at the same time others are rapidly changing. We speak of the so-called sexual revolution as an indication of change, but certain human functions and needs relating to child rearing and family life seem to endure. By the same token, broad social and political upheavals, such as the Marxist revolution in Russia in 1918, appear to be cataclysmic. Closer examination reveals, however, that the causes of such events often go back for centuries. Thus, Dewey believed that some things are fairly stable and some are subject to rapid change, whether we are speaking of biology, social institutions, or politics.

Dewey followed Rousseau's lead in seeing the importance of nature in education, although he rejected most of Rousseau's romanticism. Rousseau established three sources of education: (1) nature, the spontaneous development of our organs and capacities; (2) men, the social uses to which we put this development; and (3) things, the acquisition of personal experience from surrounding objects. Dewey thought Rousseau regarded these three factors as separate operations, independent of the use to which they were put. His naturalism differs from Rousseau's in that he believed the three factors have to be viewed in terms of their interrelationships. While Rousseau thought a child should be removed and educated "naturally" in the formative years, Dewey maintained that he should not be removed from a social environment conducive to his proper education. Thus, Dewey held that nature does not include just physical entities, but social relationships as well.

Dewey argued that if one accepts the hypotheses of the open-ended universe and a pluralistic reality, it becomes less important to develop abstract explanations and more important to examine the nature of human processes. Acceptance of the open-ended nature of things does not necessarily lead to an overly optimistic view of life, for some processes lead to human goods and some lead to human ills. However, we *can* control our own affairs, even if not in an absolute sense, and even if controlling any one state of affairs only momentarily gives respite. Dewey was not a wild-eyed optimist as some of his critics charge—he was fully sensitive to the tragic side of human affairs—but he did steadfastly maintain that we have it within our power to attain a more satisfying life. This can be done intelligently by using human processes that yield desired results. Scientific method and experimental thinking can, if used properly, help us achieve desirable ends. In fact, thinking processes are of utmost importance because Dewey felt that most human difficulties result from faulty thinking. He was vitally concerned with connecting thinking processes with social processes, and this is shown in his emphasis on social action and education.

Instrumentalism. Dewey's attention to social action and education gave his philosophy a decidedly practical orientation. Instead of dealing only with unchanging theoretical constructs, he urged that philosophy should concern itself with human problems in a changing and uncertain world. He felt that most thinkers are embarked upon a "quest for certainty" in which they seek true and eternal ideas, when what is needed are practical solutions to practical problems. This view is in accord with modern science where ideas are not immutable but are accepted on the basis of how well they solve a perplexing problem. For Dewey, ideas are *instruments* in the solution of man's problems. Thus, he sometimes preferred the word "instrumentalism" rather than "pragmatism" to designate his philosophy.

In *How We Think*, Dewey showed how ideas can be used as instruments in the solution of real problems. He described his view in five stages: (1) *a felt difficulty* that occurs because of a conflict in our experience or a hitch or block to ongoing experience; (2) *its location and definition*, establishing the limits or characteristics of the problem in precise terms; (3) *suggestions of possible solutions*, formulating a wide range of hypotheses; (4) *development by reasoning of the bearings of the suggestions*, reflecting on the possible outcomes of acting on these suggestions—in short, mulling things over; and (5) *further observation and experiment leading to its acceptance or rejection*, testing the hypotheses to see if they really yield the desired results. Although these five steps are presented in an orderly sequence, this does not mean that they are independent in a given situation or occur in any special order. They can occur together in such ways that the various steps interact with each other or become fused.

In this regard, Dewey viewed *method* rather than abstract answers as the central concern. If the universe is open-ended, if existence is precarious and uncertain, we cannot expect to locate enduring solutions; instead, we have to take each human problem as it arises. This is not to say that answers are not important, but it does recognize that they must be couched in terms of real-life situations, no two of which are exactly alike. The consequences of this fact are that we must view the place of ideas in an instrumental sense. We know that something is true or false on the basis of what it does, and what effects it has on human activity. Dewey's work at the Laboratory School at the University of Chicago not only demonstrated his concern for education, but also his belief that ideas should be tested in the crucible of real-life experience.

Individuality and Social Relations. One of the areas of Dewey's philosophy around which controversy has swelled is his treatment of individuality in the social world. This controversy is somewhat surprising and lends credence to the observation that Dewey is much "cussed" and discussed but little read. On the one hand, there have been those who claim that he exalted individuality at the expense of organized society. On the other hand, many charge that he submerged the individual under a stifling objectivity represented by technology, the scientific consciousness, and centralized social institutions. The controversy is surprising because, if one gives Dewey a fair reading, it is difficult to find that he maintains either position.

Rather than accepting the extremes of subjectivity or objectivity, Dewey tried to show that experience is first and primarily gross and macroscopic, and that distinctions of subjectivity (or individuality) and objectivity (or the social environment) come out of experience. In short, the one is not necessarily more real than the other, for Dewey viewed subject and object or individual and society in a precarious balance, a *transactional* relationship. Of course, individuality can be submerged or lost by rigid institutional restrictions, and sociality can be denied by a rampant individualism of the economic laissez-faire variety. What Dewey actually said is that individuality and sociality are interrelated, and the one cannot prosper without the other. Both are possibilities and not guarantees. In other words, we have to work to see that they are in fact actualities and not just theoretical propositions.

Dewey thought that modern industrial society had submerged both individuality and sociality. Because of the confusion of modern society, he argued, the school should be an institution where both the individual and the social capabilities of children can be nurtured. The way to achieve this is through democratic living. Individuality is important because it is the source of novelty and change in human affairs. Dewey defined individuality as the interplay of personal choice and freedom with objective conditions. To the extent that personal choice is intelligently made, then individuals exercise even greater control over their personal destinies and the objective world surrounding them. Sociality refers to a milieu or medium conducive to individual development. In Dewey's mind, there could be no true individuality without humane, democratic, and educative social conditions; consequently, the category of the social is the *inclusive* philosophic idea because it is the means by which the distinctly human is achieved. Therefore, individuality and sociality cannot be divorced in Dewey's system. They are interdependent and interrelated.

In this respect, we can better understand Dewey's ideal for the school and his rejection of those philosophies that promote a separation of individuals from institutions. The school, through democratic education, must enhance the interplay of individuality and sociality, the one supporting and enlarging the other, as in an ever-widening spiral.

Religious and Moral Development. Dewey's views on religious experience can be found in a number of his works but are most succinctly stated in *A Common Faith*, published in 1938. Dewey felt that being "religious" did not require the acceptance of supernatural beliefs or of organized religion. He thought most religions have a negative effect because they tend to separate and classify people, an untenable practice in a democratic society. He rejected both supernaturalism and militant atheism and promoted a consideration of man in the realm of nature instead. Religious ideas are rooted in man's natural needs.

Basically, Dewey thought that there are two schools of social and religious reform. One feels that the individual must be constantly watched, guided, and controlled to see that he stays on the right path, while the other believes man will control his own actions intelligently. Dewey sympathized with the latter, but he pointed out that there are no guarantees that we will exercise control intelligently. However, we *can* do so; that is, freedom is a *possibility* and not a guarantee. Human existence occurs in a context and not in a vacuum. An individual's actions are influenced by the social context, for when an individual acts, he or she always acts in some socially connected way. When man understands the connecting links between himself and his social context, when he acts to promote the desirable elements of this connection, he achieves a "religious" character. An "unreligious" attitude is that which attributes human pur-

pose and achievement to the individual in isolation from the physical and social environment.

In *Human Nature and Conduct*, Dewey proposed a "broad sweep" of
morals as these relate to all the social disciplines connected with the study of
man. He thought that not only analyzing morals but looking at them constructively was in the tradition of Hume. Moral rules should be adapted to a particular
situation in terms of their consequences; hence, each action is to be judged good
or bad in terms of its outcomes. Essentially this is an educative process, for an
awareness and concern for consequences is to be arrived at only through careful
and reflective thinking. Dewey rejected morality as a branch of knowledge based
on *a priori* reasoning or divine precept. Basically, he thought that moral traits are
to be acquired by individual participation in the social group or by learning about
morality through living.

Aesthetic Development. According to Dewey, art is a marriage between
form and matter, that is, the artist attempts to incorporate his ideas into the
object being created. Thus, the artist engages in his work until he achieves the
desired end. The artist is not only the creator but also the perceiver. However,
Dewey did not believe that art and aesthetic experiences are to be left only to the
realm of the professional artist. Everyone is capable of achieving and enjoying
aesthetic experiences provided that creative intelligence is developed through
education. Therefore, art need not be the possession of the few but available to
everyone and can be applied to the ordinary activities of life.

Dewey believed that a truly aesthetic experience is one where the person
is unified with his activity. It is an experience that is so engaging and fulfilling that
there is no conscious distinction of self and object in it; the two are so fully
integrated that such distinctions are not needed. In short, an aesthetic experience is one in which the contributions of both the individual and the environment or the internal and the external are in harmony. This kind of experience is
what Dewey called "consummatory experience," or experience that provides
unity and completion. This is human experience at its highest.

Like the Greeks, Dewey thought we should project art into all human
activities, such as the *art* of politics, and the *art* of education. Although he was
very much in favor of using the scientific method and technology in the educational enterprise, Dewey still believed that education is primarily an artistic
activity as opposed to a strictly scientific one. The desirable educator, from
Dewey's point of view, is one who seeks to unify both the mind and body of the
student, or thinking and doing. When this is achieved, education becomes the
supreme art form—the art of education.

Pragmatism as a Philosophy of Education

The pragmatic movement in American education has been one of monumental
importance. Today, many schools have implemented elements of pragmatic
ideas in one way or another, but this influence is not always connected with the

philosophy. One reason that this occurred is that pragmatism in its most influential period was often identified with radicalism and social reform. Many educators realized that this belief was a detriment to getting pragmatic ideas accepted into basically conservative and traditional schools; therefore, many progressive educators became more interested in showing the practical use of pragmatic ideas and techniques rather than having them identified with the philosophy of pragmatism. In a sense, therefore, pragmatic education came through the back door of American schools, and this factor helps to explain why pragmatic ideas and methods are often used (and misused) but are not always identified with the philosophy.

It would be a mistake to link pragmatism too closely with progressive education in all its aspects. While it is certainly true that most progressivists claim to agree with the philosophy of John Dewey, Dewey himself was often critical of the excesses of progressivism. His book *Experience and Education* was directed as much at progressivist excess as it was at tradition-bound, old-style American education. It has been pointed out many times that Dewey's name was often invoked, but his works were seldom read by all too many progressivists.

Pragmatic education as a movement began because many liberal thinkers in the 1920s felt that American education did not reflect the ideas of justice and freedom found in democratic theory. They believed that schools should be brought into tune with the spirit of these ideas and that they should reflect advances made in the physical sciences, the social sciences, and technology. These early pragmatists were stimulated by the scientific movement that began with Bacon. They believed very strongly in science, particularly in its role as an antithesis to superstition, dogmatic religion, and political paralysis.

Locke, with his emphasis on experience, also influenced pragmatic thought. His view that no ideas are innate and that experience is the primary shaper of human existence found ready acceptance into the pragmatic movement. Pragmatists stress the importance of seeing the child in relation to all the experiences he encounters in his environment, not just school experiences. They feel children must be looked at in terms of cognitive, physical, and emotional development, and in light of all the other factors that serve to influence and shape their lives.

Rousseau influenced pragmatic thinking with his emphasis on nature. Pragmatists maintain that education should be natural and related to the development of the human as a complex kind of animal. They have long championed schools where children can move about, where there is an open and a stimulating environment that brings the natural element into education.

The ideas of Bacon, Locke, and Rousseau were perhaps best synthesized by the thinking of John Dewey. Their ideas were not brought together into a meaningful whole and applied to education before Dewey's time.

Aims of Pragmatism

Dewey and the pragmatists believed that education is a necessity of life. It renews the individual so that he is able to face the problems encountered by his interaction with the environment. Civilized society exists, Dewey pointed out, because education is transmitted from generation to generation, occurring by means of the communication of habits, activities, thoughts, and feelings from the older to the younger. Without this, social life cannot survive; therefore, it should not be looked upon as the mere acquisition of academic subject matter, but as a part of life itself. Education is basically an art, and the teacher expresses the highest concept of this art when he or she keeps it from becoming routinized and lethargic. All living educates, but social living helps us to extract the net meaning from our education. Dewey, like Plato, believed people need society as a necessary part of their learning experiences, and we must guard against schools treating subject matter as if it were a thing apart from life itself.

Pragmatists do not believe that "training" is the same thing as education. We can train a child to like or avoid things without his really understanding *why* he does so. Most of the habits of animals are the result of training, but humans, unlike horses, are capable of understanding what they do, and therefore the educative process is only fulfilled when we promote understanding. Helping the child to think becomes *education* as opposed to mere training. In doing this, we appeal to language as a means of conveying ideas and helping others to reason. This language and teaching must be framed in the proper environment that has been regulated deliberately so as to achieve maximum educative effect. Dewey felt that the school should provide just this kind of environment. The school should be the place where the other environments that the child encounters—the family environment, the civic environment, the work environment, and others—are coordinated into a meaningful whole.

In the pragmatic view, then, education should not be looked upon as a preparation for life, but as life itself. The lives of children are important to children as the lives of adults are to the adults. Thus, educators should be aware of the interests and motivations of children as well as the environment from which they come. In "My Pedagogic Creed," Dewey set forth the belief that education has two fundamental sides: the psychological and the sociological. One could not be subordinate to the other because the child's own instincts and powers provide the material and starting point of all education, and the educator's knowledge of social conditions is necessary to interpret the child's powers. The educator does not know what these powers and instincts are until he or she can translate them into their social equivalents and project them into the future for insight into their consequences. In sum, Dewey believed that individuals should be educated as social beings, capable of participating in, and directing their own social affairs. This means a freer interaction among social groups as well as attention given to developing all the potentialities an individual may have for future growth. He looked upon education as a way to free the individual to engage in continuous growth directed toward appropriate social aims.

Whatever the specific aim of schooling and learning, pragmatists stress the importance of how we arrive at those aims. According to Dewey, aims should (1) grow out of existing conditions. They should (2) be tentative, at least in the beginning, and maintain flexibility. Perhaps most important of all, the aim must (3) always be directed toward a freeing of activities, an "end in view." This last suggestion is central to Dewey's idea of education. Properly speaking,

Dewey thought people—parents, students, and citizens—are the ones who have educational aims, and not the process of education. Yet there is still a sense of meaningfulness about educational aims. For Dewey, the aim of education is growth: "Since growth is the characteristic of life, education is all one with growing; it has no end beyond itself." In this regard, he was speaking of growth as an enlargement of the capacity to learn from experience and to direct future experience in a meaningful way. Here rests the importance of the third point, that education should free our activities, for only in this way can proper growth in democratic living occur.

Sidney Hook maintains that education for growth goes together with education for the democratic society. In fact, the ideals of the democratic society establish the direction in which growth should occur: the growth should support and develop the ideals of the democratic society. Intelligence is significant because it enables us to break the bonds of habit and makes it possible to devise alternatives that are more satisfying and desirable. Hook points out that growth, democracy, and intelligence are the inclusive and related aims of education.

William Heard Kilpatrick, one of Dewey's students and colleagues, maintained that the overriding concern of each individual should be that all people have "the fullest and finest life possible." What we have accomplished and the possibility of future accomplishments are always uncertain; therefore, continued progress demands intelligent effort. Education becomes involved in teaching children how to live. This is accomplished in three steps: (1) provision of opportunity to live, (2) provision for learning experiences, and (3) provision of conditions for proper character development.

The function of education, then, is to direct, control, and guide personal and social experience. Pragmatists argue that we need to make persons aware of the consequences of their actions so they may guide their actions more intelligently. In this way, people learn to control their own actions and require less outside support and direction. An educated person grows in this manner, and his growth depends on a good environment shared with others, as well as the natural flexibility inherent in the person. Schools should foster habits of thought, invention, and initiative that will assist the people in growing in the right direction; that is, toward democratic living.

According to the pragmatists, education should be an experimental enterprise as well as something that assists in social renewal. It should promote a humanistic spirit in man, as well as the desire to explore and find new answers to our present-day problems in economics, politics, and other social life. Education should promote our true individualism that will result in a diminishing of our reliance upon custom and tradition in the solving of our problems, and cause us to rely more upon intelligence to achieve our goals and interests.

Dewey pointed out that a "philosophy of education" is not the application of ready-made ideas to every problem but rather the formation of right mental and moral attitudes to use in attacking contemporary problems. Philosophy itself is "the theory of education in its most general phases." When changes occur in social life, we must reconstruct our educational program to meet these challenges. Thus, our ideas will have a pragmatic function. Learning helps us to meet environmental changes and affects our character as well. In this way, education has a moral influence and should play a vital part in helping us to become the kind of moral persons who are interested not only in promoting our own growth, but also in promoting the growth of others.

Methods of Pragmatism

Pragmatic educators prefer methods that are flexible and capable of being used in a variety of ways. By the same token, they like school buildings and furnishings that are functional. Movable furniture, furniture that fits children, folding walls, large print in books, are all things that came out of Dewey's work at the Laboratory School in Chicago. The same is true with methods, for pragmatists maintain that there is no one way to educate children; consequently, we should be aware of a variety of ways that can be used, including settings and situations from inside the school to the wider community outside.

Some pragmatists urge that teachers and students see that all knowledge is related. In schools today it is easy to understand that areas such as reading, writing, and spelling can be put under the category of language arts. We can put history, geography, and economics under the title of social studies because we can see the relationship between these areas. Furthermore, relationships can be found between social studies and language arts, and between other areas of the curriculum. This can be done by developing a "core" approach to curriculum so that students can understand how things are related. We may then have students select an area of concentration or "core" for a period of study, such as "exploration," and all the subject areas would revolve around this. The language arts, for example, would deal with the literature of exploration, including the biographies of famous explorers past and present, science fiction that gives exploration themes, and written work by students in which they express themselves creatively or by which they report the results of their inquiry into the theme of exploration. In addition, they could investigate the important place of mathematics in exploration, ranging from the practical mathematics of circumnavigating the globe to mathematical explorations of the kind done from the time of Pythagoras down to Albert Einstein and contemporary mathematicians. One could hardly study exploration without becoming involved in both the social studies and the sciences. In social studies, students would inquire into the history, the economics and politics, and the geographical considerations involved in exploration. Science itself has been one of the frontier areas of exploration and it would, of course, serve as a fundamental area of study as suggested in some of the preceding examples. Students would even examine the art of exploration, ranging from paintings with exploratory themes to students doing their own exploratory compositions. By so doing, they would be exposed to all the relevant bodies of knowledge that could be brought to bear on the theme of exploration. They would be involved with the fundamentals of knowledge in a practical and applied way so that the usefulness of knowledge would be more apparent. This approach demonstrates the relation of the various disciplines and shows students the wholeness of knowledge and helps them learn to use it in attacking problematic situations in novel and creative ways.

The teacher should constantly be aware of the motivation factor. Dewey held that children are naturally motivated, and that the teacher should capture and use the motivation that is already there. There should be an understanding, however, that all children are not at the same point and cannot be educated in the same way. Although there may be projects that motivate some students for group work, there may have to be individual projects for others.

The pragmatist is an adherent of action-oriented education; therefore, he would suggest an activity-oriented core approach, so not only would students learn they can relate various kinds of knowledge and use them to attack a problem, but they can act on them as well. To understand exploration more fully, students might visit historical sites of exploration or contemporary sites such as the Kennedy Space Center. At school, they could reconstruct past events and life situations in order to appreciate the difficulties involved in the actual occurrence better. These reconstructions could take the form of dramatizations, role playing, and model building.

Since pragmatists are concerned with teaching children how to solve problems, they feel that real-life situations encourage problem-solving ability in a practical setting. Let us suppose that in a particular class some children want to devise an energy allocation system. This becomes the problem, and children may study plans and decide how they want to go about solving it. The motivation is there in student interest, and the teacher serves primarily as a resource person concerned with helping children to get the maximum educational advantages out of the situation. But, basically, the children do it themselves, and they run into various problems about what kinds of allocation schemes to use, how to construct an equitable allocation basis, what social and economic issues must be considered, what possible alternative energy sources may be tapped, or how modern society could conserve energy better. It is in tackling such problems and trying to provide solutions that children come to understand and control their own destinies better.

In some respects, the method of learning is as important to pragmatists as what is learned. They feel that if one knows how to go about solving a problem then he is equipped to handle more remote things with which school may not be able to deal since the school does not know what kinds of life problems a person will face in the future. Pragmatists think, however, that where problems, such as those relating to marriage, the family, jobs, leisure time, and questions of peace and war, may be identified or predicted, the school should help to prepare the person to cope with them.

Pragmatic educators advocate meeting the needs and interests of the child. This has often been interpreted to mean letting him do anything he wants. "Interests and needs" do not necessarily mean the dictates of whim. Suppose a child wants to build model airplanes. Pragmatists would point out that this child's interest could be used as a motivational basis by which basic areas of the curriculum could be related. For example, he could be taught mathematics and physics in studying the principles of the airfoil. He could do this by studying man's dream to fly and the eventual realization of it. In Dewey's Laboratory School at Chicago, the principle followed was to start the child in some activity of direct interest, and then as the child encountered practical problems in the activity, to involve him in particular knowledge of the activity that in turn would lead to more general knowledge.

Pragmatists tend toward a broad education rather than a specialized one. This is why they endorse a more general education as opposed to narrow specialization. They maintain that when one breaks knowledge down into discrete elements and does not put it back together one faces the danger of losing perspective. The research chemist working on a specialized project may not be able to see the consequences of his action in the social sense. For example, after World War II, many nuclear physicists became disillusioned because their work was mainly used for destructive war-making purposes. In today's knowledge explosion it is impossible for a person to know everything, but he is capable of understanding the general operating principles of nature and social conditions that serve as guides for participation. The pragmatic approach is supposed to correct the excesses of narrow specialization. It does not oppose breaking knowledge down into its constituent elements, but it encourages us to put them back into a reconstructed whole that gives new direction and insight. It is in achieving this new wholeness that pragmatism becomes humanistic and holistic.

The concept of experimentation is basic to pragmatic philosophy. The fact that Dewey called his school at Chicago the "Laboratory School" illustrates his view that education is by its very nature experimental. Even though there are numerous guides, precepts, and maxims with regard to education, pragmatists hold that in the final analysis education is a process of experimentation because there are always new things to learn and different things to experience. Life does not stand still, and there is a constant need for improvement. This concept illustrates the pragmatic assumption of the open-ended universe where new development is a distinct possibility. Because of this, experimental education is necessary because it meets the needs of flexibility in an ever-changing world and also gives individuals security and a sense of constancy by helping them learn to understand and exercise control over the directions of change. Thus, pragmatic methods of education are not fixed, "cookbook" methods but are capable of being changed to fit changing circumstances.

Experimental method recognizes that there are no fixed or absolute conclusions; consequently, pragmatic education is really "discovery" education. Even the teacher does not always know what specific conclusions students will draw from their inquiry, although general possibilities may be known. Dewey gave the example of seven-year-old students who were cooking eggs and comparing them with vegetables and meats. If cooking eggs were simply the end, the children could have used only a cookbook. They raised this very point, but in cooking the eggs they discovered that albumen is a characteristic feature of animal foods corresponding to starches in vegetables. Thus, they had learned a very important lesson in nutrition by discovery. The teacher could have given them this information beforehand, but the lively manner of discovery established the knowledge in a much more profound way than mere telling could ever have accomplished. The students were learning the process of discovery as much as the facts uncovered. This type of learning is of twofold value: an important piece of knowledge is learned, and the skills of inquiry and self-sufficiency are developed that will benefit individuals for years to come.

One of the approaches suggested by such pragmatic educators as William Heard Kilpatrick is the "project approach" to learning. This is a systematization of the general approach Dewey used at the Laboratory School. According to Kilpatrick, a project approach results in the student's receiving a general education. Projects are decided by individual and group discussion, with the teacher as moderator. Children cooperate in pursuing the goals of the project. The essential features are those used by Dewey, but the approach is less structured, for in some cases the teacher has no idea what the outcome will be. Kilpatrick carefully pointed out that teachers can and should veto projects that are too ambitious or for which resources are lacking. He advocated that the entire time of the elementary school be devoted to the project method and that it be extended into the secondary school but in diminishing amount to make room for some specialization.

Although there may be some individual variations among pragmatists on specific aspects of method, they all agree that the proper method of education is experimental, flexible, open-ended, and oriented toward developing the individual's capacity to think and to participate intelligently in social life.

Curriculum

Pragmatists have rejected the tendency of traditional approaches to curriculum where knowledge is separated from experience and is fragmented or compartmentalized. When this happens, facts are torn away from experience and made to fit general principles that may or may not be helpful. In *The Child and the Curriculum*, Dewey maintained that the result of fragmentation has usually been to focus primary attention upon subject matter rather than on the contents of the child's own experience. In such an approach, children may be able to quote passages from Shakespeare without seeing how these can inform them about their own lives. The schools present materials to children in almost total neglect of their actual experiences. Children are often egotistic, self-centered, impulsive, and their experiences confused, vague, and uncertain, yet the materials they encounter in school present the world as well-ordered, certain, and predictable. On the other hand, Dewey criticized those who made children the only starting point, the center, and the end of education. He did not believe that everything should be subordinate to the personality and whims of children.

According to Dewey, there are two major concerns in such cases: the logical and psychological. The first emphasizes "discipline" and the second "interest." The error is to see a gap between a child's interest and necessary subject matter, for appropriate subject matter is not something fixed and ready-made outside a child's interest. The problem resides in how subject matter is organized and presented to students. For example, history is traditionally taught as something they should study simply because it is "good" for them, yet it may be remote and alien to their everyday experience. What the study of history should do is enable children to connect their own experiences, customs, and institutions with those of the past. It should liberate and enrich personal life by furnishing it with context, background, and outlook. Dewey thought that the practice of divorcing history from the present is a grievous error because it robs historical study of the capacity to provide intelligent insight into the present. A divorced history loses its value for ethical instruction. It does not give understanding to the fabric of present life and may produce callous indifference to why things become what they are.

When we look upon what a child learns as fixed and ready-made, attention is directed too much upon outcome and too little upon process. Pragmatists want to focus at least some attention on process, because ends should not be divorced from means. They assert that the means used to accomplish something dictate what the actual ends, the outcomes, really are. For example, to say that the American school should produce democratic citizens and then establish the school in such a way so that the students have almost no choice, judgment, or decision-making opportunity is, in actuality, to produce virtually anything but democratic citizens. The older generation then sits back and wonders why the young do not participate more in social and political activities. According to the pragmatist, there is little doubt as to why such conditions exist.

Pragmatists believe in a diversified curriculum. This has helped American education extend itself into many areas not previously considered its domain. For example, pragmatists have advocated studies in occupations and hygiene, and in topics such as the family and the economy. Today, schools have courses in distributive education, health, physical education, family life, and even sex education, but the actual outcome has not always been what the pragmatists want. For example, sex education courses are often taught only from a biological or physiological point of view. This is important, but pragmatists would say that human sexual behavior permeates many other human activities and should be integrated with them. How can one properly understand the meaning of so much of our great literature, for instance, without some understanding of sexual behavior?

Consequently, many pragmatists have advocated what is sometimes referred to as "problems-centered learning," the "core curriculum," the "project method," and the "problems approach." Essentially, such approaches to curriculum start with a central question, "core," or problem. Students are to attack the problem in diverse ways according to interest and need. Some may work independently, others in groups, and still others in various combinations and contexts. Information and ideas are drawn from whatever source is applicable. Resources include books, periodicals, travel, field trips, experts, and other community or human sources. The materials are then sifted and evaluated for importance, and the students draw conclusions and construct suitable generalizations concerning the problem. They evaluate their own growth and development that sets the stage for the next phase of education. In many respects, the pragmatic curriculum is a process as much as a distinct body of subject matter. Traditional disciplines are not ignored; rather, they are studied and used for the light they throw on the problem and how significant they are in aiding student growth. Pragmatic curriculum is composed of both process and content, but it is not fixed or an end in itself.

Critique of Pragmatism in Education

Pragmatism has been a very influential philosophy in America in the twentieth century. It has influenced not only education, but other areas such as law, art, economics, psychology, and religion. It is difficult, however, to separate a philosophy from the prevailing culture, and so it is hard to determine whether pragmatism shaped America or America shaped pragmatism. American culture is generally pragmatic in the popular sense of the word because Americans are concerned with workability, the "show me" attitude, and the "cash value" of propositions. It is also difficult to say that these things flow from philosophical pragmatism. Dewey's philosophy, for example, called for a rigorous attention to consequences in terms of moral and social goods and not in the crassly material- istic terms in which many Americans interpret it.

Progressive education is a case in point. Many observers equate pragma- tism with progressivism, and progressivism with the name of John Dewey. However, there is quite a bit of evidence that others had as much if not more to do with developing the progressive education movement than did Dewey. Colonel Francis Parker and G. Stanley Hall certainly loom large in the move- ment, both in practical and theoretical terms. The followers of Dewey such as William Heard Kilpatrick, John Childs, Boyd Bode, and Gordon Hullfish were also influential. Dewey was often critical of those who accepted his philosophy uncritically. At one point in his career, he openly criticized progressive educa- tors he thought had misinterpreted his philosophy. In his nineties, and shortly before his death, Dewey looked back on the history of progressive education and lamented the fact that his ideas had been taken as ready-made rubrics to be applied like mustard plaster to educational problems.

During the early twentieth century when pragmatic and progressive ideas were being developed, some people identified Dewey and his followers as subversive to the American system. For this reason, many educators repudiated pragmatic aims and techniques as too radical. Thus, pragmatists found it difficult to get their ideas widely accepted in secondary and higher education, but they were more successful at the elementary level. In many cases, the pragmatic ideas accepted were of the less threatening sort and were not recognized as being related to a philosophy. Such things as colored chalkboards, gaily colored surroundings, movable furniture built specifically for children, greater involve- ment of students in decision making, increased community involvement and support were all advocated by the pragmatists. Although Dewey primarily designed his ideas for public schools, many private and parochial schools were influenced by his philosophy.

By the late 1930s, progressive methods were sufficiently widespread, and a massive national study was launched to compare the differences between traditional and progressive schools. Known as the "Eight Year Study," and conducted between 1932 and 1940, the investigation showed that high school students in progressive schools did as well or better than those attending traditional institutions. This study that involved 30 high schools and 300 colleges aided in the adoption of progressive methods in American elementary and secondary schools. The final report on the study came out in the hectic days of World War II so that the study never received the attention it deserved.

As progressive ideas gained more acceptance, reaction to them also grew. Americans had to put education on the back burner during World War II, but the reaction blossomed again after the war. Criticisms about "soft-headed" pedagogy, "fads and frills," and "permissiveness" in progressive education were tossed about. A "back to the basics" movement picked up steam and reached a crescendo with the launching of Sputnik by the Soviet Union in 1957. This stimulated Congress to pass the National Defense Education Act in 1958 that poured millions of dollars into the schools to support the basic studies of science, mathematics, and foreign languages. Critics such as James Bryant Conant, Admiral Hyman G. Rickover, Max Rafferty, Arthur Bestor, and James D. Koener spearheaded the movement for basic education. They criticized progressivism for its alleged lack of patriotic and religious fervor, emphasis on change and relativism, and excessive freedom and lack of discipline. While many of these criticisms are shallow, they reflect on some of pragmatism's fundamental philosophical tenets.

One of the criticisms directed against pragmatism is that it deprecates acquisition of knowledge and cognitive development. It "waters down" the curriculum by advocating a "core" or "problems" approach that takes a piece of this and a bit of that discipline without ever fully exploring either one. Consequently, students are shortchanged in terms of knowledge. Furthermore, critics charge, pragmatists are oriented toward organizing studies around student interests. The result is that students lack the discipline that comes from study in the basic subject areas. Pragmatists have replaced history with "social studies," English with "language arts," and biology with "life sciences." The effort is to cater to students' interests and not to give them the basic disciplines they need. Pragmatists are too permissive in the way they bend to students whims; therefore, they leave school lacking judgment, with no depth, and have an almost total lack of direction or commitment to basic values.

Some of this criticism has merit because curriculum reform based on pragmatic ideas has usually been implemented too hastily and without adequate preparation of the teaching staff. In addition, many educators are too shallow in their interpretation of what student interests are, what is relevant, and what a problematic approach really involves. It has been pointed out on numerous occasions that Dewey's works were grossly distorted. When he said "interest," he did not mean whim or mere desire. Children have interests in understanding the society they live in whether they recognize that interest or not. It is the duty of the teacher to help students recognize these kinds of interests, and to help them make these interests personal. This is a symptomatic problem of interpreting Dewey's ideas, and it lies at the heart of his attack on dualistic thinking. He rejected any approach that only went either to the subjective side (student choice) or to the objective side (the subject matter). He argued against false separations of mind and body or individual and society. To meet student interest from Dewey's standpoint is to respect both subjective desires and objective demands, and both should be integrated into the educative process so that they are not at odds but are supportive of each other.

The same logical and interpretive problem exists with regard to Dewey's view of the place of cognitive development. Some educators have taken Dewey to mean that the intellectual and cognitive side of education are unimportant. The fact is that Dewey placed intelligence and thinking in a central position in his philosophy. He thought that cognition is developed in purposeful activity dealing with problems and arriving at solutions. He did not ignore books and the need for periodic drill. He simply rejected these as the heart and soul of education. Dewey believed that every human activity is potentially pregnant with opportunities for cognitive, emotional, aesthetic, and moral growth.

Indeed, there is a wide gap between what Dewey urged and what has often transpired in his and other philosophers' names. A case in point is the "life adjustment" movement. Some critics argue that pragmatists, and particularly Dewey, promoted an ethic of adjusting personal desires and interests to existing social and economic conditions. They say that such an outlook promotes monopolistic economics, *status quo* social divisions, and a general deadening effect. In fact, there has been a movement called the "life adjustment" movement, but there is no evidence that Dewey or any other leading pragmatist ever supported it. Dewey used the word "adjustment," but he used it in terms of people adjusting objective conditions to themselves as much as the other way around. He pointed out that people, in order to reconstruct and reorient society, first have to interact with existing conditions. In this sense, they have to adjust like any other organism, but they do it for the purpose or end of changing objective conditions and not simply to conform to what already exists.

Conservative critics have often attacked pragmatism for its "relative" and "situational" approach to life problems. They maintain that pragmatism rejects traditional values in religion, ethics, and society and tends toward values that are uncertain, changeable, and impermanent. While there is an element of truth in these charges, Dewey did not think one should reject traditional ideas and values out of hand, but that these should be considered as possible answers to any problem-solving activity. He did feel, however, that one could not afford to rely only on hand-me-down values, and that one should be constantly on the search for new ideas and values in every area of human activity. This problem is particularly apparent in the pragmatic approach to education where pragmatists support the idea that schools should maintain a constant "experimental" approach to learning. This does not mean workable approaches no matter how ancient in origin are to be scrapped, but new ideas and approaches should be sought constantly, tried, and implemented wherever feasible.

Several factors account for much of the difficulty found in pragmatic thought on education: the writing style of some pragmatists, such as Dewey, which lends itself to misinterpretation; the breadth and the lack of analytic specificity in pragmatic philosophy; the pragmatic penchant for centering on specific problems and the zeal of followers to overgeneralize the ensuing ideas and to oversimplify basic propositions; and the woeful lack of energetic attention to Dewey's philosophy itself as opposed to interpretations of it. Dewey's philosophy has not had a thoroughgoing and systematic criticism, particularly with regard to its meaning for education, because most critics have only taken on piecemeal aspects, have made polemical attacks rather than critical analyses, or have given bipartisan attacks in order to support another philosophy. Nevertheless, pragmatic philosophy, for all its problems, has been one of the enduring contributions to American education.

Dewey

"My Pedagogic Creed"

John Dewey exerted great influence on both American philosophy and American education. His interest in education was lifelong, and he wrote and spoke extensively about it. Dewey wrote the following selection in the early years of his professional career, and it shows his zeal as he sees education as one of the great social forces in human affairs.* It is not surprising that he refers to this as a "creed," for education was indeed to him one of the most important duties of the community, in fact, its paramount moral duty.

Article One—What Education Is—I Believe that—all education proceeds by the participation of the individual in the social consciousness of the race. This process begins unconsciously almost at birth, and is continually shaping the individual's powers, saturating his consciousness, forming his habits, training his ideas, and arousing his feelings and emotions. Through this unconscious education the individual gradually comes to share in the intellectual and moral resources which humanity has succeeded in getting together. He becomes an inheritor of the funded capital of civilization. The most formal and technical education in the world cannot safely depart from this general process. It can only organize it or differentiate it in some particular direction. . . .

—this educational process has two sides, one psychological and one sociological, and that neither can be subordinated to the other, or neglected, without evil results following. Of these two sides, the psychological is the basis. The child's own instincts and powers furnish the material and give the starting-point for all education. Save as the efforts of the educator connect with some activity which the child is carrying on of his own initiative independent of the educator, education becomes reduced to a pressure from without. It may, indeed, give certain external results, but cannot truly be called educative. Without insight into the psychological structure and activities of the individual, the educative process will, therefore, be haphazard and arbitrary. If it chances to coincide with the child's activity it will get a leverage; if it does not, it will result in friction, or disintegration, or arrest of the child nature. . . .

In sum, I believe that the individual who is to be educated is a social individual, and that society is an organic union of individuals. If we eliminate the social factor from the child we are left only with an abstraction; if we eliminate the individual factor from society, we are left only with an inert and lifeless mass. Education, therefore, must begin with a psychological insight into the child's capacities, interests, and habits. It must be controlled at every point by reference to these same considerations. These powers, interests, and habits must be continually interpreted—we must know what they mean. They must

---

*Selection from John Dewey, "My Pedagogic Creed," *The School Journal* 54, 3 (Jan. 16, 1897), pp. 77–80. Reprinted with the permission of the Center for Dewey Studies, Southern Illinois University at Carbondale.

be translated into terms of their social equivalents—into terms of what they are capable of in the way of social service.

Article Two—What the School Is—I Believe that—the school is primarily a social institution. Education being a social process, the school is simply that form of community life in which all those agencies are concentrated that will be most effective in bringing the child to share in the inherited resources of the race, and to use his own powers for social ends.

—education, therefore, is a process of living and not a preparation for future living.

—the school must represent present life—life as real and vital to the child as that which he carries on in the home, in the neighborhood, or on the playground.

—that education which does not occur through forms of life, forms that are worth living for their own sake, is always a poor substitute for the genuine reality, and tends to cramp and to deaden. . . .

—much of present education fails because it neglects this fundamental principle of the school as a form of community life. It conceives the school as a place where certain information is to be given, where certain lessons are to be learned, or where certain habits are to be formed. The value of these is conceived as lying largely in the remote future; the child must do these things for the sake of something else he is to do; they are mere preparations. As a result they do not become a part of the life experience of the child and so are not truly educative.

—the moral education centers upon this conception of the school as a mode of social life, that the best and deepest moral training is precisely that which one gets through having to enter into proper relations with others in a unity of work and thought. The present educational systems, so far as they destroy or neglect this unity, render it difficult or impossible to get any genuine, regular moral training. . . .

Article Three—The Subjectmatter of Education—I believe that—the social life of the child is the basis of concentration, or correlation, in all his training or growth. The social life gives the unconscious unity and the background of all his efforts and of all his attainments. . . .

—the true center of correlation on the school subjects is not science, nor literature, nor history, nor geography, but the child's own social activities. . . .

—literature is the reflex expression and interpretation of social experience; that hence it must follow upon and not precede such experience. It, therefore, cannot be made the basis, although it may be made the summary of unification.

—once more that history is of educative value in so far as it presents phases of social life and growth. It must be controlled by reference to social life. When taken simply as history it is thrown into the distant past and becomes dead and inert. Taken as the record of man's social life and progress it becomes full of meaning. I believe, however, that it cannot be so taken excepting as the child is also introduced directly into social life.

—the primary basis of education is in the child's powers at work along the same general constructive lines as those which have brought civilization into being. . . .

—there is, therefore, no succession of studies in the ideal school curriculum. If education is life, all life has, from the outset, a scientific aspect, an aspect of art and culture, and an aspect of communication. It cannot, therefore, be true that the proper studies for one grade are mere reading and writing, and that at a later grade, reading, or literature, or science, may be introduced. The progress is not in the succession of studies, but in the development of new attitudes towards, and new interests in, experience.

—education must be conceived as a continuing reconstruction of experience; that the process and the goal of education are one and the same thing.

—to set up any end outside of education, as furnishing its goal and standard, is to deprive the educational process of much of its meaning, and tends to make us rely upon false and external stimuli in dealing with the child.

Article Four—The Nature of Method—I Believe that—the question of method is ultimately reducible to the question of the order of development of the child's powers and interests. The law for presenting and treating material is the law implicit within the child's own nature. Because this is so I believe the following statements are of supreme importance as determining the spirit in which education is carried on.

—the active side precedes the passive in the development of the child-nature; that expression comes before conscious impression; that the muscular development precedes the sensory; that movements come before conscious sensations; I believe that consciousness is essentially motor or impulsive; that conscious states tend to project themselves in action. . . .

—ideas (intellectual and rational processes) also result from action and devolve for the sake of the better control of action. What we term reason is primarily the law of order or effective action. To attempt to develop the reasoning powers, the powers of judgment,

without reference to the selection and arrangement of means in action, is the fundamental fallacy in our present methods of dealing with this matter. As a result we present the child with arbitrary symbols. Symbols are a necessity in mental development, but they have their place as tools for economizing effort; presented by themselves they are a mass of meaningless and arbitrary ideas imposed from without.

—the image is the great instrument of instruction. What a child gets out of any subject presented to him is simply the images which he himself forms with regard to it. . . .

—much of the time and attention now given to the preparation and presentation of lessons might be more wisely and profitably expended in training the child's power of imagery and in seeing to it that he was continually forming definite vivid, and growing images of the various subjects with which he comes in contact in his experience. . . .

—these interests are neither to be humored nor repressed. To repress interest is to substitute the adult for the child, and so to weaken intellectual curiosity and alertness, to suppress initiative, and to deaden interest. To humor the interests is to substitute the transient for the permanent. The interest is always the sign of some power below; the important thing is to discover this power. To humor the interest is to fail to penetrate below the surface, and its sure result is to substitute caprice and whim for genuine interest.

—the emotions are the reflex of actions.

—to endeavor to stimulate or arouse the emotions apart from their corresponding activities is to introduce an unhealthy and morbid state of mind.

—if we can only secure right habits of action and thought, with reference to the good, the true, and the beautiful, the emotions will for the most part take care of themselves. . . .

Article Five—The School and Social Progress—education is the fundamental method of social progress and reform. . . .

—this conception has due regard for both the individualistic and socialistic ideals. It is duly individual because it recognizes the formation of a certain character as the only genuine basis of right living. It is socialistic because it recognizes that this right character is not to be formed by merely individual precept, example, or exhortation, but rather by the influence of a certain form of institutional or community life upon the individual, and that the social organism through the school, as its organ, may determine ethical results. . . .

—the community's duty to education is, therefore, its paramount moral duty. By law and punishment, by social agitation and discussion, society can regulate and form itself in a more or less haphazard and chance way. But through education society can formulate its own purposes, can organize its own means and resources, and thus shape itself with definiteness and economy in the direction in which it wishes to move. . . .

—it is the business of everyone interested in education to insist upon the school as the primary and most effective interest of social progress and reform in order that society may be awakened to realize what the school stands for, and arouse to the necessity of endowing the educator with sufficient equipment properly to perform his task.

—education thus conceived marks the most perfect and intimate union of science and art conceivable in human experience. . . .

—when science and art thus join hands the most commanding motive for human action will be reached, the most genuine springs of human conduct aroused, and the best service that human nature is capable of guaranteed.

Dewey

Democracy and Education

Perhaps the single most important work Dewey wrote on education was Democracy and Education, published in 1916.* His understanding of education was very detailed and complex, and he struggled to express his ideas in a language ordinary people could understand; however, he was not always successful because complex ideas are often difficult to express simply. The following selection is a lucid but general statement of Dewey's views. In it he reflects on the social nature of education and how it is necessary for individuals to enter into social relations to become educated. Communication is central to the education of individuals in social contexts, because communication enlarges experience and makes it meaningful. Education occurs in both formal and informal settings, and philosophy's role is to help achieve a proper balance between the two.

1. Renewal of Life by Transmission.— The most notable distinction between living and inanimate beings is that the former maintain themselves by renewal. A stone when struck resists. If its resistance is greater than the force of the blow struck, it remains outwardly unchanged. Otherwise, it is shattered into smaller bits. Never does the stone attempt to react in such a way that it may maintain itself against the blow, much less so as to render the blow a contributing factor to its own continued action. While the living thing may easily be crushed by superior force, it none the less tries to turn the energies which act upon it into means of its own further existence. If it cannot do so, it does not just split into smaller pieces (at least in the higher forms of life), but loses its identity as a living thing.

As long as it endures, it struggles to use surrounding energies in its own behalf. It uses light, air, moisture, and the material of soil. To say that it uses them is to say that it turns them into means of its own conservation. As long

as it is growing, the energy it expends in thus turning the environment to account is more than compensated for by the return it gets: it grows. Understanding the word "control" in this sense, it may be said that a living being is one that subjugates and controls for its own continued activity the energies that would otherwise use it up. Life is a self-renewing process through action upon the environment.

In all the higher forms this process cannot be kept up indefinitely. After a while they succumb; they die. The creature is not equal to the task of indefinite self-renewal. But continuity of the life process is not dependent upon the prolongation of the existence of any one individual. Reproduction of other forms of life goes on in continuous sequence. And though, as the geological record shows, not merely individuals but also species die out, the life process continues in increasingly complex forms. As some species die out, forms better adapted to utilize the obstacles against which they struggled in vain come into

---

*Selection from John Dewey, *Democracy and Education* (New York: Macmillan, 1916), pp. 1–9. Reprinted with the permission of the Center for Dewey Studies, Southern Illinois University at Carbondale.

being. Continuity of life means continual readaptation of the environment to the needs of living organisms.

We have been speaking of life in its lowest terms—as a physical thing. But we use the word "life" to denote the whole range of experience, individual and racial. When we see a book called the *Life of Lincoln* we do not expect to find within its covers a treatise on physiology. We look for an account of social antecedents; a description of early surroundings, of the conditions and occupation of the family; of the chief episodes in the development of character; of signal struggles and achievements; of the individual's hopes, tastes, joys and sufferings. In precisely similar fashion we speak of the life of a savage tribe, of the Athenian people, of the American nation. "Life" covers customs, institutions, beliefs, victories and defeats, recreations and occupations.

We employ the word "experience" in the same pregnant sense. And to it, as well as to life in the bare physiological sense, the principle of continuity through renewal applies. With the renewal of physical existence goes, in the case of human beings, the re-creation of beliefs, ideals, hopes, happiness, misery, and practices. The continuity of any experience, through renewing of the social group, is a literal fact. "Education, in its broadest sense, is the means of this social continuity of life." Every one of the constituent elements of a social group, in a modern city as in a savage tribe, is born immature, helpless, without language, beliefs, ideas, or social standards. Each individual, each unit who is the carrier of the life-experience of his group, in time passes away. Yet the life of the group goes on.

The primary ineluctable facts of the birth and death of each one of the constituent members in a social group determine the necessity of education. On one hand, there is the contrast between the immaturity of the newborn members of the group—its future sole representatives—and the maturity of the adult members who possess the knowledge and customs of the group. On the other hand, there is the necessity that these immature members be not merely physically preserved in adequate numbers, but that they be initiated into the interests, purposes, information, skill, and practices of the mature members: otherwise the group will cease its characteristic life. Even in a savage tribe, the achievements of adults are far beyond what the immature members would be capable of if left to themselves. With the growth of civilization, the gap between the original capacities of the immature and the standards and customs of the elders increases. Mere physical growing up, mere mastery of the bare necessities of subsistence will not suffice to reproduce the life of the group. Deliberate effort and the taking of thoughtful pains are required. Beings who are born not only unaware of, but quite indifferent to, the aims and habits of the social group have to be rendered cognizant of them and actively interested. Education, and education alone, spans the gap.

Society exists through a process of transmission quite as much as biological life. This transmission occurs by means of communication of habits of doing, thinking, and feeling from the older to the younger. Without this communication of ideals, hopes, expectations, standards, opinions, from those members of society who are passing out of the group life to those who are coming into it, social life could not survive. If the members who compose a society lived on continuously, they might educate the new-born members, but it would be a task directed by personal interest rather than social need. Now it is a work of necessity.

If a plague carried off the members of a society all at once, it is obvious that the group would be permanently done for. Yet the death of each of its constituent members is as certain as if an epidemic took them all at once. But the graded difference in age, the fact that some are born as some die, makes possible through transmission of ideas and practices the constant reweaving of the social fabric. Yet this renewal is not automatic. Unless pains are taken to see that genuine and thorough transmission takes place, the most civilized group will relapse into barbarism and then into savagery. In fact, the human young are so immature that if they were left to themselves without the guidance and succor of others, they could not even acquire the rudimentary abilities necessary for physical existence. The young of human beings compare so poorly in original efficiency with the young of many of the lower animals, that even the powers needed for physical sustentation have to be acquired under tuition. How much more, then, is this the case with respect to all the technological, artistic, scientific, and moral achievements of humanity!

2. Education and Communication.— So obvious, indeed, is the necessity of teaching and learning for the continued existence of a society that we may seem to be dwelling unduly on a truism. But justification is found in the fact that such emphasis is a means of getting us away from an unduly scholastic and formal notion of education. Schools are, indeed, one important method of the transmission which forms the dispositions of the immature; but it is only one means, and, compared with other agen-

cies, a relatively superficial means. Only as we have grasped the necessity of more fundamental and persistent modes of tuition can we make sure of placing the scholastic methods in their true context.

Society not only continues to exist *by* transmission, *by* communication, but it may fairly be said to exist *in* transmission, *in* communication. There is more than a verbal tie between the words common, community, and communication. Men live in a community in virtue of the things which they have in common; and communication is the way in which they come to possess things in common. What they must have in common in order to form a community or society are aims, beliefs, aspirations, knowledge—a common understanding— like-mindedness as the sociologists say. Such things cannot be passed physically from one to another, like bricks; they cannot be shared as persons would share a pie by dividing it into physical pieces. The communication which insures participation in a common understanding is one which secures similar emotional and intellectual dispositions— like ways of responding to expectations and requirements.

Persons do not become a society by living in physical proximity, any more than a man ceases to be socially influenced by being so many feet or miles removed from others. A book or a letter may institute a more intimate association between human beings separated thousands of miles from each other than exists between dwellers under the same roof. Individuals do not even compose a social group because they all work for a common end. The parts of a machine work with a maximum of coöperativeness for a common result, but they do not form a community. If, however, they were all cognizant of the common end and all interested in it so that they regulated their specific activity in view of it, then they would form a community. But this would involve communication. Each would have to know what the other was about and would have to have some way of keeping the other informed as to his own purpose and progress. Consensus demands communication.

We are thus compelled to recognize that within even the most social group there are many relations which are not as yet social. A large number of human relationships in any social group are still upon the machine-like plane. Individuals use one another so as to get desired results, without reference to the emotional and intellectual disposition and consent of those used. Such uses express physical superiority, or superiority of position, skill, technical ability, and command of tools, mechanical or fiscal. So far as the relations of parent and child, teacher and pupil, employer and employee, governor and governed, remain upon this level, they form no true social group, no matter how closely their respective activities touch one another. Giving and taking of orders modifies action and results, but does not of itself effect a sharing of purposes, a communication of interests.

Not only is social life identical with communication, but all communication (and hence all genuine social life) is educative. To be a recipient of a communication is to have an enlarged and changed experience. One shares in what another has thought and felt and in so far, meagerly or amply, has his own attitude modified. Nor is the one who communicates left unaffected. Try the experiment of communicating, with fullness and accuracy, some experience to another, especially if it be somewhat complicated, and you will find your own attitude toward your experience changing; otherwise you resort to expletives and ejaculations. The experience has to be formulated in order to be communicated. To formulate requires getting outside of it, seeing it as another would see it, considering what points of contact it has with the life of another so that it may be got into such form that he can appreciate its meaning. Except in dealing with commonplaces and catch phrases one has to assimilate, imaginatively, something of another's experience in order to tell him intelligently of one's own experience. All communication is like art. It may fairly be said, therefore, that any social arrangement that remains vitally social, or vitally shared, is educative to those who participate in it. Only when it becomes cast in a mold and runs in a routine way does it lose its educative power.

In final account, then, not only does social life demand teaching and learning for its own permanence, but the very process of living together educates. It enlarges and enlightens experience; it stimulates and enriches imagination; it creates responsibility for accuracy and vividness of statement and thought. A man really living alone (alone mentally as well as physically) would have little or no occasion to reflect upon his past experience to extract its net meaning. The inequality of achievement between the mature and the immature not only necessitates teaching the young, but the necessity of this teaching gives an immense stimulus to reducing experience to that order and form which will render it most easily communicable and hence most usable.

3. **The Place of Formal Education.**—There is, accordingly, a marked differ-

ence between the education which every one gets from living with others, as long as he really lives instead of just continuing to subsist, and the deliberate educating of the young. In the former case the education is incidental; it is natural and important, but it is not the express reason of the association. While it may be said, without exaggeration, that the measure of the worth of any social institution, economic, domestic, political, legal, religious, is its effect in enlarging and improving experience; yet this effect is not a part of its original motive, which is limited and more immediately practical. Religious associations began, for example, in the desire to secure the favor of overruling powers and to ward off evil influences; family life in the desire to gratify appetites and secure family perpetuity; systematic labor, for the most part, because of enslavement to others, etc. Only gradually was the by-product of the institution, its effect upon the quality and extent of conscious life, noted, and only more gradually still was this effect considered as a directive factor in the conduct of the institution. Even to-day, in our industrial life, apart from certain values of industriousness and thrift, the intellectual and emotional reaction of the forms of human association under which the world's work is carried on receives little attention as compared with physical output.

But in dealing with the young, the fact of association itself as an immediate human fact, gains in importance. While it is easy to ignore in our contact with them the effect of our acts upon their disposition, or to subordinate that educative effect to some external and tangible result, it is not so easy as in dealing with adults. The need of training is too evident; the pressure to accomplish a change in their attitude and habits is too

urgent to leave these consequences wholly out of account. Since our chief business with them is to enable them to share in a common life we cannot help considering whether or not we are forming the powers which will secure this ability. If humanity has made some headway in realizing that the ultimate value of every institution is its distinctively human effect—its effect upon conscious experience—we may well believe that this lesson has been learned largely through dealings with the young.

We are thus led to distinguish, within the broad educational process which we have been so far considering, a more formal kind of education—that of direct tuition or schooling. In undeveloped social groups, we find very little formal teaching and training. Savage groups mainly rely for instilling needed dispositions into the young upon the same sort of association which keeps adults loyal to their group. They have no special devices, material, or institutions for teaching save in connection with initiation ceremonies by which the youth are inducted into full social membership. For the most part, they depend upon children learning the customs of the adults, acquiring their emotional set and stock of ideas, by sharing in what the elders are doing. In part, this sharing is direct, taking part in the occupations of adults and thus serving an apprenticeship; in part, it is indirect, through the dramatic plays in which children reproduce the actions of grown-ups and thus learn to know what they are like. To savages it would seem preposterous to seek out a place where nothing but learning was going on in order that one might learn.

But as civilization advances, the gap between the capacities of the young and the concerns of adults widens. Learning by direct sharing in the pursuits of grown-ups becomes increasingly difficult except in the case of the less advanced occupations. Much of what adults do is so remote in space and in meaning that playful imitation is less and less adequate to reproduce its spirit. Ability to share effectively in adult activities thus depends upon a prior training given with this end in view. Intentional agencies—schools—and explicit material—studies—are devised. The task of teaching certain things is delegated to a special group of persons.

Without such formal education, it is not possible to transmit all the resources and achievements of a complex society. It also opens a way to a kind of experience which would not be accessible to the young, if they were left to pick up their training in informal association with others, since books and the symbols of knowledge are mastered.

But there are conspicuous dangers attendant upon the transition from indirect to formal education. Sharing in actual pursuit, whether directly or vicariously in play, is at least personal and vital. These qualities compensate, in some measure, for the narrowness of available opportunities. Formal instruction, on the contrary, easily becomes remote and dead—abstract and bookish, to use the ordinary words of depreciation. What accumulated knowledge exists in low grade societies is at least put into practice; it is transmuted into character; it exists with the depth of meaning that attaches to its coming within urgent daily interests.

But in an advanced culture much which has to be learned is stored in symbols. It is far from translation into familiar acts and objects. Such material is relatively technical and superficial. Taking the ordinary standard of reality as a measure, it is artificial. For this measure is connection with practical concerns. Such material exists in a world by itself, unassimilated to ordinary customs of thought and expression. There is the standing danger that the material of formal instruction will be merely the subject matter of the schools, isolated from the subject matter of life-experience. The permanent social interests are likely to be lost from view. Those which have not been carried over into the structure of social life, but which remain largely matters of technical information expressed in symbols, are made conspicuous in schools. Thus we reach the ordinary notion of education: the notion which ignores its social necessity and its identity with all human association that affects conscious life, and which identifies it with imparting information about remote matters and the conveying of learning through verbal signs: the acquisition of literacy.

Hence one of the weightiest problems with which the philosophy of education has to cope is the method of keeping a proper balance between the informal and the formal, the incidental and the intentional, modes of education. When the acquiring of information and of technical intellectual skill do not influence the formation of a social disposition, ordinary vital experience fails to gain in meaning, while schooling, in so far, creates only "sharps" in learning—that is, egoistic specialists. To avoid a split between what men consciously know because they are aware of having learned it by a specific job of learning, and what they unconsciously know because they have absorbed it in the formation of their characters by intercourse with others, becomes an increasingly delicate task with every development of special schooling.

Selected Readings

Bayles, Ernest. *Pragmatism in Education*. New York: Harper and Row, 1966.
    A short introduction to the pragmatic style of philosophizing, this book tries to explore major tenets in pragmatism and their relationship to the educational process.

Childs, John L. *Education and the Philosophy of Experimentalism*. New York: Century, 1931.
    This book aims at developing a pragmatic approach toward educational problems. It gives the historical development of pragmatism and has served as a guide for those who wish to understand educational problems from a pragmatic point of view.

Dewey, John. *Democracy and Education*. New York: Macmillan, 1916.
    Dewey believed that this work was the most complete statement of his philosophy. It has been one of the most influential books on education written in the twentieth century.

———. *Experience and Education*. New York: Macmillan, 1938.
    This is one of Dewey's most concise statements on education in which he criticizes excesses of the progressive movement and misinterpretations of his ideas. He attacks either/or thinking as debilitating to educational theory and maintains that a philosophy of experience must be central.

Kilpatrick, William H. *Education for a Changing Civilization*. New York: Century, 1926.
    Kilpatrick promotes the use of pragmatic method in educational practices. He sees the use of this philosophy as a way of improving both man and society.

Plato
(427-347)

Aurelius   St. Augustine
(121-180)   (354-430)

RECONSTRUCTIONISM

The philosophy of reconstructionism contains two major premises: (1) society is in need of constant reconstruction or change, and (2) such social change involves both a reconstruction of education and the use of education in reconstructing society. It is not unusual for those who are involved with change, particularly the kinds of immediate and necessary changes that every age seems to require, to turn to education as the most effective and efficient instrument for making such changes in an intelligent, democratic, and humane way. Reconstructionists advocate an attitude toward change that encourages individuals to try to make life better than it was or is. In our own age, particularly, reconstructionism could strike a responsive chord, because we are faced today with a bewildering number of problems regarding race, poverty, war, ecological destruction, and technological inhumanity that call for an immediate reconstruction of all our existing religious and philosophical value systems. Ideas and values that once seemed workable for religion, family life, and education no longer seem as viable as they once were. Twentieth-century man is bewildered not only by the changes that have already taken place, but also by the prospect of future changes that must be made if we are to cope adequately with these problems. While there have always been persons of intelligence and vision who thought about and promoted social change, only in recent times there has been the development of a systematic outlook called reconstructionist philosophy.

120

1500AD	1900AD

More
(1478-1535)

St. Simon
(1760-1825)

Marx
(1818-1883)

Counts
(1889-1974)

Illich
(1926-   )

Fourier
(1772-1835)

Freire
(1921-   )

Dewey
(1859-1952)

Owen
(1771-1859)

Brameld
(1904-   )

4

RECONSTRUCTIONISM
AND
EDUCATION

Historical Background of Reconstructionism

There have been reconstructionist ideas in one form or another throughout history. Plato, in preparing his design for a future state, the *Republic*, was a "reconstructionist" philosopher. He outlined a plan for a just state in which education would become the building material for a new and better society. Plato believed that his state would be eminently desirable. He proposed radical departures from the customs of his Greek contemporaries, such as sexual equality, communal child rearing, and rule by a philosopher-king. In the *Laws*, he envisioned a time when interest charges would be forbidden, profits would be limited, and mankind would live friend-to-friend. Although Plato's attempts to establish such a society failed, perhaps he was simply ahead of his time.

The Stoic philosophers, particularly in their concern for a world state, promoted a "reconstructionist" kind of ideal. Marcus Aurelius, a Roman

121

emperor and philosopher, maintained that he was a citizen of the world, not of Rome. This concept is one that reconstructionists articulate today in their attempts to minimize nationalistic fervor and chauvinism.

Many of the Christian philosophers, such as Augustine, preached reconstructionist reforms in order to bring about an ideal Christian state. The kinds of reforms Augustine asked for in *The City of God* were intended for man's soul rather than his material being, but they had ramifications that carried over to the material world as well. Theodore Brameld, a major contemporary reconstructionist, states that Augustine raised several difficult questions that later utopian philosophers endeavored to answer, such as whether or not the course of history encourages us to believe our ideal goals finally may be reached. Thomas More, Thomas Campanella, Johann Valentin Andreae, Samuel Gott, and other Christian utopian writers also proposed things we might do to bring the state into better accord with Christian thinking.

The writings of eighteenth- and nineteenth-century Utopian socialists, such as Comte de Saint-Simon, Charles Fourier, and Francois Noël Babeuf advocate reconstructionist ideals through the development of various forms of socialism. Robert Owen and Edward Bellamy were greatly influenced by the industrial revolution and saw the use of technology not for the production of wealth per se, but for improving the lot of mankind throughout the world. It was Karl Marx, decrying the harm done to workers by the dehumanization of the industrial system, who pictured a reconstructed world based upon an international communism.

It is interesting to note that Karl Marx received a Ph.D. in philosophy, yet wrote extensively about economics. Marx deplored armchair philosophical thinking, and like the reconstructionists, believed that education should not be an ivory-tower affair but a method of changing the world. In his *Thesis on Feuerback*, Marx wrote: "Philosophers have only interpreted the world differently; the point, however, is to change it."

Marx had studied Hegel intensively, but where Hegel saw the dialectical movement of the Universe in idealist terms, Marx saw it in terms of the clash of economic forces. These forces manifest themselves today by pitting the worker against the capitalist system. Education has been used as a way of maintaining the *status quo* because it has supported the interests of the ruling class. However, Marx believed that education can also be used to overthrow those interests and place the proletariat in control. At such a time, Marx felt, the power of the state will begin to wither and eventually will be replaced by a true rule of the people.

According to Marx, education has been an insidious device used to indoctrinate people into accepting and supporting the attitudes and outlooks of the moneyed interests. Although money is seemingly neutral, laborers are robbed of their freedom by exchanging work and production for money, a condition of which workers are usually unaware. Thus, workers are exploited by the system, their productive abilities appropriated in exchange for the symbolic value of money. Education is a means to entrench this system by promoting the interests of the ruling class using both the formal and informal or "hidden" curriculum that encourages subservience and docility. This is accomplished through the ways schools are controlled by elite governing authorities, and the schools in turn control students through rules and regulations, discipline procedures, and the curriculum. Textbooks are censored when they challenge conventional views on economics and government as well as sex, religion, and other touchy issues. Teachers, often without even realizing it, promote conventional biases in many subtle ways, attitudes, and practices. Students control each other through peer group pressures that can be powerful and unconscious influences. Just as education can be used to enslave us, however, it can also be used, if properly understood, to free us. To do this would mean overthrowing our present economic system and instituting a new kind of education oriented toward raising social consciousness of economic controls that would enable each person to be an end and not a means.

Although World Wars I and II turned men's thoughts away from optimistic pictures of future worlds and spawned such dystopias as Aldous Huxley's *Brave New World* and George Orwell's *1984*, there were still reformers and optimists such as Bertrand Russell, whose *Principles of Social Reconstruction* listed steps that man might take in order to avoid a nuclear holocaust. Today, various groups propose ways to change the world and eliminate racism, poverty, and war. Some advocate the use of conditioning or "behavioral engineering" (as in B. F. Skinner's *Walden Two*) to make important and significant changes in everyday life through advancing technical skills. In *Beyond Freedom and Dignity*, Skinner maintains that we cannot afford "freedom" in the traditional sense, and we must resolutely engineer a new social order based on the technology of behavior.

When we examine proposals from Plato to Skinner, we find that they recommend education as a primary instrument for social change. Plato, for example, thought of education as the *sine qua non* of the good society; Marx saw it as a way to help the proletariat develop a sense of "social consciousness"; Christian writers advocated the use of education as a means of inculcating religious faith and ideals; and modern technocrats see it as a way to promote technical change and provide individuals with the necessary skills for living in an advanced technological society. In *Walden Two*, Skinner depicted a community of highly trained technicians, engineers, artists, and agronomists who are educated or conditioned to a high level of proficiency. This is certainly a far cry from the romantic heritage of Henry David Thoreau's *Walden* and Jean-Jacques Rousseau's *Emile*, but even Rousseau saw his finished product (as did John Locke in *Some Thoughts Concerning Education*), as a person who would later guide society along newer and better paths. Locke's "gentleman" was to lead by virtue of his breeding and education, while Rousseau's "Noble Savage" would lead because of his purity and naturalness. They all looked for social change through education.

In the United States, a number of people have seen education as a tool for social reform: Horace Mann, Henry Barnard, William Tory Harris, Francis Parker, and John Dewey. Dewey saw education as an instrument for changing both man and society, and particularly, in the 1920s and 1930s, his philosophy became identified in the minds of many people with radical social reform. Dewey's pragmatism was linked with a rejection of absolutes and an acceptance of relativism, and it rankled many who thought (and some who still do) that education was in the grip of forces destined to lead American society down the liberal path to eventual destruction. Though Dewey's philosophy is more readily identified today with moderate "progressivism," at its peak it was often identified with radicalism.

Modern reconstructionism is basically pragmatic in nature and owes a tremendous debt to Dewey's philosophical ideas. Reconstructionists promote such things as the scientific method, problem solving, naturalism, and secular humanism. The point of divergence between reconstructionists and pragmatists is not in relation to their common base, but rather in an interpretation of how the pragmatic method should be used. Although pragmatism advocates continuous change and a forward-looking approach to the problems of man and society, it has become (in the hands of many who call themselves progressivists) a tool for helping people to "adjust" to society rather than to change it. One can explain this attitude partly by reference to the immigrants coming to America in the early 1900s who needed to be "adjusted" to American language and customs to bring them more into the "mainstream" of American society. There was and always will be a need for education to "adjust" people to social and cultural values, but reconstructionists do not believe that this is the primary role education should undertake. Education from the reconstructionist's point of view is to serve as a tool for immediate and continuous change.

Although much has been written about Dewey's radicalism in politics, philosophy, education, and other areas, he has also been interpreted to have viewed education as a way of making evolutionary as opposed to revolutionary progress toward social change. Dewey envisioned these changes occurring within the democratic fabric of society as it existed, or as it would evolve, rather than through the major revolutionary changes many reconstructionists believe are necessary. Whereas some pragmatists support the idea of dealing with problems within the existing framework of society, many reconstructionists hold that while this may be a reasonable approach for some problems, it is often necessary to get outside the general bounds of the contemporary value system in order to look at our problems afresh without traditional restraints. Utopian writers have pointed out, and perhaps understood better than anyone else, that many of the great problems of society cannot be solved without changes in the structure of society itself. Many utopians and reconstructionists (and in all fairness, Dewey himself) believe that some of the things we consider evil are really part of the institutions to which we give allegiance, and we cannot hope to eradicate such evils without changing these institutions fundamentally. Many of us are perplexed when we hear that Socrates, the "gadfly of Athens," chose to face death rather than oppose the laws of Athens as they then existed. Some reconstructionists charge that pragmatists appear to have accepted the Socratic compromise: pragmatists have championed change, but not at the price of alienating those who gradually need to be persuaded into accepting orderly and systematic movement through established democratic institutions.

Dewey, for example, seemed to be somewhat reluctant to advance education much faster than society itself could be advanced. The reconstructionists maintain that modern man may not have the luxury of such delay. Thus, while reconstructionism has its roots in past philosophical systems and philosophers, it attempts to strike out in more radical directions than its predecessors.

Philosophy of Reconstructionism

Reconstructionism is not precisely a philosophy in the more traditional meaning of philosophy; that is, it does not seek to make detailed epistemological or logical studies. As indicated, reconstructionism is more concerned with the broad social and cultural fabric in which we exist. We might say that reconstructionism is almost a purely social philosophy. Its leading exponents are not so much professional philosophers as they are educational and social activists. They concentrate on social and cultural conditions and how these can be made more palatable for full human participation.

George S. Counts and Theodore Brameld are two people who have exemplified this outlook. Of the two, Brameld has come closest to the more traditional role of the philosopher, having written in considerable depth about the philosophical nature of reconstructionism. Counts was the educational activist-scholar whose interests were wide ranging, and while not lacking in philosophical knowledge, his writings and professional activities were more broadly concerned with social activism itself.

George S. Counts (1889–1974). Counts came from a rural background and spent most of his adult life in some of America's major universities and intellectual circles. He engaged in extensive travel and study abroad, especially in the Soviet Union. He was a personal acquaintance of John Dewey and was influenced a great deal by that philosopher's social activism side.

Counts's major work on reconstructionism is a small but widely read book, *Dare the Schools Build a New Social Order?* First delivered as three public lectures before a national group of educators, the central theme of *Dare the Schools* struck American educators with force. Counts had returned from the Soviet Union in 1930, where he had made a detailed study of that country's struggles. Seeing the United States bogged down in the social confusion of the Depression (a condition Counts thought was inexcusable and needless), he sought to awaken educators to their strategic position in social and cultural reconstruction. Counts's central message was that while education had been historically used as a means of introducing people to their cultural traditions, social and cultural conditions were so altered by modern science, technology, and industrialization that education must now be used as a positive force for establishing new cultural patterns and eliminating social evils. He implied that educators must envision the prospects for radical social change and actually implement those prospects. Count argued that educators should give up their comfortable role of being supporters of the *status quo* and should take on the more difficult tasks of social reformers. Further, he expressed some dissatisfac-

tion with the course of progressive education, charging that it had identified itself
with the "liberal-minded upper middle class." He stated:

> If Progressive Education is to be genuinely progressive, it must emancipate itself
> from the influence of this class, face squarely and courageously every social
> issue, come to grips with life in all of its stark reality, establish an organic relation
> with the community, develop a realistic and comprehensive theory of welfare,
> fashion a compelling and challenging vision of human destiny, and become less
> frightened than it is today at bogies of *imposition* and *indoctrination*.

Counts's thesis that the school take responsibility for social renewal met
with heated opposition. He was roundly criticized and condemned as a Soviet
sympathizer. Critics pointed out that the school, a relatively weak institution,
could not accomplish so great a task; but Counts's view was not tied solely to the
school, and his radicalism went much deeper. Indeed, he pointed out that the
school should not promote any one reform, but rather it should "give our
children a vision of the possibilities which lie ahead and endeavor to enlist their
loyalties and enthusiasms in the realization of the vision." To him, all social
institutions and practices should be scrutinized critically, and the school serves
as a reasonable means whereby a rational scrutiny can be made. The actual
reform, however, must be culture-wide and thorough.

Counts was the author of numerous books (over nine of them on Soviet
culture and education) and hundreds of articles. He influenced many students,
educators, and social reformers. His philosophical influence has been confined
primarily to philosophy of education, and within that to the philosophy of
reconstructionism, but, nonetheless, it has been an influence of considerable
proportions.

Theodore Brameld (1904–   ). The person who has been most influential in building reconstructionism into a more fully developed philosophy of
education is Theodore Brameld. The author of many books, including *Toward a
Reconstructed Philosophy of Education*, *Education As Power*, and *Patterns of
Educational Philosophy*, Brameld has taught philosophy and philosophy of
education, lived and taught in Puerto Rico, and held posts in some of America's
major universities.

Brameld views reconstructionism as a crisis philosophy, not only in terms
of education but of culture as well. He sees humanity at the crossroads—one
road leads to destruction and the other to salvation, but only if we make the
effort. Above all, he sees reconstructionism as a philosophy of values, ends, and
purposes. While he has definite ideas about which road we *should* take, he
points out that he is by no means sure which road we *will* take.

According to Brameld, we are confronted with mass confusion and
contradictions in modern culture. We have at our disposal immense capacity for
good on the one hand, and a terrifying capacity for destruction on the other. We
must establish clear goals for survival. In broad terms, this calls for a world unity.
We must forego narrow nationalistic bias and embrace the community in a
worldwide sense. This will involve world government and world civilization "in

which peoples of all races, all nations, all colors, and all creeds join together in the common purpose of a peaceful world, united under the banner of international order." One major activity for philosophy would be an inquiry into the meanings of different conceptions of this central purpose of world unity. We need a democratic value orientation, an orientation in which "man believes in himself, in his capacity to direct himself and govern himself in relation to his fellows." It would involve, in terms of world government, majority policy making and provision for minority criticism. A basic means by which these goals may be achieved is through education.

Basically, Brameld attempts to provide us with alternative possibilities for a new society. In *The Open Society and Its Enemies*, Karl Popper wrote about a piecemeal engineering approach versus the utopian approach to the problems of society. Popper was clearly in favor of the former that fosters the view of an open society where many possibilities are explored. He opposed the utopian approach because he felt that long-range goals may become fixed and unyielding to change. However, Brameld sees great value in the use of both approaches, that is, both utopian ends and piecemeal means. He recognizes the need for piecemeal engineering on a daily basis, but this should be directed toward some goal, even though goals may be changed from time to time. It is true, as Popper showed, that goals can become inflexible, but for Brameld this does not have to be true, and he is as opposed to absolutes in goal setting as he is to absolutes in anything else. He is a dreamer as well as a worker, and his proposals are more visceral than provable in any complete sense because he is a person who has certain presuppositions about the continued perfectibility of individuals and society.

Brameld has been active in advancing proposals for consideration and implementation, and he sees the use of the utopian concept as a technique for both establishing useful goals and orienting people toward an acceptance of change itself. Reconstructionists tend to look upon problems in a holistic way. They understand that problems overlap and in solving one problem we may only create new ones; however, they maintain that if people can be encouraged to see problems in a broader perspective, the chances of eliminating them are greatly enhanced. Reconstructionists charge that the piecemeal engineer, for all his good intentions, is often only putting Band-Aids on problems rather than solving them, and perhaps unwittingly prepares the ground for other problems to come.

The argument has often been advanced that there is no empirical way to determine what the good society should be, and that the reconstructionist operates on premises that are more a matter of wish fulfillment than anything else. No one, Brameld included, can say what the good society should be in any definitive sense. While he is aware and appreciative of the empirical approach, he maintains that the results of scientific achievement should be used as broadly as possible for the benefit of mankind. However, he is quite critical of the fact that science—no less than politics, education, and economics—is often dealt with in too narrow a scope. Scientific technology is involved in making war and killing more efficiently than ever before. In our own country, horrible deaths through automobiles and industrial machinery are another part of the price we pay for living in a highly mechanized society. Scientific technology is also used in making cigarettes and alcohol and in developing harmful chemicals used on food and crops. Technology is often used in industry in ways that belittle and dehumanize workers. Brameld certainly is not opposed to the advancement of science and technology, but he does feel that their advancement should depend upon humane use. He is aware that the determination of what is humane is difficult but maintains that through education we can be encouraged to see human events in a much broader fashion. There is no denying that, basically, reconstructionists such as Brameld are future-oriented and optimistic people. This is not to state that there is any certainty the future can be made better than the present, or that there are underlying forces of class struggle or spirit such as in the Marxian or Hegelian sense that are propelling us toward a higher point; rather, reconstructionists hold the belief that the future *can* be better *if* people adopt an attitude to work to make it better.

In recent years, a number of individuals and organizations have continued to push for ideas and reforms in accord with a reconstructionist philosophy. Brameld maintains that although the late Saul Alinsky is hardly regarded as an "educator" in the professional sense, he may have contributed far more richly to the education of grass-roots Americans than any number of superintendents of schools and professors of education. For example, in Buffalo, Alinsky taught poor people to unite against unemployment in favor of equal opportunity for every employable adult.

There are several other people who serve as change-agents of democracy. Ralph Nader has long fought for consumer protection and has maintained that there can be an end to mass injustice if enough private citizens become *public* citizens. John Gardiner and Common Cause have shown how individuals can work together to eliminate social injustices and improve the political process. Buckminster Fuller has been widely applauded for developing plans for future awareness and control of technology. Lewis Mumford has dedicated a great deal of time to analyzing contemporary civilization and suggesting alternatives.

In addition, there are some organizations that agree with many of the reconstructionists' ideas. The Council for the Study of Mankind has been seeking to analyze and interpret the meaning of a "planetary" notion of the human species. The World Law Fund has developed "world order models" as designs for world law. Both the Council for the Study of Mankind and the World Law Fund have enlisted a variety of students in schools and colleges for their projects. The World Future Society is another organization consistently seeking to examine futuristic trends as well as to develop models in government, marriage, and education as guides to human behavior. Basically this organization is concerned with a study of alternative futures and receives both private and public support for its activities.

One finds a strong inclination toward utopian or futuristic thinking in reconstructionist philosophy. Reconstructionists have a penchant for utopian thinking that manifests itself in their desire for an ideal world free of hunger, strife, and inhumanity. They believe that planning and thinking about the future is a good way of providing alternative societies for people to consider and feel that this kind of thinking should be promoted in schools where teachers can encourage students to become future oriented.

Alvin Toffler, who coined the term "future shock," points out that people today are suffering mental and physical breakdowns from too much change in too short a period of time. These breakdowns are revealed in the number of heart attacks, ulcers, nervous disorders, and similar ailments of modern people. To combat "future shock," Toffler feels that "future studies" should be a part of the curriculum on every level of schooling. Some forms that this curriculum could take might include students preparing scenarios, engaging in "think-tank" thinking, role playing, computer programming of "futures games," and conducting futures fairs and clubs.

In *Learning for Tomorrow*, Toffler says, "So long as the rate of technological change in such a community stays slow, so long as no wars, invasions, epidemics or other natural disasters upset the even rhythm of life, it is simple for the tribe to formulate a workable image of its own future, since tomorrow merely repeats today." Today we know this is no longer true; yet, our educational systems often deal with the world as a static system. The problem is reminiscent of that recounted in *The Saber-Tooth Curriculum* where the author shows that little or no change is necessary in education until the encroaching glacier makes current practices out of date. Today, we still continue to teach theories and practices that are no longer useful in improving or maintaining the life of the tribe. Toffler says that even now "most schools, colleges and universities base their teaching on the usually tacit notion that tomorrow's world will be basically familiar: the present writ large." We realize that this is most unlikely. It is more probable that the future will be radically different from the world as we now know it. Still, we continue to educate people not for a future time, not even perhaps for a present time, but for a past time.

James Herndon, in *How To Survive in Your Native Land*, noted that while his classes were engaged in new and creative activities, other classes in the same school slaved over lessons about Egypt. One could compile a lengthy catalog of obsolete courses that should be replaced with those more germane to today's and tomorrow's needs. For example, schools emphasize penmanship instead of typing, forbid students to use calculators in mathematics classes, teach spelling and the diagraming of sentences instead of creative writing, drill pupils in phonics instead of teaching speed-reading, and so on. The inordinate attention they give to maintaining the *status quo* may represent the attitude of those who really run the schools—our school boards and our state legislatures. Frequently, such organizations promote a more conservative viewpoint and fail to see the need for change in education if it is to keep up with changes in society at large. This idea has been stressed by such educational reconstructionists as George Counts and Theodore Brameld, who emphasize the change aspect.

Reconstructionists, understandably enough, are critical of contemporary society. They point out the contradictions and hypocrisies of modern life.

Education, they feel, should help students deal with these problems by trying to orient them toward becoming agents of change. Counts, for example, suggested that educators should enter areas, such as politics, where great change can be achieved. He also suggested that teachers run for political office or become active in organizations that promote change. Reconstructionists feel that students should think more about such things as world government, a world without schools, and approaches to ending war, bigotry, and hunger.

Although most educators have not seriously heeded the philosophy advocated by reconstructionists, some have become aware of the great need for change. During the last two decades, there was a rash of school programs sparked by cries of "relevance" and "innovation." Teachers were encouraged to innovate, although innovation was often of the most trivial kind, and relevance was interpreted to mean relevance to a system that was in decay. Very few of the programs developed during this period changed education in any lasting way. Their lack of seriousness has today led to a counterreaction among parents and other lay people who are calling for a return to basics and the kind of authoritarian school structure that existed some fifty years ago.

In many quarters, however, there is a more sober assessment being made of the needs of education, not only for today but also for tomorrow. The World Future Society has sponsored numerous workshops for teachers in an effort to get them to think about the future. Such workshops have spawned a number of the programs on the future found in elementary and secondary schools. Educators are now becoming increasingly aware that they are educating students who must function as productive citizens many years after their days in the classroom. It was this kind of concern that led Dewey to point out that the facts we teach children today may be out of date by the time they graduate. Thus, he emphasized a problem-solving method that he felt would be as useful in the future as it is in the present.

There has been a great deal of speculation about where our schools are headed as well as about what course they *should* follow in the years ahead. Some futurists have suggested such things as longer hours for preschoolers, extending formal education from birth to death, selective breeding to raise IQs, and increased use of electronic media to aid learning.

Long-range predictions usually start with birth technology. It is possible that future prospective parents will be able to predetermine the sex of their child and to program his intelligence, looks, and personality. Several apparently healthy "test-tube babies" have already been born and embryo transplants may become widespread. Parents may be able to select twins or triplets. Children may be born in artificial wombs. Parents may one day purchase embryos in a "babytorium." Some children may even have more than two biological parents. (Experiments with the embryos of mice have shown that if several embryos are placed into a dish they form a single embryo. This embryo, when implanted in another mouse, produces offspring having the characteristics of each mouse and all of its accompanying genetic traits.) There is also the possibility of cloning, the production of several people or even an infinite number who are exactly alike. Such developments most certainly would have a profound effect upon education and would necessitate changes in the way we look at children.

As future children grow up, they may receive more of their education at home through various media, such as television, tapes, radio, and movies. There may also be twenty-four-hour day-care centers where parents can leave children for extended periods of time, visiting them only when they choose.

Ivan Illich goes even further in *Deschooling Society*. He suggests that we need no schools at all. Illich, who makes a distinction between schooling and education, believes that education should be spread throughout society rather than being conducted only in special buildings provided for that purpose. He feels that people could be educated on the job, at home, and wherever they may be during their day-to-day activities. Illich has also proposed the use of "learning webs" where people can pool information and talents with others. Some critics point out that we once went through a period in our history without schools or with few schools. Others see Illich's idea as having great implications for the future; they contend that special buildings set aside for elementary, secondary, and higher education may be passé. Certainly, many changes are on the way for education; undoubtedly efficiency and quality will be enhanced.

Educators may approach the teaching of the future in a variety of ways. In order to get students to think about the future, some courses raise questions such as these: Where will you be in ten years? What are some long-range projections regarding the status of the family? What major changes do you see occurring in the years ahead? In some schools there is even a game called "What If?" It asks such questions as "What if your eyes were closed and you opened them in the future? What would be the first thing you would see?", or "What if there were no schools and everyone had to find his own education? Where would you begin?"

An interesting experiment is being conducted in some schools where students work on projects that examine their possible life on Mars. Questions are posed about what laws they would enact. How would they manage limited food and air supplies? What activities might they engage in on Mars? Students can be asked to develop an ideal society, focusing on such areas as economics, politics, social patterns, and so forth. They might even prepare a wheel showing how all of these various activities would interrelate to develop an efficient and harmonious society. At one school, students were asked to write their own obituaries, stating the cause of death, the year they died, and major activities performed during their lifetimes. (One creative student reported that his death was caused by a monkey wrench dropped by a careless robot.)

Students can engage in making short- and long-range forecasts using a variety of forecasting techniques. As part of this assignment, they could evaluate the forecasts of others. Students can be asked to write scenarios or science fiction stories. They might even be encouraged to think about the future in terms of such present-day facts as the following: 1. The United States' population has only 6 percent of the world's population but consumes 30 percent of the world's energy output; 2. 10 percent of the world's population is white while 90 percent is black or yellow; 3. the average length of time people of the United States spend in any large city is four years. These and other facts may encourage interest in the future and serve as the basis for report writing and discussion. Students might also use these facts as springboards for dramatizations and role-playing.

Many students seem to have a natural interest in the future, and teachers can use this interest to motivate them in the study of mathematics, science, and art. Some children who are not "turned on" by traditional approaches may be motivated by the novel and direct appeal of future concerns.

Since the world of tomorrow will be run by the children of today, it is vital that we encourage young people to be concerned about the future and instill in them the idea that they can help shape that future according to their own goals and aspirations. Rather than view it as something that just happens, we need to look at the future as something that we can, by our own efforts, make into a world of beauty and infinite promise.

As a recent movement in education, reconstructionism has influenced educators in thinking anew about the role of education. Reconstructionists have been in the vanguard of those seeking to make education a more active social force. They have championed the role of the educator as a primary change-agent and have sought to change schools in ways that would contribute to a new and better society. Since reconstructionism is a relatively new movement in education, it is difficult to assess its impact fully at this time.

Reconstructionism as a Philosophy of Education

Perhaps the most outstanding characteristics of reconstructionist educators are their views that modern man is facing a grave crisis of survival, that the educator must become a social activist, and that the school occupies a strategic position in meeting the crisis and providing a necessary foundation for action.

Education and the Human Crisis

Today, there are a number of educators who call themselves reconstructionists. The Society for Educational Reconstruction was established in 1969 to further reconstructionist ideals on a wider scale. A policy statement released by SER sets forth the two basic objectives of reconstructionism: democratic control over the decisions that regulate human lives and a peaceful world community. They believe educators everywhere ought to be helped to present their deepest social concerns to their students with optimum effectiveness. They encourage leaders who are able to apply reconstructionist values to experimental educational programs in the school and community.

The members of SER believe that most approaches to educational and social reform are luxuries we can no longer afford. From their perspective, we cannot wait for the kinds of gradual reform advocated by most philosophies, particularly when our very survival may depend on the immediate steps needed to make society more humanistic and productive. Indeed, it appears that we are living in an age of crisis, and progressivism, which once promised so much, seems to be an outmoded way of dealing constructively with present issues. As reconstructionists point out, we now have the power to extinguish ourselves and all living creatures from the face of the earth, and unless some way is found to integrate our technological developments with the highest principles of human rights, all our cogitations and discussions will become as mere rhetoric. Our schools have failed to take on this task. As one reconstructionist has put it, "What academic concept will students be 'discovering' when the computers press the nuclear button?"

The reconstructionists see the primary struggle in society today between those who wish to preserve society as it is, or with very little change, and those who believe that great changes are needed to make society more responsive to the needs of man. Such a struggle is not limited to the United States; it is an international crisis of great proportions. This crisis demands concerted and well-planned action. Central to this needed action, the reconstructionists believe, is the crucial role of the educator and the schooling institution.

If we assess the role of educators nationally and internationally in this time of crisis, we may conclude with the reconstructionists that most educators are, at their worst, linked with the forces of reaction, and, at their best, only liberalized. Many teachers come from the middle class, and from families where the parents seldom suffered loss of income from unemployment, where they usually did not have to worry about where the next meal was coming from, and where their parents could afford to send them to college. Most of them attended schools where they were taught traditional "genteel" attitudes toward life and society. As a reward for such endeavors, they obtained positions where they have continued the teaching of preestablished materials in preestablished ways. Evidence indicates that such teaching has failed to reach minority groups, to change racial attitudes, to create change-oriented individuals, to develop humane attitudes, or to solve the problems of poverty, repression, war, and greed. One might even argue that instead of solving such problems, education as it presently exists has actually served as a partner in perpetuating these problems. It has provided specialists for warfare and for Wall Street, and it has aided the conspicuous consumer. Under such conditions, reconstructionists maintain that we have indeed forgotten that education should create change, and by our very actions use it as a means for keeping things as they are.

For educators to make real changes in society, reconstructionists urge them to become involved in affairs outside their own classrooms and schools. In a book entitled *The Nature of Teaching*, Peter Schrag challenged Counts's treatise of 1932 by the very fact that educators are not located at those points in society where fundamental political and economic decisions are made. Although Counts did suggest that teachers run for political office and engage in social issues outside the classroom, the number of teachers who have done so is pitiably small, and those who have, seem to have acted not for the purpose of advancing the cause of education or to enact great social reforms, but for personal gain or some other self-interest.

Some critics feel that teachers should not take part in social and political affairs because schools should be neutral places, and teachers may lose objectivity by playing a partisan role; however, as the French philosopher, Jean-Paul Sartre, has pointed out, there are no neutral positions and not to act is still to act by default. Teachers by their deliberate nonaction stand responsible for the absurdities all around us in the same sense that good Germans were responsible for Nazi atrocities. There are no neutral positions, and even if there were, most reconstructionists would agree that "the hottest spot in hell is reserved for those who in times of moral crisis remain neutral."

Nobuo Shimahara, who challenged the neutrality in higher education after the student uprisings at Columbia University in the late sixties, also explored this issue. In an article appearing in the January 1969 issue of *School and Society*, Shimahara stated that the appeal to neutrality as an attempt to resolve the dilemma was futile and obsolete. Why? Colleges and universities are politically influenced to a significant degree and occasionally adulterated by politicians. Research in an advanced university, for example, is determined, more or less by the structure of investments of private industries and the order of political priorities in government. University trustees and alumni usually influence local or national political and economic power and strongly influence university direction and basic policies. The university inevitably reflects the national political and economic structures, a factor that should not be concealed.

Reconstructionist educators tend to think of themselves as radical educational reformers as opposed to reactionary conservatives, timid moderates, or weak-hearted liberals. In the last few decades, there have been an increasing number of educators who have called for radical changes in our educational aims and methods; among them are Herbert Kohl, Kenneth Clark, Paul Goodman, A. S. Neill, Ivan Illich, and Neill Postman. However, only a few seem to have fully comprehended the fact that radical changes in education cannot occur without radical changes in the structure of society itself. Sociologists such as Christopher Jencks point out that educational reforms cannot be made apart from wider social reforms. It is generally true that educational reform follows social reform and rarely if ever precedes or causes it. What this means is for an educator to engage in educational reform effectively, he must perform a dual role: educator and social activist. There should be no separation between the two roles, for the reconstructionist educator is one who is committed enough to act upon those things taught in the classroom. This is also what it means to be a citizen in the fullest sense of that term, although what we are talking about here is world citizenship rather than national citizenship. Acting as a citizen implies that one is not only a participating member of society, but also is a person who continually searches for better values and an end to those aspects of society that are degrading and harmful. It also implies becoming an individual who is willing to act in ways to bring society more in line with those better values.

The idea of an educator as an action-agent, particularly as a social activist, seems disturbing to some people. Reconstructionists explain that there is no real need to separate knowledge and action. Knowledge should lead to action, and action should clarify, modify, and increase knowledge. This point is illustrated by a painting that hangs on the third floor of the New York Public Library in New York City. It shows some monks busily working on their Bible safe inside the monastery, while outside knights are burning down houses and cutting off the noses of the slower taxpayers. The monks saw no need to use what knowledge they had for the improvement of man in *this* world. It is true that action without thought leads to detrimental ends, but its opposite, thought without action, is no more defensible. Thus, educators, because of their nonintervention in the course of human affairs, have contributed to some extent to the problems presently facing us on a worldwide basis. Actions are no more perfect than ideas, but placing an idea into action allows us, as Dewey argued, to reassess it in the world of human experience and through subsequent thought make it a better idea. Basically, reconstructionists would like to link thought with action, theory with practice, and intellect with activism.

The Role of the School

Americans have asked a lot from their schools. When driver education needed to be taught, the schools took it on, just as they have taken on sex education, home economics, drug education, and many other tasks. The belief, however, that in so doing educators and the schools are leading society in some better way, may be erroneous. The schools are fulfilling a need that by virtue of their organized and specialized structure they can do better than any other institution. Yet, basically, schools have remained the same, and the idea that we are advancing society by making education more "relevant" or "accountable" is only to say that we are making it more "relevant" to *status quo* needs or more "accountable" to vested interests as they presently exist. To think that the changes recently undertaken to make school curricula more open or flexible will also result in necessary societal changes may be called wishful thinking. Such changes do not often succeed in altering the power structure as much as in maintaining or advancing it.

There is a great need in education today to view the schools in much wider perspective. Such a movement cannot simply be a movement in "life adjustment," "relevancy," "accountability," or "open education," since these only prolong ideas and institutions that are in need of change. To be effective, this movement must be a more radical approach that seeks through a variety of methods to change existing social institutions, including the school, in ways that make them more responsive to human needs. Such a movement must begin with the view that the school does not exist apart from society but within it, and the reconstruction of society will occur not *through* the school but *with* it. This requires educators who are willing to explore new possibilities through action. It requires teachers who can see alternatives and who have some conception of a better world. It demands a school institution freed from the old traditional ideological framework so that it can project new goals and values. It needs individuals—teachers and students—who are moral in the sense that there is no conflict between the well-thought ideas and well-planned actions they are willing to perform on a daily basis. This means insisting on the idea that people can change society through individual and collective effort, for not to be involved is to assist in the perpetuation of values and systems that are archaic, unworkable, and dehumanizing. We live in a world where nuclear destruction is possible at any moment, where there is air, water, and sound pollution, where the population explosion grows more threatening every day; a world where there are worsening racial relations, international misunderstandings, and political idiocy on an international scale.

America has embarked upon a program of mass education unparalled in human history. It has succeeded to the extent that we have taught a vast number of people who would have been denied schooling in many other countries. Our methods of teaching, while still far from ideal, have vastly improved. Reconstructionists maintain, however, that our schools are still looking backward rather than forward. In 1900, about 60 percent of our human power rested on physical strength. Today, only about 6 percent is manual. Education was slow to move in a direction that enabled it to cope with such changes. It must now redouble its efforts in order to face the time ahead when even greater changes will occur. We need, as difficult as it may be, to provide people with education for a future we do not know—one that will most likely be more complex than our present circumstances.

The problem of goal setting in society and in the schools is important because, although we have many people who are busily engaged in the affairs of life, much of what they do is harmful to themselves and others. We have people working to turn out missiles, new methods of warfare, unnecessary luxuries, and all the rest. They do not lack initiative, drive, and productivity. However, is there any purpose in all this? The problem is a moral one. Reconstructionists view all our actions in a moral context, for everything we do has consequences for the future. Actions in the schools must be directed toward goals that are basically humane and result in better social consequences for all.

Ivan Illich, a priest turned social reformer, recently struck a new radical note. In Cuernavaca, Mexico, Illich founded the Center for Intercultural Documentation (CIDOC), where he and other scholars studied and explored radical alternatives. In *Deschooling Society*, he charged that modern societies, such as the United States, have become too dependent upon established institutions, particularly with regard to education. Schools certify and license parasitical interests. They hold a monopoly over the social imagination, controlling standards for what is valuable through their degree-granting powers. It has come to the point that knowledge is suspect unless certified by schooling. The social and human results create psychological impotence and the inability to fend for ourselves.

What we must do, Illich maintained, is to detach learning from teaching, and create a new style of education based on self-motivation and new linkages between learners and the world. Educational institutions have become too "manipulative"; what is needed is a "convivial" system of education that promotes, rather than selectively controls, educational access by helping learners arrange for their own education. This new system would have "learning networks" of information storage and retrieval systems, skill exchanges, and peer-matching capacities. It would provide learners with available resources at any time in their lives, it would recognize those who want to share what they know and connect them with those who want to learn it, and it would provide opportunities for the open examination of public issues. "Deschooling" would liberate access to education, promote the sharing of knowledge and skills, liberate individual initiative, and free individuals from institutional domination.

While Illich's book did not bring forth a massive disestablishment of the schools, it did help many persons reevaluate their beliefs about education and schooling. The idea that there are many paths to education and that formal schooling is not the only or necessarily the best way in every instance, received a renewed emphasis.

A similar cry for reform was heard from Paolo Friere, whose *Pedagogy of the Oppressed* shows how education has been used to exploit poor people. Friere suggested that the ideal teacher is a friend of those he educates. Through subtle techniques, he enables adult students to become cognizant of the forces that exploit them and to become aware of how they can use education and knowledge as a means to improve their lives. Friere criticized the traditional or what he called the "banking" concept of education where people learn something they may then recall for future use. Students are not required really to *know* anything, they just memorize information presented by the teacher. Instead, Friere wanted education to be involved with the real and present everyday problems of people. If poor people need better health, then education ought to help them comprehend or construct ways in which to secure it.

Aims of Reconstructionism

Basically, reconstructionism emphasizes the need for change. It is utopian oriented in the idea of goals directed toward a world culture or civilization. Yet, it is also flexible, because it holds that goals can be modified in process as we see problems and blocks along the way. Whatever the specific educational goals, one thing seems fairly certain: we need social *change* and social *action*.

The idea of promoting change is based on the notion that individuals and society can be made better. One may see in this idea the kind of evolutionary development or Hegelianism connected with Dewey's philosophy; that is, we can assist in the process of moving things from a less desirable to a more desirable state. Thus, reconstructionists would like to involve people more as change-agents, to change both themselves and the world around them. They are opposed to abstract or armchair philosophies where the emphasis is more on knowing than on doing. Reconstructionists do not believe that there is any conflict between knowing and doing, for all actions should be well thought out in advance. Dewey once said that burly sinners run the world while the saint sits in his ivory tower. Reconstructionists would like to see an end to the ivory tower mentality, with everyone involved in some way in social action. They see education as something that includes both individuals and society. The education that one generally receives in today's schools, based as it is on competition, tends to isolate and separate people. Reconstructionists do not think we can separate school from the rest of society or individuals from each other. They strive for unity rather than fragmentation.

When Counts wrote *Dare the Schools Build a New Social Order?*, he

provided a rallying cry for reconstructionists. He criticized the direction progressivism had taken in its life-adjustment phase and its failure to act on critical
issues of the day. He argued for a new progressivism that would be more active
and take the lead in social change. When we look at the situation today, we find
that schools and educators are still not leaders of change and often serve to
prevent it. Even when society has moved ahead in accepting insignificant social
customs, the school often continues to preserve the outmoded styles. Counts
urged educators to begin taking the lead in obtaining power and exercising that
power for the good of society. Educators should become more involved in social
causes. In this way, they would be involved in improving their own education and
would serve to educate others far more than in any classroom activity.

World community, brotherhood, and democracy are three ideals that
reconstructionists believe in and desire to implement in schools and in society.
Schools should foster these ideals through curricular, administrative, and
instructional practices. While schools cannot be expected to reconstruct
society by themselves, they can serve as models for the rest of society by
adopting these ideals.

Methods of Reconstructionism

Reconstructionists are very critical of most of the methods presently used in all
levels of schooling. This occurs because the old methods reinforce traditional
values and attitudes underlying the *status quo* and resistance to change. In such
circumstances, the teacher becomes an unwitting agent of entrenched values
and ideas. There is a "hidden curriculum" underlying the educational process in
which students are shaped to fit preexisting models of living. To the extent that
teachers are ignorant of this factor, they continue to nurture and sustain the
system through the teaching techniques and processes they use. For example,
school boards or states approve the textbooks that teachers must use in their
classrooms, and teachers who accept and use these adopted materials without
question become party to a devious kind of indoctrination. Often such textbooks are approved because they are noncontroversial or contain distortions
popular to the dominant culture such as subtle economic, racist, or sexist ideas.

Instructional tools such as texts and teaching techniques and processes
are guilty of subtle influences on learners. For example, where teachers are
viewed as dispensers of knowledge and students as passive recipients, the way is
paved for students to accept uncritically whatever is presented. Passivity on the
part of students deprives them of any creative role in analyzing and constructing
materials, or in making judgments and decisions. Perhaps this kind of problem is
most readily seen in the area of social studies. What often passes as social
studies is really little more than nationalistic bias that reinforces chauvinistic
tendencies. Prefabricated teaching materials with the questions and answers
already established result in making students think alike and uncritically about
society, the economy, and the political structure. Social studies are designed to
encourage good citizenship, but a built-in bias of what good citizenship is almost
guarantees a narrow and provincial outlook among students.

It is regrettable that fewer than half of the citizens of the United States bother to vote in national elections. Usually not more than 70 percent of the *registered* voters actually go to the polls, and they make up only a portion of citizens who *could* vote if they bothered to register. Local elections are even more poorly attended and some issues do not receive even a 15 percent turnout. Polls show that few citizens know who their United States senators are, and even fewer know the names of their congressmen. Studies have been made showing that citizens do not know what the branches of government are. Citizens, for the most part, take a passive attitude toward government. Although they may complain about high taxes, inefficient government, and the low quality of public officials, they do not often exercise their rights to change these things.

The failure to vote is only an indication of a deeper problem according to the reconstructionist. In addition to voting, citizens need to work for candidates they believe in, or to run for office themselves. Reconstructionists want to see activism rather than the passivity that presently exists.

Education should be directed toward arousing interest in public activism. For example, one political science professor allowed his class to spend a semester working for the candidates of their choice. These students learned more about the political process through active participation than they could have by reading sterile books or attending lectures. Reconstructionists would heartily endorse this kind of approach for at least a portion of the students' formal education.

In order to carry out this kind of activist educational program, teachers must be freed from their own passivity and fears about actively working for change. They must begin focusing on critical social issues not usually found in textbooks or generally discussed in schools. One useful tactic would be propaganda analysis or what Neill Postman and Charles Weingartner call "crap detecting." Rather than being passive purveyors of knowledge, teachers must become critical, analytical, and discriminating in judgment. They should also encourage this same kind of development on the part of students. In this way, reconstructionism helps develop democratic approaches to social problems by allowing students to cope with social life intelligently. In fact, democratic procedures should be used on *every* level of schooling. This means that the student will play an active part in the formulation of objectives, methods, and curricula used in the educational process. Perhaps the most important facet of a student's education is the development of decision-making abilities, and reconstructionists maintain that this cannot be accomplished outside democratic educational practices.

Curriculum

Reconstructionists favor, first, that students get out as much as possible into society where they can both learn and apply learning. Brameld recommends that as much as half of a student's time should be spent outside the traditional school structure, learning at some place other than a school. Reconstructionists favor such programs as the Parkway Plan in Philadelphia and Metro in Chicago where this method has been in operation. The traditional classroom setting may have some value, but the important thing is to get students to use what they learn, and traditional schools do not always encourage this.

One of the ways of organizing curriculum is a modification of the core plan advocated by progressivists that Brameld calls "the wheel" curriculum. According to Brameld, the core may be viewed as the hub of the wheel, the central theme of the school program. The spokes represent related studies such as discussion groups, field experiences, content and skill studies, and vocational studies. The hub and the spokes support each other while the rim of the wheel serves in a synthesizing and unifying capacity. While each school year would have its own "wheel," there would be continuity from year to year with each "wheel" flowing into and strengthening the other. Although each year would be different, it would also inherit the problems and solutions from previous years and would move on to new syntheses. Brameld thinks that the reconstructionist curriculum is both a "centripetal" and "centrifugal" force. It is centripetal because it draws the people of the community together in common studies and centrifugal because it extends from the school into the wider community. Thus, it has the capacity to help bring about cultural transformation due to the dynamic relationship between school and society.

In terms of curriculum, reconstructionists favor a "world" curriculum with emphasis on truth, brotherhood, and justice. They are opposed to narrow or parochial curricula that deal only with local or community ideas and ideals. They favor studies in world history as well as explorations into the contemporary work of the United Nations and other world agencies. The curriculum should be action oriented by engaging students in projects such as collecting funds for worthy causes, informing citizens about social problems, and using petitions and protests. Students can learn from books, but they can also learn from activities, such as voter registration drives, consumer research, and anti-pollution campaigns where they can make a genuine social contribution while they are learning.

Reconstructionists realize that it is all too easy to be enculturated so that we are not aware of the problems of other nations. They would encourage learning the language and the mores of other people. They would also encourage reading the literature of other nations as well as newspapers and magazines that deal with issues on a worldwide basis. In some schools, considerable attention is given to other nations with special activities designed to inform students about other cultures and customs. Sometimes students dress up in the costumes of other nations, serve their food, and engage in other activities that provide better understanding and cultural relationships. Reconstructionists want teachers to be internationally oriented and humanitarian in their outlook. They should be experts in getting students engaged in action projects of all kinds. When a student is involved in some social activity, then that curriculum can produce far more learning than most classroom lectures.

Not only should students become oriented to other cultures, but they should also become future oriented and should study proposals for future development. They need to plan activities that lead to future goals. Most of our schools today, as Alvin Toffler points out, are backward looking and do not face the future properly. People must learn to confront the future; consequently, teachers should encourage students to construct plans for future societies with some cognizance of problems regarding population, energy, transportation, and so on. They could visit with various communal organizations where futuristic alternative life styles are being practiced.

Reconstructionists reason that if people are sincerely interested in society and education, then they will be at those pivotal places where decisions are made. They strongly urge community action and promote the kind of education to assist people in obtaining social and human rights. The work of Saul Alinsky in Chicago demonstrates this kind of education. Alinsky helped people to participate in activities designed to raise social consciousness about their problems and to learn how to attack such problems effectively. Likewise, reconstructionists think people should be involved in both community and world affairs, and they should become efficient and effective activists for continuous social reform.

Critique of Reconstructionism in Education

Reconstructionists believe their approach is a radical departure from pragmatism. This is true in terms of the positions many pragmatists have taken on social, economic, and political issues. However, it is misleading to say that Dewey did not champion radical solutions. He argued that solutions to social problems must be thought out carefully and experimentally with an ever-watchful eye on possible consequences. The results of his approach may be that Dewey was a cautious radical, a reflective champion of social change. Critics have often attacked reconstructionism for a lack of Dewey's caution, charging that the reconstructionist analyses of social problems and the accompanying remedies do suffer from shallowness and superficiality. Often reconstructionists, in their strong desire for change, are precipitous in their recommendations for reform. The charge has been made that this precipitousness results in a great deal of talk and controversy concerning aims and methods in education, but little effect. One can point to the actual effects pragmatism has had on schools, but it is extremely difficult to discern any concrete impact from reconstructionism. Perhaps this occurs because pragmatists' recommendations are easier to accept and less radical on the surface, but it may be due to the depth and feasibility of their proposals. By the same token, the reconstructionists' lack of impact may be directly attributable to the fact that their recommendations are not popular with the mass of people or with the majority of educators.

In many respects, reconstructionists have a romantic notion of what the schools can do. Recent studies by historians such as Michael Katz and Colin

Greer, and by sociologists such as James Coleman and Christopher Jencks show that our expectations of what the schools can do have far outstripped the actual benefits accrued. Indications are that schools cannot directly affect income, racial acceptance, and equality of opportunity. Counts believed that great social reforms could be achieved when educators banded together, but it is questionable whether teachers could ever obtain such power or use it in the best way. Counts argued that teachers should engage in political action and thus provide a moral basis for social change. However, in light of the educators who do run and achieve political office such a premise can be questioned seriously. Educators are rarely different from other politicians, or they are generally co-opted by the very forces they seek to destroy.

Another charge leveled against the reconstructionists is that their view of democracy and decision making is questionable. They start with the premise that change is needed, and often they state the goals the change should take before they start the journey. This is quite different from Dewey's conception of open-endedness and of the initimate relation between means and ends. Reconstructionists advocate world law, but there is evidence that people accept laws to the extent that the laws respect basic cultural patterns and are formulated by the people themselves or their representatives. Because of the diversity of world cultures, it is doubtful that a universal code to which every cultural group would pay allegiance could be constructed at this time. Not only does a world law code disregard cultural diversity, but it assumes that it is good to centralize the regulation of human behavior. Reasonable and intelligent objections to such centralization may be raised by people of a different philosophical persuasion. There is the notion that change and novelty itself come about because of individual variation, and any centralization on a world scope may have detrimental consequences for social change. Indeed, it may result in the destruction of cherished ideals in reconstructionism itself concerning change. We do not really know if world law is possible or desirable, for there has not yet been sufficient study and experimentation. The United Nations is perhaps mankind's most notable experiment in this regard, but its power of control in terms of warfare, international intrigue, and even starvation and economic injustice is almost negligible. Reconstructionism's noticeable utopianism has some advantages, but it also may take our eyes off immediate problems to focus them on some ideal end.

There is evidence that reconstructionists have been co-opted by the very forces they once sought to overcome. They once fought vigorously for the social welfare programs of the liberals of the early and mid-twentieth century. They argued for unemployment insurance, welfare, unionism, the graduated income tax, social security, unemployment insurance, and the extension of tax-supported education beyond public elementary and secondary schools to community colleges and state universities. They have accomplished their aims, and these programs are now part of the *status quo*; however, reconstructionists have failed to come up with new programs and goals to capture the imagination and nerve of the activist sector. In effect, the World Future Society has presented more alternative solutions to the world's problems in recent years than has reconstructionism. As a consequence, many of reconstructionism's thrusts now have the sound of a tired refrain, and its forcefulness has been dissipated.

Despite reconstructionism's less noticeable profile, its call for action still remains. Despite liberal reform efforts of an earlier time, problems seem to endure and may even be more complex than they were formerly. Today, people do not speak about crises, but "mega-crises" that seem immune to the best planned reforms. Americans traditionally have been opposed to long-range planning, and we seem to "muddle" through with a "crisis mentality" that does not act until a problem is upon us. Computer simulation of world trends show us moving toward a series of mounting crises as world population and runaway industrialization deplete natural resources and spoil the environment. The Club of Rome report is only one notable call to action about this kind of problem. This group of 100 industrialists, scientists, economists, educators, and statesmen attempted to stimulate concerted and international political action in a rational and humane direction. They established graphic projections of impending disasters in population, food supply, and nonrenewable resources unless direct action was taken in the near future. *The Limits of Growth*, a book based on their initial work, predicts global catastrophe within the next century if present rates of growth continue. In their second report, *Mankind at the Turning Point*, they describe two great gaps—one between man and nature and the other between the rich countries of the northern hemisphere and the poor countries of the south. These findings and conclusions stress the need for the immediate and radical changes on a worldwide basis sounded by the reconstructionists. The crises and impending disasters on the horizon have been anticipated by reconstructionists for many years and really should not take us by surprise. Those critics who have accused reconstructionists of being alarmists may now need to reconsider. If anything, it appears that the reconstructionists erred not in terms of being alarmists, but by failing to sound a stronger warning. Today, many people are unaware of the extent and depth of our problems, and reconstructionists can rightly claim that schools and educators have not been forthright in informing the public of the nature of the difficulties.

Reconstructionist philosophy has been an available antidote to the easy virtues of materialism, established cultural values, and social adjustment. While reconstructionist theories are not always accepted, they can stimulate and provoke thinking about critical issues. They have provided visions of a more perfect world and have suggested means of attaining them. It is, perhaps, a shortcoming of other philosophies that do not have future goals, either short-range or long-range. Concern for social values, humane justice, the community of man, world peace, economic justice, equality of opportunity, freedom, and democracy are all significant goals for reconstructionism, things in which the world is sadly lacking. If it is true that reconstructionists are impatient and precipitous in their desire to eliminate social evils, it is understandable in a world still filled with hate, greed, bigotry, and war.

Counts

Dare the School Build a New Social Order?

George S. Counts, many of whose ideas loom large in the reconstructionist lexicon, was one of the most radical progressive educators. He thought the aim of education should be social reform and urged teachers to throw off their "slave psychology" and work for the good of the people. Counts was identified with the progressive movement in education but became disenchanted with its rhetoric for change but reluctance to act. In the following selection, written in 1932 in the depths of the Great Depression, Counts calls to educators to "reach for power" and initiate changes in society. The words still have a decidedly contemporary ring.*

[Education] . . . must . . . face squarely and courageously every social issue, come to grips with life in all of its stark reality, establish an organic relation with the community, develop a realistic and comprehensive theory of welfare, fashion a compelling and challenging vision of human destiny, and become less frightened than it is today at the bogies of *imposition* and *indoctrination*. . . .

This brings us to the most crucial issue in education—the question of the nature and extent of the influence which the school should exercise over the development of the child. The advocates of extreme freedom have been so successful in championing what they call the rights of the child that even the most skillful practitioners of the art of converting others to their opinions disclaim all intention of molding the learner. And when the word indoctrination is coupled with education there is scarcely one among us possessing the hardihood to refuse to be horrified. . . .

I believe firmly that a critical factor must play an important role in any ade-

quate educational program, at least in any such program fashioned for the modern world. An education that does not strive to promote the fullest and most thorough understanding of the world is not worthy of the name. Also there must be no deliberate distortion or suppression of facts to support any theory or point of view. On the other hand, I am prepared to defend the thesis that all education contains a large element of imposition, that in the very nature of the case this is inevitable, that the existence and evolution of society depend upon it, that it is consequently eminently desirable, and that the frank acceptance of this fact by the educator is a major professional obligation. I even contend that failure to do this involves the clothing of one's own deepest prejudices in the garb of universal truth and the introduction into the theory and practice of education of an element of obscurantism. . . .

There is the fallacy that the school should be impartial in its emphases, that no bias should be given instruction. We have already observed how the individ-

*Selection from George S. Counts, *Dare the School Build a New Social Order?* (New York: Arno Press and the *New York Times*, 1969), pp. 9–12, 19, 27–29, 31–37.

ual is inevitably molded by the culture into which he is born. In the case of the school a similar process operates and presumably is subject to a degree of conscious direction. My thesis is that complete impartiality is utterly impossible, that the school must shape attitudes, develop tastes, and even impose ideas. It is obvious that the whole of creation cannot be brought into the school. This means that some selection must be made of teachers, curricula, architecture, methods of teaching. And in the making of the selection the dice must always be weighted in favor of this or that. Here is a fundamental truth that cannot be brushed aside as irrelevant or unimportant; it constitutes the very essence of the matter under discussion. Nor can the reality be concealed beneath agreeable phrases. . . .

If we may now assume that the child will be imposed upon in some fashion by the various elements in his environment, the real question is not whether imposition will take place, but rather from what source it will come. If we were to answer this question in terms of the past, there could, I think, be but one answer: on all genuinely crucial matters the school follows the wishes of the groups or classes that actually rule society; on minor matters the school is sometimes allowed a certain measure of freedom. But the future may be unlike the past. Or perhaps I should say that teachers, if they could increase sufficiently their stock of courage, intelligence, and vision, might become a social force of some magnitude. About this eventuality I am not over sanguine, but a society lacking leadership as ours does, might even accept the guidance of teachers. Through powerful organizations they might at least reach the public

conscience and come to exercise a larger measure of control over the schools than hitherto. They would then have to assume some responsibility for the more fundamental forms of imposition which, according to my argument, cannot be avoided.

That the teachers should deliberately reach for power and then make the most of their conquest is my firm conviction. To the extent that they are permitted to fashion the curriculum and the procedures of the school they will definitely and positively influence the social attitudes, ideals, and behavior of the coming generation. In doing this they should resort to no subterfuge or false modesty. They should say neither that they are merely teaching the truth nor that they are unwilling to wield power in their own right. The first position is false and the second is a confession of incompetence. It is my observation that the men and women who have affected the course of human events are those who have not hesitated to use the power that has come to them. Representing as they do, not the interests of the moment or of any special class, but rather the common and abiding interests of the people, teachers are under heavy social obligation to protect and further those interests. In this they occupy a relatively unique position in society. Also since the profession should embrace scientists and scholars of the highest rank, as well as teachers working at all levels of the educational system, it has at its disposal, as no other group, the knowledge and wisdom of the ages. . . .

This brings us to the question of the kind of imposition in which teachers should engage, if they had the power. Our obligations, I think, grow out of the social situation. We live in troublous times; we live in an age of profound change; we live in an age of revolution. Indeed it is highly doubtful whether man ever lived in a more eventful period than the present. In order to match our epoch we would probably have to go back to the fall of the ancient empires or even to that unrecorded age when men first abandoned the natural arts of hunting and fishing and trapping and began to experiment with agriculture and the settled life. Today we are witnessing the rise of a civilization quite without precedent in human history—a civilization founded on science, technology, and machinery, possessing the most extraordinary power, and rapidly making of the entire world a single great society. Because of forces already released, whether in the field of economics, politics, morals, religion, or art, the old molds are being broken. And the peoples of the earth are everywhere seething with strange ideas and passions. If life were peaceful and quiet and undisturbed by great issues, we might with some show of wisdom center our attention on the nature of the child. But with the world as it is, we cannot afford for a single instant to remove our eyes from the social scene or shift our attention from the peculiar needs of the age. . . .

Consider the present condition of the nation. Who among us, if he had not been reared amid our institutions, could believe his eyes as he surveys the economic situation, or his ears as he listens to solemn disquisitions by our financial and political leaders on the cause and cure of the depression! Here is a society that manifests the most extraordinary contradictions: a mastery over the forces of nature, surpassing the wildest dreams of antiquity, is accompanied by extreme material insecurity; dire poverty walks hand in hand with the most extravagant living the world has ever known; an abundance of goods of all kinds is coupled with privation, misery, and even starvation; an excess of production is seriously offered as the underlying cause of severe physical suffering; breakfastless children march to school past bankrupt shops laden with rich foods gathered from the ends of the earth; strong men by the million walk the streets in a futile search for employment and with the exhaustion of hope enter the ranks of the damned; great captains of industry close factories without warning and dismiss the workmen by whose labors they have amassed huge fortunes through the years; automatic machinery increasingly displaces men and threatens society with a growing contingent of the permanently unemployed; racketeers and gangsters with the connivance of public officials fasten themselves on the channels of trade and exact toll at the end of the machine gun; economic parasitism, either within or without the law, is so prevalent that the tradition of honest labor is showing signs of decay; the wages paid to the workers are too meager to enable them to buy back the goods they produce; consumption is subordinated to production and a philosophy of deliberate waste is widely proclaimed as the highest economic wisdom; the science of psychology is employed to fan the flames of desire so that men may be enslaved by their wants and bound to the wheel of production; a government board advises the cotton-growers to plow under every third row of cotton in order to bolster up the market; both ethical and æsthetic considerations are commonly overridden by "hard-headed business men" bent on material gain; federal aid to the unemployed is opposed on the ground that it would pauperize the masses when the favored members of society have always lived on a dole; even responsible leaders resort to the practices of the witch doctor and vie with one another in predicting the return of prosperity; an ideal of rugged individualism, evolved in a simple pioneering and agrarian order at a time when free land existed in abundance, is used to justify a system which exploits pitilessly and without thought of the morrow the natural and human resources of the nation and of the world. One can only imagine what Jeremiah would say if he could step out of the pages of the Old Testament and cast his eyes over this vast spectacle so full of tragedy and of menace.

The point should be emphasized, however, that the present situation is also freighted with hope and promise. The age is pregnant with possibilities. There lies within our grasp the most humane, the most beautiful, the most majestic civilization ever fashioned by any people. This much at least we know today. We shall probably know more tomorrow. At last men have achieved such a mastery over the forces of nature that wage slavery can follow chattel slavery and take its place among the relics of the past. No longer are there grounds for the contention that the finer fruits of human culture must be nurtured upon the toil and watered by the tears of the masses. The limits to achievement set by nature have been so extended that we are today bound merely by our ideals, by our power of self-discipline, by our ability to devise social arrangements suited to an industrial age. If we are to place any credence whatsoever in the word of our engineers, the full utilization of modern technology at its present level of development should enable us to produce several times as much goods as were ever produced at the very peak of prosperity, and with the working day, the working year, and the working life reduced by half. We hold within our hands the power to usher in an age of plenty, to make secure the lives of all, and to banish poverty forever from the land. The only cause for doubt or pessimism lies in the question of our ability to rise to the stature of the times in which we live.

Our generation has the good or the ill fortune to live in an age when great decisions must be made. The American people, like most of the other peoples of the earth, have come to the parting of the ways; they can no longer trust entirely the inspiration which came to them when the Republic was young; they must decide afresh what they are to do with their talents. Favored above all other nations with the resources of nature and the material instrumentalities of civilization, they stand confused and irresolute before the future. They seem to lack the moral quality necessary to quicken, discipline, and give direction to their matchless energies. In a recent paper Professor Dewey has, in my judgment, correctly diagnosed our troubles: "the schools, like the nation," he says, "are in need of a central purpose which will create new enthusiasm and devotion, and which will unify and guide all intellectual plans."

Brameld

Education As Power

Theodore Brameld is an "elder statesman" of reconstructionist thought. Like Counts, he was also in the progressivist camp but felt restricted by its inactivity and lack of radical commitment. He wrote many books but perhaps Education As Power *best illustrates his view that change is necessary if we are to meet the challenges that face us on the horizon.* Brameld would like to see curriculum changes at all levels of education—from kindergarten through the university. He has been particularly concerned with the control of education and advocates more democracy and radical departures than most staid boards of education and controlling interests would dare countenance. In this particular selection, he examines the necessary connection of means and ends to achieve a "far-reaching reconstructive approach to education."*

First of all, since the reconstructionist, being a crisis philosopher, places heavy stress upon clear, unequivocal goals and purposes, the primary task of education is that of formulating, implementing, and validating such purposes. This contention is tied up with what was said above about the importance of values, for all purposes are saturated with values.

The reconstructionist, accordingly, is searching for what we earlier called, in common with some American social scientists, a value orientation. Is it possible to develop a value orientation that is sufficiently defensible and unified to give us the purposes we now need— one that can galvanize and channel our activities?

Where are such purposes to be found? They will not, I think, be found merely through philosophic analysis. They will be found, if at all, through understanding the abnormal nature of our time, and through recognition of

what is required by such a time.

Now there is one requirement today which overshadows all others. . . . This is a world civilization so powerful, so unified, and so committed to the values we shall presently describe that it can successfully combat and destroy the forces which could lead to the destruction of mankind. World civilization is the great magnetic purpose which education requires today. What does this purpose mean?

Vast problems at once arise when one seriously considers such an encompassing purpose. Certainly it becomes a primary task of education to attack the gigantic difficulties in the way of achieving world civilization. For, as these difficulties are analyzed, the meaning of world civilization itself becomes more and more clear.

Despite the hazards of generalizing about reconstructionism, one thing can be said now that will indicate how it is different, in substantial degree at least,

---

*Selection from Theodore Brameld, *Education As Power* (New York: Holt, Rinehart and Winston, Inc., 1965), pp. 32–40.

from other philosophies on our continuum: the purpose of a world civilization is a *radical* purpose. It is radical in that it is a thoroughgoing and future-directed goal for mankind. Thus far in its history, mankind has never achieved a world civilization—not even remotely. The world has been split into warring camps that expend much of their energy and resources in hating each other and trying to destroy each other. Hate and destruction are disvalues that often seem to have been more conspicuous in the life of man than the values of love and cooperation and construction. Hence, to propose such a goal as world civilization in which peoples of all races, all nations, all colors, and all creeds join together in the common purpose of a peaceful world, united under the banner of international order, is truly a radical purpose. I suggest to my fellow teachers that should they devote themselves to this great purpose, and in turn help young people to assume responsibility for its achievement, they will become radical teachers. And this, says the reconstructionist, is precisely what they should become.

One more point about the meaning of this supreme purpose may be made in a preliminary way. It is obvious that many people in the world are already prepared to agree on the purpose of world civilization. Where they disagree is on the nature of the world civilization that they favor. For the communist, for instance, the idea of world civilization is perfectly congenial, provided that the civilization is built on communist principles. The remarkable Pope John XXIII also wanted a world civilization. But of course he wanted it in terms of the perennialist conception of man and the universe.

So it is necessary to go further. We need to inquire into the precise meanings of different conceptions of the central purpose. Education should carefully consider, for example, what the communist is advocating. Any school system which prevents children from studying communism fairly, objectively, and thoroughly is not a responsible school system. The same is true in the study of, let us say, the proposals of the Roman Catholic Church; we need to understand critically and comparatively what it advocates also. Similarly we should understand as fully as we can the purpose of world civilization which reconstructionists, or people close to them in viewpoint, most strongly favor.

The essence of this purpose centers in the conception of democracy. We should carefully examine what democracy means. It is, of course, the hope of reconstructionists that if enough people understand what democracy really means, rather than resorting to superficial labels that sound pleasant but mean little, they will come to agree that the kind of world civilization they want most is a democratic world civilization. Here again, we are brought back to the question of value orientations, because democracy itself points toward a definite value orientation.

What, then, is the nature of a democratic value orientation? At least this: it is one in which man believes in himself, in his capacity to direct himself and to govern himself in relation to his fellows. Politically, this means that a world civilization of the kind reconstructionists advocate is one in which fundamental policies are determined by the majority of people of the world, and in which, at the same time, minorities have the right to criticize and to dissent from policies established by the majority. This does not mean dissent in the sense of disregarding or disobeying such policies, but in the sense of having the privilege of criticizing them and attempting freely to persuade the majority that they are wrong.

Democracy as a political philosophy, therefore, is also bipolar. It cannot possibly function unless both of these principles are constantly at work: majority policy making and minority criticism. Each is necessary to the other. The value orientation behind this bipolarity is a deep conviction that human beings, ordinary human beings in the long run, have more common sense and good judgment with regard to what is ultimately good for them than any one else does—any leader or group of leaders, no matter how allegedly benevolent or wise they may claim to be. Unless we earnestly believe this, and unless we as teachers have profound confidence in the capacity of the majority of people to make the best basic decisions regarding policy, we do not accept democracy. . . .

We have focused thus far upon ends and purposes. But reconstructionism is not just a philosophy of ends—indeed, all philosophies of education worthy of the name are also concerned with means. For education, as an agency through which cultures transmit and modify themselves, is inevitably a process, too. Consequently, we must ask: What is the reconstructionist view of education as means?

For one thing, education as means is only strong when education as an end is strong. We need to know what we want, where we want to go, what our objectives are. Then we can begin to work out ways by which to achieve them. Here is one of the points at which the reconstructionist modifies the progres-

sivist philosophy. The latter emphasizes that ends emerge out of the means we use: if we develop effective means, the ends will eventually come into view. The reconstructionist philosophy emphasizes more strongly that means are also shaped by the ends we decide upon and commit ourselves to. That is, if we are clear about where we are going, we will be more likely to develop the necessary processes by which to get there. To be sure, ends and means are necessary to each other. Nevertheless, education should now concern itself much more deeply and directly than hitherto with the great ends of civilization.

Another definite characteristic of the reconstructionist approach to means, one which could make some claim to distinctiveness, is its stronger-than-average insistence upon the limitations in man's rationality. In many ways, man possesses tremendously powerful unrational drives, both within himself and in his relations with other men. If we are to channel the forces of education effectively toward achievement of such a great purpose as democratic world civilization, it is necessary for us to recognize and utilize these powerful unrational forces—the forces of emotion, the forces of hostility and conflict, as well as the forces of love and harmony. Reconstructionism searches for fresh insights into the nature of man, individually and collectively, in order to understand how he may capitalize upon his energies to the utmost in behalf of imperative new goals.

Where may we search for these resources? Two in particular stand out as intellectual mountain peaks of the last hundred years. The first is the young science of psychiatry. Here, of course, one immediately thinks of that giant in the study of man's emotional complexities, Sigmund Freud (although others as diverse as Carl Jung and Harry Stack Sullivan may also occur to you). More firmly than the other major philosophies of education, reconstructionism contends that sophisticated awareness of these complexities is now so necessary that no teacher can be competently prepared for his work unless he is acquainted with the main principles and practices of this rapidly growing science.

The second major resource for understanding the unrational dimension of man's nature is to be found in those social sciences which examine the phenomena of group behavior, especially class behavior. Here the greatest of all pioneers is, I think, Karl Marx, a profound student of society who exposed the unrational behavior of people, not as individuals, but in their organized social and economic relations. The modern teacher needs to become familiar with the chief contributions of Marx and of later scholars who have modified his interpretation.

Thus the reconstructionist philosophy of education insists upon analysis of the unrational factors in life, both from the point of view of the individual and from the point of view of the group. This is not to say that education as means wishes merely to encourage the release of these unrational factors. This is to say that education as an agency of cultural rebuilding cannot effectively operate rationally unless it takes into full consideration the strength of the unrational. There is a paradox here. It is sometimes contended that the Marxist has no respect for rationality because he stresses the conflicting and sometimes violent nature of the struggle between classes. But this contention overlooks a

deeper assumption in Marxian theory: men can never become rational as long as they conceal from themselves their own unrational social behavior. Freudians maintain the same paradox with regard to the individual.

Socrates said twenty-five hundred years ago, "Know thyself." Marx might have said, "If thou art to know thyself, become conscious of thy class relationships." Freud might have said, "To know thyself, examine thy inner emotional forces." The reconstructionist wishes to transform education into a powerful means for social change toward world civilization. But to accomplish this we must learn how to estimate and direct our energies on all levels of personal and cultural nature. The means are ultimately rational, to be sure, but only if and when they succeed in recognizing the power of the unrational.

Let me try to put together what I have been saying. Both the progressivist and the reconstructionist strongly believe in education as cultural modification. They urge you and me as teachers, and as potential if not actual leaders in education, to regard our institution as an agency of change as well as an agency of stabilization. . . .

But let me say now that the reconstructionist point of view means fundamental alteration in the curriculum of the schools all the way from kindergarten up through the high schools, the colleges, and adult education. The processes of learning and teaching will also be radically altered. Finally, the control of education, including its administration and policy-making, will have to be changed. Thus, the curriculum, the teaching-learning process, and the control of education will all undergo transformation. This, again, is what is implied by a democratically radical philosophy. A philosophy which endorses minor, patchwork changes cannot achieve the required goals. Only a far-reaching, recon- structive approach to education as both ends and means will serve an age such as ours.

Selected Readings

Brameld, Theodore. *Toward a Reconstructed Philosophy of Education.* New York: Dryden, 1956.

This book is one of the most complete statements by a leading reconstructionist and explores the development and uses of reconstructionism as a philosophy of education.

_____. *Patterns of Educational Philosophy: Divergence and Convergence in Culturological Perspective.* New York: Holt, Rinehart and Winston, 1971.

The author connects the need for philosophy with the contemporary "crisis in culture," that reflects his deep interest in philosophical and cultural anthropology and their relation to education. An attempt is made to establish a critical perspective for reconstructionism in contrast to other philosophies.

Counts, George S. *Dare the Schools Build a New Social Order?* New York: John Day, 1932.

This work is a challenging attack on the *status quo* and the misuses and distortions of progressive educational thought. The book is still timely, and its well-written contents continue to stimulate thought.

Shimahara, Nobuo, ed. *Educational Reconstruction: Promise and Challenge.* Columbus, O.: Charles E. Merrill, 1973.

This collection of reconstructionist writings deals with significant educational and social problems and is one of the most complete recent statements of the need for reconstructionist thought today.

Protagoras
(480-410)

EXISTENTIALISM⎯⎯⎯⎯⎯⎯⎯⎯⎯⎯⎯⎯⎯⎯⎯⎯⎯⎯⎯⎯⎯⎯⎯⎯⎯⎯⎯⎯⎯⎯⎯

Existentialism is one of the newest modern philosophies; hence, it has had only recent application to educational theory and the problems of education. The roots of this philosophy can be found as far back as the Sophists, but as "existentialism" it is usually traced to the nineteenth century to Søren Kierkegaard, the Danish philosopher, and Friederick Wilhelm Nietzsche, a German. In the twentieth century, it has been further developed by such figures as Martin Heidegger, German; Karl Jaspers, also German; Martin Buber, the Israeli philosopher-theologian; and Jean-Paul Sartre, the French philosopher. In America, its application to education has developed since the 1950s, in its early stages by such educational writers as George Kneller and Van Cleve Morris. More recently, educators such as Maxine Greene and Donald Vandenburg have explored existentialist themes and have attempted "phenomenological" analyses of educational problems.

Buber   Sartre
(1878-1965)   (1905-1980)

Jaspers
(1883-1969)

Heidegger
(1899-1976)

Kierkegaard   Marcel
(1813-1855)   (1889-1973)

5

EXISTENTIALISM
AND
EDUCATION

Existentialist Philosophers and Their Thought

Existentialism offers a puzzling array of interpretations, so that it is often difficult to sort out a consistent set of meanings. Part of this difficulty occurs because it is such a new philosophy and is spread across so many different nationalities and cultural contexts. Its seemingly tortured and mixed varieties may be due to the very nature of the existentialist credo—the lonely, estranged, and alienated individual caught up in a meaningless and absurd world. In order to understand what the existentialists themselves are attempting to say, we shall examine the particular thought systems of four representative existentialist philosophers: Kierkegaard, Buber, Heidegger, and Sartre.

Søren Kierkegaard (1813–1855). Kierkegaard's childhood was spent in close association with his father who demanded that his children excel in intellectual matters. Under the eye of his father, young Kierkegaard learned to act out the plots of literary works, became proficient in Latin and Greek, and developed the habit of pursuing ideas for intellectual satisfaction. As a young man, he studied Hegel and revolted against his systematization and adherence to a society-oriented outlook. Kierkegaard chose instead to search out individ-ual truth by which he could live and die. His ideas were largely passed over in his own time because of his eccentric views and his ascetic nature. For one thing, he was a devout Christian who attacked conventional Christianity with a ven-geance, producing biting literary works such as *Attack upon Christiandom*. For another, he believed that Christianity had become warped by modern times, for modern conventional Christianity seemed to perpetuate such human absurdi-ties as war. Obviously, these views did not endear him to the religious establish-ment. He called for a "leap of faith" in which modern man would accept the Christian deity, even though there is no proof that such a God exists and even though there is no rational way to know Him. It is only through the "leap of faith" that modern man can begin to restructure his life and truly live out the principles of Christianity.

Kierkegaard's category of philosophical study is the lonely individual against an objective and science-oriented world. He was acid in his criticism of science and what it has wrought, and he felt that it is the scientific penchant for objectivity that has largely driven modern man away from a viable Christian belief. Man has embraced objectification and this has led him to become group centered, or in the words of some contemporary American sociologists, "other-directed." Instead, Kierkegaard argued for the subjective individual who makes his own choices, eschewing the scientific demand for objective proof. This unfounded subjectivity calls for a "leap of faith," in which one must abandon reason and accept groundless belief.

Kierkegaard was not concerned with "being" in general but with individ-ual human existence. He believed that we need to come to an understanding of our souls, our destiny, and the reality of God. He attacked Hegelian philosophy and other abstract speculation for depersonalizing individuals by tending to emphasize thought rather than the thinker. He believed that the individual is confronted with choices in life that he alone can make and for which he must accept complete responsibility.

Kierkegaard described three stages on "life's road." The first is the aesthetic stage where we live in sensuous enjoyment and where emotions are dominant. The second, the ethical stage, occurs when we arrive at the "universal human" and achieve understanding of our place and function in life. The third stage is the religious, which for Kierkegaard was the highest, where we stand alone before God. There is an unbridgeable gulf between God and the world that we must somehow cross through faith. This takes passion, and passion is sorely lacking in modern life. We achieve such passion not through reflection but through understanding ourselves as creatures of God.

Kierkegaard believed that education should be subjective and religious, devoted toward developing individuality and the individual's relationship with God. He opposed vocational and technical studies because they are directed primarily toward the secular world of objectivity.

Although Kierkegaard was largely ignored in his own time, his writings and thoughts were revived in the twentieth century because it has been in the present century that Kierkegaard's fears of an unchecked and raging objectification and technological revolution seem to have become largely realized. World wars, with their ever-increasing engines of death and destruction, characterize this century, and the rise of totalitarianism and loss of individuality seem to go along with this objectification. Thus, Kierkegaard's thought appears to many European and American intellectuals to point the finger most aptly at the true condition of modern man. Through the efforts of such thinkers, the word "existentialism" has gained familiarity with increasing numbers of people.

Martin Buber (1878–1965). Martin Buber, the Israeli philosopher-theologian, was one who took Kierkegaard seriously and began to develop his own system of thought. Although born and educated in Europe, Buber immigrated to Palestine to join in the attempt of the Jewish people to reclaim their homeland. Perhaps this struggle epitomized the human predicament for Buber because his writings reflect the need for mutual respect and dignity among all human individuals. Buber's best-known book is *I and Thou*, a work that seeks to get at the heart of human relations.

In *I and Thou*, Buber described how man is capable of relating and identifying with the outside world. There is an objective relationship characterized as "I-It." In this relationship, the individual views something outside himself in a purely objective manner, as a thing to be used and manipulated for selfish ends. Man needs to look upon his fellows in terms of the "I-Thou" relation; that is, he must recognize that each and every individual has his own intense, personal world of meaning. To the extent that this personal or subjective reality of each individual is discounted or ignored, then man will continue to suffer from the absurdities in which he is caught. It is from the standpoint of I-It that inhumanity, death, and destruction are foisted upon man by man.

Buber found men treated as objects (Its) in business, religion, science, government, and education. Many students today feel that they are only social security numbers or numbers of holes punched in computer cards. In college classes of two hundred or more, it is not surprising that this concern becomes reinforced when the teacher cannot remember a student's name or perhaps not even know who is enrolled in the class. He assigns material, marks papers, and gives grades, but student and teacher each go their own separate ways. When the student leaves that class he is replaced by another equally anonymous organism. Buber did not feel that it had to be this way. In an I-Thou relationship between teacher and student, there is a mutual sensibility of feeling: there is empathy. This is not a subject-to-object relationship as in an I-It relationship but rather a subject-to-subject relationship: one in which there is a sharing of knowledge, feelings, and aspirations. It is a relationship in which each person involved is both teacher and learner, sharing what he has with the other. Buber believed that this kind of relationship should pervade the educational process at all levels as well as society at large.

Buber thought that a series of I-Thou relationships constitute a continuum with man at one end and God at the other. Man does not turn aside from the course of his life to find God. Both the divine and man are related, and through man's communication with his fellow human beings, he experiences a reciprocal subjectivity that makes his life more spiritual. The existence of mutuality between God and man cannot be proven, just as God's existence cannot be proven. Yet man's faith both in God and his fellowman are witness of his devotion to a higher end.

The humanism of Buber has had a profound impact on many thinkers in recent times, not only in philosophy and theology, but in psychology, psychiatry, literature, and education. In fact, Buber was one of the few existentialists who wrote specifically about education, especially the nature of the relations between teacher and student. He was careful to point out that education, like many other areas, could also consist of an I-It relationship in which the student is treated as an object. What Buber really wanted was the kind of education where the teacher and student, while differing in kinds and amounts of knowledge, were on an equal footing in terms of humanity, and where each person in the relationship is both teacher and learner. Buber believed that the most desirable educational situation is one where friendship—the epitome of an I-Thou relationship—can exist.

Martin Heidegger (1889–1976). Heidegger was born in Messkirch, Germany, and was reared in the Catholic faith. He spent much time wandering in the hills and woods of the Black Forest, and later did much writing and thinking there. He attended the University of Freiburg where he was influenced by Kantian philosophy and later by the teachings of the philosopher Edmund Husserl, who developed the philosophical method known as phenomenology. This method that most of the leading existentialist philosophers have used means, in Husserl's words, "to go back to the things themselves," that is, to examine pure consciousness after the everyday world has been discounted. When this has been done, certain essential features remain that indicate to us the very nature of our being if we will but make the effort to study it. Heidegger adopted this methodology and extended its usage. In his mature years, he became famous as a professor of philosophy at the University of Freiburg, where he taught many young philosophers including Jean-Paul Sartre, who probably was his most renowned student. His works and teachings have influenced many philosophers throughout the world and his major work, *Sein und Zeit* (*Being and Time*), was published in 1927.

Although Heidegger did not accept the label "existentialist" for his thought, many observers have credited him with extending existentialist think - ing into new areas. On several occasions, he took pains to state that his major category of investigation was Being, and not necessarily the lonely estranged individual. Be that as it may, Heidegger's starting point was what he called "being-in-the-world," or lived experience at the individual-environment (world) level. The individual existent is *Dasein*, and it is the analysis of *Dasein* to which Heidegger devotes a great deal of space. Thus, although Heidegger's intent and purpose is to investigate Being, his analysis largely rests on the individual constructing his own world of meaning.

Individual existence, or being-in-the-world, is comprised of three basic aspects. The first of these is the individual experiencing his world as a surrounding environment (*Umwelt*). *Umwelt* is not just the physical environment in the objective sense; rather, it is the environment *as experienced* by the individual. Thus, *Umwelt* is not strictly an objective experience. The second aspect of being-in-the-world is the experience of others, or fellowman (*Mitwelt*). *Mitwelt* is the complicated ground of social relations, for not only does the individual experience others in his own subjective way, but others are also subjectivities with their own personal viewpoints. The third aspect of being-in-the-world is where the individual becomes aware of himself as a distinct and subjective existent (*Eigenwelt*). This is the intensely personal level encountered when one poses a question such as "Who am I?" It is in encountering such a fundamental question that the individual comes face-to-face with existential anguish and anxiety, for there is no apparent answer at the level of lived experience. There are no laws, guidelines, or objective reality that automatically give it to us. Each person must answer the question for himself, or at the level of true individuality, "*I* must decide, for this life is *mine* and no one else's." *Eigenwelt* is, to say the least, a humbling experience. It is part of the human condition, and to the extent that we seek our meanings in objective reality or passively let "society" push us into various behavior patterns, we are only postponing the necessity to make our own individual commitments and stands.

This brief exposition of Heidegger's *Dasein* analysis in no way does justice to his complex philosophy. In fact, he himself found it extremely difficult to find words adequate to describe the intricacies of Being from the standpoint of the individual existent, and he has been soundly criticized for the terminology and style in which he wrote. He had to attach particular meanings, weighty and intricate, to such words as *Dasein* and *Eigenwelt* that complicate any understanding of his thought. This complexity is further heightened for those who must read him in English translation, for one will encounter many words, such as *Dasein*, for which there is no accurate English equivalent. Nonetheless, there is no substitute for a thorough study of Heidegger's works for those who wish to understand some of the ideas of this philosophical pioneer.

For Heidegger, man is a being who comes into the world without his own consent. He is without justification or reason for being. He is confronted with his own nothingness. This creates anxiety as a primary feature of human existence. It is burdensome, but it also provides us with the avenue with which to become aware of our own existence. An awareness of existence involves the individual in confrontations with fear, dread, conscience, guilt, nothingness, and death. While these themes may sound morbid, they are the themes that give human existence its meaning as distinctly human *being*. To the extent that an individual escapes confronting the question "Who am I?" or avoids affirming the existential fact that "I am," he is "unauthentic," not facing the authentic human predicament. To be authentic and affirm that "I am," an individual must face the truth as he is able to discover it, live life in the face of death, and construct his meaning as a human existent by committing himself to authenticity.

Heidegger did not write specifically about education, but his thought has a great deal of promise in helping the educator better understand the intense personal side of existence. The question "Who am I?" is a profound and troubling question, one that most of us face more or less in a blind panic during the adolescent years, and one that is probably never fully answered. We might say that this condition lies at the heart of the identity crisis each person encounters at various times in his or her life.

Jean-Paul Sartre (1905–1980). Of all the leading existentialist philosophers, probably the best known is Jean-Paul Sartre. Born in France, he was brought up in a home where he was encouraged to develop his intellectual talents. At a very early age he began to write, emphasizing the predicaments of the human condition. Influenced a great deal by his grandfather who was a language teacher, Sartre himself aspired to become a teacher of philosophy. He was an excellent student, and after completing his education in France went to Germany where he studied with Martin Heidegger in the 1930s. He later settled in Paris, where he became a professor of philosophy. At the same time, he pursued his literary ambitions, writing several novels and plays that became best-sellers in Europe. But Sartre, like so many others, was caught up in the destructive web of World War II. He joined the French Army and was captured by the Germans early in the war. After the fall of France, he was allowed to return to Paris on parole, and it was there that he joined the underground French Resistance. The Nazis were brutal and swift in their punishment of captured Resistance fighters: men and women in the Resistance were constantly faced with instant death, and it was in this kind of situation that Sartre's thinking on the absurdity and meaninglessness of individual existence was sharpened.

Even in the face of the Nazi death machine, Sartre was able to write and publish a major philosophical work in 1943, *L'Etre et le Neant* (*Being and Nothingness*). It stands as one of the most original philosophical treatises to be written in the twentieth century, and it is Sartre's most thorough philosophical statement.

It investigates consciousness (being-for-itself) and the objects of consciousness (being-in-itself). Consciousness, or being-for-itself, is the reflection and negation of the objective world. It is as if human consciousness tries to be its objects, as in the case of the self-conscious person who literally tries to be the role he is playing, or the "dedicated" teacher who tries to be the essence of all teachers. Such attempts, of course, are always failures, for consciousness, or individuality, cannot really be what it is not. Being-for-itself always transcends, negates, or goes beyond being-in-itself. This means that human consciousness or individuality is free. In a sense, it could be said that consciousness deals with the *meaning* of things and not with raw objectivity or things-in-themselves.

In his philosophical works, Sartre views the human predicament in terms of the lonely individual in an absurd world. Essentially, he views human existence as primarily meaningless, for we are thrown into the world totally without meaning, and any meaning that we encounter in the world we must construct ourselves. The development of meaning is an individual matter, and since both the world and the individual are without meaning, we have no justification for existing. There is no God to give existence meaning (Sartre was an atheist), nor is there any realm of ideas or independent physical reality with its own independent and immutable meaning. Humanity, individually and collectively, exists without any meaning or justification except what we ourselves make.

Sartre's point of view is very austere, at least when compared with, say, idealism or realism, and it is very pessimistic when compared with pragmatism. Yet, it would be an error to take this notion too far. Sartre states that "existence precedes essence," and means that if we are indeed without meaning when we are born, we can fashion our own meaning in the world in any way we see fit. According to Sartre, if there is no God, no First Cause, then there is nothing to prevent us from becoming whatever we desire, because there is no predeter-mined self or essence. The same can be said for physical reality and science, for Sartre sees science as a human creation, no better or no worse in and of itself than any other creation. Thus, when we step back and view ourselves as we really are, we see that *nothing* determines us to do anything, for all the absolutes, rules, and restrictions are simply the puny and absurd creations of humans. If there are no primal restrictions, then there is no determinism. Everything is possible. Man is absolutely free, or as Sartre puts it in his own characteristic terminology, "man is condemned to be free."

Human freedom is awesome, for if we are totally free, we are also totally responsible for our choices and actions. In other words, we cannot do some-thing and then claim it was God's will, or was caused by the laws of science, or that society made us do it. We are free; therefore we are totally responsible. We have no excuse. We have *no exit*.

If one thinks seriously about this existentialist proposition, he or she may come to understand that human existence is a sword that cuts two ways. Existence today may be characterized by war, disease, hunger, or starvation on the part of many, and conspicuous consumption on the part of a few. There is ignorance, racial strife, and a host of the most severe and depressing conditions that make up the human predicament, but who is responsible? Is it God? Is it the law of supply and demand? National honor? No. Man himself is responsible. If we can create war, we can also create peace. And if we can, through absurd economics, create conditions of starvation by allowing a few individuals to control the wealth of a country, we can also likewise redistribute the wealth so that no one need starve. In other words, if we are the creators of our ills, we can also create a better and more humane way of living. It is up to us. All we have to do is make our choices and act accordingly; however, these choices and actions are not easy, for if we attempt to change these conditions, those who benefit from them will resist us. Sartre did not disregard existing society and customs, for he was well aware that many individuals do not see anything wrong with war, or the surplus controlled by a few, or even starvation.

We may argue that while all of this is true, we do have to contend with nature and scientific law. Sartre would answer by pointing out that "nature," "law," and "science" are themselves meanings created by man. We may then object that while this is true for science and scientific laws, surely we cannot ignore nature, man's oldest enemy that thwarts him at every turn. But that which we call "nature" is itself meaningless and without justification, and it is man who gives it meaning as "nature." Witness how the "laws" of nature have changed through the ages: once it was accepted that the world was flat, but this has changed. No one would want to stake his or her life on the proposition that people will view the world a thousand years from now in the same way they do at the present. What this points to is that even nature itself is endowed with meaning by human beings. Through this endowment we come to control nature, however limited this control may be. We say we cannot control nature because we do not understand it, but it makes just as much sense to say we do not control nature because we have not given it sufficient meaning. Scientific investigation is, after all, nothing more than the striving to endow the natural world with meaning so that we can control our own lives better. Here again, we are even responsible for the meaning of nature.

Lest we begin to think that Sartre makes man into God, it should be pointed out that this is just the opposite of his view. Instead, he says man tries to be God, but since God does not exist, this is only further evidence of man's absurdity. In fact, Sartre calls man a "useless passion" when he tries to set himself up as God.

Much of the foregoing may sound strange to our ears. We are used to thinking differently about existence, if we bother to think about it at all. We may tend to view life as a "bowl of cherries," or we may go the other way and become cynical pessimists who bemoan our fate. Sartre is really trying to call our attention to what is obvious: we *can* make a difference, but not without choosing our goals and working toward them. It could be said that every advance humans have made, every humane act committed, has happened because some individual or group of individuals chose to make it happen and then struggled to achieve that choice. Few if any of the things we achieve come about by accident. Even those events that occur by accident show Sartre's insight, because they are *accidents*, meaningless in and of themselves. They depend on humans to experience them, suffer, undergo, endure, or enjoy them. It is *man* who gives them their meaning *for* man.

Critics have pointed out that existentialism in general and Sartre's philosophy in particular lack an adequate social base to treat institutions such as the school, and this factor has hampered more thorough application of existentialist thought to the problems of education. Sartre, who was perhaps the most individualistic of all the existentialist philosophers, eventually came to align himself with Marxist theory, although he did not adopt a doctrinaire Marxist position and preferred to think of himself as an independent. This happened primarily because, as Sartre put it, his theory could not stand alone, for it needed Marxism for completion; and Marxism needed the humanizing influence of the existential perspective. Apparently, Sartre came to agree that individuals can find value in participation in the social and political process.

Existentialism in Modern Life

The theme of individuality points to the great concern existentialists have for the role of the individual in life. They attempt to describe individuality in all its phases, and they feel that it is best characterized by a person making choices and committing himself through action. Accordingly, such choices should be preceded by a questioning attitude that might engender such questions as: Who am I? Where am I going? What should I do? Existentialists believe people should be encouraged to see the paradoxes and absurdities that are simply a part of life. One such paradox is that we are everything and nothing. Each person thinks he is important and unique, and in a sense he is, but he is born and he dies without any independent external justification. Existentialists also describe human anxiety. They believe being involved with life means taking stands, being committed, being out in the open, visible and vulnerable, and all of that requires a great amount of tension. It is interesting to note that Sartre, for example, lived these ideas and took many controversial and unpopular stands. On the issue of Algerian nationalism, he promoted independence, and his home was bombed as a result. He often praised Castro and was part of a War Crimes Tribunal that accused former President Lyndon Johnson of war crimes in the Vietnam war. This made many Americans so angry with Sartre that they rejected his ideas out of hand.

The existentialists view the individual as a being who first exists and then defines his or her essence, for it is from individuals that all ideas, values, and institutions come. This is radically different from Platonic idealism where all ideas or essences are in a realm preexisting and independent from man. For the existentialist, however, the individual does not discover ideas; rather, he creates them. Thus, the ideas and institutions that are in existence today are all human products, and the existentialists agree that some deserve praise and some rebuke. Concepts like beauty, truth, and justice are all man-made. Some existentialists hold that even the idea of God is a man-made idea, and this helps to explain why we generally have anthropomorphic ideas about deities. The existentialist view of man can be illustrated by the story in Victor Hugo's book, *Eighteen Fifty-Seven*, of a huge gun getting free of its moorings in the bottom of a ship. It bangs against the sides of the ship and threatens to sink it. One sailor leaves his post, finally secures the gun, and saves the ship. He is rewarded by the captain for this action and then shot for leaving his post. Similarly, existentialists think man deserves rewards for some of his actions while he deserves punishment for others.

Existentialists are firm believers in commitment and action and hold that both work together; if we are not willing to act upon our beliefs, then we are not committed to them. They are very critical of jargon. They know, for example, that most people say they favor truth, justice, and peace. What happens however, when we ask these people what they have *done* for peace, for truth, for justice? Generally, we find they have done very little, and from an existential viewpoint this indicates people do not really believe in the things they say, for they are unwilling to *act* upon them. Existentialists maintain that the failure to act because all the facts may not be in or because we want to maintain neutrality is a moral cop-out. In a very real sense, not making a decision *is* making a decision. Often, in our failure to act, we allow someone else to make the decision for us. Sartre tells the story of a young woman who goes out on a date with a young man who takes her hand in his. She thinks that if she moves her hand it will break the charm of the moment so she allows the man to take "liberties," all the while lying to herself about the real reasons for his actions. She makes no decision, or at least this is what she tells herself. In effect, this woman is operating in "bad faith," for the truth is that we all make choices constantly, whether we recognize it or not. We choose and we must take responsibility for choosing. This is one of the key things to which Sartre called our attention. If each individual is honest, he will recognize this and become a more morally responsible individual by not placing blame, rationalizing, or hiding from the dilemmas of the world.

Consider the case of a young man who consistently refused induction into the armed forces. He was called before his local draft board to explain his action. He presented his case well, explaining that he had always been opposed to war and could not in good conscience accept any form of military service. The head of the draft board heard his appeal but did not think it was valid. He ordered the young man to report for induction and said if the youth failed to do so, then he would see that he was prosecuted to the fullest extent of the law. Who is the existentialist? We might say that both of them are. However the young man would not be acting "authentically," according to the existentialist, if he were fabricating excuses only to get out of the dangers of military service. Likewise, the head of the draft board would not be acting "authentically" if he privately agreed with the young man but would prosecute him simply because the law demanded it.

Although an individual may be a conservative and an existentialist, existentialism has been more associated with left-wing elements of society. For the most part, existentialist ideas are opposed to conformity and the middle-class establishment. This concern for individual rights appealed to university students and other young people in the 1960s who wished to create their own identity in hair styles, clothing, music, and other things. Movies like *The Graduate* and writings like Theodore Roszak's *The Making of the Counter-Culture* and Charles Reich's *The Greening of America* described their struggle. The student protests, particularly against the Vietnam war, were also representative of the existentialist concern for commitment and action, where many students were willing to risk life and limb for their beliefs.

Existentialism has affected many areas of thought. There has been the development of a strong movement in existential psychiatry, and there is even a journal by that name. Essentially, it is a nondirective approach and is similar to the thought espoused by Carl Rogers and Abraham Maslow.

Rogers, for example, believes that teachers should risk themselves for their students in classroom experimentation. The teacher should look for the "potentiality and wisdom of the person" and work for self-directed change on the part of the learner. The risk involves not only the individual teacher's sense of self, but a willingness to trust the learner. This means he must be a "facilitator of learning" to help release students' potential. Rogers is against the concept of teaching as showing, guiding, or directing; rather, the teacher should "prize" the learner and make him or her feel worthwhile. This can be accomplished through prizing the feelings and opinions of the student, and it involves the development of what Rogers calls "empathic understanding." The result of successful educa- tion and living should be a "fully functioning person."

Although Maslow talks about a hierarchy of needs, he differentiates between basic needs and "metaneeds." Basic needs are primary: the need for air, food, protection from danger, and a familiarity with the environment. Meta- needs transcend these basic needs and involve a personal reaching or growing to realize one's potential. These metaneeds include such things as belonging- ness, esteem, and aesthetic needs. They are necessary, in Maslow's view, to help us become "self-actualized" persons: persons who are realistically oriented, autonomous, and creative. Maslow also differentiates between pseudo-self- actualization and authentic self-actualization. Pseudo-self-actualization is the undisciplined release of impulses, for example, someone who behaves like a spoiled child. An authentic self-actualized person says "I've considered my feelings and yours too." The central idea is that people should be encouraged to make their own decisions, respect themselves, and treat others with compas- sion. Life is full of paradox and contradiction, and no single life-style is necessar- ily the true one. To recognize the existentialist frame of reference is to recognize individual differences and variation.

The intensity of modern life has brought on increasing tension and anxiety. The nature of individual choice, individual action, and commitment is such that anxiety is very real and present in every human being, regardless of his station in life or his particular ideology. This feature of modern life is of great concern to existentialists and has been treated extensively in their works. Some critics have castigated the existentialists for their inordinate amount of attention to anxiety, charging that they dwell too much on the tragic, the perverse, and the morbid side of life and exclude the more hopeful and optimistic themes. Existen- tialists reply that too many people wrongly emphasize the optimistic, the good, and the beautiful, all of which creates a false impression of existence. For example, if a friend from out of town visits, his host usually takes him to the beautiful spots, the parks, the museums and art galleries, and the best restau- rants. He does not take his guest to the slums, the depressing areas of poverty, and places where extensive suffering is going on. Without experiencing these things, the visitor gets a one-sided picture of the city as it really is. Existentialists feel it is time to balance the scales, but even more fundamentally, they think that the tragic side of life more nearly illustrates human existence where "the chips are down" and the individual must face up to his or her condition. We have no recourse but ourselves. Our very existence is one of anxiety.

Strange as it may sound, Christian theologians have found existentialism to be a fresh breeze in a musty environment. It was Nietzsche, one of the early architects of existentialism, who proclaimed that God is dead. In addition, Christianity has traditionally had a strong streak of optimism in its promise of eternal salvation. There are many existentialists who agree with Karl Marx that religion is the opiate of the masses, pointing toward some supposed heaven and keeping our attention diverted from the real problems of the world. The result is that the masses are brutally exploited by the few. It will be recalled that another founder of existentialism—Kierkegaard—found Christian belief to be characterized by anxiety, anguish, and doubt. Christian existentialist theology has embraced these themes, holding out to the believer the proposition that anxiety and doubt are real and necessary experiences to be encountered in living the Christian life.

Gabriel Marcel, a French religious existentialist, wrote about the Christian experience of the "subjectivity" or "presence" of others. This presence should not be treated as a mere object of experience, but as a fellow human in line with, perhaps, the theme of the Golden Rule. The idea of "presence" has similarities to Buber's I-Thou concept. It also resembles Sartre's "being-for-itself" and "being-in-itself," but Marcel was more attuned to the characteristics and necessities of social relations than was Sartre. Marcel recognized anxiety and "baseless" choice, and he held that while a person's belief is always subject to doubt and questioning, he is not totally isolated from all other existence and needs to be open to the "presence" of others.

Other Christian thinkers, such as Paul Tillich, examined human nature in all its ambiguity. Tillich questioned what man ought to be in an "age of anxiety." His answer was that we must have "the courage to be" in spite of fate, death, meaninglessness, and despair. The "courage to be" is based on a belief in God when God has "disappeared," and it involves a faith underlined by resulting doubt. Thus, courage becomes a necessary characteristic of the believer in order to sustain belief.

The impact of existentialism upon modern Christianity has been notable. It has thrown new light on the mystical aspects of religion and reduced the emphasis on the material side of life, and it has helped many persons to make religion more a matter of personal commitment and inner conviction.

Existentialism has had a broad impact on twentieth century life. It is a philosophy that does not mince words and is not afraid to take on the sacred cows of Western culture, but in so doing it has often encountered opposition and misunderstanding. Some critics have even questioned whether existentialism should be considered a philosophy. Certainly it is not systematic in the traditional pattern, but it still has a strong claim as a philosophy in the tradition of Socrates. Just as Socrates was the "gadfly" of Athens, pricking the consciences and "shells of decency" of the Athenians, so also do the existentialists call us to examine our personal lives and break away from superficial beliefs and uncommitted action.

Existentialism as a Philosophy of Education

Existentialism is one of the most individualistic philosophies. There are many kinds of existentialism, and existentialist writers often resent being lumped together. Despite their protests, however, there are many areas of similarity in their thinking as well as specific differences.

Aims of Existentialism

Existentialists believe that most philosophies of the past have asked man to think deeply about abstractions that had little or no relationship to life. Scholastic philosophy, where thinkers debated such questions as how many angels could sit on the head of a pin, might be a case in point. The answers to such questions provided nothing except perhaps some psychological satisfaction at winning a debate through argumentation. Even then the answers were unprovable. Existentialists reject this approach to ideas. They feel that their philosophy is one where the individual is drawn in as a participant. We explore our own feelings and relate ideas to our own lives. Consequently, in an existentialist education the emphasis is not on scholarly debate, but on creation; that is, one can create ideas relevant to his own needs and interests.

Existentialists such as Sartre tell us that "existence precedes essence." First comes the individual, and then the ideas the individual creates. Ideas about heaven, hell, God, are all human inventions. Even theistic existentialists admit that ideas about God are unprovable even though they might parallel something in existence. Thus, the individual can be given credit for the creation of concepts like peace, truth, and justice, but blamed for things like bigotry, war, and greed. Since people are the creators of all ideas, this focuses as much attention upon humans as the ideas themselves, and if it is true that we have created ideas that are harmful in practice, then likewise we can create new ideas to replace them.

Because the individual human is so important as the creator of ideas, existentialists maintain that education should focus upon individual human reality. It should deal with the individual as a unique being in the world, not only as a creator of ideas, but as a living, feeling being. Most philosophies and religions, existentialists charge, tend to focus on the individual only as a cognitive being. The individual is this, but he or she is also a feeling, aware person, and existentialists think that this side deserves attention.

Existentialists assert that a good education would encourage individuals to ask such questions as, Who am I? Where am I going? Why am I here? In dealing with these questions we would have to recognize that the individual is an emotional and irrational creature as much or more than he or she is one who is unemotional and rational. The individual is always in transition, so that the moment when one thinks he knows himself is probably the moment to begin the examination all over again.

Most educational philosophies up to this point have emphasized the concept of a person as a rational being in a rational world. Much of this stems from the Aristotelian notion that we can understand our place in the universe, and that this understanding is primarily a result of sharpening our powers of intellect through the use of reason and observation. Even through the Age of Enlightenment, there was a strong conviction that we could steadily increase our knowledge and power over the universe. Yet, with this rise of rationality we continued to be plagued by wars, inhumanity, and irrationality, often perpetrated by those who believed that they had attained a mastery of logic and philosophy. For the modern existentialists, World War II was a watershed in such irrationality and inhumanity, and existentialists, particularly in France and Germany, began to take a new look at human nature. They began to reexamine such things as death, courage, and reason. Reason, often used to justify the great amount of death and destruction inflicted by war, was particularly scrutinized. Existentialists found that reason was used to justify cruelty and aggression to the extent that millions of Jews were sent to the gas chambers for what some Nazis thought were rational motives. Reason was used to defend these actions so that a person could say he or she was only following orders, that it was not his or her decision, or that it was done for better worlds to come.

Existentialists believe that a good education is one that emphasizes individuality. It attempts to assist each of us in seeing ourselves with our fears, frustrations, and hopes, as well as the ways in which we use reason for good and ill. The first step in any education, then, is to understand ourselves.

Existentialists maintain that the "absurd" side of life needs serious exploration. Perhaps what we take to be a rational explanation of the universe is our own application of what we think is rational. It is difficult to see things as they really are, objectively, as if we came from another planet. Yet, if we did so, how strange many things would seem that we take for granted, such as women walking on little stilts that they call shoes, and men wearing flashy colored material around their collars that they call ties. Further areas of absurdity might be explored such as the pierced ear on which to dangle bright shiny objects, or the efforts of some who hate blacks to change their skin coloring to dark tan in the summer. Are these rational acts, or do we use our reason to say that they are rational?

In recent years, an area of playwriting known as the theater of the absurd has grown steadily. Eugene Ionesco, Samuel Beckett, Edward Albee, and others, have written plays that fall into this genre. The threater of the absurd is about life, magnifying and emphasizing certain aspects of it in ways to show its irrationality and absurdity. In the play *Who's Afraid of Virginia Woolf*, we see a married couple who spend a great deal of time attacking each other, and who have become very skillful at it through practice. Seemingly, such people remain together for the purpose of developing greater ways of hurting each other. We are not encouraged through our own kind of education to see the absurdities of life; rather, the good side is emphasized. For example, most reading books for children focus upon the uniformity and reliability of existence. They show children in settings where there is no marital conflict, war, hunger, or death. Existentialists feel that a vital part of one's education is to examine the perverted and ugly side of life, the irrational as well as the good side. Yet, in education we are always covering up. Apparently we do not believe that a child should be exposed to such human realities as death, and so we tell him that his dead grandfather went on a long trip or that he is away. We lie to children about birth, about sex, about money, and about a host of other things. Existentialists believe in a truthful kind of education where there is no cover-up, where children learn about many facets of life whether good or bad, rational or irrational.

Existentialists feel that education should foster an understanding of anxiety. It is certainly true that many people are frustrated by life, but often it has been caused by the kind of education that did not prepare them for a world of conflict. What existentialists mean by anxiety is an awareness of the tension of existence. When one is involved in life, when one is an acting person, he is bound to feel some tension through involvement. Existentialists point out that there is no tension after death, and that some people are trying to make their own lives like death by avoiding conflict at all cost. The opposite of death is life, and life for the existentialist requires some degree of tension. The degree of living can be measured by the amount of tension that is felt. Though Marx talked of religion as the opium of the people, Christian existentialists say that the true Christian is a person in conflict; he is a person who must constantly wonder if what he believes is really true, and if he is acting enough in support of those beliefs.

Existentialists argue that education should promote a sense of involvement in life through action. They believe that persons should be encouraged to be committed and take stands even though the rational basis of any stand is always incomplete. They think further that one's commitment might be judged by the action or actions he is willing to take in its behalf. Thus, the existentialist would not ask whether one says that he is truthful, brave, and just, but what he has done that is truthful, brave, and just. They believe more in deeds than words. It is a tough philosophy, and existentialists are appalled by the amount of verbiage they find in the world supporting all the "good" things, even though the practices of the world belie this. They desire a world in which our highest concepts are put into practice, not only in personal life, but in the world at large.

Methods of Existentialism

Existentialists are extremely disturbed at what they find in most educational institutions. They point out that much of what passes for education is simply propaganda stuffed down the throats of a captive audience. Moreover, much of what we call education is actually harmful in that it prepares students for conspicuous consumerism or make them cogs in the machinery of industrial technology. Instead of helping to bring out individuality and creativity, education stifles and destroys them.

The first thing that most existentialists want is a change in our attitude about education. Instead of seeing it as something a student is filled with or something that he is measured against or fitted into, the existentialist suggests that we first look at students as individuals and that we allow them to take a positive role in the shaping of their own education and life. It is true that every student brings to school a background of experiences that will influence personal decisions, but by and large, existentialists urge that schools and other institutions be free places where students are encouraged to do things because they want to do them. Some writers, such as Van Cleve Morris, look at *Summerhill* as a sketch of the kind of education existentialists prefer. At Summerhill a student does not have to attend class if he does not want to, and there are no grades or examinations unless students request them. It is an environment where students are encouraged to make their own choices and are free to do so. Summerhill has its rules and regulations, some made by the children and some made by the administration, but basically it is a free institution as compared with most other schools.

For the existentialist no two children are alike. They differ in the information, personal traits, interest, and desires they have acquired. It is ridiculous to think they should have the same kind of education. Yet all too often we find children not only lumped together, but taught the same things that are supposedly appropriate to their grade level. There has been much concern with "mass man," "the lonely crowd," and "a nation of sheep," but our educational institutions still foster conformity and obedience. Many existentialists are disturbed by the emphasis that some educators put upon education for adjustment. Although Dewey believed that education should be in the forefront of change, he also recognized the need to prepare the child for existing society while working for change. Some "progressive" educators, however, under the guise of pragmatic philosophy, made "life adjustment" the primary focus of education and promoted education that stifled both individuality and social change.

Existentialists criticize the schools for not being truthful, realistic, and objective. Much education is a fraud in which the truth is hidden or obscured from the student. History is presented from the point of view or bias of a particular culture. Economics, geography, and other areas are not studied objectively as much as they are studied from a definite ideological point of view. Indeed, one might argue that the curriculum contains many hidden biases depending upon the particular culture in which the education takes place. In addition to biases that are not made clear, criticized, or explored, the school often promotes questionable notions about religion, death, birth, and sex. Existentialists believe that such practices, even when a child is young, cannot be condoned. For those who argue that knowing the facts of birth or death may be harmful to a child in terms of creating anxiety or fear, existentialists argue that often just the reverse happens; not knowing the true situation causes more anxiety than the facts. A. S. Neill has pointed out that many children felt relieved of their concern about birth when he told them point-blank what it involved.

Existentialists would like to see an end to the manipulation of the student. Teachers control children along predetermined paths using behavioral techniques of reward and punishment. Existentialists would like the children to choose their own paths from the number of options available to them. Furthermore, existentialists do not believe that the effort in education to make children successful as businessmen, lawyers, or engineers is necessarily the right course. They think other choices, even if they have less social prestige, should also be open to children as alternative life-styles without the onus of inferiority or failure. Schools should foster choice making from among alternatives, and not prescribe the kinds of choices people should make.

To some existentialists the word "school" has a very bad connotation. School seems to imply that education only goes on in a particular setting or institution and nowhere else. They would like to see a societal attitude toward education in which it not only takes place in particular buildings, but also throughout society in places of business, factories, military establishments, and personal affairs. Such ideas have been forcefully stated by Ivan Illich in *Deschooling Society*, and find favor with many existentialists. Education should not be limited to particular institutions and to particular hours. It should be universal, the education of the public in the truest sense of the word.

Schools often contain uniform materials, curriculum, and teaching. Although educators have talked quite a bit about promoting individuality in education, most programs and teaching methods have tended to become more alike. Existentialists argue for diversity in education, not only in curriculum, but in the way things are taught. Some students, they point out, learn well through one approach, and others through another. Many options for learning should be open to them. Some school critics hold that the growing bureaucracy in education has been a factor in producing sameness, and some now feel that local control is one answer to this problem. By giving individual school districts the right to determine their own curriculum and ways of teaching, they argue, we will promote diversity and originality. Other critics say, however, that this plan would give local school districts the right to impose cultural biases and local prejudices.

Existentialists are concerned with the role of teacher or educator in the learning process. They believe that every teacher should be a student and every student a teacher. Martin Buber discussed this in detail in his description of his I-Thou and I-It concepts. In the I-It relation, a teacher treats a student as someone to direct and fill up with knowledge. The student is an object to be manipulated. Followers of Buber support an I-Thou approach where both student and teacher learn from each other, and where the relation is more friend to friend.

It should be apparent from the foregoing that there is no absolute method of education for the existentialist. Ideally, the student should be encouraged to teach as well as to learn for himself, and whatever method serves this purpose is a desirable one. Education should help to enhance individuality, and when it does this it is good education. Too much schooling may promote other-directedness rather than inner-directedness. Most education is still too coercive to allow students to explore and create without having to do so along prescribed directions to reach a particular end. Too many teachers believe there is a "right" answer, and they reward or punish the student depending upon the answer he or she gives. The existentialist teacher maintains that the purpose of education is not to find right answers, but to explore possibilities.

It could be said that the exploration of possibility is the hallmark of any educational method that is legitimately linked to existentialism. Existentialists view the individual as always "in situation"; that is, he or she is always in some setting where choice is a necessity and is made from among several possibilities. Indeed, it is hard to conceive of any meaningful human experience where there is no possibility of choice or variation. It is this very necessity of choice, without any absolute guidelines, that gives the human condition its characteristic of anxiety. If we could always choose with clarity and certainty, there would be no anxiety. Sartre spoke of the "blind panic" of childhood, and it could be said that baseless choice is at the roots of that panic. Education should help the individual deal with the blindness and panic by helping him realize that he is what he chooses. In other words, education may not dispel the anxiety of choice, but it can help us better decide on what we will be by recognizing that through our choices we become what we are.

Van Cleve Morris connects existentialist theory with the idea of responsibility. This agrees with Sartre's view of baseless choice. We are what we are because we, and we alone, choose it. This is true whether we choose intelligently or ignorantly. The fact remains, we are what we choose. From an educational standpoint, this implies that individuals should be educated to make choices as intelligently as possible, even though there is always uncertainty, anxiety, and the possibility of tragic outcome.

Children always seem to have questions about life, death, and the dilemmas of human existence. Teachers should avoid giving dogmatic answers to such questions; rather, they should help the students explore human experience with these ultimate questions, and explore them from a variety of viewpoints. Teaching methodology in this instance would not be didactic or hortatory, but facilitative.

Perhaps the most significant thing the educator can foster through his methodology is commitment. Existentialists point out that many people attempt to avoid choice making and commitment and to that extent avoid becoming "authentic" individuals who act upon the basis of reflective beliefs. Morris and Kneller both point to Socrates as the prototype of the "authentic" individual who acted out deep-seated beliefs about man and society. In the same fashion, we should encourage students to emulate the Socratic model by committing themselves to causes in which they believe. The teacher of today can serve as a model to students just as Socrates served as a model to students in ancient Greece by his continued moral participation in social issues. Thus, students might well choose to participate in causes such as the UNICEF campaign, to solicit funds for the Red Cross and community agencies, and to join various political or even protest campaigns. They might support minority rights, freedom movements, children's and women's liberation, and other areas.

Without dismissing the importance of group activities, existentialists are concerned about the possible tyranny of the group. Numerous studies have shown how individual viewpoints can be altered and even reversed to fit the consensus of the group. Often when groups are first formed, individual members find a fulfillment and share common purposes. Then, after common purposes are met, group unity begins to crumble. Sartre, for example, has described how groups can exert terror tactics over individuals by forcing conformity to group goals through both covert and overt forms of pressure. Teachers should be constantly aware of group tyranny and should exercise their judgment on how best to use groups to benefit the individuals who compose them. For the most part, however, existentialism's attention is focused on the individual whether he or she works alone or in a group. The goal is to help individuals achieve their chosen ends, evaluate those ends, and know how to act on them. It is not whether an individual belongs to a group or not, but whether one's actions and ends are one's own, authentically chosen and acted upon.

Curriculum

It is interesting that most existentialist philosophers have had lengthy and rigorous educations. Most of them taught at one time or another, usually in a university setting. They have been concerned with the humanities primarily and have written extensively in that genre. Through the humanities the existentialists have tried to awaken modern man to the dangers of being swallowed up by the megalopolis and a runaway technology. This seems to have taken place because the humanities contain greater potential for introspection and the development of self-meaning than other studies.

The humanities loom large in an existentialist curriculum because they deal with the essential aspects of human existence such as the relations between people, the tragic side of human life as well as the happy, the absurdities as well as meaning. In short, existentialists want to see man in his totality—the perverted as well as the exalted, the mundane as well as the glorious, the despairing as well as the hopeful, and they feel that the humanities and the arts do this better than the sciences.

Existentialists, however, do not have any definite rules about what should comprise the curriculum. They believe that student choice, that is, the student-in-situation making a choice, should be the deciding factor. For example, at Summerhill a student can decide to take courses, take a particular kind of course, or not take any courses at all. While Summerhill is not really an institution operated on the basis of existentialist philosophy, it has many practices that seem agreeable with existentialist theory.

Existentialists do not look down at such subjects as vocational training, home economics, or sex education. If an individual thinks that a particular program or course has meaning, then there should be an opportunity for him to take that subject. Because the needs and interests of people are varied and complex, existentialists advocate a curriculum that has many possibilities. The use of minicourses as a way of providing a variety of experiences for elementary and secondary school students is one way in which this might be achieved. Another is to have the student design or construct his or her own curriculum with the school providing the materials and facilities for individual interests. Some existentialists suggest that an excellent educational task is to have the student write a book or make a movie about personal interests in life.

Existentialists have no qualms about teaching students fundamentals because they believe that fundamentals can be very useful to individuals in making decisions about their lives. However, fundamentals should not be taught in isolation from life or from the "affective" side of development. In some educational institutions today there is talk about "confluent" education where attention is given to both cognitive and affective development, and this approach seems to be more in line with existentialist thinking than traditional attitudes toward curriculum.

Existentialist educators have been very much interested in curriculum reform and have suggested a variety of alternatives for educators to ponder. Their attention to the unlimited potential for individual development has been of crucial concern in their educational philosophy.

Critique of Existentialism in Education

Existentialist philosophy has been hailed as a helpful antidote to American education, especially where that education has become dominated by an organizational mentality and the continuing bureaucratization of the American school. Existentialism's challenge that man must not be beguiled by the technological society has been heeded by many younger members of society, the so-called counterculture described by Theodore Roszak. This challenge has awakened us to the tragedy and absurdity of life, and to the lonely, baseless existence of modern man. It has been a needed medicine for contemporary Americans who have never experienced the direct effects of widespread hunger, devastating war, or widescale genocide. Most American philosophies have an optimistic tone, and existentialism has served the purpose of sounding a sobering note—sobering but not hopeless.

If it is sobering it also calls us to reexamine our culture in terms of its rampant materialism, its robotization of the worker, its antiintellectualism, and its devastating effect on individuality. Probably no modern philosophy devotes as much concern to individuality in political, social, and economic life as existentialism. It speaks to modern man in terms that distinctly belong to the twentieth century and the enduring human predicament. It encourages us toward self-examination in a world that tends to force us outward to nonpersonal concerns.

Today we are constantly bombarded by advertisements that induce us to be something other than what we are. Individuals are manipulated by church, school, family, business, industry, government, and other institutional forces. Existentialism points to the possibility that we can refuse these enticements and seductions, that we are free to choose ourselves if we will but exhibit the courage. We do not have to be pawns buffeted about like helpless victims without succor. Even though our efforts to resist may be puny, may end in death, the individual human being is forged in the struggle to overcome such forces.

With regard to education, existentialists have been among the most severe critics. They have condemned the school as a dehumanizing force that indoctrinates the individual and steals personal initiative. It is as if the school's main function is to process human beings as a canning factory processes tuna. Everyone comes out alike. While the analogy may exaggerate the actual case with schools, the existentialist criticism calls our attention to a definite problem of magnitude. Teachers and students are both victims of this condition, and modern society cannot hope to find itself if its educational institutions are aligned against individual identity, personality, and well-being. Rather than uplifting individuality, the schools have all too often submerged it.

Although these concerns seem new to many people, the message has been sounded before. No less a figure than John Dewey attempted to call

America's attention to what he termed "America, Incorporated" and the "lost, submerged individual." C. Wright Mills spoke of the dangers of the "power-elite" and the effects of an increasing economic oligarchy seeking to control all facets of American life. Yet, existentialism's cries seem to have been heard where older voices went unheeded. Perhaps this occurred because existentialism's ideas are communicated in art forms that ordinary people can understand, in painting, sculpture, drama, and novels. Existentialism does not use the language of abstruse professors in ivory towers; its message is often heard in the streets, the factories, and the offices.

While this popularization has been a blessing of sorts, there have been some rather strong drawbacks. For one thing, in the youth rebellion of the 1960s and 1970s, existentialist jargon and cliches were mouthed but little substance went with them. The "hip" culture of the coffee houses and university campuses was often little more than a passing fad. Existentialist revolt came to mean wearing the costume clothing of "beatniks" or "hippies," thumbing noses at the middle class through smoking pot and engaging in sexual promiscuity, and other such behavior patterns. Instead of fundamental social revolution, there were sporadic and symbolic seizures of university presidents' offices or classroom buildings, hardly the centers of political, economic, or military power. The heart of the existentialist message of man's humanity, his tragic condition, his fragile but still enduring hope was often lost in the adolescent clamor of rebellion.

In education, this turn of events is perhaps best shown by the glorification of "the individual." Yet, this glorification has often been of an abstract individual. We glorify "the individual" to the exclusion of the real-life needs of particular, concrete, live children. Some educators have rejected all order, discipline, and study in the guise of promoting true individuality. They have preached an individualism that is often harmful to real individuals because it promotes selfishness, egoism, and disregard for others. "Spoiled brats" have sometimes been the result. The existentialists have called upon us to become aware of our existence as authentic beings, but this has been corrupted by the "do your own thing" ethic. These corrupters seem to be ignorant of Sartre's reminder that while an individual may do anything, his actions are a message to people that they may do likewise. If man is totally free, Sartre cautioned, he is also totally responsible, and this is an awesome responsibility for any individual.

Repeated criticisms of the individualistic and nihilistic character of existential thought have led some adherents to strike off in new directions. Building a more adequate method to investigate educational problems from an existential perspective has been a recent development. This is called the "phenomenological method," and it relies heavily on the works of such philosophers as Edmund Husserl and Martin Heidegger. Donald Vandenburg, a leading figure in this methodological movement advocates analyzing problems from the standpoint of the lived experience of the child, that is, the child's world, existence, and experiences. The method tries to understand and develop a more adequate theory of what Vandenburg has called "the chronological development of inwardness and outwardness," that is, understanding how a person's consciousness is developed or educated from his own perspective.

This method investigates phenomena related to the expansion, development, and integration of conscious existence through learning. By learning is meant a "coming to know things," and "being aware of something of which one was not previously aware." Thus, educational phenomena are those things generating awareness of conscious existence. There is still an individual empha- sis on the lived world of the child, but the focus is not so much on doctrinaire notions of a nihilistic life-style as on methodological steps toward understanding how an individual comes to be whatever he or she is in the modern world.

Existentialist ideas of education do not mean that individuals cannot learn from others, cannot profit from discipline, or cannot gain from formal study in school. Existentialism, however, insists that these are not the only ways we can create new avenues and identities. While existentialism's influence has helped foster the movement known as "alternative education," proponents sometimes seem to forget that formal study—even the three Rs—is an alterna- tive open to consideration. Existentialist philosophers have sought and are seeking to open our eyes to human possibility and not necessarily to make narrow, doctrinaire ideologues out of us. Such an outcome would be anathema to both the letter and spirit of existentialism.

Sartre

Existentialism and Humanism

Jean-Paul Sartre was a prolific writer and produced major works in a number of different areas including novels, plays, and formal philosophical treatises. In the following selection, he offers a defense of some of his ideas, and in the course of this defense presents some central themes of his philosophical views.* He claims that existentialism is indeed humanistic and provides insight into human freedom and human responsibility. Although Sartre did not write directly about education, his views have been applied to learning, curriculum, and the ethical aspects of education.

My purpose here is to offer a defense of existentialism against several reproaches that have been laid against it.

First, it has been reproached as an invitation to people to dwell in quietism of despair. For if every way to a solution is barred, one would have to regard any action in this world as entirely ineffective, and one would arrive finally at a contemplative philosophy. Moreover, since contemplation is a luxury, this would be only another bourgeois philosophy. This is, especially, the reproach made by the Communists.

From another quarter we are reproached for having underlined all that is ignominious in the human situation, for depicting what is mean, sordid or base to the neglect of certain things that possess charm and beauty and belong to the brighter side of human nature: for example, according to the Catholic critic, Mlle. Mercier, we forget how an infant smiles. Both from this side and from the other we are also reproached for leaving out of account the solidarity of mankind and considering man in isolation. And this, say the Communists, is because we base our doctrine upon pure subjectivity—upon the Cartesian "I think": which is the moment in which solitary man attains to himself; a position from which it is impossible to regain solidarity with other men who exist outside of the self. The *ego* cannot reach them through the *cogito*.

From the Christian side, we are reproached as people who deny the reality and seriousness of human affairs. For since we ignore the commandments of God and all values prescribed as eternal, nothing remains but what is strictly voluntary. Everyone can do what he likes, and will be incapable, from such a point of view, of condemning either the point of view or the action of anyone else.

It is to these various reproaches that I shall endeavour to reply to-day; that is why I have entitled this brief exposition "Existentialism and Humanism." Many may be surprised at the mention of humanism in this connection, but we shall try to see in what sense we understand it. In any case, we can begin by saying that existentialism, in our sense of the word, is a doctrine that does render human life possible; a doctrine,

*Selection from Jean-Paul Sartre, *Existentialism and Human Emotions* (New York: Philosophical Library, 1957), pp. 9–18.

also, which affirms that every truth and every action imply both an environment and a human subjectivity. The essential charge laid against us is, of course, that of over-emphasis upon the evil side of human life. I have lately been told of a lady who, whenever she lets slip a vulgar expression in a moment of nervousness, excuses herself by exclaiming, "I believe I am becoming an existentialist." So it appears that ugliness is being identified with existentialism. That is why some people say we are "naturalistic," and if we are, it is strange to see how much we scandalise and horrify them, for no one seems to be much frightened or humiliated nowadays by what is properly called naturalism. Those who can quite well keep down a novel by Zola such as *La Terre* are sickened as soon as they read an existentialist novel. Those who appeal to the wisdom of the people—which is a sad wisdom—find ours sadder still. And yet, what could be more disillusioned than such sayings as "Charity begins at home" or "Promote a rogue and he'll sue you for damage, knock him down and he'll do you homage"? We all know how many common sayings can be quoted to this effect, and they all mean much the same—that you must not oppose the powers-that-be; that you must not fight against superior force; must not meddle in matters that are above your station. Or that any action not in accordance with some tradition is mere romanticism; or that any undertaking which has not the support of proven experience is foredoomed to frustration; and that since experience has shown men to be invariably inclined to evil, there must be firm rules to restrain them, otherwise we shall have anarchy. It is, however, the people who are forever mouthing these dismal proverbs and, whenever they are told of some more or less repulsive action, say

"How like human nature!"—it is these very people, always harping upon realism, who complain that existentialism is too gloomy a view of things. Indeed their excessive protests make me suspect that what is annoying them is not so much our pessimism, but, much more likely, our optimism. For at bottom, what is alarming in the doctrine that I am about to try to explain to you is—is it not?—that it confronts man with a possibility of choice. To verify this, let us review the whole question upon the strictly philosophic level. What, then, is this that we call existentialism?

Most of those who are making use of this word would be highly confused if required to explain its meaning. For since it has become fashionable, people cheerfully declare that this musician or that painter is "existentialist." A columnist in *Clartés* signs himself "The Existentialist," and, indeed, the word is now so loosely applied to so many things that it no longer means anything at all. It would appear that, for the lack of any novel doctrine such as that of surrealism, all those who are eager to join in the latest scandal or movement now seize upon this philosophy in which, however, they can find nothing to their purpose. For in truth this is of all teachings the least scandalous and the most austere: it is intended strictly for technicians and philosophers. All the same, it can easily be defined.

The question is only complicated because there are two kinds of existentialists. There are, on the one hand, the Christians, amongst whom I shall name Jaspers and Gabriel Marcel, both professed Catholics; and on the other the existential atheists, amongst whom we must place Heidegger as well as the French existentialists and myself. What they have in common is simply the fact that they believe that *existence* comes before *essence*—or, if you will, that we must begin from the subjective. What exactly do we mean by that?

If one considers an article of manufacture—as, for example, a book or a paper-knife—one sees that it has been made by an artisan who had a conception of it: and he has paid attention, equally, to the conception of a paper-knife and to the pre-existent technique of production which is a part of that conception and is, at bottom, a formula. Thus the paper-knife is at the same time an article producible in a certain manner and one which, on the other hand, serves a definite purpose, for one cannot suppose that a man would produce a paper-knife without knowing what it was for. Let us say, then, of the paper-knife that its essence—that is to say the sum of the formulae and the qualities which made its production and its definition possible—precedes its existence. The presence of such-and-such a paper-knife or book is thus determined before my eyes. Here, then, we are viewing the world from a technical standpoint, and we can say that production precedes existence.

When we think of God as the creator, we are thinking of him, most of the time, as a supernal artisan. Whatever doctrine we may be considering, whether it be a doctrine like that of Descartes, or of Leibnitz himself, we always imply that the will follows, more or less, from the understanding or at least accompanies it, so that when God creates he knows precisely what he is creating. Thus, the conception of man in the mind of God is comparable to that of the paper-knife in the mind of the artisan: God makes man according to a procedure and a conception, exactly as the artisan manufactures a paper-knife, following a definition and a formula. Thus each individual man is the realisation of a certain con-

ception which dwells in the divine understanding. In the philosophic atheism of the eighteenth century, the notion of God is suppressed, but not for all that, the idea that essence is prior to existence; something of that idea we still find everywhere, in Diderot, in Voltaire and even in Kant. Man possesses a human nature; that "human nature," which is the conception of human being, is found in every man; which means that each man is a particular example of an universal conception, the conception of Man. In Kant, this universality goes so far that the wild man of the woods, man in the state of nature and the bourgeois are all contained in the same definition and have the same fundamental qualities. Here again, the essence of man precedes that historic existence which we confront in experience.

Atheistic existentialism, of which I am a representative, declares with greater consistency that if God does not exist there is at least one being whose existence comes before its essence, a being which exists before it can be defined by any conception of it. That being is man or, as Heidegger has it, the human reality. What do we mean by saying that existence precedes essence? We mean that man first of all exists, encounters himself, surges up in the world—and defines himself afterwards. If man as the existentialist sees him is not definable, it is because to begin with he is nothing. He will not be anything until later, and then he will be what he makes of himself. Thus, there is no human nature, because there is no God to have a conception of it. Man simply is. Not that he is simply what he conceives himself to be, but he is what he wills, and as he conceives himself after already existing—as he wills to be after that leap towards existence. Man is nothing else but that which he makes of himself. That is the first principle of existentialism. And this is what people call its "subjectivity," using the word as a reproach against us. But what do we mean to say by this, but that man is of a greater dignity than a stone or a table? For we mean to say that man primarily exists—that man is, before all else, something which propels itself towards a future and is aware that it is doing so. Man is, indeed, a project which possesses a subjective life, instead of being a kind of moss, or a fungus or a cauliflower. Before that projection of the self nothing exists; not even in the heaven of intelligence: man will only attain existence when he is what he purposes to be. Not, however, what he may wish to be. For what we usually understand by wishing or willing is a conscious decision taken—much more often than not—after we have made ourselves what we are. I may wish to join a party, to write a book or to marry—but in such a case what is usually called my will is probably a manifestation of a prior and more spontaneous decision. If, however, it is true that existence is prior to essence, man is responsible for what he is. Thus, the first effect of existentialism is that it puts every man in possession of himself as he is, and places the entire responsibility for his existence squarely upon his own shoulders. And, when we say that man is responsible for himself, we do not mean that he is responsible only for his own individuality, but that he is responsible for all men. The word "subjectivism" is to be understood in two senses, and our adversaries play upon only one of them. Subjectivism means, on the one hand, the freedom of the individual subject and, on the other, that man cannot pass beyond human subjectivity. It is the latter which is the deeper meaning of existentialism. When we say

that man chooses himself, we do mean that every one of us must choose himself; but by that we also mean that in choosing for himself he chooses for all men. For in effect, of all the actions a man may take in order to create himself as he wills to be, there is not one which is not creative, at the same time, of an image of man such as he believes he ought to be. To choose between this or that is at the same time to affirm the value of that which is chosen; for we are unable ever to choose the worse. What we choose is always the better; and nothing can be better for us unless it is better for all. If, moreover, existence precedes essence and we will to exist at the same time as we fashion our image, that image is valid for all and for the entire epoch in which we find ourselves. Our responsibility is thus much greater than we had supposed, for it concerns mankind as a whole. If I am a worker, for instance, I may choose to join a Christian rather than a Communist trade union. And if, by that membership, I choose to signify that resignation is, after all, the attitude that best becomes a man, that man's kingdom is not upon this earth, I do not commit myself alone to that view. Resignation is my will for everyone, and my action is, in consequence, a commitment on behalf of all mankind. Or if, to take a more personal case, I decide to marry and to have children, even though this decision proceeds simply from my situation, from my passion or my desire, I am thereby committing not only myself, but humanity as a whole, to the practice of monogamy. I am thus responsible for myself and for all men, and I am creating a certain image of man as I would have him to be. In fashioning myself I fashion man.

Morris

Existentialism in Education

Van Cleve Morris was one of the early advocates of an existentialist approach to educational theory and practice. In the following selection, Morris outlines some of the basic ideas expounded by existentialist thinkers. He focuses on three major concerns of existentialism (subjectivity, paradox, and anxiety) that he thinks would serve as theoretical structures in a proper theory of education. Summerhill is the existentialist school that he believes comes closest to the ideal, although he recognizes that from the existentialist perspective, any formal schooling has definite shortcomings.*

Existentialism's very name suggests the central importance of the word "exist." Unfortunately, it is not an easy word to understand, despite its frequent appearance in everyday talk. One pathway into its meaning is through the private, subjective awareness we each have of our own selves as existing in the world.

The first thing to exist is me. This may be ungrammatical and seemingly arrogant, but it is the best way to plunge to the heart of the seminal existential concept. What it means is this: All philosophizing begins with an existing being aware of his own existing. Every thought he thinks, *every* word he places on paper, *every* act he commits, derives *its* existence from *his* prior existing.

One of the ridiculous puzzles of philosophy has been the question: Do I really exist? It is ridiculous because it is not a problem; no philosopher genuinely doubted his own existence. And we must certainly include in this generalization Descartes himself. Descartes' logic seemed to be impeccable, and he appeared to be really sincere in trying to prove his own existence. But his argument was deceptive, flawed by a subtle error:

Descartes wanted to develop an argument to support the contention "I am." In approaching this problem, he decided to begin by wiping the slate clean and doubting the existence of everything, including himself. What he could not doubt the existence of, however, was his own doubting. So he came up with the classic "*Cogito, ergo sum*" ("I think, therefore I am"). But it is obvious even to an untrained mind that in uttering the first "I" Descartes had already assumed his conclusion "I am." What is the sense, therefore, of going through this solemn syllogism only to find at the end of it a "startling truth" that you have already uttered by the very first sound your lips have made? To think that centuries of philosophy have been bewitched by the *Cogito*!

Some philosophers have tried to save Descartes by insisting that what he really meant by the *Cogito* was not "I think" but rather something like "Think-

*Selection from Van Cleve Morris, *Existentialism in Education* (New York: Harper and Row, 1966), pp. 12–13, 15–17, 23–25, 147–50.

ing is going on here." This turns out to be even more precarious. For in the formulation "Thinking is going on here, therefore, I exist" we have uttered a *non sequitur* of the most outrageous sort. Nothing existential follows from the remark "Thinking is going on here." All that follows is the question: Who is speaking? We are driven back inevitably to the first Cartesian "I."

The "I" comes first. I am the first existent, "the first thing that is." The utterance "I exist" must necessarily precede any other sentence I wish to say. "In the beginning was the Word, and the Word was the pronoun 'I.' " All else must wait upon this.

The priority of the existential "I" is therefore a starting hypothesis. It is a hypothesis only, since there is no conceivable way to verify it. But, as hypothesis, it arouses no doubt or skepticism. Of all the propositions I can utter, the assertion "I am" is by all measure the one of which I am most certain.

The hypothesis is central to all forms of Existentialism and may be generalized with the dictum: "Existence precedes essence." What this phrase means is that the *fact* of my existing is antecedent to any other fact or any other understanding I may have of the world, including the understanding of my own essence. Likewise, the *fact* of man's presence in the world is antecedent to any other fact that may be uttered about the world. . . .

Paradox consists in holding two contrary views of the significance of our own existing. One of these views may be explained in the following way: When I awake to the fact of my existing, when I recognize the absolute priority of the pronoun "I" in the structure of my life and world, I am struck by the fact that this "I" that I know seems to be the only one of its kind in existence. There is an absolute uniqueness of the phenomenon of my own selfhood. I peer out on the world with all its apparent order and system. It seems to contain a multivariety of items, all of them understood under their own rubrics and categories, like the items in a Sears, Roebuck catalog. Yet, I know that I am really different from all else I behold there. I am not to be found under any of the rubrics. I am not in the catalog; there is no entry for me in the index; the world apparently "does not carry that item." The reason is that there are no rubrics under which I could be classified. Or, better, I *am my own rubric*, the only instance of this item in existence, a singular phenomenon never to be repeated. Never again this particular arrangement of protoplasmic molecules, never again this particular origin or history, never again this particular set of traits and attitudes. Never again shall another Van Cleve Morris come into the world. What am I to make of this uniqueness, this one-and-only-oneness? Do not most of us translate it into a positive quality, a basic value, a characteristic to be glad of? To be one of a kind, to be a single instance, is to be a phenomenon worthy of attention in the world.

There is an irony to the fact that most religions and philosophies and some political theories, most notably Western democracy, have made so much of the uniqueness of the individual and the sanctity of the person. We are reminded, over and over again, of Kant's imperative that each man is to be treated as end, never as means. And the American ethic, from Jefferson to the present, has reiterated the injunction that each person is precious, the individual always superior to the state. The irony is that we already *know* it! No one has to convince us of the truth of this principle. It is somehow known and believed by each one of us even before anyone says it.

Sometimes the most prosaic of metaphors helps to illuminate our attempt to convey profound ideas. For example, we often remark in commenting on an unusual friend or acquaintance, "Yes, he's quite a person. They threw away the mold when they made that fellow!" Doesn't everyone think of himself in terms of this metaphor?

No matter what happens, I shall always insist that my own existing, my being an "instance" of man, is an unrepeatable datum in the world. Furthermore, I am permanent, a datum written with indelible ink into the cosmic ledger book, never to be erased or expunged. It may be in very small print, but it is there forever. I assign to myself, therefore—without any assistance from Christian doctrine or democratic preachments—an absolute value and an ultimate worth. I count, I matter in the scheme of things. My existing makes a difference; the cosmos wouldn't be quite the same without me.

This is one side of Existential paradox. The other side: My existence is a big joke, a huge delusion! Each of us recognizes, when we reflect on it for a moment, that we count for absolutely nothing. The cosmos does not require our presence. Not in the slightest. Look around you—funerals every day! And what does it matter? Isn't the loss made up somehow, by putting others in the vacated places?

If I were to fall into the Chicago Drainage Canal, which flows near Chicago Circle, and wash down the Mississippi River into the Gulf, what difference would it make? There would, I presume, be some stir. The University community would be jostled, ever so slightly;

there would necessarily be a reassignment of my responsibilities to others until a replacement could be found. (One can always hope that the flag might fly at half-staff for a day or so.) Certainly my loved ones, those close to me, would grieve, and there would be concentric circles of sorrow extending outward among them. But the intensity of the sorrow would decrease "by the square of the distance"; by the time it reached my last cousin, it would have faded into nothing.

Sooner or later, the loss would be forgotten. My friends would put it out of mind and return to work. The University would run the flag back up the flagpole and would find a replacement—because I *am* replaceable. And my family and relations would adjust to a world without me. In time, all would heal over, and my "I," the content of my selfhood, would be lost, expunged from existence. The ideas I had expressed would be forgotten; the words I wrote would molder in the libraries. Eventually all would go "down the drain." And men living a hundred or five hundred years from now would have no inkling that I had been here.

So, I will eventually be erased from the universe. I do not particularly like to think about it, but I must recognize this truth. In the end, the significance of my presence in the world will inevitably reduce to that absolute zero usually reserved for Centigrade thermometers at $-273.16°$, where all molecular movement has to come to a stop. That will be the situation: In ten, or a hundred, or five hundred years, all residual effects of my existence shall have disappeared, all "motions" shall have expended their last quantum of energy, and the fact of my presence, while still a fact, shall have been emptied of significance, my meaning in the world finally exhausted and spent.

This, then, is the paradox, and every man must live with it. It is to know two things about oneself: (1) that one is of absolute value in the world, and (2) that one is of absolutely no value whatsoever. These two truths are contradictory, but they are both true. It may be that they are known to an individual in different ways; perhaps my subjectivity tells me the first and my empirical reason tells me the second. But that is beside the point. I believe them both, and at once. . . .

A few pages back, it was pointed out that we could conceive of the nothingness of chairs and worlds. And we have seen in the section just above that we are able not only to *conceive* of nothingnesses but actually to *experience* them— indeed, to become the very vehicle for their emergence. However, in all of these illustrations, we have been considering the existence or nonexistence of phenomena beyond our own skin. Can we as easily open up for consideration the existence or nonexistence of our own selves?

The question is ridiculous on its face. Of course not! I can stand aside and speak in a very scholarly way about the being or nonbeing of chairs or Pierres. I can conceive of them and deliberately experience them as absent from the world. I can even dare to speak of the nonbeing of the world itself, so long as I maintain a safe distance—so long, that is, as I don't include myself. But if I am *in* the world, and if the world could pass into nonbeing, then obviously I would have to go. And this prospect, different in kind from the others, simply cannot be contemplated in the same mood or spirit.

Why not? The reason is this: If I am in

no doubt whatsoever about assigning the characteristic of "existence" to my own selfhood, then "nothingness" must be absolutely excluded from consideration; it cannot be entertained as an option. My awareness of my own existence is, shall we say, "puncture proof." However, although I seem to be absolutely invulnerable to all suggestions that I do not exist, I am absolutely defenseless against the suggestion that some day I might not exist. To recognize, in the certainty of one's own existence, that this existence need never have occurred or, equally, that this existence could pass away in a flicker and indeed may disappear eventually with no loss is to be overcome by an emotion of the most overpowering sort. . . .

Anxiety, in this context, is not to be confused with Freudian or psychoneurotic anxiety. That form of the ailment, what we might speak of as the psychosocial form, concerns the low-order problem of being out of adjustment with one's social environment. A "nothingness" has crept in, to be sure, but it is a nothingness occasioned by warped rapport with one's fellow man, and as such is theoretically curable. If one is cut off from psychic communication with others, the anxiety thus engendered has a cause which is, in theory, capable of being located and identified. And the psychiatrist or psychoanalyst can undertake therapeutic measures aimed at identifying and removing the cause.

The situation is entirely different with what we are now calling existential anxiety. It is an anxiety of the most profound sort, signifying alienation not merely from one's fellow human beings but from the world, from the very ground of existence. This form of anxiety does not seem to have any identifiable cause. There is no specifiable "nothingness," if you will, which can be pointed to and of which it might be said, "Here, doctor, here is the difficulty." And hence, there appears to be no suitable therapy. The malady is a kind of *ultimate ache* for which conventional psychiatric medicine has no specific. . . .

Has anyone ever really organized a school designed to function on behalf only of the individual learner? As we all know, Progressive schools have often claimed this distinction, but I think in our latter-day assessment of their efforts we may conclude that they ultimately fell prey to the "socializing" theory of child development. They fostered the growth of individualism, but only in social terms, only in terms of the individual's relation to other members of the group or to the group itself.

Is there a school which has succeeded in holding "the others" at bay? A possible candidate is Summerhill, a small private school in England at Leiston, Suffolk, about 100 miles from London. The school is now over forty years old, having been founded in 1921 by A. S. Neill, who has served as its original director but who is now over eighty and semi-retired.

For forty years "Neill," as his students call him, has been testing a hazardous hypothesis. Does freedom work? Suppose you had a school in which there were no rules, no requirements, no homework, no regulations, no roll taking, no grades, no academic expectations, no tests, no institutional code of decorum, no social conventions. Suppose all you had were a small "campus," some living quarters, some classrooms, half a dozen teachers, and forty to fifty youngsters ranging in age from five to seventeen. It would be a small but thoroughly free and open society, with no

institutional "ethos" to adjust to and no organizational hierarchy to please. It would be, rather, merely a collection of separate individuals dealing with one another, old and young alike, as free and autonomous persons. Could anything like "education" possibly occur there? Neill has found that the answer is "Yes." And the story of his work is told with warmth and compelling dedication in the most recent and most famous of his many books, *Summerhill—A Radical Approach to Child Rearing.*

The school draws its students from an admittedly atypical clientele. For one thing, there are tuition, boarding, and rooming fees; . . . which . . . exert a selective influence over admissions. For another, the school seems to attract many youngsters who have been in revolt against other kinds of schools, who have failed to adjust to institutional life, and who have been transferred by their parents to Summerhill. In the telling, Mr. Neill finds the greatest satisfaction in the rehabilitation of these youngsters. They come to Summerhill full of hate—for parents, for teachers and principals, for authority. Their previous encounter with learning has been so thoroughly associated with compulsory duties that they are at war not only with adult authority but with the very act of learning itself. They hate books, they hate study, they hate learning!

Their enrollment in Summerhill represents a traumatic and sudden "decompression" in the scholastic environment. All the pressures associated with "going to school" are abruptly lifted, and their customary response is precisely what one might expect—they play hooky, refuse to attend any classes or do any work; they indulge to the full their child impulses to play and play all day long. Neill lets them.

Sooner or later, though, they voluntarily take up their studies again. This interval Neill appropriately calls "recovery time"; it sometimes goes on for months. "The recovery time is proportionate to the hatred their last school gave them. Our record case was a girl from a convent. She loafed for three years. The average period of recovery from lesson aversion is three months."

After the child is rehabilitated, he continues to be as free to determine his own routine and learning schedule as he was during his "recovery" period. He studies what he likes with the teachers he likes. He discovers himself in full responsibility for his own learning.

There is a timetable—but only for the teachers. The children have classes usually according to their age, but sometimes according to their interests. We have no new methods of teaching, because we do not consider that teaching in itself matters very much. Whether a school has or has not a special method for teaching long division is of no significance, for long division is of no importance except to those who want to learn it. And the child who wants to learn long division will learn it no matter how it is taught.

What more apt way of stating the principle of "appropriation" implicit in Existentialist epistemology!

The school is also remarkable for its social freedom. The life of the community is in the hands of those who live in the community, the smallest child's vote exactly equal in strength to Neill's and to each teacher's. Punishment is meted out to individuals, not on grounds of having broken a school rule but rather on grounds that the culprit is interfering with the lives of others. If damage is done to school property, it is handled as a violation of Neill's private property

and restitution must be made. If there is football in the lounge, it is treated as a disturbance of the peace and an invasion of others' rights of quiet and privacy. Even sex has no special containing bonds. Boys and girls are left alone, and relations between them appear to be healthy. Neill's approach to the matter exemplifies the only grounds for discipline, viz., infringing the freedoms of others: "I met them [two teen-age lovers] late one night and I stopped them. 'I don't know what you two are doing,' I said, 'and morally I don't care, for it isn't a moral question at all. But economically I do care. If you, Kate, have a kid, my school is ruined.' "

There are rules, but only a few and those few reserved for palpable hazards: There is no swearing in town (permitted on campus), no running on the roof; no child may carry a gun or other weapon that can injure; and arson is automatically punishable. Except for these and a few others, all legislated by the self-governing General School Meeting of all Summerhill citizens, young and old, the life at this amazing institution is free, in both the "freedom from" and the "freedom to" sense of this word. As in any society, large and small, expectations and anticipations of others' behavior do develop. But at Summerhill the expectations are all person-to-person, I-Thou phenomena. The institutional is played down, the personal is played up. It is a close approximation of a society of subjectivities—free, autonomous, independent selfhoods, each determining the essence and meaning of his own life.

Neill has created a remarkable community on the basis of an exceedingly simple but powerful idea. He admits it has a lot of Freud in it: A free child is a happy child. A happy child does not fear or hate; he can love and give. The loving, giving child can live positively. Neill would be a more thoroughgoing exemplar of Existentialist education if he were to make one further, final argument which is implicit in his work: The free child eventually becomes the *responsible* child; it is freedom itself which makes this awareness possible. He who becomes responsible becomes capable of authenticity. Neill is creating authentic individuals.

Summerhill's graduates are proving out this thesis. Although there are some failures—some for whom a Summerhill education simply does not "take"—the preponderance of graduates are, in Neill's and society's terms, successes. They are living advertisements for the school: motion-picture cameramen, cooks and dietitians, ship's stewards, physicians, university professors, all of them self-directing and self-moving because they took charge of their own lives early and know what it means to be responsible for one's own career as a human being.

Selected Readings

Greene, Maxine. *Teacher as Stranger: Educational Philosophy for the Modern Age.* Belmont, Ca.: Wadsworth, 1973.

This is an engaging work that combines a literary analysis of existentialist themes with philosophical and educational concepts. It is an exploratory work that many readers will find stimulating.

Kneller, George F. *Existentialism and Education.*

This book is one of the first efforts to give a systematic treatment to the relationship of existentialism to education. It has been widely used but also widely criticized for its systematization of the philosophy.

Morris, Van Cleve. *Existentialism in Education.* New York: Harper and Row, 1966.

A comprehensive overview of existentialism as a philosophy of education, this work tries to provide some insight into possible uses of existential thought. Like Kneller, Morris has been vigorously criticized for treating existentialist thought as another "ism."

Sartre, Jean-Paul. *Existentialism and Human Emotions.* New York: Philosophical Library, 1974.

This is a short compilation of writings from among some of Sartre's best-known philosophical works. It is an excellent introduction to Sartre's ideas as well as to his style of philosophizing.

Troutner, Lee. "Making Sense out of 'Existential Thought and Education:' A Search for the Interface," in *Philosophy of Education*, 1975. Proceedings of the thirty-first annual meeting of the Philosophy of Education Society. San Jose, Ca.: Philosophy of Education Society, 1975. Pp. 185–99.

This paper explores the contributions of existential thought to education. The author sketches possible future contributions existentialism can make.

Vandenberg, Donald. *Being and Education: An Essay in Existential Phenomenology.* Englewood Cliffs, N.J.: Prentice Hall, 1971.

This work is different in that it does not present existentialist thought as another "ism." Instead, it attempts to apply phenomenological method to selected problems in education.

BEHAVIORISM

Behaviorism is not generally considered a philosophy in the same sense that idealism, realism, pragmatism, and other such thought systems are. It is most often classified as a psychological theory, a more specialized and less comprehensive theory than a systematic philosophy. At the same time, behaviorism has been given increasing attention and acceptance in the field of education, so that in many instances it has extended into areas ordinarily considered the domain of philosophy. These extensions include theoretical considerations dealing with the nature of man and society, values, the good life, and speculations or assumptions on the nature of reality.

Perhaps no psychological theory can escape dealing with philosophical assumptions and implications. For an extensive period of time, psychology was thought to be a philosophical study, and only in recent times have most psychologists come to think of themselves as scientists. Indeed, the leading proponents of behaviorism do consider themselves scientists, perhaps more justifiably laying claim to that title than some other schools of psychology. Be that as it may, most psychologists at some point in their endeavors encounter questions of a philosophical nature. Much psychological theory rests upon assumptions about human nature that have had a long career in the history of philosophy. Behaviorism, even though it lays claim to an objective scientific orientation, is no less involved with philosophical questions than other psychological theories.

An attempt is made in this chapter to show some of the connections of behaviorism with past philosophical systems and how these have influenced modern behavioristic theory. In addition, exploration is made of philosophical themes in behaviorism, primarily as these are given in the works of B. F. Skinner. Finally, an effort is made to show the educational uses and implications of behaviorism, or in terms of education, what might be more appropriately referred to as behavioral engineering.

6

BEHAVIORISM
AND
EDUCATION

Philosophical Bases of Behaviorism

Behaviorism has its roots in several philosophical traditions. It is related to realism, largely in terms of the realist's thesis of independent reality that is similar to the behaviorists' belief that behavior is caused by environmental conditions. Behaviorism also is indebted to materialistic philosophy, such as that promoted by Thomas Hobbes, who held that reality is primarily matter and motion, and all behavioral phenomena are capable of being explained in those terms.

Realism

Behaviorism's connection with realism is primarily with modern realism and its advocacy of science. However, there are some similarities to classical realism. For example, Aristotle thought we reached form or essence through the study of particulars. The behaviorists believe we can understand human behavior by a meticulous study of particular behaviors. Indeed, they expand this approach to the effect that human "nature" (if there be such) can be explained by what traditionally has been thought to be only a particular aspect of human nature—behavior. In addition, there is no "internal" reality of the human hidden from scientific discovery for the behaviorists, because what is real is external, factual, and observable behavior capable of being known.

Thus, one of the realist elements of behaviorism includes going from particular, observable facts (particular behaviors) to "forms," or the laws of behavior. Behaviorists think the human traits of personality, character, integrity, and so forth are the results of behaving in certain ways. These traits are not internally determined by each individual but come about by behavior patterns developed through environmental conditioning. The emphasis on environment shows another realist leaning toward the importance of the discernible, factual, observable aspects of the universe. In other words, by understanding particular behaviors and how they are caused by environmental circumstances, we can detect the patterns and processes by which behavior comes about. Thus, it is possible, the behaviorists maintain, to discern the laws of behavior and thereby come to exercise control over human behavior. It is possible, then, to construct a technology of behavior.

Of course, these notions about behavior would be foreign to Aristotle, but it is possible to see similarities between him and the behaviorists in at least the basic framework. The connection becomes even more apparent with more recent versions of realism, especially the realism that came about with the advent of modern science. For example, Francis Bacon, in his efforts to develop an inductive scientific method, held that we must reject indubitable dogmas in favor of an inquiry approach that seeks meaning in the facts as we find them. Behaviorism holds that we should cease accentuating the mind, consciousness, or soul as the causal agent of behavior and look rather to the facts of behavior, or that which is observable and capable of empirical verification. This consideration is not only Baconian but is representative of contemporary realism.

The idea of the "laws" of behavior, while having similarities to Aristotelian and Baconian realism, is strongly similar to Alfred North Whitehead's contention that the philosopher should seek out the patterns of reality. Behaviorists do this by seeking the processes and patterns through which behavior is shaped. Once they have sufficient understanding of these, they maintain, it will be possible to engineer more effectively the kinds of people and social conditions we want.

Materialism

Materialism has its roots in Greek philosophy, but as it exists today it is essentially the theory developed along with modern science in the sixteenth and seventeenth centuries. Basically, materialism is the theory that reality can be explained by the laws of matter and motion. We can see that behaviorism is definitely a kind of materialism, for most behaviorists view man in terms of his neurological, physiological, and biological contexts. Beliefs about mind, consciousness, and soul, they say, are relics of a prescientific age. The behaviorists seem to be saying that body is material, and behavior is motion. Thus, man can be known from the standpoints of matter and motion.

Elements of behaviorism are akin to some aspects of mechanistic materialism. This philosophical perspective also dates back several centuries. For the materialist, man is not a partially supernatural being above nature (as some religious persons might hold), but rather, he is a part of nature; and even though he is one of the more complex natural organisms, he is capable of being studied and is governed by natural law just as any other natural creature.

Thomas Hobbes (1588–1679). Thomas Hobbes was an earlier exponent of mechanistic materialism. Hobbes was personally acquainted with some of the greatest figures of his day, including Descartes, Galileo, and Kepler. He learned a great deal about philosophy and science from these men, but he was also a first-rate thinker in his own right. Hobbes was a thorough-going determinist, and he rejected the elements of self-determination and free will in the thought of Descartes. In most respects, he was more at home with the thinking of Galileo and Kepler. He applied some of their ideas about the physical universe to man and social institutions. Life is simply motion, Hobbes held, and one can say a machine has life, even if an artifical one. By the same token, an organized society is like a machine: it has an artificial life that has to be maintained. Even biological natural life is mechanistic in the sense that it operates according to its own design.

For Hobbes, man's psychological makeup can be explained in mechanistic terms. Man experiences objects by their qualities (color, odor, texture, and so forth) through sensation. Sensation is physical, what is sensed is quality, and quality is motion. Even imagination, according to Hobbes, is motion. The same can be said for thinking. Therefore, all that truly exists is matter and motion, and all reality can be explained in terms of mathematical precision.

Behaviorism's close affinity with mechanistic materialism lies in several areas. For one thing, both materialists and behaviorists believe that we behave in certain ways according to our physical makeup. Bodily functions occur in certain objectively describable and predictable ways. Because of this physical makeup, we are capable of numerous motor responses. Organs and limbs operate according to known physiological processes. The brain, for instance, contains no soul, but does contain physiological and neurological materials and processes because chemical and electrical process make up a large part of the brain's functions. However, it is body-in-situation that is significant, for here there is *human* behavior or motion. The significant thing is to observe behavior (motion) of a body in an environment (supporting material conditions). While this is not precisely what the behaviorists say, the similarity to mechanistic materialism is obvious. A difference is that for the behaviorists, human behavior or motion is *the* significant datum, and knowledge of matter is crucial because it helps us understand behavior itself.

Early Behaviorists

Ivan Pavlov (1849-1936).   Pavlov was an eminent experimental psychologist and physiologist in pre-Soviet Russia. He was noted for his studies of the reflex reaction in humans and animals and devised a number of conditioning experiments. He found that when a bell is rung each time a dog is fed, the dog is conditioned to associate the sound of the bell with food. Consequently, when the bell is sounded the dog's physiological makeup reacts in such a way as to expect food. Pavlov was the father of conditioning theory and was also a strong opponent of the Freudian interpretation of neuroses throughout his life.

Pavlov's conditioning studies show how both realism and materialism are related. For the dog, bodily response is not based on something mental going on inside the dog; rather, the response is made on the basis of conditioning, and conditioning can be explained by external circumstances. This lay at the heart of Pavlov's opposition to Freudianism. Of course, it could be argued that Freud recognized conditioning by his extensive work on the influence of early childhood and family training. The difference is, however, that Freud claimed this influence resides in a mentalistic unconscious, an "inner" thing. Pavlov wanted an explanation based on controllable external conditions that require no inner source of action. This illustrates both realism's affinity for an independent reality and materialism's claim that things can be explained in terms of matter and motion.

Modern behaviorists hold that Pavlov was headed in the right direction, but that his explanations were too simplistic. Pavlov only considered conditioned reflex behavior whereas modern behaviorists use operant conditioning that includes action on the part of the organism being conditioned. The organism can act to change his environment, and the resulting changes reinforce the behavior of the organism in some way. The modern view tends more toward a two-way flow while Pavlov only showed it one way. His pioneering nevertheless has been of crucial importance.

John B. Watson (1878-1958). Watson repudiated the introspective method in psychology as delusive and unscientific. He relied solely on an observational technique restricted to behavior. He believed that the fears people have are conditioned responses to the environment. In a number of successful experiments, he conditioned people to be fearful and then deconditioned them. He thought of the environment as the primary shaper of behavior and maintained that if he could control a child's environment he could then engineer that child into any kind of person desired. Following his work with infants in the maternity ward of Johns Hopkins Hospital in Baltimore, he announced: "The behaviorists believe that there is nothing within to develop. If you start with a healthy body, the right number of fingers and toes, and the few elementary movements that are present at birth, you do not need anything else in the way of raw material to make a man, be that man a genius, a cultured gentleman, a rowdy, or a thug." Watson was very influential, and the strong movement in American psychology toward behaviorism is often directly attributed to him.

Watson was even more materialistic than preceding behaviorists. He thought the chief function of the nervous system is simply to coordinate senses with motor responses. Thus, the brain is only a part of the nervous system and not the seat of mind or consciousness or a self-active entity. He thought that the senses not only gain knowledge of the world but are also instruments in guiding activity for successful maintenance of life. In rejecting mentalistic notions of mind and consciousness, Watson also rejected concepts such as purpose, feeling, satisfaction, and free will because they are not observable and therefore not capable of scientific treatment or measurement.

Behaviorism and Positivism

Watson's penchant for giving acceptance only to those things directly observable set a pattern for those who came after him. E. L. Thorndike was solidly within Watson's outlook when he proclaimed that anything which exists, exists in some quantity capable of being measured. These kinds of thinking have been influential in psychology and have had their parallels and influences in and from philosophy. One movement that has given a philosophical basis to positions such as Watson's and Thorndike's is known as positivism.

Philosophical positivism was initiated by Auguste Comte, often referred to as the founder of modern sociology. His objective was to reform society, and he argued for a positive social science to achieve this end. He thought that by applying scientific principles to social conditions systematically, we would be able to recognize the laws constituting the social order, their evolution, and the ways to apply them more systematically. This could be accomplished through discovering the real and exact knowledge of society. The test of value of this knowledge would be the extent to which it helps us change the material world and society to more desirable conditions.

Comte divided history into three periods, each characterized by a particular way of thinking. The first is the *theological* in which things are explained by references to spirits and gods. The second period is the *metaphysical* in which events are explained by causes, inner principles, and substances. The third or *positive* period is the highest stage where man does not attempt to go beyond observable and measurable fact.

Comte's thought influenced subsequent thinkers to use science in devising social policy. Behaviorists are squarely in this tradition because Watson's statements concerning how he could produce any kind of person from a reasonably healthy child have been taken seriously by contemporary behaviorists. No longer is science the province of intellectuals and gentlemen of leisure, but it is now viewed as the key to the better society. It is interesting that in some quarters psychology, sociology, and similar disciplines are no longer referred to as the social sciences, but as the *behaviorial* sciences. This change in terms has occurred because behavior is the objective, observable human element susceptible to scientific manipulation.

While earlier positivism was founded on the science of the nineteenth century, contemporary positivism has been more interested in the logic and language of scientific concepts. This has been exemplified most by the school of thought called logical positivism. It has dealt with areas familiar to both behaviorism and the older positivism, but it is primarily known for its work on the logic of propositions and the principle of verification.

The movement began in the early decades of the twentieth century and has often been identified with a group of European philosophers, mathematicians, and scientists known as the "Vienna Circle." It included such figures as Rudolf Carnap, Herbert Feigl, Felix Kaufmann, and others. Bertrand Russell and Ludwig Wittgenstein, although not members of the group, had close philosophical ties to it. The circle has since dissolved, and its members have dispersed into several different directions. Basically, the impetus of logical positivism has been to develop a unity among the sciences by devising a consistent set of logical or linguistic phrasings and structures. This effort has come about in order to rectify the language difficulties encountered in scientific investigation. An investigation can often be sidetracked or misled by the words and statements used. For example, our words and statements should reflect the facts of the situation under discussion. Suppose we are studying an educational problem, and our problem is largely involved with self-concept. Suppose we cannot discover that there really is such a thing as self in the sense of mind or consciousness. Then what we need to do is examine what we really mean by the signification "self." This word is so colored by prescientific and metaphysical considerations that its usage is vague, even with tinges of the theological soul. If we are truly scientific, we want an objective statement of the problem in terms so that an objective resolution of the problem can be made. In other words, we must specify in clear terms what we are talking about.

The connection of this philosophical "school" of thought with behaviorism is that behaviorists seek a language framework that more accurately reflects the facts of behavior to them. Rather than using the word "self" to signify personal identity or the characteristics of an individual, the behaviorists speak of "conditioned" or "reinforced behavior," "repertoire of behavioral responses," or perhaps "operant conditioning" in regard to the specific organism we may call John Jones. Self or self-concept are too much tied to mentalistic constructs, and we are in danger of being misled in the direction of imputing certain mysterious, internal, driving forces to John Jones to explain his behavior.

Logical postivists are sensitive to the fallacies into which the wrong uses of language can get us. What we should do, they maintain, is make meaningful statements conveying information regarding the observable, verifiable facts of the situation. In the context of both behaviorism and logical positivism, it is one thing to make a statement such as, "There are matches in this box," and quite another thing to state, "There is a self-concept in John Jones." We can verify whether there are matches in this box by opening the box and examining it. There are either matches or there are no matches. We cannot operate on John Jones and find that self is a fact. First, it would be ridiculous to cut John Jones open. Second, it makes more sense to observe John Jones's behavior to see what stimulates him to behave as he does. The behaviorist maintains that because we do not know very much about behavior and because of our lack of knowledge, we wrongly impute meaning to behavior by reference to an "inner man," a self, mind, consciousness, soul, or some such hidden entity that "causes" the behavior. Even the most meticulous and rigorous scientific experiments have not been able to locate this "inner man." Behaviorists and logical positivists alike would agree with the British philosopher, Gilbert Ryle, who maintained that traditional meanings of mind really infer a "ghost in the machine" (or a mind in the body).

Coupled with their concern for more linguistic precision, logical positivists have also championed what is called "the principle of verifiability." This principle means that no statement should be taken as truthful unless it can be verified empirically or it is at least capable of being verified. For example, a statement about angels is not verifiable in any scientific way, nor is it capable of being verified at some future date because of the very nature of the statement. Even those who believe in angels do not maintain that they can be verified by science. However, such a statement as "There is life in outer space" may not be capable of immediate verification, but it is certainly within man's technical capacity to find out in the near future. Thus, logical positivists try to discourage non-sense statements and promote language and thought that is more controllable and rigorous. The behaviorist, mindful about careless linguistic and logical statements, seeks to avoid absurd theories. There are observable, factual behavior and environmental conditions, and we must describe them in objective, logical, and accurate terms.

Philosophical Aspects of Behaviorism

B.F. Skinner (1904-   ). Skinner was born in Susquehanna, Pennsylvania. He studied at Hamilton College and Harvard and later taught at the University of Minnesota and at Indiana University where he was chairman of the department of psychology before returning to Harvard as professor of psychology. He is sometimes referred to as "the high priest of behaviorism." In other instances, he is more sympathetically referred to as one of the most important contemporary psychologists. Without a doubt, Skinner's work and influence have certainly caught attention and comment, even though opinions have ranged from bitter criticism to disciple-like emulation. There are very few persons knowledgeable about Skinner's work who are neutral about it.

Skinner himself has often debunked philosophical approaches to psychology. He thinks a great deal of error and misunderstanding have come about because philosophers have tried to deduce an understanding of man from *a priori* generalizations, or they have been "armchair scientists" content with introspection. He claims, on the other hand, to base his findings on observations and controlled scientific experiment. Yet, he has often found it necessary to make statements about such traditional philosophical topics as human nature and the good society. In fact, Skinner is not necessarily the sterile scientist in the laboratory, for he is also a dreamer and a utopian. It is possible to discern a strong element of social radicalism in his writing. In the brief overview of his thought that follows (taken largely from his book, *Beyond Freedom and Dignity*), some of these ideas will be explored.

Human Nature

Traditionally, the study of human nature has been an important aspect of philosophical endeavor. It has been central to the metaphysics of many great philosophers and has been of considerable influence in the philosophical treat-ment of ethics. Skinner maintains that less philosophical speculation and more "realistic" observation of behavior is necessary, but he still poses the question, "What is man?"

Skinner attacks what he calls the traditional views of man. Those views have imputed all kinds of internal drives, forces, or otherwise mysterious actions to "autonomous man," forces such as aggression, industry, attention, knowing, perceiving, and so on. Traditionally, such capacities were assumed to be there somewhere, hidden from direct scrutiny, and were said to make up (at least in part) the very essence of human nature. Skinner, on the other hand, maintains that aggression, for example, is not inherent in our nature in the sense that we will automatically harm or damage others. It makes just as much sense to say that we behave in a manner we call aggressive because that behavior is rein-forced by particular environmental contingencies. For Skinner, the contingen-cies of reinforcement themselves explain the aggressive behavior quite apart from some assumed internal or genetic force within man.

Let us explore an example. In wartime, it is often discovered that some persons commit acts we call depraved. In the Vietnam war, some American soldiers indiscriminately killed a number of noncombatant women and children. When the event was made known in America, there were outcries of disbelief and horror. In searching for answers to why this had occurred, some observers said that these actions only indicated evil human nature. A widely publicized court martial was held, and an officer was found guilty of having participated in the massacre. From a Skinnerian point of view, we could say that however deplorable the behavior, finding a guilty culprit and punishing him does not get at the real problem. Punishment may extinguish certain kinds of behavior, but it is usually ineffective. Does a soldier under combat conditions kill others because he is basically evil? Or does it make more sense to observe his behavior in terms of the environmental contingencies and the reinforcement of particular aggres-sive behaviors in those conditions? While it is true that all soldiers do not kill noncombatant civilians, it also seems very likely that noncombatant civilians would not have been killed by combatant soldiers if there had been no war, no behaviors of combatant soldiering, and no existing environmental conditions that would make warlike behavior rewarding. We may say that the evil lies in making war, training people to kill, and maintaining and securing conditions that make such behavior rewarding, and not in some innate evil within man.

Let us take another example: knowing. Skinner says that the traditional view sees an autonomous man, who in perceiving the world around him, reaches out or acts upon that world in order to know it, to "take it in," to "grasp it." The implication is that the action and initiative come from the autonomous man, but Skinner maintains that the reverse is the case. Knowing is really a case of the environment acting on us. We perceive and know to the extent that we respond to stimuli from environmental contingencies. For instance, we may respond to heat, light, color, and so forth according to the arrangement of contingencies. As Skinner puts it, we move in or out of sunlight depending upon how hot or cold it is. Thus, we come to know sunlight, heat, and cold. Sunlight figures in how we arrange time, set schedules, and perform certain activities. Our knowledge of the sun, heat, and light is expanded to the extent we behave in relation to these environmental conditions and are reinforced by that behavior. Too often we think knowing is a cognitive process, but it is behavioral and environmental, neurological and even physiological.

Some critics say behaviorism cannot deal with individual conscious-ness—with awareness of oneself. They insist that there is an "inner realm" that the behaviorist ignores. Skinner says this charge is a serious one that cannot be lightly passed over, and holds that thus far self-observation must be included in any comprehensive analysis of human behavior. What is at stake, however, is what an individual knows when he or she does this self-analysis. For Skinner, what one knows in this respect is difficult to comprehend because it is largely a matter of responding to the natural contingencies of individual circumstances. We respond to our own internal stimuli (without much awareness), as in behav-ior such as walking, jumping, and running. To the extent that we really *know* these behaviors and their causes, we must do more than merely respond to them. This kind of knowing would involve systematic study beyond a mere internal soliloquy and would include bodily functions, environmental conditions, and contingencies.

Knowing one's desires, beliefs, and feelings, the things usually thought to be most private, is more difficult. For one thing, we lack the necessary verbal tools to accomplish this. Without verbalization in some form, behavior is largely unconsciousness, and Skinner maintains that consciousness in the verbal awareness sense is a social product and not within the range of a solitary individual. Really knowing this "inner realm" is difficult because we have not developed appropriate verbalization of it. We are too prone to rest the case on our conviction of an inner or autonomous man. We have not effectively uncov-ered the contingencies of reinforcement in order to describe this personal awareness. It is as if, we may say, we hug our privacy to us and refuse to understand it.

Skinner attempts not to deny personal awareness, but rather to affirm that when and if we really come to know it, *what* we know will not be essentially different from external objects. That is, the *what* or content of the knowledge will be that which is observable. In Skinnerian terminology, that content will be knowledge of behavior and contingencies of reinforcement and not the old catchall of a mind, soul, consciousness, or an "inner man."

Skinner's reply to the charges of his critics that he is destroying or abolishing man is that a scientific analysis in no way destroys man, for no theory destroys that about which it is a theory. What is too often destructive is actual human behavior, not a theory. Skinner puts it thus: "What is being abolished is autonomous man—the inner man, the *homunculus*, the possessing demon, the man defended by the literature of freedom and dignity." What is left is the real, observable human organism who is biological and animal. Although Skinner maintains that humans are not machines in the classic sense, he holds that we are machinelike in the sense that we are a complex system behaving in lawful, observable ways. But even if the humans are simply animal and mechanical, Skinner is fascinated by their complexity, their uniqueness and intricacy.

Skinner believes the importance lies in human behavior and how it makes us what we are. Perhaps the most accurate description of Skinner's view is that we are both controller and controlled. Another way of putting it is that, in a very real sense, we are our own makers. It is Skinner's position that we have developed through two processes of evolution; one is the biological process from which we evolved, and the other is the cultural process of evolution that we have largely created. It is perhaps this latter process that is most important and intriguing for Skinner. He points out that our environment today is largely contrived, not natural, and it is an environment we have wrought. This environment contains the significant contingencies of reinforcement that makes us *human*. In this respect we may say that we are our own makers, and while we are doing the making, we are being made or we are in the making.

The Good Society through Cultural Design

There is a paradox involved in Skinner the person. On one hand, he appears to be a hard-nosed scientist, dealing only with factual, observable behavior. On the other, he seems to be the utopian dreamer. Perhaps the best statement of Skinner's utopian ideals is expressed in his work, *Walden Two*, a fictional account of a futuristic social experiment.

In *Beyond Freedom and Dignity*, however, Skinner gives a nonfictional descriptive account of his views. Accordingly, the important thing is the social environment. We may even say that for Skinner, social environment *is* culture. This position is in opposition to those who say that culture is essentially ideas or values apart from human behavior. Basically, behavior carries the ideas and values of a culture, and it transforms, alters, and changes a culture. In a large sense, cultural evolution is an evolution of behavioral practices that are established within a social milieu or a milieu of contingencies of reinforcement. So we may say that in cultural evolution, what actually evolves are practices set in a social context.

Skinner makes a strong case for controlled cultural evolution. In the historical past, we had a confused sort of control, often as not blind and accidental. We did not fully understand the nature of the control or how it could be more effectively used. Skinner maintains that controls are needed to make us more sensitive to the consequences of our behavior. Reinforcement follows behavior: it does not precede it (even though most human behavior is conditioned by previous reinforcement). Behavior develops in directions that are positively reinforced; consequently, we should be controlling, devising, or using contingencies that reinforce desired behaviors. In short, control lies at the crux of sensitivity to the consequences of our behavior.

Skinner admits that we do not really know the *best* way to rear children, to educate effective citizens, or to build the good society, but he does maintain that we can develop *better* ways than we now have. If we want to change culture or individuals, we must change behavior; and the way to change behavior is to change the contingencies, that is, culture or social environment.

What are contingencies of reinforcement? Simply put, contingencies are the conditions in which behavior occurs; they reinforce it and influence the future direction and quality of behavior. For example, we cannot drive an automobile unless an automobile actually exists. The behavior of automobile driving is contingent upon an actual automobile. Furthermore, the manner in which we drive is contingent upon numerous other conditions, such as the functions and capacities of that particular automobile, road and traffic conditions, and a host of other supporting conditions. Finally, driving an automobile does things for us. It gets us to a desired destination, helps us earn a living, increases our range of mobility. What an automobile does for us is rewarding, and our behavior of driving automobiles is reinforced. Some of these conditions serve as particularly strong contingencies. It seems reasonable to say that a great deal of the trouble with the operation of motor vehicles, such as speeding, comes about because of a lack of understanding and control of the contingencies.

Skinner states that contingencies of reinforcement are hard to discern in many instances. For one thing, we are not used to viewing human situations in behavioral terms (or else we fail to recognize the behavioral point of view). For another, our understanding is at least hampered, if not misled, by holding to such notions as autonomous man. We have not developed sensitivity to the *conditions*, the contingencies, in and with which behavior occurs. But Skinner maintains that contingencies *are* accessible (even if difficult), and as we progressively come to understand the relation between behavior and environment, we will discover new ways of controlling behavior. It is possible, as further understanding is developed, to design and control not just isolated behaviors and their contingencies, but a whole culture.

Skinner views the educational process as one of the chief ways of designing a culture, and his attention is also directed at numerous other institutions. He believes that positive reinforcement can induce us to begin to alter and control our schools and other institutions. Man's behavior is shaped in the direction of reward; that is, behavior is reinforced to the extent that its consequences are good or bad. Good consequences are positive reinforcement and bad consequences are negative or aversive reinforcement. A problem arises in that mankind is too often ignorant of long-range consequences. What is immediately positive reinforcement may have negative effects at a later time. We need to examine cultural contingencies critically in light of likely consequences.

The critical analysis of culture is a matter not to be taken lightly. It is easier to proceed on a piecemeal basis because planning and foresight of consequences are simplified. Thus, it is easier to change particular teaching practices than a whole educational establishment, and it is easier to change one institution than a whole culture. For Skinner, the greatest mistake is to stop trying.

The big questions, however, are: What is the good society? How do we get it? Who is to say what is good? Finally, who controls the good society? Such questions as these have been the stumbling blocks to social or cultural recon-struction throughout history. In more recent times, these questions are believed to be outside the realm of science, for as the claim goes, science deals with what is, while questions revolving about a "good society" deal with what ought and ought not to be. Such questions are involved with value judgments and not with matters of fact. This would seem to rule out any part for the behavioral scientist or other scientists.

On the contrary, Skinner expresses his consternation about why value judgments are any more remote from scientists than from any other human beings, and he rejects the claim. He poses this question as a more suitable one: "If a scientific analysis can tell us how to change behavior, can it tell us what changes to make?" To Skinner, this is a question about the behavior of those who advocate and promote changes. In other words, people act to effect changes for reasons, and among these reasons are behavioral consequences. To say we would like a culture in which war-making is absent is to say we would like to eradicate war-making behavior. Whatever the behavioral consequences considered in efforts to effect change, these consequences include things people call good or of value. Thus, we can see that, for Skinner, the good society and values are within the domain of the behavioral scientist precisely because those goods and values are involved in behavior, even based in it and coming out of it.

It seems reasonable to observe that as a behavioral scientist Skinner may be solidly involved with the good and value, but it makes just as much sense to say that he is also behaving like a philosopher and dealing with philosophical issues. Rather than quibble over what label should be applied to Skinner, the central fact is that he does become involved in the areas of the good and value, and these are intricately woven into his views of achieving a better culture or social environment.

What, then, is good and of value from the Skinnerian standpoint? Simply put, to classify something as "good" is to classify it as a positive reinforcer. We say certain foods are "good" because they give us positive reinforcement (they are pleasing, delicious, palatable, healthful, and so forth), and we tend to seek out and eat "good" food. By the same token, some foods are "bad" because they do not taste good, are unhealthful, and are undesirable, so we avoid them. But tastes vary, and what is positively reinforcing to one may be negative to another. This applies in many areas such as things that feel good or bad, look good or bad, sound good or bad, and so on. Skinner calls these goods "personal goods."

There are other goods to be considered, those which Skinner calls "goods of others," and they refer to more social-like behaviors even though they may also flow from personal goods. Most societies have found rampant dishon-esty to be negatively reinforcing. Although the dishonest individual may find it rewarding, measures have been instituted by the social group to control individual behavior to the extent that dishonesty is met with aversive or negative measures, while honesty is praised and rewarded. (Of course, there have been and are some groups where dishonesty is rewarded when it is conducted against an outsider or enemy.)

There is still one further kind of good that Skinner calls "the good of culture." This good induces the members of a culture to work for the survival and enhancement of that culture. Generally, such goods may have dim cultural and genetic roots. We do not always know why we work to support our culture or to change it for what is deemed a better state of affairs. As Skinner points out, we are faced with so many problems of magnitude today that immediate changes are needed for our very survival. We are confronted with nuclear warfare, overpopulation and starvation, and environmental pollution, all of which if allowed to run rampant can mean disaster. Change does not occur simply because of the passage of time, but because of what *occurs* while time passes. Thus, we are thrown back to behavior. All change is not necessarily good and valuable, and neither is behavior. But directed and intended change depends upon behavior aware of its consequences. We may phrase the behavioral context of the goods of culture in this way: If we are reinforced by human survival, and if human survival depends upon the cultural and physical environment in which we exist, then we will work for human survival by designing culture to that end. Skinner seems to say there is little choice. We must act.

What, then, is good? That which is positively reinforcing in terms of the personal, social, and cultural survival contexts. What is of value? That which has desired reinforcing effects. The good society is one that gives personal satisfaction, supports social interaction, and furthers our survival. The good society is valuable, and the way to achieve it is through the proper design of the culture; that is, through the proper arrangement and development of the contingencies of reinforcement.

Skinner maintains we need a sophisticated science and technology of human behavior. Although such a development would be morally neutral and could be misused and abused, he believes that it has a definite survival value. The survival value will not insure against abuse, but he feels survival will go a long way in aiding desirable usage. When we survey the plight of the modern world and the brink on which we totter, we may be strongly inclined to agree with Skinner.

Behaviorism as a Philosophy of Education

The principles of behaviorism and the techniques of behavioral engineering go back at least to Pavlov and Watson, but B. F. Skinner has pioneered their implementation in many fields of contemporary life. Skinner sees behaviorism extending into politics, economics, and other social organizations. He has strongly championed it as a method in education that is more practical and produces greater results than any other method. It is an approach that is growing in popularity and is being used with increasing frequency, particularly in areas of special education and with disadvantaged children.

Aims of Behaviorism

Although many people disapprove of the concept of behavioral engineering, it has increasingly become a part of our educational process. One might even argue that conditioning has always gone on in education, though it has not been labeled as such. Teachers have conditioned students to sit up straight and to be quiet through looks, grades, and physical punishment. When students are emotionally disturbed, conditioning is one way to develop a step-by-step program through rewards (or punishment) so that they are led to achieve complex patterns of behavior. At some institutions for the emotionally disturbed, students can earn tokens and use them to buy things, a drink, playtime, or even time away from the institution. The way a student acquires tokens may be very diverse. He may obtain them for staying in his seat, for doing a certain amount of required work, or for approved social behavior. Critics often state that it is undesirable for children to be extrinsically rewarded for every action, but Skinner responds by saying that extrinsic rewards are necessary when other methods do not work, or do not work as well, though they should be replaced by more intrinsic rewards at a later date.

Behaviorists have a conception of the child as an organism who is already highly programmed before he comes to school. This programming is accomplished by, among other things, parents, peers, siblings, and television. Most of the programming he has received may have been bad programming but he has been receptive to it, and has absorbed a lot of it. For example, Skinner believes that one of the reasons people have trouble making moral decisions is that the programming they have received on morality has been very contradictory.

Skinner would like to replace the erratic and haphazard kind of conditioning that most people receive with something that is systematic and meaningful. First, some kind of agreement must be reached about just what is meaningful and important towards which children ought to be conditioned. This point raises a storm of controversy since it seems to indicate that some people will decide how other people will be conditioned. Skinner maintains that one of our obligations as adults, and particularly as educators, is to make educational decisions and then to use whatever methods we have at our disposal, conditioning being the best, to achieve them. He believes we should try to create a world of brotherhood and justice, and if conditioning can help, it should be used.

We can easily see that the way children are presently being conditioned in school is not satisfactory. Either the teacher does not condition systematically or else reinforcement does not follow immediately. Skinner would like teachers to see that what they are doing generally involves some kind of conditioning; hence, they had best learn how to do it more effectively.

One of the points of contention between Skinner and many other people is that they see education and conditioning as two different things. Education presumably represents a free mind being exposed to ideas that one may look upon critically and accept or not accept, whereas conditioning is seen to represent the implementation of certain specific ideas in the pupil's mind with or without his critical consent. Skinner does not draw any distinction between education and conditioning. He does not feel that the mind is free to begin with. Whatever kinds of critical judgment or acceptance of ideas a student makes are already predicated on ideas with which he has been previously conditioned.

Since so much of our education at present involves rote or memory learning, Skinner feels that mechanical electronic devices also have a very useful part to play. Usually the programs prepared for electronic devices such as teaching machines have been structured in ways that provide for a more systematic learning, and they provide the kinds of immediate reinforcement that Skinner feels is lacking in present-day education. Teaching machines may take very different forms but they are all based on the theory that we should reward the kinds of responses we want, and we should do it immediately.

Behavioral engineering, one might argue, has been based primarily on experiments with laboratory animals. There are some who claim that Skinner's experiments with animals are not applicable to humans and to human educa- tion; but Skinner argues that man is an animal, although more advanced, and the basic difference between man and other animals is one of degree and not of kind.

The primary aim of behavioristic techniques is to change behavior and point it in more desirable directions. The argument is immediately raised as to whether one should go in a special direction. The question is, who decides what changes and what direction. Skinner replies that we are already controlled to a large degree by genetic forces, parental upbringing, schooling, peer groups, the media, the church, and society. He argues that the question of control is not a good one; that is to say, we may feel free and even actually be free relatively speaking, but we are always controlled by something, though we may assist in the kind of control that is exercised over us. Thus, Skinner does away with the concept of innate freedom by saying that man has always been controlled, though we have not always been aware of the control and the direction in which it leads.

One thing primarily wrong with control is not that it has always existed, but that it has been random and without any real direction. We have been controlled by politicians for their own ends and purposes, and by business interests for their own profits, but such controls have been implemented in ways that were directed toward base ends and unfortunately in ways that served for self-negation. Skinner advocates control and thinks that a new society can be shaped through control. This means someone must be in charge to make sure the control is exercised efficiently toward the highest aims we can establish. At the present time we have many kinds of control, but they are directed toward war, consumerism, superstition, and greed. Skinner points out that we have been talking for years about a world directed toward peace, brotherhood, and freedom, and now, for the first time, we have in our hands a method for bringing about such things. Not to use control for such high purposes, he believes, would be immoral.

Skinner is a strong advocate of education, although many critics argue that what he means by education is not education but "training." Skinner charges that much of what passes for education is not good education because it is not reinforcing, it does not properly motivate students to progress and does not deal with immediate reinforcement. When a child takes a spelling test, for example, he is very interested in knowing what responses are right or wrong at the time of the test. When the test is returned to him a week later he has usually lost interest. Skinner maintains that the child should know immediately when he is right or wrong, and this is why he has championed such methods of immediate reinforcement as programmed learning and teaching machines.

Although many behaviorists use positive and negative methods of rein-forcing behavior, Skinner advocates positive reinforcement. Aversive (or nega-tive) reinforcement, although it may be effective, often has many bad side effects. The same results can be achieved through rewarding good behavior rather than punishing bad behavior. For example, in experiments to train pigeons to perform certain activities, the pigeons are rewarded with food when they pick the proper square. To discontinue such behavior, it is simply a matter of stopping the reward. The behavior may continue for a short time after it is no longer rewarded, but eventually it will cease. Some behaviorists would punish the pigeon with shocks or similar devices, but Skinner maintains that the most effective procedure is to withdraw reward. It could be argued that depriving the organism of reward for a particular task is punishment, but in most situations Skinner would not agree; it is simply a matter of ceasing to reward a specific behavior.

Many people argue that the aim of behavioral engineering is to turn out robots, people who are at the beck and call of others who control them. Skinner counters that this is not true, for when we look around at our present world we find that most people are controlled by forces of which they are unconscious. He believes that we live in a world where advanced technology in conditioning can be used to improve human life if we use it in the right way. In *Walden Two*, we are shown a world where technology is used to make people better, more humane, creative, and even more individualistic. Skinner does not believe that individual-ity can exist apart from social development. The title *Walden Two* seems to indicate that Waldens such as Thoreau's are somewhat romantic in nature and impractical in today's world. Skinner is attempting to show us what technology can do when it is used wisely.

It is interesting to note in *Walden Two* that the only unhappy person is Frazier, who is the conditioner of others. He is aware that he is in control, and whatever decisions he makes involve numerous conflicts. Skinner points out that one who is conditioned may not assent to or be aware that he or she is conditioned. We are all conditioned anyway, and we could even assist in our own conditioning. We do this when we reward ourselves for doing something right and punish ourselves for doing something wrong. The development of personal habits depends to a large extent on conditioning techniques that we our-selves use.

Methods of Behaviorism

According to the behaviorist, the teacher has a great many rewards or rein-forcers at his disposal: praise, a smile, a touch, stars, M & Ms or what have you.

In some schools, paper money or tokens are used as reinforcing mechanisms. Many people have questioned the use of such extrinsic rewards, but behavior-ists claim they are only to be used in place of intrinsic ones that should be encouraged later. Studies indicate that rewards need not be given every time, for they can also be effective on an intermittent basis. One example might be a situation where a child would be called upon three successive times to answer spelling words but then would not be called upon again. We see the child raise his hand to answer the first question, and he answers it correctly. He does the same for the second spelling word, and the third. However, he is not to be called on again. He may continue to raise his hand several times even though he is not being called upon. If we called upon him only occasionally, we could probably get as strong a response as if we called upon him every time.

One might briefly describe a procedure for behavior modification in the ordinary classroom as follows: (1) specify the desired outcome, what needs to be changed, and how it will be evaluated; (2) establish a favorable environment by removing unfavorable stimuli that might complicate learning; (3) choose the proper reinforcers for desired behavioral manifestations; (4) begin shaping desired behavior by using immediate reinforcers for desired behavior; (5) once a pattern of desired behaviors has been begun, slacken the number of times reinforcers are given; (6) evaluate results and reassess for future development.

Suppose, for example, a teacher has a problem with a student who constantly runs in the hallways, endangering other students and himself. For safety reasons, the teacher wants to modify the behavior so that running ceases, and the objective will be evaluated successfully when the student stops running. Investigation shows that the student runs in part because he must go all the way to the other end of the building for his next class and fears that the time span for class change is too short. Also, he seems to like to run. The teacher works to get the student's class time shortened so he can be excused early. He begins to compliment the student when he does not run, and the students' classmates are less negative toward him because he is not constantly bumping and jostling them in the hall. Because the student gets more positive reinforcement from his peers, the teacher finds it less necessary to compliment him. In addition, the student finds that he can make it to class on time if he does not dawdle, even without extra time. Finally, because he now finds walking more rewarding than running, extrinsic reinforcers are no longer needed or can be reduced. Evaluation by the teacher shows that the desired behavior has been fairly well achieved and that it may eventually be possible to stop all external reinforcers completely for the student's running problem. This does not mean that the teacher loses interest in the problem, for he or she may check periodically to see if the student's desired behavior is being continued. One might also observe that this approach has reinforced the teacher's behavior. The positive success reinforces the teacher to use this technique in similar instances.

Skinner thinks that one of the most effective kinds of instruction may be done through the use of teaching machines. He is often referred to as the "father of the teaching machine" and has done significant research in this area. In one type of machine, there is a question area that may ask, for example, "Who was the first president of our country?" There is a place for the student to write in his answer, and his answer appears under a glass case at the top of the machine when he pushes a button. The student can then check his answer against the machine and if he is correct he is rewarded by the machine that reinforces him to remember the answer. The series of questions in a teaching machine are related to each other and are usually arranged in sequences of increasing complexity. Skinner thinks learning should take place in small steps and succeeding ques- tions should have some relationship to the preceding ones. He prefers a student to have nothing but success. He should simply go on if he misses a question or two. If he misses too many questions then he probably does not belong on that particular program. Some of the early teaching machines rewarded the child with candy or spoke to him, but recent studies indicate that getting the right answer is often reward enough.

Other more sophisticated teaching machines are designed primarily for adults. One machine has a large amount of material on microfilm that the student must read. After reading the material, the student is asked to choose one of several possible answers. If he presses the correct answer he goes on to the next frame. If he presses the wrong answer, however, there are two contrast- ing views about what should happen. Skinner thinks that to make the student repeat the materials is too much punishment, and if he misses the answer the machine should still go on to the next frame. Other behaviorists, such as S. J. Pressey, maintain that repeating the material is not too much punishment and that the student should get the right answer before the machine moves to the next frame. This process is made as painless as possible in some machines, and if the student presses the wrong button, the machine will go to a frame that tells him why he selected the wrong answer and then refer him back to reread the material.

Some teaching machines are also "branching" machines; that is, they contain material for average, slow, and bright students. If a student completes exercises one through ten without making a mistake, the machine may have him jump the next ten lessons because they are repetitious. If a student makes a single mistake, he will have to do the next ten, and if he makes two mistakes, he may be referred to a remedial program before he can begin at lesson one again.

According to the behaviorists, the advantages of machine learning are many: immediate reinforcement is given, the programmed material is written by competent people, and the learning takes place in many small steps so that the student can avoid making mistakes. One major objection to the teaching machine is that while it might be very good in teaching factual material, it cannot teach material of a more conceptual or creative nature. Skinner disputes this and claims that we can develop programs to teach very complicated ideas as well as create machines that provide reinforcement every time the child gives what is considered a more creative answer.

Behavioral engineering has many implications for modern education and raises many important philosophical questions regarding control and demo- cratic procedures. Its increasing application and apparent effectiveness, how- ever, may make it a vital force in the educational process. Nothing seems to bring out more ire among educators than a discussion of behavioral engineering as applied to education. Skinner has always been interested in education, has written about it, spoken to educational groups, and has done pioneering work in the field. In one interview, he remarked that he had planned to put more about education in *Walden Two* but had misplaced the section he had written on it. Skinner's views about education must be seen as an integral part of his overall views concerning man and society. Basically, he believes that education must be seen not simply as giving people information, but as a controlling power over the lives of people. Many have related Skinner's ideas to those of Aldous Huxley (*Brave New World*) and George Orwell (*1984*), and although Skinner maintains that his ideas about conditioning are different and more humanitarian, he would not deny that the forces for control as discussed by Huxley and Orwell are in existence. We might even be inclined to think, if we observe modern life closely, that many of the things discussed by Huxley and Orwell have been in existence for some time. Some of the things in *1984*, such as video to watch people's daily lives, have been used in industry, education, and government. Skinner is not so much opposed to the controls that have been developed or proposed, as to the misuse of them.

Today, we can see wide varieties of behavioral techniques already in use. All these methods rest essentially on a particular theory: we first determine the kind of behavior we want, and then we get it repeated by reinforcing it through various rewards. In classroom situations, the same process may be employed by using praise or with tangible rewards such as candy or tokens. Some educators seriously question the use of such rewards, but behavioral engineers argue that they are to be used sparingly and only to the point where the student learns to reward himself without outside tangible rewards. One finds, for example, a number of tangible rewards used with special education students where children are rewarded for staying in their seats for a certain time or doing a particular amount of work. Carl Bereiter and Siegfried Engelmann have used behavioral techniques with disadvantaged students who supposedly have poor learning abilities. Other psychologists have used such techniques for purposes ranging from toilet training to piloting aircraft.

The essential thing about any of these techniques, however, is that whatever reward is used should be systematic and immediate. Skinner and others believe that a primary problem with most education at present is a definite lack of immediate reinforcement.

Critique of Behaviorism in Education

Interest in the use of behavioral engineering has been steadily increasing in many walks of life. Business, churches, the military, and schools have felt its impact, and it is becoming more and more prevalent to assess growth in these areas by their success with behavioral techniques. Probably the most outstanding feature of this approach is that it is "scientific." It is based on a great deal of research, and researchers can point to measurable success using this method. It has been increasingly used in education since the 1960s, and many educators are zealous supporters of behavioral techniques that they are using in their classrooms. In areas such as special education teachers find the concept of immediate rein-forcement particularly useful in controlling and directing children with motor and mental handicaps. Even within the ordinary classroom, however, one hears about M & Ms, a token economy, and positive and·negative reinforcements as effective aids in the educational process. Even Skinner's air crib, designed as a behavior-reinforcing mechanism for the early life of the child, has been used by some parents in an effort to influence child behavior at the earliest stages of life. Behaviorism's popularity has arisen because its techniques seem to work when so many other approaches fail. Furthermore, the approach used by many behavioral engineers, Skinner in particular, tries to avoid any aversive methods of education, and this fact appeals to many modern educators. Children also seem to respond well to a method that provides both incentives and rewards for their achievements. Teaching machines are popular with some teachers and students and are effective and efficient ways of imparting knowledge in a given area, with the range of areas steadily increasing.

Not only do behavioral engineers suggest the use of their methods in education but in social life as well. Skinner, for example, has taken the possibili-ties of his theories into the area of social and cultural reform. He sees behavioral engineering applicable on a global scale, maintaining that it is possible to solve problems of hunger, warfare, and economic upheaval if we will do so through the development of a technology of behavior. Many people scoff at Skinner's recommendations and launch vitriolic attacks on his theories, particularly where he holds that man has no inherent freedom and dignity. They say that if his suggestions are followed, Orwell's 1984 will be a certainty. Skinner replies that his theory is perhaps the only hope for survival in our technologically complex age. We have come to the point where we can no longer afford the old luxuries of self-centeredness, violence as a way of life, the wealth of a few at the expense of the many, and the old philosophical and theological notions about man's inner makeup that support these old luxuries. Freedom and dignity in the old sense are emotive ideas that generate strong support, but Skinner maintains that these ideas are too often used for hiding a multitude of sins. Aggressiveness, for example, is often said to be a part of man's inner makeup and nothing can be done about it because "you can't change human nature." To Skinner, such easy escapes and superficial assumptions are regrettable. The net result is to give up before we begin because aggressiveness is a learned behavior and can be unlearned or extinguished if we take an intelligent approach in controlling it.

Many critics charge that Skinner's theories belittle and limit man, but there is a strong argument that his views are optimistic, holding the promise that man can become practically anything through proper behavioral engineering. From the Skinnerian standpoint, there is little in man's inner makeup that limits development in a variety of creative ways. For these reasons, the Skinnerians maintain it is possible to build the good society with good people in the foresee-able future if we have the fortitude to plan and cooperate in this venture. When all is said and done, the controls will be on the environment, on the contingencies of reinforcement, and in this way man is indirectly controlled. While some critics see Skinner's *Walden Two* as the kind of brave new world Huxley wrote about, Skinner maintains that it is an idealization of the behaviorally engineered society where happiness and good will prevail.

Behavioral techniques have been found to be highly successful in the laboratory, but legitimate questions may be raised about their applicability to human society where so many variables and unknowns exist. In the laboratory it is possible to maintain rigorous control, but control is extremely difficult in the rough and tumble out-of-doors world. Behaviorists are probably on soundest grounds when they are dealing with the step-by-step procedures of learning. It is certainly reasonable to construct a theory that ignores or discounts man's inner nature because it may open up new insights into the study of man. It may work and work beautifully, but this still does not mean that there may not be innate capacities or characteristics in man that are being overlooked. Skinner has said that "no theory destroys what it is a theory about," and this is an idea that cuts both ways. To say that man has no inner freedom and dignity does not destroy such inner freedom and dignity if in fact they do exist.

While behaviorists make some questionable assumptions about man, they also make them about the nature of the universe. One assumption under- girding much of their thinking is that the universe operates in mechanistic terms. They view the scheme of things as orderly, regular, predictable, and hence, controllable. Serious questions have been raised as to whether the universe operates this way or whether behaviorists impose this notion of order upon the inscrutable face of the universe. This penchant for order and regularity is most noticeable in behaviorists' efforts to develop a technology of behavior patterns. They may be trying to make an exacting approach out of something based on highly questionable assumptions. This drive for exactness seems to be modeled after the physical sciences, but there are those knowledgeable in the physical sciences who maintain that exactness is much overrated even there. In other words, behaviorists may be constructing their theory on the shifting sands of the quest for certainty.

Perhaps one of the most glaring weaknesses critics point to is the social policy recommendations of behaviorists such as Skinner. They may be on very sound ground when they are describing how learning takes place or how behavior is altered in small, sequential steps in the laboratory or classroom. But when they take the quantum leap from the laboratory to broad social, political, and economic conditions, critics begin to flinch. Skinner recommends a group of planners and controllers for the reshaping of man and society. There does not seem to be sufficient and systematic work to back up such a recommendation. The controllers sound very much like the psychologist in the laboratory, but again there is much difference between the laboratory and society at large. History is replete with examples of individuals and groups who thought that they and only they could lead society in the proper direction. History is also replete with the disasters and ill effects of such thinking. In so many respects, there seems to be little difference between deriving the powers of government from divine authority, the laws of dialectical materialism, or the laws of behavior.

One recurring question is, "Who controls the controllers?" Skinner maintains that the controlled exert influence over the controllers, just as the behavior of school children affects the teacher's behavior. In other words, the directions of the behavior of the controlled sets the conditions to which the controllers react. This seems to be a very weak argument because the initiative is loaded in favor of the controllers who have social, political, intellectual, and economic power concentrated in their hands. It seems to be very predictable that the powerless ones of the Skinnerian society will be just as manipulated (even if "for their own good") as in any other authoritarian structure.

Although Skinner and other behaviorists strongly maintain that their aims and methods are not ones that belittle us or eclipse inner feelings and purposes, the charge that their programs result in a robotization of man has some basis. From the point of view of some critics, behaviorists seem to ignore what is truly human in favor of a new view of human nature that is more mechanistic in scope. Frazier, the character Skinner depicts as the founder of *Walden Two*, says he is the only unhappy one in the controlled society because he is the only one who was not reared there. If we were to give most people the option of being Frazier with all his frustrations, hopes, and fears versus the new engineered man of *Walden Two* with all his blissful ignorance of the controls exerted on him, it seems that many people would choose the former.

Skinner

Beyond Freedom and Dignity

Skinner is the most important behaviorist living today. Following the leads of Pavlov and Watson, he constructed a science of behavior based on operant conditioning. While much of his work has been based on laboratory experiments, he has also discussed the social and political consequences of his theory. In the following selection, Skinner argues against traditional notions of freedom and dignity of the human being, views that are often supported by various philosophies.* He claims that such notions can be socially harmful, particularly the notions of permissiveness championed by some philosophical and educational schools of thought. At the same time, his rejection of permissiveness does not imply resort to punishment; instead, he argues for control based on the principles of a technology of behavior.

Those who champion freedom and dignity do not, of course, confine themselves to punitive measures, but they turn to alternatives with diffidence and timidity. Their concern for autonomous man commits them to only ineffective measures, several of which we may now examine. . . .

A method of modifying behavior without appearing to exert control is represented by Socrates' metaphor of the midwife: one person helps another give birth to behavior. Since the midwife plays no part in conception and only a small part in parturition, the person who gives birth to the behavior may take full credit for it. Socrates demonstrated the art of midwifery, or maieutics, in education. He pretended to show how an uneducated slave boy could be led to prove Pythagoras' theorem for doubling the square. The boy assented to the steps in the proof, and Socrates claimed that he did so without being told—in other words, that he "knew" the theo-

rem in some sense all along. Socrates contended that even ordinary knowledge could be drawn out in the same way since the soul knew the truth and needed only to be shown that it knew it. The episode is often cited as if it were relevant to modern educational practice. . . .

Intellectual, therapeutic, and moral midwifery is scarcely easier than punitive control, because it demands rather subtle skills and concentrated attention, but it has its advantages. It seems to confer a strange power on the practitioner. Like the cabalistic use of hints and allusions, it achieves results seemingly out of proportion to the measures employed. The apparent contribution of the individual is not reduced, however. He is given full credit for knowing before he learns, for having within him the seeds of good mental health, and for being able to enter into direct communication with God. An important advantage is that the practitioner avoids re-

---

*Selection from B. F. Skinner, *Beyond Freedom and Dignity* (New York: Alfred A. Knopf, 1971), pp. 83–97, 99–100.

sponsibility. Just as it is not the midwife's fault if the baby is stillborn or deformed, so the teacher is exonerated when the student fails, the psychotherapist when the patient does not solve his problem, and the mystical religious leader when his disciples behave badly.

Maieutic practices have their place. Just how much help the teacher should give the student as he acquires new forms of behavior is a delicate question. The teacher should wait for the student to respond rather than rush to tell him what he is to do or say. As Comenius put it, the more the teacher teaches, the less the student learns. The student gains in other ways. In general, we do not like to be told either what we already know or what we are unlikely ever to know well or to good effect. We do not read books if we are already thoroughly familiar with the material or if it is so completely unfamiliar that it is likely to remain so. We read books which help us say things we are on the verge of saying anyway but cannot quite say without help. We understand the author, although we could not have formulated what we understand before he put it into words. There are similar advantages for the patient in psychotherapy. Maieutic practices are helpful, too, because they exert more control than is usually acknowledged and some of it may be valuable.

These advantages, however, are far short of the claims made. Socrates' slave boy learned nothing; there was no evidence whatever that he could have gone through the theorem by himself afterward. And it is as true of maieutics as of permissiveness that positive results must be credited to unacknowledged controls of other sorts. If the patient finds a solution without the help of his therapist, it is because he has been exposed to a helpful environment elsewhere.

Another metaphor associated with weak practices is horticultural. The behavior to which a person has given birth grows, and it may be guided or trained, as a growing plant is trained. Behavior may be "cultivated."

The metaphor is particularly at home in education. A school for small children is a child-garden, or kindergarten. The behavior of the child "develops" until he reaches "maturity." A teacher may accelerate the process or turn it in slightly different directions, but—in the classical phrase—he cannot teach, he can only help the student learn. The metaphor of guidance is also common in psychotherapy. Freud argued that a person must pass through several developmental stages, and that if the patient has become "fixated" at a given stage, the therapist must help him break loose and move forward. Governments engage in guidance—for example, when they encourage the "development" of industry through tax exemptions or provide a "climate" that is favorable to the improvement of race relations.

Guidance is not as easy as permissiveness, but it is usually easier than midwifery, and it has some of the same advantages. One who merely guides a natural development cannot easily be accused of trying to control it. Growth remains an achievement of the individual, testifying to his freedom and worth, his "hidden propensities," and as the gardener is not responsible for the ultimate form of what he grows, so one who merely guides is exonerated when things go wrong.

Guidance is effective, however, only to the extent that control is exerted. To guide is either to open new opportunities or to block growth in particular directions. To arrange an opportunity is not a very positive act, but it is nevertheless a form of control if it increases the likelihood that behavior will be emitted. The teacher who merely selects the material the student is to study or the therapist who merely suggests a different job or change of scene has exerted control, though it may be hard to detect.

Control is more obvious when growth or development is *prevented.* Censorship blocks access to material needed for development in a given direction; it closes opportunities. De Tocqueville saw this in the America of his day: "The will of man is not shattered, but softened, bent, and guided. Men are seldom forced . . . to act, but they are constantly restrained from acting." As Ralph Barton Perry put it, "Whoever determines what alternatives shall be made known to man controls what that man shall choose *from.* He is deprived of freedom in proportion as he is denied access to *any* ideas, or is confined to any range of ideas short of the totality of relevant possibilities." For "deprived of freedom" read "controlled."

It is no doubt valuable to create an environment in which a person acquires effective behavior rapidly and continues to behave effectively. In constructing such an environment we may eliminate distractions and open opportunities, and these are key points in the metaphor of guidance or growth or development; but it is the contingencies we arrange, rather than the unfolding of some predetermined pattern, which are responsible for the changes observed.

Jean-Jacques Rousseau was alert to the dangers of social control, and he thought it might be possible to avoid them by making a person dependent not on people but on things. In *Emile* he showed how a child could learn about

things from the things themselves rather than from books. The practices he described are still common, largely because of John Dewey's emphasis on real life in the classroom.

One of the advantages in being dependent on things rather than on other people is that the time and energy of other people are saved. The child who must be reminded that it is time to go to school is dependent upon his parents, but the child who has learned to respond to clocks and other temporal properties of the world around him (not to a "sense of time") is dependent upon things, and he makes fewer demands on his parents. . . .

Another important advantage of being dependent on things is that the contingencies which involve things are more precise and shape more useful behavior than contingencies arranged by other people. The temporal properties of the environment are more pervasive and more subtle than any series of reminders. A person whose behavior in driving a car is shaped by the response of the car behaves more skillfully than one who is following instructions. . . .

But things do not easily take control. The procedures Rousseau described were not simple, and they do not often work. The complex contingencies involving things (including people who are behaving "unintentionally") can, unaided, have very little effect on an individual in his lifetime—a fact of great importance for reasons we shall note later. We must also remember that the control exercised by things may be destructive. The world of things can be tyrannical. Natural contingencies induce people to behave superstitiously, to risk greater and greater dangers, to work uselessly to exhaustion, and so on. Only the countercontrol exerted by

a social environment offers any protection against these consequences.

Dependence on things is not independence. The child who does not need
to be told that it is time to go to school
has come under the control of more
subtle, and more useful, stimuli. The
child who has learned what to say and
how to behave in getting along with
other people is under the control of
social contingencies. People who get
along together well under the mild contingencies of approval and disapproval
are controlled as effectively as (and in
many ways more effectively than) the
citizens of a police state. Orthodoxy
controls through the establishment of
rules, but the mystic is no freer because
the contingencies which have shaped
his behavior are more personal or idio-
syncratic. Those who work produc-
tively because of the reinforcing value of
what they produce are under the sensitive and powerful control of the products. Those who learn in the natural
environment are under a form of control as powerful as any control exerted
by a teacher.

A person never becomes truly self-
reliant. Even though he deals effectively
with things, he is necessarily dependent
upon those who have taught him to do
so. They have selected the things he is
dependent upon and determined the
kinds and degrees of dependencies.
(They cannot, therefore, disclaim responsibility for the results.)

It is a surprising fact that those who
object most violently to the manipulation of behavior nevertheless make the
most vigorous efforts to manipulate
minds. Evidently freedom and dignity
are threatened only when behavior is
changed by physically changing the environment. There appears to be no
threat when the states of mind said to be
responsible for behavior are changed,
presumably because autonomous man
possesses miraculous powers which enable him to yield or resist. . . .

Beliefs, preferences, perceptions,
needs, purposes, and opinions are other
possessions of autonomous man which
are said to change when we change
minds. What is changed in each case is a
probability of action. A person's belief
that a floor will hold him as he walks
across it depends upon his past experience. If he has walked across it without incident many times, he will do so
again readily, and his behavior will not
create any of the aversive stimuli felt as
anxiety. He may report that he has
"faith" in the solidity of the floor or "confidence" that it will hold him, but the
kinds of things which are felt as faith or
confidence are not states of mind; they
are at best by-products of the behavior
in its relation to antecedent events, and
they do not explain why a person walks
as he does.

We build "belief" when we increase
the probability of action by reinforcing
behavior. When we build a person's
confidence that a floor will hold him by
inducing him to walk on it, we might not
be said to be changing a belief, but we
do so in the traditional sense when we
give him verbal assurances that the
floor is solid, demonstrate its solidity by
walking on it ourselves, or describe its
structure or state. The only difference is
in the conspicuousness of the measures. The change which occurs as a
person "learns to trust a floor" by walking on it is the characteristic effect of
reinforcement; the change which occurs
when he is told that the floor is solid,
when he sees someone else walking on
it, or when he is "convinced" by assurances that the floor will hold him depends upon past experiences which no

longer make a conspicuous contribution. For example, a person who walks on surfaces which are likely to vary in their solidity (for example, a frozen lake) quickly forms a discrimination between surfaces on which others are walking and surfaces on which no one is walking, or between surfaces called safe and surfaces called dangerous. He learns to walk confidently on the first and cautiously on the second. The sight of someone walking on a surface or an assurance that it is safe converts it from the second class into the first. The history during which the discrimination was formed may be forgotten, and the effect then seems to involve that inner event called a change of mind.

Changes in preference, perceptions, needs, purposes, attitudes, opinions, and other attributes of mind may be analyzed in the same way. We change the way a person looks at something, as well as what he sees when he looks, by changing the contingencies; we do not change something called perception. We change the relative strengths of responses by differential reinforcement of alternative courses of action; we do not change something called a preference. We change the probability of an act by changing a condition of deprivation or aversive stimulation; we do not change a need. We reinforce behavior in particular ways; we do not give a person a purpose or an intention. We change behavior toward something, not an attitude toward it. We sample and change verbal behavior, not opinions.

Another way to change a mind is to point to reasons why a person should behave in a given way, and the reasons are almost always consequences which are likely to be contingent on behavior. Let us say that a child is using a knife in a dangerous way. We may avoid trouble by making the environment safer—by taking the knife away or giving him a safer kind—but that will not prepare him for a world with unsafe knives. Left alone, he may learn to use the knife properly by cutting himself whenever he uses it improperly. We may help by substituting a less dangerous form of punishment—spanking him, for example, or perhaps merely shaming him when we find him using a knife in a dangerous way. We may tell him that some uses are bad and others good if "Bad!" and "Good!" have already been conditioned as positive and negative reinforcers. Suppose, however, that all these methods have unwanted by-products, such as a change in his relation to us, and that we therefore decide to appeal to "reason." (This is possible, of course, only if he has reached the "age of reason.") We explain the contingencies, demonstrating what happens when one uses a knife in one way and not another. We may show him how rules may be extracted from the contingencies ("You should never cut *toward yourself*"). As a result we may induce the child to use the knife properly and will be likely to say that we have imparted a knowledge of its proper use. But we have had to take advantage of a great deal of prior conditioning with respect to instructions, directions, and other verbal stimuli, which are easily overlooked, and their contribution may then be attributed to autonomous man. A still more complex form of argument has to do with deriving new reasons from old, the process of deduction which depends upon a much longer verbal history and is particularly likely to be called changing a mind.

Ways of changing behavior by changing minds are seldom condoned when they are clearly effective, even though it is still a mind which is apparently being changed. We do not condone the changing of minds when the contestants are unevenly matched; that is "undue influence." Nor do we condone changing minds surreptitiously. If a person cannot see what the would-be changer of minds is doing, he cannot escape or counterattack; he is being exposed to "propaganda." "Brainwashing" is proscribed by those who otherwise condone the changing of minds simply because the control is obvious. A common technique is to build up a strong aversive condition, such as hunger or lack of sleep and, by alleviating it, to reinforce any behavior which "shows a positive attitude" toward a political or religious system. A favorable "opinion" is built up simply by reinforcing favorable statements. The procedure may not be obvious to those upon whom it is used, but it is too obvious to others to be accepted as an allowable way of changing minds.

The illusion that freedom and dignity are respected when control seems incomplete arises in part from the probabilistic nature of operant behavior. Seldom does any environmental condition "elicit" behavior in the all-or-nothing fashion of a reflex; it simply makes a bit of behavior more likely to occur. A hint will not itself suffice to evoke a response, but it adds strength to a weak response which may then appear. The hint is conspicuous, but the other events responsible for the appearance of the response are not.

Like permissiveness, maieutics, guidance, and building a dependence on things, changing a mind is condoned by the defenders of freedom and dignity because it is an ineffective way of changing behavior, and the changer of minds can therefore escape from the charge that he is controlling people. He is also exonerated when things go wrong. Autonomous man survives to be credited with his achievements and blamed for his mistakes. . . .

The freedom and dignity of autonomous man seem to be preserved when only weak forms of nonaversive control are used. Those who use them seem to defend themselves against the charge that they are attempting to control behavior, and they are exonerated when things go wrong. Permissiveness is the absence of control, and if it appears to lead to desirable results, it is only because of other contingencies. Maieutics, or the art of midwifery, seems to leave behavior to be credited to those who give birth to it, and the guidance of development to those who develop. Human intervention seems to be minimized when a person is made dependent upon things rather than upon other people. Various ways of changing behavior by changing minds are not only condoned but vigorously practiced by the defenders of freedom and dignity. There is a good deal to be said for minimizing current control by other people, but other measures still operate. A person who responds in acceptable ways to weak forms of control may have been changed by contingencies which are no longer operative. By refusing to recognize them the defenders of freedom and dignity encourage the misuse of controlling practices and block progress toward a more effective technology of behavior.

Selected Readings

Bereiter, C., and Engleman, S. *Teaching Disadvantaged Children in the Preschool.* Englewood Cliffs, N.J.: Prentice-Hall, 1966.

This is a well-known attempt to develop behavioral techniques for use in preschool settings with disadvantaged children. While not basically philosophical in scope, the book shows how aspects of behaviorism can be applied to education.

Pavlov, I. P. *Conditioned Reflexes.* London: Oxford University Press, 1927.

Pavlov's work is a classical study of conditioning that has had great influence on the historical development of behaviorism.

Skinner, B. F. *Beyond Freedom and Dignity.* New York: Knopf, 1971.

This book attacks the notion that freedom or dignity in its present forms are inherent or necessary for human fulfillment. It is a comprehensive exposition of the implications of Skinner's theories for man and society.

_____. *Walden Two.* New York: Macmillan, 1948.

Skinner presents a picture of what behavioral engineering might be like in communal form. It is a fictional treatise that has attracted a wide audience of readers from scientists to utopian-minded thinkers.

Thoresen, Carl E., ed. *Behavior Modification in Education.* The Seventy-Second Yearbook of the National Society for the Study of Education, Part One. Chicago: The National Society for the Study of Education, 1973.

This volume is a very readable collection of scholarly essays that offer critical analyses of behavior modification. They range from techniques of classroom teaching to a philosophical study of behaviorism.

ANALYTIC PHILOSOPHY

One of the more recent developments in philosophy is called the "analytic move-ment." Analytic philosophy is not a systematic philosophy as is idealism, realism, or pragmatism. Indeed, most analytic philosophers take pains to repudiate iden-tity with a systematic philosophy, for they say that the system approach in philosophy has brought more problems than solutions to human affairs. For the most part, analytic philosophers seek to clarify the language, concepts, and methods we use in the more precise activities of life, such as science. Analytic efforts at clarification also have been extended into less defined kinds of activity such as education.

Clarification is the one simple unifying theme in analytic philosophy. The underlying assumption of the analysts is that most philosophical problems of the past were not really problems concerning ultimate reality or truth, goodness, and beauty, but problems located in confused language, warped or unclear meanings, and conceptual confusion. Genuine knowledge, most analysts claim, is the business of science, not philosophy. The true role of philosophy is critical clarification.

There are several kinds of approaches within the general movement of analytic philosophy, and the general movement itself has undergone a somewhat puzzling historical evolution. Basically, philosophical analysis has always gone on. Socrates was analyzing when he investigated the meaning of justice. But the modern movement of analytic philosophy has its more immediate roots in several recent philosophical developments. To try to fit these developments into any one mold is to alter the actual facts of the situation: consequently, what follows may at times appear connected and at other times disconnected. This, however, only reflects what has occurred and is still occurring in the analytic movement.

The first part of this chapter will attempt to show the evolution of analytic philosophy from the late nineteenth and early twentieth century to the present, and the second part is concerned with the way that philosophical analysis has been applied to educational theory and philosophy of education.

Moore
(1873-1958)

Russell
(1872-1970)

Wittgenstein
(1889-1951)

Ayer
(1910-   )

Peters
(1919-   )

Ryle
(1900-1976)

7

ANALYTIC PHILOSOPHY AND EDUCATION

The Analytic Movement in Philosophy

The analytic movement has undergone an evolution stemming in part from the influence of contemporary realism as it was being shaped at the turn of the century by G. E. Moore and Bertrand Russell. Furthermore, analysis largely has been developed in the Anglo-American cultural context, although several of its exponents, primarily of Germanic-Austrian origin, came from Continental Europe. This latter aspect, however, was to have its impact mainly in Britain and the United States, for the Germanic-Austrian figures came to these two countries as they found Naziism repulsive and Continental social conditions restrictive. A second influence that came from the Continent and finally merged for the most part with the Anglo-American analytic movement was logical positivism. This was a philosophical school of thought originally identified with a group of philosophers known as the "Vienna Circle."

219

More recently, the analytic movement, comprised of persons of many stripes, including many formerly associated with logical positivism, has often been identified with the name "linguistic analysis," and most of its advocates were greatly influenced by Ludwig Wittgenstein.

This part of the chapter will explore the roots of analysis in realism, as represented by Moore and Russell; the impact of logical positivism on analysis, as represented by A. J. Ayer; and its evolution into linguistic and conceptual analysis, as represented by the later writings of Ludwig Wittgenstein and the work of Gilbert Ryle.

Realism and the Early Analytic Movement

It should not be assumed that realism is the parent of the analytic movement, but there is, nonetheless, a strong family resemblance. By the same token, it would not be accurate to say that G. E. Moore and Bertrand Russell invented the analytic movement, for there were contemporaries equally capable, aware, and involved in this movement, but Moore and Russell stand as perhaps the most representative of the new train of thought.

George Edward Moore (1873–1958). Moore, an Englishman, was instrumental in the development of twentieth-century realism and one of its outgrowths, philosophical analysis. He exerted quite a bit of influence on Bertrand Russell and is often credited with heading Russell toward a realist orientation when Russell had become infatuated with Hegelian idealism. Moore and Russell became good friends and philosophical colleagues, but gradually a difference emerged. Moore's realism went in the direction of common sense and ordinary language while Russell's went toward science, mathematics, and formal language.

A Defense of Common Sense is one of Moore's better known works. Primarily, he was interested in the things we say in ordinary life. He believed that most common sense things are true and that we know what we are talking about in ordinary, common sense language. Many philosophers, on the other hand, had made a career out of disputing common sense. However, in both ordinary language and in philosophy, there are many statements that can neither be proven nor disproven, and Moore saw as his task not the discovery of the truth or falsity of the propositions of ordinary language and philosophy, but an analysis of the meaning of propositions. By analysis, he thought the way would be cleared toward a better understanding of the truth and propriety of what we say and write.

Moore's investigations went primarily into ordinary language because he felt that there were better reasons for accepting it than philosophical propositions. For one thing, ordinary language deals with the common sense, everyday world. Its statements and propositions are about commonly encountered matters of fact and real-life experiences. Ordinary language and common sense deal with the real, and have done so over the centuries, withstanding the test of time. Moore sought to analyze commonly used terms such as "good," "know," and "real." We all know what these words mean when we use them in ordinary, common sense language. In simple terms, it could be said that Moore believed we have a concept of "good" already in mind before we use it, but knowing the meaning (or having the concept) and analyzing the meaning are two different things. Analysis of the meaning would help us clarify the propriety of the meaning, or we might say, its "goodness of fit."

This illustrates the value of Moore's philosophical task: how often are we thrown into all kinds of difficulties and troubles because of our confusion over meaning? Many, if not most, of the problems of the modern world are due to misunderstanding and confusion over ideological positions, political beliefs, and so forth, all of which depend heavily on key word meanings and concepts. Moore sought to analyze the meanings of key words so as to shed light on the nature of the confusion. Consequently, he became very much involved in ethical meanings, and in one of his most important books, *Principia Ethica*, he analyzed the various meanings we have in mind when we use the word "good."

Let us explore this further in light of the above statement about ideological and political confusion. It is probably safe to assume that most serious-minded political theories incorporate notions or concepts about what is good. It is often the case, however, that what one theory holds to be good is quite different from what another theory may hold. Take, for example, economic considerations in political theories. Marxist theory believes that collective ownership of the means of production results in certain desirable ends or goods. Other political theories maintain that private ownership is one of the supreme goods. In other instances, a political theory may contain internal inconsistencies and even contradictions about what is good. It may be said that a great deal of human strife exists in the world today from such confusions over the various meanings of the word "good."

While the preceding examples in no way show the sophisticated manner in which Moore carried out his analysis, they do shed light on the nature of the problem he was tackling. From Moore's standpoint, the philosophers themselves were often guilty of the confusion, as they attempted to wrest meaning from common sense and ordinary language and make that meaning remote and abstract. We may say that for Moore, common sense knows "where the shoe pinches," while abstract theories do not. He accused philosophers of abusing language when they took it from common, ordinary usage and meaning. But it was not just meaning that Moore was after; he was after the *analysis* of meaning. His characteristic approach was to analyze a given concept (or meaning) in light of similar concepts and to distinguish one from another more precisely.

Moore's influence receded for some time due to the development of Russell's more formalistic analytic approach and later that of the logical positivists. In recent times, however, people have been returning to elements of Moore's work.

Bertrand Russell (1872-1970). Whereas Moore regarded analytic philosophy as the analysis of meanings in ordinary language and common sense, Russell developed a more formal logical analysis akin to the exact sciences and necessitating a precise vocabulary. In *Principia Mathematica*, by Russell and Alfred North Whitehead, mathematics was reduced to a logical language. Russell held that mathematics gives us a clarity and a logic that is not found in the general uses of language, and since language is such an important part of our life, we do need to try to make it more precise and clear. Aristotle had been responsible for the development of classical logic using principally the syllogistic method. Aristotelian logic was primarily a logic of classes, such as we find in the syllogism. Russell's logic, however, dealt with the relationship of propositions to each other: "If it is raining, then the streets are wet." The clauses "it is raining" and "the streets are wet" both express propositions that have a certain relationship, or what Russell called "implication." *Principia Mathematica* attempted to demonstrate that mathematics is, in fact, a part of logic. Russell further held that language has a basic logical structure similar to that of mathematics. Thus, he hoped that mathematical logic could be used to provide philosophy with an instrument for clarifying the meaning of language with precision.

Russell distinguished between what he called "atomic sentences" and "molecular sentences." An atomic sentence is a sentence with no parts that are themselves sentences. Thus, "Mary is human" is an atomic sentence; and the sentence "Mary and Betty are going shopping" is a molecular sentence since it is a complex sentence containing two parts, each of which is itself a sentence: "Mary is going shopping," and "Betty is going shopping." Molecular sentences are created out of atomic sentences by connective words such as "and," "or," and "if." Russell thought we could analyze any molecular sentence into a set of atomic sentences with the logical connectives. Thus, the meaning of a molecular sentence could be explained by breaking it down into its constituent atomic sentences. This is often referred to as Russell's "logical atomism."

Accordingly, when an atomic sentence is true, the subject denotes an individual thing or object, and the predicate refers to some characteristic of this thing or object. In showing that atomic sentences refer to such objects and characteristics, we are informed that the world is made up of *facts* and that all facts are *atomic* in nature and can be described by an atomic sentence. Russell believed that there are no *molecular* facts in nature since connectives "and," "or," "if . . . then," are only linguistic devices used to combine atomic sentences in various ways. Atomic sentences are "syntactic" only. There are no general facts either, such as "All men are mortal," since this can be reduced to the atomic sentences "Mary is mortal," "Betty is mortal," and so on for every individual.

Russell dealt with what he called the "Theory of Descriptions," in which he attempted to show that philosophers, through the faulty analysis of language, had been led by specious arguments into believing that the sorts of things that ordinary men regard as fiction or nonexistent in some sense actually do exist. For example, we seem to make true statements when we say "Captain Ahab pursued the white whale." This is true in a sense even though there really was no Captain Ahab or white whale. Russell put it this way: "How is it possible for there to be such a sentence as 'The present king of France is wise,' when there is no king of France?" Russell dealt with this kind of problem by making a distinction between the "grammatical form" of a sentence and its "logical form." Thus, the grammatical structure leads us to believe that the phrase "the present king of France" is logically the subject term and "is wise" is the predicate term, and that this is an atomic sentence. But this sentence is not "logically" of the subject-predicate form. When analyzed, we have the following three sentences:

1. Something is current monarch of France.
2. Not more than one thing is current monarch of France.
3. Whatever is current monarch of France is wise.

Each of these three sentences is a "general" sentence, not an atomic one. There are no proper names: instead, we have such generalities as "something," "whatever," and so forth. Thus, "the present king of France" is not logically a proper name, though it might function to form a grammatical point of view. In pointing out that "the present king of France" is logically a "general" sentence and not an atomic one, Russell showed that such a phrase has no relationship to any object in the world, and thus, it has no meaning on its own. If we translate a sentence into logical language, its meaning becomes clear. If it turns out not to be of the subject-predicate form, then there is nothing its grammatical subject will refer to directly, since in the perfect language every subject term will denote an actual object in the world, and every predicate term will denote an actual characteristic of that subject.

His efforts to construct a logical language, or a more perfect language that is objective and oriented to the facts of science, shows the difference between Moore and Russell. Russell wanted a formal, logical language. In fact, he preferred to call his approach "logical analysis."

The term "analytic" takes on special meaning for Russell. A great deal of the philosophy of the past had been "synthetic"; that is, it had tried to take disparate parts or issues and synthesize them into a "great answer" or a "block system." Russell argued that philosophers already had their great answers in hand and tried to make the disparate parts fit into the answers in an erroneous fashion. He believed that the way out of trouble was to discard block universe conceptions in favor of taking on issues one at a time. By reducing each issue or problem to its smallest parts (its "atoms," so to speak), clarity and precision of meaning could be gained. This is Russell's analytic approach—to whittle each problem down to its constituent parts, and then to examine each part in detail to pick out its essential features. Thus, rather than arriving at great answers or syntheses, we have small but significant and well-worked analyses. We get to the truth this way. Science does this, according to Russell, and philosophy should do it, too. Russell's analytic approach is *reductive*. It reduces propositions to their smallest bare-bones significance. It is also *empirical*, for the bare-bones significance of a proposition must square with reality, or with the facts of the case. This is demonstrated by the example about the king of France. It is useless to talk about the king of France if there is, in fact, no king. If there is no king, this nonexistent king cannot possibly be wise. This, in effect, illustrates Russell's condemnation of the synthetic, "grand manner" philosophy of the past. There has been too much talk and system building around nonexistent, nonwise "kings" or great answers.

In fact, this aversion for a "systems" or "grand manner" approach to philosophy fairly well characterizes the analytic movement as a whole. Analysts oppose categorization of ideas into philosophical systems, preferring to view ideas as overlapping and not belonging to any single viewpoint. Thus, they feel a "systems" or "ism" approach defeats the purpose of the kind of thinking philosophy should promote. They prefer to analyze language meaning and to clarify ideas rather than to categorize them.

Although Russell helped to develop philosophical analysis, his interest in analysis was primarily from a methodological standpoint. His orientation was strongly in realism. Russell's emphasis on fact, his insistence on going to the atomic as opposed to molecular and general propositions, show his acceptance of the realist's thesis of independence. We should point out that a figure of Russell's stature is difficult to pin into any school. He willingly gave up positions and renounced views when he discovered what to him were errors. At the end of his life he was still making the philosophical quest, still searching for wisdom wherever that search led and whatever sacred ox was gored. That his influence has extended in many directions is testimony of his virtue as a thinker.

Both Moore and Russell show the strong roots of analysis in realism: Moore for his insistence on anchoring analysis in the ordinary world of facts and sense experience, and Russell for his insistence on the scientific model of a logical, orderly, and systematic treatment of particulars. The analytic movement still has much of this realist orientation, although most modern analysts reject identity with any system.

Logical Positivism and Analysis

Logical positivism originated with a group of European philosophers, scientists, and mathematicians. They formally designated themselves as the "Vienna Circle" in 1929 and began publishing a journal, *Erkenntis*. The members of the circle included Moritz Schlick, Rudolph Carnap, Herbert Feigl, Felix Kaufmann, and A. J. Ayer. The works of Bertrand Russell, especially the *Principia Mathematica*, exerted some influence on this group, as did the earlier works of Ludwig Wittgenstein, especially his *Tractatus Logico-Philosophicus*. Perhaps the most notable feature of the members of the group was their fascination with the progress of modern scientific method, especially the theory of relativity, and what has been called "the principle of verification"; that is, no proposition can be accepted as meaningful unless it can be verified on formal grounds (that is, logic and mathematics), or verified on empirical or sense-data grounds. The former shows their indebtedness to modern mathematics and logic and the latter their indebtedness to modern empirical science. After several years they encountered difficulties with the principle of verification, however, for in their zeal they had given it a very narrow and rigorous application that ruled out any consideration of unverifiable propositions. It was found that some of the fundamental assumptions of science itself are unverifiable in the rigorous application the logical positivists used. The important weight given to empirical sense-data presented problems, too, for such data depend on human beings observing some phenomenon, and this lets in the subjective element of perception. What one encounters is the *observation* of the object or phenomenon and not the objective reality of the thing itself as Kant maintained with "*das Ding an sich.*" Thus, there is always this probable error of subjectivism, and this particularly sticky problem led to various splinterings within logical positivism. For this reason, in more recent years, there have been very few people who identify themselves with logical positivism, for its assumptions have proven to be per-haps too simple, and its methodology too rigid. Nonetheless, it has exerted an influence not to be discounted, even though as a philosophical position its career was short lived.

In terms of its influence on the analytic movement, several things need to be pointed out about logical positivism. Two leading figures will be used for illustration: Ludwig Wittgenstein and A. J. Ayer.

Ludwig Wittgenstein (1889-1951). Wittgenstein's connection with logi-cal positivism stems from his earlier works, primarily the *Tractatus Logico-Philosophicus*. In this book, he argued that the natural sciences are the primary source of true propositions and the primary means of finding new facts. Philoso-phy should not see its role as the discoverer of truth, but rather as an activity to solve dilemmas, elucidate problems, and clarify ideas obtained from other sources. A true proposition might be referred to as an "atomic proposition" that reveals the particular structure and arrangement of objects and facts. The philosopher should not concern himself with the *truth* of the data but should deal with the *language* and *statements made about* the data. Thus, we need to specify what we can and cannot say, that is, the limits of language.

Wittgenstein was born in Austria, and raised by rather rigid parents who expected only excellence from their children. His father wanted Ludwig to become an engineer, so he studied engineering first in Berlin and later in Manchester, England. He specialized in aircraft propulsion and consequently developed a deep interest in pure mathematics as an outgrowth of his work.

While in England, he was introduced to the mathematical logic of Russell, and soon went to Cambridge and became a student and personal friend of Russell. His studies, philosophical research, and association with Russell were interrupted by World War I. He returned to Austria, served in the Austrian army, and was captured on the Italian front. He completed most of the work on *Tractatus Logico-Philosophicus* while serving in the army. It was also during this time that he apparently had some sort of mystical experience, for after the war, he returned home, gave away his considerable wealth, and became an elemen-tary school teacher.

The Wittgenstein of the *Tractatus* was an even more rigorous empiricist than Russell, and this may account for his appeal to logical positivism. He thought the only significant use of language was to picture the facts or to state tautologies, and beyond this he thought language was nonsensical. During the 1920s, he again came into contact with Cambridge intellectual circles, and in

1929, he moved to Britain and became a British subject. He began revising his philosophy and by the mid-thirties arrived at an altered position that was to have profound effects on Anglo-American philosophy thereafter.

Although in his later works Wittgenstein repudiated or revised some of the above views, the members of the Vienna Circle understood his early views to mean that philosophy primarily should be an activity that tries to clarify concepts. They, too, believed that philosophy does not produce propositions; it merely clarifies the meaning of statements, showing some to be scientific, some mathematical, and some nonsensical. Thus, every significant statement is either a statement of formal logic (which includes mathematical statements) or a statement of science. Other statements may be "partial," "emotive," "pictorial," or "motivational" but are not cognitive. Philosophy should show the limits of language, try to make propositions intelligible, and provide clarity. Again, the insistence is not on the development of truth, but on the meaning of propositions as they presently exist.

The principle of verification was adopted by the Vienna Circle and stands as one of its chief devices. The members believed that all propositions must be verifiable either by logic or sense perception statements. An example of a logical statement would be "Fathers are males," a logically true statement based on the terms employed. On the other hand, "Fathers are workers" is not necessarily true or meaningful. This kind of proposition is meaningful only if it can be verified empirically by sense experience. Proponents of logical positivism made a distinction between what they called "analytic" and "synthetic" sentences. Sentences whose truth logically follows from their meaning, such as the statement "All bald-headed men have no hair," are called analytic. Sentences that have some sort of empirical investigation for their confirmation are called "synthetic," such as the statement "John has brown hair."

The positivists believed that all analytic sentences are in the realm of formal logic—they are true because of their structure—and all synthetic statements belong to science, requiring empirical investigation for their validity. It should be pointed out that analytic sentences do not refer to the world the way synthetic sentences do. We cannot, for example, infer that the items mentioned by the terms of an analytic sentence actually exist. Thus, from the analytic statement "Mermaids are women," we cannot infer that there are any actual mermaids in existence, but the statement "This cat is white" can be verified by checking the facts of the situation. The logical positivists thought that analytic sentences are "trivial," whereas synthetic ones are "informative." Analytic statements are only true by definition, while synthetic statements make actual claims about reality that can be verified as true or false.

Care should be taken here with the terms "analytic" and "synthetic." The positivists were not using the term "synthetic" in the older meaning. They, too, were as suspicious as Russell had been of the old "philosophy in the grand manner" that sought to construct "great answers" and elaborate systems out of a synthesis of conflicting ideas. To both Wittgenstein and the logical positivists, the old manner of synthesis was too metaphysical. For Wittgenstein, metaphysical statements are nonsensical. The only *sayable* propositions are the propositions of natural science. The logical positivists took Wittgenstein's position to mean that true propositions must be capable of empirical verification. Wittgenstein, however, was interested in the limits of language—what is sayable. He himself did not anchor his position on empirical verification. Apparently, the logical positivists understood his statement about natural science to mean "the empirically discoverable" or "what can be verified by the senses." At any rate, they arrived at the "principle of verification"; consequently, they gave a rather exalted position to "synthetic," "informative" statements because these can be verified by the empirical approach.

Alfred Jules Ayer (1910-   ). A. J. Ayer is one who seriously sought further to combine logical positivism with analytic approaches. He was educated at Eton and Oxford, taught for a number of years at the University of London, and became a professor at Oxford in 1959. He was a prominent member of the Vienna Circle and has sought to interpret logical positivism to the English-speaking world not only through teaching and writing, but also through radio and television.

Ayer has attempted to reconcile and order the principle doctrines of analysis from the works of Russell, Wittgenstein, and the Vienna Circle. He views the task of philosophy to classify language, distinguish genuine propositions from others, and explain the meaning and justification of propositions by their reductive analysis into basic statements about immediate experience. Ayer has used the principle of verification to show that religious, evaluative, and metaphysical utterances are not propositions.

In *Language, Truth and Logic*, Ayer used the verifiability criterion of meaning. Accordingly, a sentence will be factually significant to a given person if and only if he knows how to verify the propositions that it purports to express; that is, if he knows what observation would lead him under certain conditions to accept the proposition as being true or to reject it as being false. Thus, it must be possible to describe what sorts of observations would have to be made in order to determine whether a sentence is true or false. If some observations can be made that will be relevant in determining the truth or falsity of a sentence, then the sentence will be significant; if not, it will be meaningless. In the sentence "Angels have silver wings," there would not seem to be any *observation* that could confirm or deny this proposition, and thus it is meaningless. This is quite different from a statement such as "There are men on Mars," for while it is not verifiable at the present, it is at least capable of being verified at some point in the future.

Ayer thinks philosophy would do well to abandon the metaphysical "grand manner" approach, especially where that approach starts with first principles and then constructs a deductive system from them as a complete picture of reality. The problem with this approach is that first principles are taken to be logically certain. What makes more sense, according to Ayer, is the inductive approach in which any derived generalizations are viewed as only probable and hypothetical. More to the point, the most valuable thing philosophy can do is to reveal the criteria that are used in showing whether a proposition is true or false. The truth or falsity of any proposition must be determined by empirical verification, not philosophical clarification.

Recently, Ayer has softened somewhat on the finality of the verification principle due to the criticism directed at the rigorous application he and the logical positivists used. Consequently, he has ceased to identify himself with any definable school of thought, but he does retain some elements of the empirical approach of logical positivism. It has been suggested that Ayer could most aptly be called an "analytically minded empiricist."

Linguistic Analysis

"Linguistic analysis" is the name many observers prefer when discussing the current state of analytic philosophy. This is due to a general trend in the last few decades to get away from trying to construct an ideal language as precise as the scientific model of mathematics or trying to construct too rigid a set of rules for ordinary language. Perhaps tacking the word "linguistic" in front of analysis is still a far from accurate way to describe the current scene. Indeed, many kinds of analysis are going on, and development is under way in many directions, but "linguistic" still has a ring of accuracy to it. The task is as much a linguistic one as it is a matter of formal logic or some brand of positivism.

The trend noted above may be credited to the later works of Ludwig Wittgenstein as much as any one figure, for in his mature stage his viewpoint opened considerably to recognize many uses of language. Hence, "linguistic" becomes an apt term to signify this approach to philosophy.

Some mention has been made of Wittgenstein in this chapter, yet his ideas deserve additional attention because of the complexities of his career and thought as well as the confusing development of philosophical analysis. The "later Wittgenstein" set new directions in philosophy that had a profound impact on linguistic analysis.

These views first came to light in written form as mimeographed notes on lectures he had delivered to students in the early 1930s. Called *The Blue and the Brown Books*, they were not published until after his death. The basic ideas of these works appeared in a much expanded and revised form as *Philosophical Investigations*, also published posthumously. Of all his writings, perhaps the most simple and easiest to read is *The Blue Book*.

Wittgenstein's revised philosophy no longer took the narrow view of language but saw language comprised of indefinite possibilities of usage. In effect, he was saying that we must get at the context of any language usage, and in order to understand the meaning of a language, we may construct "language games." He thought most philosophical "problems" were not really problems at all, but puzzlements brought about by linguistic confusions. The proper issue was these puzzlements and how most of us had gotten locked into certain language uses early in life from which we could not readily escape. We are, in Wittgenstein's view, like flies in a bottle, haphazardly flitting about and banging against the walls in our confusion. The role of philosophy, then, should not be to construct explanations about reality and so forth, but to solve the puzzles of linguistic confusion. Philosophy should be viewed as a method of investigation (although no specified, singular method) that results in pure description, and language should be seen as having no necessary or ideal form.

Historically, philosophy has posed such questions as "What is real?" "What is meaning?" and so forth. Wittgenstein thought these kinds of questions only led to mental cramp. It is better to ask "What is an explanation of meaning?" than "What is meaning?" Thus, he focused on the explanation of meaning, or the meaning of meaning. According to Wittgenstein, we get into problems, when upon hearing a word, we immediately begin to look for its meaning in some corresponding object. What we ought to do is look at the word itself, the sign, the statement, and examine the context of its usage. Usage depends on the meaning of signs (that is, names or words) in relation to other signs within a system of signs; in short, within a language. According to Wittgenstein, understanding a sentence involves understanding a language. (By language, he did not mean English, French, or German, for any of these can have many languages within them in terms of usage and context.)

Let us take an example of a word over which philosophers have long argued: "thinking." According to Wittgenstein, the meaning of "thinking" varies. When confronted with the word, most of us may associate it with mind and mental activity. However, what happens when we begin to explain what we mean by the sign "thinking"? Is it hidden away inside the cranium? If we could open someone's head while he was thinking, could we see it? Likely, we would see physiological things. What do we do when "thinking" is going on? Some suggestions may come easily to mind: writing, reading, speaking. Is thinking done by the mouth and larynx? Why do we say "mind" is doing the thinking? Where is its locus, its seat? Really, we can only explain thinking by signifying agents such as the brain, hand, and larynx. Wittgenstein did not question that thinking also went on in the brain, but he maintained that when we try to describe thinking in words and statements, we signify agents of thinking and draw *analogies* from them. We try to sum all these up into a general term such as "mind" and then relate this to a thing or object. For centuries, philosophers have argued about mind, mental, and thinking, and trying to locate and delineate them. Wittgenstein suggested that the puzzle is really a linguistic one. We became fascinated with a linguistic form when we thought we had a problem with a thing.

Part of this difficulty, Wittgenstein maintained, is that we have come to crave generality, a concept that is linked to a number of philosophical puzzlements. Philosophers have taught that we should look for commonality in all things that can be brought under a general term. The tendency to generalize is rooted in our forms of expression. Words have come to possess the meaning of a general image of things associated with, or corresponding to, the words. The result is a confusion of the things named with the names themselves—the words. We have also come to confuse, as in the case of "thinking," mental processes and mechanisms with states of consciousness or awareness. Part of this is due, Wittgenstein thought, to our preoccupation with the method of science that seeks to reduce the explanations of natural phenomena to the smallest possible number of natural "laws" or principles, or if you will, scientific generalizations. He stated that this preoccupation is the source of metaphysics in philosophy. For Wittgenstein, it is not the proper business of philosophy to reduce anything, to produce generalizations, or to offer grand explanations. Philosophy's business is to be purely descriptive.

Wittgenstein believed that the problem with modern philosophy is the "contemptuous attitude towards the particular case." For example, we use the word "kind" a great deal. This shows our penchant for generalization, for we quickly want to subsume something under a larger heading. When confronted with strange words about something, a quick reaction is to ask, "What kind of thing is it?" as if we had to subsume it under some heading of animal, vegetable, or mineral before we could understand the meaning of the word properly. Let us go back to the philosopher's plight with the word "thinking." We want to locate it, and in our analysis we describe several cases of thinking. But there is still something lacking, because it is virtually impossible to define thinking in a manner to cover all cases so that the word truly designates a general class. In actual usage, the word has no sharp boundary. To Wittgenstein, the idea that we must find a common element in all applications of a word or statement is a hindrance to philosophical investigation. It has led philosophers to the grievous error of dismissing the concrete particular.

Furthermore, Wittgenstein held that the explanation of the meaning of a word depends upon the actual context of usage and the language structure being used. If we attempt to construct generalizations, then we are thrown into the pit of drawing analogies from one context to another, relying on conventions rather than specifics of behavior, devising criteria and symptoms of usage, and then arbitrarily picking one convention, criterion, or symptom as more important than another. In effect, we are reduced to constructing arbitrary and abstract rules and procedures that get away from the concrete usage and meaning in context. We come to view language according to the mathematical rules of calculus. However, actual language is very rarely done like calculus. The craving for generality leads to abstract exactness that gives rise to philosophical puzzlements and linguistic confusion.

Wittgenstein believed that in actuality words have no true meaning given to them by some independent power. They have the meanings *people* give them. Thus, we cannot scientifically investigate what a word *really* means, and we cannot tabulate strict rules of usage. It is also fruitless to construct an ideal language to replace ordinary language: rather, an ideal language should remove the trouble of someone thinking he had gotten *the* exact usage of an ordinary word. Thus, Wittgenstein rejected any *necessary* form of language.

In actual usage, we construct and play "language games," or "systems" of communication. The understanding of language is as varied as the games. What makes anything a language, anyway? Commonality or generality is necessarily involved, but it is a commonality like a family resemblance and not the complete picture of the family. Wittgenstein thought we could invent our own language games to help us understand actual usage by showing the similarities and differences of a language. These constructed games would be used to examine actual and possible uses of language in various contexts.

Wittgenstein had no systematic doctrine, no rules of procedure, and no lockstep "grand manner" approach to philosophizing. This makes his philosophy difficult to comprehend because we are accustomed to seeing answers put forth and explanations offered for the world's origin and destiny. Wittgenstein would have none of this and asserted that philosophy needs to be purely descriptive. We may say his view recommends uncorking the bottle and letting the fly out to see where it will go.

Gilbert Ryle (1900-1976). Ryle was born, reared, and educated in England. Early in his philosophical career he was attracted to certain aspects of continental philosophy, especially Husserl's work, but by the age of thirty-one, Ryle had become well versed in philosophical analysis. He viewed analysis as a matter of finding the sources of linguistic confusion by examining some of the continually perplexing problems in philosophy, such as the mind-body dualism. His work on the use of the words "mind," "mental," "thinking," "knowing" and related words made him probably one of the most influential and widely read contemporary British philosophers. His best-known work is *The Concept of Mind* that stands as one of the more famous books in twentieth century philosophy.

In *The Concept of Mind*, Ryle attacked the Cartesian doctrine of splitting off body and mind. The doctrine holds that body is in the realm of matter, susceptible to and subject to the laws of matter. It is capable of objective study, and its behavior can be publicly observed and measured. On the other hand, there is mind, hidden from view, a private, secret realm. It is subjective, and while an individual may have access to his own mental operations, he cannot examine another's objectively. Thus, while the material body can be scientifically studied, mind is not available to science but is amenable to a special subjective method of investigation called introspection. Ryle disputed these contentions, calling the theory "the dogma of the Ghost in the Machine." It is false in principle, he maintained, because it is a "category mistake," and the dogma he referred to as "the philosopher's myth."

According to Ryle, a "category mistake" occurs when one allocates concepts to logical types to which they do not belong. He gave the example of the visitor who came to Oxford and was shown the various colleges, laboratories, libraries, offices, and so forth. The visitor then asked, "But where is the university?" This is a category mistake, for the visitor was allocating the concept of university to the same logical type as its constituent colleges. In the case of Oxford, university is a collective logical type and college is a "constituent element" logical type. A similar kind of category mistake can be made with the word "institution." We speak of marriage as an institution and we speak of Harvard University as an institution, but there is a world of difference between the logical meanings of the term "institution" in these cases.

How did the mind-body confusion come about? According to Ryle, the science developed by Galileo and others maintained that certain mechanical laws of matter governed every object occupying space. Descartes, being concerned with science, could accept such laws, but as a philosopher, he could not accept a mechanistic theory for human mind. Mental was not the same as mechanical, but its exact opposite. This is a category mistake because it puts body and mind under the same logical type in the manner of exact opposites. Both are things, but things of entirely different natures. If body is a machine then mind is a "non-machine." The belief that mind and body (or mind and matter) are at polar positions came about because of the belief that they are both of the same logical type, although opposites. Ryle was not trying to absorb the one into the other by saying it is either all material or all mental. He held that while the dogma is an absurd one, we *are* justified in making distinctions between physical activity and mental activity. It all hinges on the *sense* in which we are speaking.

Perhaps most of the problem belongs to the confusion engendered by words such as "mind," "mental," "thinking," and similar mentalistic terms. Certainly, Ryle maintained, we may legitimately describe "doing long division" or "thinking things over" as mental activity. We err, however, when we ascribe any sense of place to mental activity. We picture "in the head" when we say mental activity. This is what Ryle called the "intellectualist legend" that intelligence is some internal operation. Yet we can be justified in speaking of mental activity "in the head" if we understand that we are speaking metaphorically. One does not necessarily do arithmetic "in the head," for he can do it just as well (if not better) by speaking it out loud or writing it on a paper. The same can be said of imagined noise. We can "hear" music "in our heads." Who has not had a tune that he has heard over and over "in his mind"? If someone else placed his ear against the head of the subject he could not hear it, but if the subject were actually speaking or singing out loud, it could be heard by means of cranial bone vibrations. The tune we say metaphorically is "in our minds" is not really in our heads. A great deal of confusion over the mind-body "problem" results from mixing the literal sense with a metaphorical one.

A related problem can be found associated with the term "knowing." "Knowing" and "knowledge" have long been of concern to philosophers, and epistemology (theory of knowledge) has traditionally been one of the main disciplines of philosophy. Yet we have encountered all sorts of problems with understanding "knowing" because of our confusion with it. Ryle maintained that we have confused "knowing that" and "knowing how." "Knowing how" is having the capacity to perform, being able to do, and so forth. But, Ryle pointed out, knowing that so and so is the case does not mean that we necessarily know how to *do* it. In the same way, to be able to perform or do does not mean that we necessarily understand the purposes and reasons for doing. All too often we have assumed that knowing and knowledge are too much on the side of "knowing that." This has resulted in the ignorant approach to formal education whereby we assume that by "cramming the heads" of students with facts and "knowledge," they will be able to go out into the world and perform successfully. A more healthy concept of knowing and knowledge would be that to know in the best sense is to "know that" *and* "know how."

Many problems have developed that go back to the mind-body dualism. These can even be traced back to Plato, who extolled the mental over the material, to the churchmen who extolled soul (mind) over body, and to Descartes who devised the *cogito*. Ryle pointed out the fault was not so much that of Descartes as it was of a long philosophical and theological tradition. Furthermore, he thought that myths such as the mind-body dualism have their uses. The creation of myths helps us get around many difficulties. It has been observed on a number of occasions that modern science would never have been accepted in Christiandom if the Cartesian myth had not been developed, for it helped reconcile scientific findings with theological dogmas.

Perhaps we will need new myths to get around science's dogmas. New methods of investigation will need to be devised to replace our current ones. At any rate, Ryle's analysis is instructive in helping us wend our way through the linguistic confusions in which we find ourselves.

Philosophical Analysis and Philosophy of Education

Although philosophical analysis is generally thought of as a new development, all philosophies deal with the analysis of concepts, meanings, and problems to some extent. One can certainly see a great concern for analysis in the writings of Plato, Aristotle, Kant, and Descartes. The dialectic, for example, is not only a method for arriving at truth, but also a method for eliminating contradictions that stand in the way of truth. Francis Bacon talked about the Idol of the Marketplace being the most troublesome of all, for as he put it " . . . men believe that their reason governs words, but it is also true that words react on the understanding, and this it is that has rendered philosophy and the sciences sophistical and inactive."

The argument has been made many times that our thinking is governed in whole or in part by language and meanings of words. It is difficult to conceive of thoughts without language and what thinking we do can only be expressed in some kind of language. Some people believe that without language symbols, whether mathematical, verbal, written, pictured, or gestured, we would have no means of communication, and hence, no mind. Many analysts say that since thinking is so dependent on language, thinking problems are also language problems resulting from faulty usage and lack of clarity.

The use of analytic philosophy in education has some direct bearing on students, but perhaps it is most useful for teachers in helping them clarify what *they* propose to do with students. The consequence of this use of analytic philosophy is not to develop some new educational "ism" or ideology, but to help us to understand the meanings of our ideologies better. The benefits accrue to students as a result of a clarified and more meaningful approach to the educational process.

An illustrative example is the educator's confusion with the word "knowing," an example given by Ryle. We have confused "knowing that" with the complete picture of knowing; consequently, once having "filled students' heads" with all kinds of data, we assume our task is finished. Ryle pointed out, however, that knowing also includes "knowing how," or being able to do and perform with data. In one sense, this involves the old problem of the separation of theory ("knowing") from practice ("doing"), a problem to which John Dewey devoted quite a bit of discussion. Dewey spoke of the philosophical dichotomy between knowledge and action, or knowing and doing. In other words, he maintained that knowing and doing have been artificially separated. The knowing side is similar to "knowing that," and the doing side similar to "knowing how." Dewey thought these two should go together as much as possible, particularly with regard to the education of the young. The "learning by doing" slogan so often voiced by progressive educators has at least some of its roots in Dewey's thought. We learn or gain knowledge by becoming actively or physically involved with significant tasks. In fact, it could be said that the dichotomy goes back to the ancient Greeks who talked about "areté" and "techné" (virtue and skill).

Take, for example, the learning of bicycle riding. The prospective rider needs to know that the vehicle is steered by turning the handle bars in the desired direction and shifting body weight to maintain balance. He must also know that the bicycle's momentum must be maintained at a minimum speed in order for the vehicle to remain operative. But so far, our prospective rider only knows that certain things must be done in order to ride successfully. We may say he *knows that* there are certain specific "principles" of bicycle riding. He has, so to speak, the "theory" of bicycle riding. Every cyclist realizes, however, that he must also know *how* to ride a bicycle; he must have a practical knowledge of cycling, and this involves the actual, out-of-doors *doing* of riding a bicycle. Educators have too often stopped with the "knowing that" aspect of knowing. Students get the theory but not the practice.

A more complex example would be the objective of producing democratic citizens, dear to the hearts of many Americans. American schools have largely accomplished the task by informing students that there is something called democracy, and in the United States this is usually associated with government, American history, and such things as the right to vote. As a general rule, however, very few students ever get to *be* democratic by *doing* things democratically. We require that they have hall passes, that they get permission to speak, and that they abide by restrictive rules that they usually have had no voice in constructing. They know that there is something called democracy, but they do not know how to be democratic. It is readily apparent why there seems to be so little democracy actually practiced in American life: most people have not had the opportunity to know *how*. In education, our usage of the term "knowing" has had a very narrow meaning: we have been confused about knowing because we have too arbitrarily restricted its meaning so as to exclude considerations about knowing extending far beyond a mere cognitive or intellectual knowing.

Thus, many analysts maintain that analytic philosophy has an important role to play in education because so much of education deals with logic and language. Teachers and students constantly deal in generalizations and value judgments about educational materials that need to be examined critically. The analyst emphasizes that the role of language is learning, and there is a need to apply criteria for evaluating and clarifying the statements we make, a need which goes beyond the traditional studies of grammar. There are some educators who feel that language analysis should be the primary role with which philosophy of education is concerned. Their thesis is based on the idea that deliberate education should become more precise and scientific, and analysis offers one way in which to do this. They are quick to point out that other philosophies of education are usually based on metaphysical assumptions that are highly questionable and too often result in prescriptions for education that are more emotive than anything else. Primarily, such educational philosophers believe that students should study the language *they* (the students) use to describe and justify the meanings they apply in life.

It is certainly true that language is a very important part of our lives. It is doubtful that we could even think without languages since our thinking usually parallels language concepts: bad thinking may be, in many cases, a poor use of language. There are some educators who protest that language analysis should only be a small part of philosophy, but philosophical analysts point out that the problems of language are so numerous, diffuse, and complex, that the desired analytical study is a major undertaking of great significance. It is their contention that many educational problems are largely language problems, and if we can solve the language problems, we can, in effect, better solve the educational problems.

Language as an educational problem goes far beyond the confines of the school or classroom into practically all facets of life. Not only is language a prime concern for students in terms of curriculum, textbooks, and other conveyances of knowledge, but it is an integral concern in one's everyday life. Perhaps one of the special needs of modern life is a greater sensitivity to the place of language. People's behavior is influenced to a great extent by the language they encounter, for language serves as a stimulus to all kinds of behavior. For example, Hitler came to power partly because of his ability to manipulate language. Contemporary totalitarian regimes maintain their power to a great extent through a careful control of the language media, for they fear the consequences of an unfettered language.

George Orwell, in his novel, *1984*, wrote about the development of a language called "Newspeak" where behavior could be controlled through linguistic techniques. For example, Orwell described a method known as "doublethink" whereby one could learn to hold two contradictory points of view at the same time. Thus, war is peace and love is hate. He also talked about "crimestop" whereby a person could be so conditioned to linguistic control that he could mentally prevent entertaining any idea hostile to the state or "Big Brother." One can find many examples of these techniques in modern government when officials try to cover up existing problems by using language or corrupted versions of language to protect their power and vested interests.

We can sympathize with the position of the philosophical analyst when we think of the barrage of advertising, sloganeering, and cliché thinking to which people are daily exposed. Since most people have had little training in logical thought, they are easy victims for the misuse of language to make them buy something, vote a certain way, or support a particular position. There are any number of language devices to which people are daily exposed, many of which are effective in influencing their thinking. Determined persons representing vested interests have learned these devices and have found them so effective that they have used (or misused) them to persuade other people to behave in various ways. Books like Vance Packard's *The Hidden Persuaders* show how easily people can be manipulated and influenced by advertisers and politicians and how the methods used are often very subtle and ingenious. Theodore White's *The Making of the President* points out how a variety of techniques, including the manipulation of language, may be used to elect a candidate to political office.

A further example is the term "the law." Many people say you should or should not do certain things because "it is the *law*." But what is the law? Laws change from time to time, or differ from one country or state to another. Further, they are subject to interpretation, and thus a law as determined by one court may be overturned by another. In effect, it could be said that "the law" is an abstraction developed for a mythical person. Critics charge that lawyers prefer that the laws remain vague and abstract, for this gives them something to interpret and manipulate for clients, and leads to an abundance of lengthy court cases.

Therefore, for reasons both practical and philosophical, analysts argue that we should be sensitive to language problems and attempt to make our language more precise and clear. This is a laudable goal, but also very difficult to achieve, for words have as many meanings as users intend them to have.

Language usage affects both students and teachers. Teachers often become unwilling tools of other interests as they employ language in the educational process. The teacher teaches primarily with language, and because of its many possibilities, can use it in a variety of ways to influence the child. The teacher expresses ideas and information through language (including gestures), and the way he or she uses it has a profound effect, often unrecognized, unintended, or even unconscious. The Marxists have charged that teachers in capitalistic societies are so caught up in the system in which they are teaching that they cannot see that they are indoctrinating their students with the values inherent in a particular economic system.

By the time a child reaches adolescence he is conditioned to the "language games" of education and may use language in similar ways to manipulate others. Language is employed in textbooks, in films, and other media, and the choice of words, the size of letters, the kinds of grammatical construction (including what is left out), all contribute to a certain effect on a child's mental development. It is interesting, for example, that in many social studies texts critical discussions of various political, social, and economic policies have been omitted because they might offend some pressure group by presenting such policies in an unfavorable light. The textbooks children use in schools are not written in a vacuum and reflect many biases.

Educators themselves are victims of language devices contrived to get them to think or vote in certain ways, and also to develop particular attitudes about education, children, and society. Teachers seem as susceptible to specious language devices concerning social issues as anyone else, and there is an enormous amount of sloganeering generated in the educational profession. We talk about "the whole child," "open schools," and use many other slogans. Some critics have asked: Who ever taught half a child? What does "open" really mean? We talk about "accountability" as if to show that we are businesslike, and about having a "philosophy" when we generally mean a list of socially accepted maxims. We talk about the "democratic process" in instances where there is little or no democracy, about "individuality" when it is seldom allowed, and about "freedom" only within narrowly prescribed limits. Often, the case is similar to the sense of *1984*: we say "peace" when we mean war, "truth" when we mean falsehood, and "justice" when we mean injustice.

Philosophical Analysis and the Aims of Education

Philosophical analysts are very interested in improving both the educator's concepts about education and how he uses them. One of the first steps is to become acutely aware of language and its potential. Once we do this, the chances are better that we will have a greater concern for the sensitive use of language in the educational process.

Analysts believe that educators should be attuned to the logical complexities of language. Language is a complex cultural development, and words have a variety of meanings and use. What do words such as "knowing," "mind," "freedom," and "education," really mean? While most analysts do not believe that words have inherent meanings, they do insist that we can use them in more precise ways to reflect accurately what is intended. Many concepts have an emotive effect that must be taken into consideration: words such as "justice," "patriotism," "honor," and "virtue" that may give a "halo" or "hurrah" effect to statements about the aims of education.

For example, let us take the concept of "education." Some analysts, such as R. S. Peters, insist that one cannot legitimately speak about the "aims" of education since if education is initiation into worthwhile activities, it already has all the aims it needs. Making statements about what education *should* do is to make prescriptions, an activity most analysts reject as outside the realm of analytic philosophy. Peters has questioned the use of the concept of "education" in general and has attempted to show how confusing the usage of the word has been. It has been pointed out how Ryle attempted to show that the meaning of "knowing" could be more inclusive than it is ordinarily used by educators. Wittgenstein stated that words do not necessarily have an inherent, objective meaning; rather, they mean whatever the user intends them to mean. Peters, Ryle, and Wittgenstein caution us to examine the context and precision of our word usage. In short, the analysts do not attempt to prescribe any particular kind of education as much as they seek to clarify the conceptual devices employed by the educator, the processes of using them, their underlying presuppositions, and the purposes involved.

It seems that the use-value of words determines their meanings as much as any dictionary definition. In fact, dictionary definitions of words are altered periodically by practical use. Language itself is changing and evolving: one can neither define a word forever, nor prescribe its meaning for everyone else. The educational consequence of this, the analysts claim, is that one must see concepts, word meanings, and statements about education in their practical context as opposed to a theoretical, prescriptive construction.

Teachers constantly call for practical solutions to educational problems. But this concern with "practicality" is itself open to analytic inquiry: just what is the meaning of "practical" in this instance? Often, the "practical" teacher wants a technique, a gimmick, to apply to and solve his dilemma. It is reasonable, however, to observe that such "practical" solutions are often theoretical in the worst sense. Techniques are sometimes used indiscriminately. They are applied generally and universally in situations for which they were not designed; however, they are deemed "practical" because their mechanics are known and they are capable of being acted upon. "Achievement" is a rubric by which many educators swear, and the worth of any educational activity is judged upon students' achievement scores. "Achievement" in such instances is usually understood to be a "practical" outcome of one's education, but such emphasis may serve to retard one's education if the meaning of achievement is vague and unclear. Suppose one wants to learn how to play the piano, and the educator says that the "practical" approach is to proceed by achievement in learning to play scales. However, such a method may result in the student's learning to play scales but not in developing his ability to play the piano or in sustaining his interest. We may pose the question: how "practical" is this approach?

It can be seen how our use of words is intimately connected with the presuppositions underlying their use. In the case above, what was believed to be practical was in fact not very practical at all. The proposition that one learns to play the piano by achievement in playing scales is itself theoretical and not always supported by factual circumstances (although playing the scales may *help* achieve the goal). Similar conditions exist with regard to numerous educational prescriptions.

Thus, rather than prescribing aims to be achieved in the educational process, the analyst prefers to look at what we mean by education in the first place and what advantages may accrue from a clarified concept of education. R. S. Peters has spoken about the "justification" of education rather than mere aims. He points to at least four considerations that help us situate the meaning of education in order to arrive at better educational aims. These are (a) education is more than mere specialized skills because it includes developing one's capacity to reason, justifying beliefs and conduct, knowing the "why" as well as the "what" of things, and organizing experience in terms of systematic conceptions; (b) education is more than mere specialized knowledge and includes developing one's cognitive perspective, expanding moral understandings, and developing aesthetic appreciations; (c) education includes doing and knowing things for their own sake, for the joy of doing and knowing; and (d) education is the process by which people are initiated into their particular life-styles. Thus, in speaking about education, we must never forget that *means* figure in the meaning as well as *aims*. Peters aptly illustrates the problem of speaking about the aims of education when the meanings of education are so diverse. If we are truly going to be intelligent and reasonable in establishing aims in education, then we need to clear the ground to arrive at what we mean by education before we can reasonably construct particular aims. It may be that aims belong to particular teaching strategies and not to some esoteric word of confused meanings such as "education."

Dewey once said that "aim" was akin to a target and implies a definite goal or outcome. Peters agrees with Dewey and points out that if "aim" refers to specific outcomes, then it is ridiculous to speak of the "aims of education" as if these were universally agreed upon norms. It is more the case, where in any given historical period, the meanings of education have particular norms built into them by practical use. Thus, when people ask for the aims of education, they really are requesting clarification and specification of their particular contemporary norms. Any number of aims of education are possible depending upon the kinds of life people think are most important at any given time in history. Today, for instance, Peters says that there are some worthwhile overall aims such as "growth" and "the self-realization of the individual." But aims of this sort have their roots within a cultural system that supports individualistic thought patterns. They point to autonomy and self-actualization as important, whereas another cultural epoch and historical period may view these as minor or not even recognize them at all.

Analysts such as Peters believe that we must separate the process of formulating aims in education from the general question, "What is *the* aim of education?" This question is not an apt one because its answer must either be conceptually true or persuasive. It falls into timeworn rubrics such as "good citizenship is the proper aim of education," or "one of the cardinal aims of education is worthy home membership." The analyst thinks such statements only confuse the issue, for then we are pushed to define "good citizenship" or what "worthy home membership" really is. As Wittgenstein pointed out, we no sooner hear something uttered than we begin searching for its objective or existing equivalent.

Israel Scheffler has critically analyzed how the word "relevance" has been so misused or overused so as to complicate rather than clear up educational dilemmas. Practically everybody would agree that education ought to be relevant. Being for relevance is like being for mother love and apple pie. But what is relevant? Scheffler maintains, in fact, that the primary task of education is not relevance; rather, it is to support and insure a society dedicated to ideals of free inquiry and rationality. Thus, it is not the aim of education we must seek, but an understanding of what kinds of desirable aims there are, what the possibilities are of achieving them, and what kinds of consequences we may expect from acting on them. These latter considerations are not within the province of the philosopher of education as much as they are within the province of sociologists, psychologists, scientists, political leadership, and ordinary citizens. The philosopher's role is simply to clarify and criticize meanings involved.

Philosophical Analysis and Methods of Education

Analysts are concerned that both the methods and materials of contemporary education undergo a serious analytical study. While most analysts avoid prescribing what should or should not go on in the educational process, they are very interested in seeing that both the educator and student critically examine the curriculum from the standpoint of materials, methods, policies, and procedures.

Analysts are aware that methods and media of all kinds educate the child in many ways. Although educators should understand that words and concepts are value laden, they do not always seem to operate with an awareness of this fact. When the McGuffey readers were used in the early 1900s, for example, they not only taught reading skills, but also particular values concerning church, patriotism, and family. Readers of the "Dick and Jane" type of books that came later supposedly attempted to provide a more neutral kind of material that was value free. Neutrality was not achieved, however, for "Dick and Jane" readers contained a number of assumptions about male-female roles, children's rights and their relationship to society, and dominant social class themes.

It can be seen, then, that the analyst does not attempt to say whether a child should read McGuffey or Dick and Jane; rather, he examines the meaning of the claims made regarding the merits of such activities. Instead of saying what a child *should* read, think, study, or learn, the analyst examines what we mean by the words "think," "read," or "learn" and the statements we make regarding these words. Some analysts avoid not only prescriptive statements about what students ought or ought not do, but also statements of value about the impor-tance of such activities.

For example, there has been a great deal of concern in contemporary education about the "Right to Read" and the necessity of reading in adult life. The analysts would not question whether people should have a "right to read," but what is meant by the terminology and the statements made regarding this "right." There are a number of meanings involved in the way the words are used, and these must be viewed against the conditions and circumstances of contem-porary society. It has been suggested that the "Right to Read" campaign is supported by the various publishing industries who have vested interests in maintaining reading behavior. This support has to be considered in light of the great advances that have been made in the electronics media that modify the kinds and extent of reading skills needed. Another point of view is that the "Right to Read" campaign is fostered by reactionary political interests in order to take attention from more reform-minded social programs involved in education such as the attempts to desegregrate American society through educational means.

In addition, programs of the nature of the "Right to Read" campaign in-volve prescriptions that all children "ought" to read. When questioned about why children ought to read, advocates provide such answers as "to obtain a job," "to maintain a high standard of living," or for "leisure activities," all of which may or may not be desirable justifications. These "oughts" imply long-range considerations about the value of reading that may not withstand systematic scrutiny.

In regard to this particular slogan—the "Right to Read"—the analyst is not primarily interested, philosophically speaking, about whether persons do or do not actually have such a moral "right," but what is meant by the slogan. Even though a particular analyst may personally agree that people should have the right to read, he does not attempt to prescribe that right from the standpoint of philosophy itself. To the analyst, prescription is not the business of philosophy. Thus, in analyzing the meaning of "Right to Read," the analytic philosopher would seek to build an explanation of the various uses of the concept—the language "games" being played—showing inconsistences, emotional reactions, contradictory assertions, and external influences that shed light on implied meanings.

Some analysts advocate devising *paradigms;* that is, constructing models of logic that serve to help us clarify and order our concepts. This is similar to Wittgenstein's idea of "language games in some respects" but differs in that a paradigm has a rather specific use. It is "tailor-made," so to speak, for particular kinds of problems. Gordon Eastwood has described an appropriate analytic paradigm as one that has "a syntactically and semantically appropriate language system" that should be prescriptive only to the extent that it "enable(s) the formation of hypotheses to guide research for facts not now known." In this regard, paradigms are useful for looking at educational problems in an objective, nonpartisan, and unemotive way.

Eastwood has even suggested that large-scale paradigms be used, and he has criticized many analytic philosophers of education who direct their attention to small (or what Eastwood calls insignificant) problems. Instead, philosophy of education must be concerned with theory building in education from the standpoint of emphasizing the logical foundations of theory, and Eastwood argues that we must envision this task from an appropriate paradigm standpoint to approach it in any adequate sense.

Jerome Popp has noted that one may choose different paradigms for different purposes, and it is not necessary to choose global or universal paradigms. At the same time, however, he cautions that consistency seems preferable to wild eclecticism. Popp recognizes that the search for large-scale paradigms involves to some extent "world view" outlooks that are very close to old "grand manner" philosophy. It could be argued, for example, that the paradigm approach contains the seeds of destruction for the analytic approach to philosophy. It eschews the large-scale point of view, but it needs the larger picture to give coherence and meaning to its task.

Jonas Soltis has observed that, in the late 1950s and early 1960s, we underwent a shift from a "pragmatic paradigm" to an "analytic paradigm." Pragmatic philosophy could no longer deal adequately with urgent contemporary problems, and so students of philosophy turned to the new paradigm of analysis that seemed more in line with the concerns of the day. However, apparently analysis is now coming to suffer from similar shortcomings, and it must shift its focus from small-scale problems to larger, more encompassing ones.

Henry J. Perkinson talks about education in terms of various *functions:* intellectual, moral, emotional, aesthetic, political, and economic. Looking at education in such terms helps us to see education in all its multifaceted aspects. Rather than viewing education as a confusing, conflicting series of activities, the paradigmatic approach helps us to isolate activities and examine specific aspects of those activities as we have never before been able. Thus, Eastwood's suggestion falls in line with the way science operates, but as Perkinson points out in *The Possibilities of Error: An Approach to Education*, there is no single critical method, only different approaches. The critical approach only looks for what is wrong. The use of paradigms can help us to examine existing theories, remove inconsistencies, modify actions, and replace institutions.

One of the areas with which analysts have spent much time is the activity of teaching. Paul Hirst has shown the need for empirical research on the effectiveness of different teaching methods. Most methods, he claims, are based on little more than hunches and personal prejudices. Hirst states that teachers need to be clear about the nature of the central activity in which they are professionally involved. How, for example, do we characterize teaching from other activities? Is a teacher teaching when he sharpens a few pencils and breaks up squabbles among the children? One must admit, says Hirst, that teaching is a "polymorphous" activity; it may take many different forms. To know that teaching is going on we must clarify the aims and the intentions so that each activity is seen in a clear relationship to those aims. Successful teaching seems to be teaching that brings about desired learning. Yet, this desired learning could result from conditioning or indoctrination. If one wishes to study the difference between conditioning and indoctrinating he should postulate a perfect case of each in its most literal and ordinary use. Then we can understand the differences of the meaning of each term, that is, conditioning or indoctrinating. Even though there will be differences, there will also be similarities of meanings for each term with which everyone will agree, thus clarifying the meaning of each term. The clarified agreed-upon meanings become the different modes of teaching by which actual cases are compared. Thus, teaching methodologies are established based on teaching modes that serve as benchmarks or standards of minimal performance. If one were to ask, "How would you teach X to someone?", then reference could be made to the appropriate mode. Of course, disagreements as to proper modes could continue to arise so that there may be several other models on how to teach.

It should be pointed out that analysis is an ongoing activity. Conclusions are not arrived at full-blown and axiomatic. They do not precede investigation but flow from it. The major thrust of analytic philosophy is to try to arrive at clarified principles, agreements, and conclusions, rather than to start with them. In this sense philosophical analysis follows in the footsteps of the Socratic view of philosophy as the search for wisdom.

Philosophical Analysis and Curriculum

Analysts such as Richard Pring point out that terms such as integrated studies, integrated curriculum, unified knowledge, broad fields of experience, and problem solving are confusing and misleading. Such statements or phrases as "the seamless coat of learning," and "the unity of all knowledge" lack clarity of meaning and certainly possess no inherent value in and of themselves. Conversely, phrases such as "traditional," "subject matter," and "compartmentali-zation" are not necessarily bad in and of themselves. These slogans and phrases dealing with curricula have been used to set up straw men polarized along conceptions of good and bad.

Curriculum used to be viewed as something established in order to achieve certain ends, but it seems that today the ends flow from the curriculum itself. Hugh Sockett maintains that throughout the literature on curriculum there is a great deal of talk about taking means to ends and conceiving of the relation between means and ends as contingent. Sockett argues that what must be maintained as central to any account of curriculum, aims, and objectives is human intentionality, or our conception of what we are doing. Therefore, our conceptions must be clear.

Philosophical analysts are aghast at the flippant manner in which educa-tional plans are made. Curriculum planning is too often superficial and badly planned. Cultural bias is almost the only rationale one can discover in too many curriculum plans. There seems to be little systematic or careful planning done. Often this is not the fault of the persons involved so much as it is the faulty language, confused meanings, and unclear purposes involved. We not only need to examine present curricula in terms of these problems, but we need to promote an ongoing critical attitude toward curriculum restructuring in which meanings and purposes are made clear.

Pring says that the foremost philosophical problems in curriculum and curriculum integration are what meanings are involved, what assumptions are made about knowledge, what the forms of knowledge are, what the interrela-tionship between these forms is, and what the structural unity of language is. Thus, we see that any concern with curriculum goes far beyond the idea of plugging subject areas into a switchboard of school programs. Unfortunately, today we have many people who see curriculum reform very narrowly and give little attention to the deeper questions involved. Analysts believe that greater attention must be given to the philosophical aspects and have encouraged greater work in this area.

Critique of Analytic Philosophy in Education

It is true that analysis has been an indispensable part of philosophizing since its inception, and every serious philosopher has done analysis to some degree. There is always a need for clarifying ideas and refining concepts. Much in the writings of philosophers from Plato to the present points to the need to use language carefully and to avoid inconsistencies and illogicalities. It is undoubt-edly true that a major problem is the confusion in understanding provided by unclear or careless language. It is easy to document the misuse of many words and concepts such as "liberal," "conservative," "God," and so forth. History is replete with instances of how the misuse of words and the misunderstanding of meanings have led to internal strife, religious differences, and even full-scale wars. Some analysts maintain that since language is so important to thinking, it is almost inconceivable that we could think at all without it. They further observe that confused thinking may well be the poor use of words in the thinking process.

One of the functions of philosophy is to develop a critical attitude toward language, and meaning, and this is certainly something that analysts have fostered. Rather than accept ready-made answers, clichés, and slogans as solutions for educational and social dilemmas, they have supported an approach that insists that all ideas and issues be examined every step along the way. Analysts are wary of "the grand manner of philosophizing" in which there is a cry for synthesis and simple solutions to very complicated problems. The analyst is skeptical of a utopian attitude toward problems in which emotive or predetermined ends may lead our thinking awry. He is also fearful of the emotional factors that may overshadow clear and dispassionate thinking. This is not to imply that analysts are cold and unemotional people, but they are well aware of the dangers of passionate and fuzzy thinking.

Critics of analytic philosophy of education have pointed out that while analysis has helped educators clarify and define some educational problems better, this may be too limited a view to meet the demands of our changing, complex culture. Shying away from prescription has helped to make philosophers of education more wary of grandiose statements, but at the same time some critics point to the fact that while philosophers have ceased to prescribe, many other people such as psychologists and sociologists continue to make grand prescriptions. There seems to be little evidence that these latter sources for contemporary educational prescriptions are necessarily superior to the philosophical sources. Indeed, some persons say that they are worse.

One of the things that frustrate critics of philosophical analysis is that it is difficult to ascertain what analysts really want in terms of education. In fairness to philosophical analysts, it should be emphasized that they have seldom claimed or pretended to introduce any prescriptive maxims for educational practice itself. Yet, while analysts claim their only wish is to clarify language, it is extremely difficult for many critics to see that their work has really achieved any great clarification. It is true that analysts have uncovered ambiguities and misconceptions in education. But where do we go from there? Wittgenstein wanted to "let the fly out of the bottle," but where does the fly go once it gets out? Suppose we had a nicely clarified and precise language with regard to education. Possibly the purely descriptive and analytic approach can give us positive clarity about what we are doing in education, but if we are doing the wrong things to begin with, the wrongness is not necessarily corrected simply by language clarification. To maintain that language clarification itself will reveal inhumane and wrong educational practice is, it seems, to express a mystical belief in the power of language at the expense of action. This should not be misunderstood, however, because we *should* clarify our ideas and statements. Clarification, however, does not rule out prescriptions and recommendations about the problems of life. Indeed, it should help us to arrive at better formulated and constructed recommendations that do not necessarily have to come from science.

Perhaps part of the critic's frustration lies in the efforts of some philosophical analysts to say that true philosophy can only be analytic, or that analysis inevitably leads to the death of traditional philosophy. Where, then, do our visions come from? Surely, philosophy is not the only historical source for social renewal, and it is evident that many philosophical recommendations and utopian schemes are nonsensical, unworkable, and even completely inhumane. However, it seems just as certain that philosophy has as great a role to play in formulating social and educational policy as any other intellectual pursuit. Dewey, in his quaint way, remarked that "while saints introspect, burly sinners rule the world." Analysts have seemed to be content to quarrel over the meanings of terms, phrases, and statements while the world around them paid respect to their efforts by simply ignoring them. It could be said that philosophical analysis is little more than a new form of scholasticism, where instead of arguing about how many angels can stand on the head of a pin, analysts debate about how the words "should" and "ought" may be used. One disgruntled critic charged that when someone points his finger at a problem, the analysts study the finger rather than the problem.

While analysts eschew prescriptive and *a priori* assumptions, it seems, that in general, philosophical analysis has its own underlying and incipient assumptions or prescriptions. The penchant for paradigmatic models betrays a hidden assumption that there are clear, certain, and specifiable ways of doing things. This seems very close to philosophical realism's belief in a reality with its own inherent and universal principles. For example, Paul Hirst has stated that we need to know about the effectiveness of different teaching methods, but that " . . . without the clearest concept of what teaching is, it is impossible to find appropriate behavioral criteria whereby to assess what goes on in the class-room." This assumes that a clear concept of teaching can be uncovered. It also assumes that teaching can be assessed on the basis of "appropriate" behavioral criteria. The assumptions are these: there is a clear form of teaching, and there are appropriate teaching behaviors, and these things have an existence that can be studied, described, classified, and objectively duplicated. This is very close to the position of scientific realism.

No doubt we can construct teaching models that can be taught and duplicated. This fact is no proof that such models are desirable, of any consequence, or really useful. Because something can be done is no grounds logically, morally, or socially for doing it. Clarity and logic do not equal rightness, perfection, or certainty.

The analysts have attacked pragmatists, existentialists, reconstructionists, and others because they prescribe certain things and make normative judgments. But pragmatism, for example, tried to make us sensitive to the means-ends continuum; that is, that the actual ends achieved are continuous with, and contingent upon, the actual means used. Analytic approaches also may help us clarify actual means and ends, but aversion to making normative judgments as philosophers seems to be a classic case of the philosophical problem of the "failure of nerve."

Analysts have attempted to redefine the work of philosophy by refuting the old "grand manner" or "systems" approach. This effort has had some very healthy effects because it helps us to stop thinking in terms of categories and schools of thought. The analytic movement has helped philosophers develop and implement more refined linguistic and logical tools. The problem with analysis is, critics charge, that the tools have become an end in themselves quite apart from the practical uses to which they could be put.

Martin

"On the Reduction of 'Knowing That' to 'Knowing How' "

In this selection, Jane R. Martin, a contemporary American eaucator, further attempts to clarify Gilbert Ryle's famous distinction between "knowing that" and "knowing how."* Martin demonstrates how the techniques of analytic philosophy may be used to examine crucial philosophical concepts in terms of education. She distinguishes between several kinds of knowing and suggests how they may enter into the teaching process. Without proposing what should be taught or who should teach it, Martin maintains that there are several kinds of "knowing that" and "knowing how," and she examines the further implications of Ryle's distinction for both theory and practice.

The distinction between "knowing how" and "knowing that," which Gilbert Ryle makes in Chapter 2 of *The Concept of Mind*, is the point of departure for this paper. Ryle's object in writing *The Concept of Mind* was to discredit once and for all Cartesian dualism, or what he calls "the Myth of the Ghost in the Machine." The particular aim of Chapter 2 is to show that "there are many activities which directly display qualities of mind, yet are neither themselves intellectual operations nor yet effects of intellectual operations. When we describe such activities, we are not referring to a "second set of shadowy operations." According to Ryle, intelligent practice, that is, "knowing how," is not a "step-child of theory." On the contrary, theorizing, that is, "knowing that," is "one practice amongst others and is itself intelligently or stupidly conducted." In distinguishing between "knowing how" and "knowing that" Ryle hopes to correct the intellectualist doctrine which tended to view all knowing as "knowing that." He strongly opposed

the view that intelligent performance must be preceded by an intellectual acknowledgment of rules or criteria, that a person must "preach to himself before he can practice."

Ryle's distinction is clearly relevant to the problems of teaching and learning. For example, the learning of skills need not be preceded by knowledge of rules: men knew how to reason correctly before the rules of correct reasoning were formulated by Aristotle. Knowledge of rules is not sufficient for the performance of a skill: we do not say that a boy knows how to play chess if he can recite the rules but cannot make the required moves. In judging a performance we must look "beyond," not "behind," the performance. This does not mean we seek an occult cause for a skillful performance, but rather that a single sample of behavior is not sufficient to attribute "knowledge how" to an actor; we must take account of past record and subsequent performance as well.

Because of its simplicity and apparent

---

* Selection from Jane Rowland Martin, "On the Reduction of 'Knowing That' to 'Knowing How,' " in *Language and Concepts in Education*, ed. B.O. Smith and R.H. Ennis (Chicago: Rand McNally Company, 1961), pp. 399-404.

obviousness, the distinction between "knowing how" and "knowing that" has great appeal, but like any dichotomy it gives rise to much controversy and perplexity. Hartland-Swann has argued that "knowing that" can be reduced to "knowing how." Let us grant that his reduction holds if "knowing how" and "knowing that" are used to refer to a rather limited range of dispositions. Once "knowing that" is reduced to "knowing how," however, a distinction must be made between two types of dispositions subsumed under "knowing how."

It is of practical importance to analyze the various types of "knowing how" and "knowing that" sentences in ordinary speech and to make such differentiations as are necessary, even if the simplicity of Ryle's dichotomy or Hartland-Swann's reduction is thereby lost. Just as Ryle has drawn our attention to the dangers to education inherent in the reduction of "knowing how" to "knowing that," one may point out dangers inherent in a reduction of "knowing that" to "knowing how" if analysis is discontinued at that point. It would seem no more desirable to teach mathematical or historical facts as if they were skills like swimming than to teach swimming as if it were Latin or geometry. And an equally grave mistake would be to teach moral judgments and rules of conduct as if they were either Latin or swimming.

RYLE'S DISTINCTION

In order to formulate Ryle's distinction between "knowing how" and "knowing that" as clearly as possible, it is necessary to ascertain the meaning of the terms "knowing how" and "knowing that." Ryle calls "know" a capacity verb, and thus it is safe to conclude that he would call both "knowing how" and "knowing that" capacities also. (Ryle

differentiates capacities from tendencies, although both are dispositions. A tendency implies not only that something could be the case, but that it would be the case regularly when the appropriate conditions are realized; a capacity implies the ability to do something under specified conditions but does not imply frequency or regularity.) At no time does he say exactly what he means by the two types of knowing. From the examples he adduces and several of his statements, however, it is possible to determine that "knowing how" refers to skills or operations, for example, knowing how to play chess, knowing how to theorize, knowing how to speak Russian; and that "knowing that" refers to one's "cognitive repetoire," that is, to knowledge of factual propositions, as for instance, knowing that Sussex is a county in England, knowing that *Messer* is the German word for knife.

It is essential to note that Ryle assimilates all "knowing how" to the model "knowing how to perform a task" and all "knowing that" to the model "knowing that such and such is the case," for we then realize that his distinction is of a more limited nature than we might at first have thought. In ordinary language the phrase "knowing how" is often used when performances are not involved, and the phrase "knowing that" is found in sentences which do not refer to knowing factual propositions. For example, we say, "Johnny knows how a motor works," "I know how Eisenhower felt on election night," and "Jones knows how the accident happened." We also say, "Smith knows that he ought to be honest," "The child knows that he should be quiet when someone is speaking," and "Johnny knows that stealing is bad." None of these examples fits Ryle's paradigms for "knowing how" or "knowing that."

To summarize, Ryle's distinction between "knowing how" and "knowing that" is really a distinction between "knowing how to perform skills" and "knowing propositions of a factual nature." When Hartland-Swann discusses the question of the reducibility of "knowing that" to "knowing how," he too, I believe, is viewing "knowing how" and "knowing that" in this way. Thus in discussing his reduction one must not assume that it holds for all "knowing that" sentences. In fact, I think we will find that such sentences as "Johnny knows that he ought to be quiet" and "Jones knows that he should be honest" cannot be reduced to Ryle's and Hartland-Swann's "knowing how." This problem will be discussed in Section 3. First those sentences to which Hartland-Swann's reduction applies will be analyzed.

TWO KINDS OF "KNOWING HOW"

Hartland-Swann maintains that Ryle's distinction between "knowing how" and "knowing that" proves to be unstable when subjected to analysis. Every case of "knowing that," he says, is a case of "knowing how." This follows from the fact that "know" is a dispositional term. If I understand him correctly, what he means is that if we call the statement "Johnny knows that Columbus discovered America" dispositional, then it must be translatable into some such form as "Johnny knows how to answer the question 'Who discovered America?' or 'What did Columbus discover?' correctly." The only alternative to this inclusion of "knowing that" in the "knowing how" category, Hartland-Swann feels, would be to give up the dispositional analysis of "know."

I think one must agree with Hartland-Swann that a dispositional analysis of "knowing that" entails a translation of a "knowing that" sentence into a "knowing how" sentence of the type illustrated above, that is, knowing how to answer a question or to state a fact. It would be a mistake, however, to end the analysis of "knowing" with this reduction, for granted that "knowing that" can be reduced to "knowing how," there is still a fundamental distinction to be made within Hartland-Swann's new, expanded "knowing how" category. The basis for this distinction lies in the fact that two very different sorts of dispositions are subsumed under "knowing how."

Let us consider for a moment the case of Jones who was witness to the murder of Y. Without doubt Jones knows that X murdered Y, and this, in turn, means he knows how to state that X murdered Y and knows how to answer the question "Who murdered Y?" Yet it seems intuitively obvious that there is an essential difference between his knowing how to answer the question "Who murdered Y?" and his knowing how to swim or speak French. That is to say, the difference between the capacity involved in knowing how to state that X murdered Y and the capacity involved in knowing how to swim is more basic than the difference between the capacities involved in knowing how to swim and knowing how to do logic, or in knowing how to ice skate and knowing how to play the violin.

I would like to suggest that the feature which distinguishes these two kinds of capacities from each other is *practice*. That is, "knowing how to swim" is a capacity which implies having learned how to swim through practice; "knowing how to answer the question 'Who murdered Y' " is a capacity which does not imply having learned how to answer the question through practice. When Jones was a witness to the murder, he knew immediately that X murdered Y and did not need to practice stating facts or answering questions. Similarly, when Jones looks out his window and sees rain falling, he knows that it is raining without any sort of practice in saying "It is raining" or answering the question "What is the weather like right now?" To be sure, if he knows that it is raining, he *is able* to state certain facts and answer certain questions, but his capacity to do so does not imply that he has practiced doing so. On the other hand, Jones could not know how to swim or speak French unless he had at some time practiced swimming or tried to speak French. If Jones tells us he knows how to swim we are justified in asking him if he has ever tried to swim. If he answers "No" to our query, his assertion will be discredited. But if Jones tells us that he knows that X murdered Y, it surely would be nonsensical for us to ask him if he has practiced that assertion or tried to answer questions on the subject before.

If, as I propose, the difference between the two types of capacities subsumed under "knowing how" is based on the notion of practice, some interesting consequences follow. If knowing how to swim requires learning to swim through practice, then we usually would not consider the practice itself to be swimming. The practice may consist in kicking and arm waving and, if all goes well, these will gradually approach swimming. Although the point at which the practice in swimming becomes swimming is not for us to determine, it is interesting to consider the case of the individual who practices just up to the point where he actually swims and then gets out of the water. I think we could say of him that he knows how to swim even though he has not yet actualized this capacity by swimming.

Just as there may be cases of knowing how to swim which are not cases of swimming, so there may be cases of swimming which are not cases of knowing how to swim. For example, it is conceivable that Jones falls into the water one day and swims to shore although he has never practiced or tried to swim before. We cannot deny that he is swimming, but we might well wish to deny that he knows how to swim. In the case of swimming, of course, it is logically possible but in fact unlikely that there would be a performance of the skill which had not been preceded by practice. If, however, we think of a skill such as hitting the target, we realize that it is not too unusual for a novice to hit the bull's-eye without any previous practice. In such a situation we would maintain that although he hit his mark he does not "know how" to hit it. For we would expect someone who knows how to hit the target to hit it again. In other words, hitting a target is an occurrence which may be due to accident or luck; knowing how to hit a target is a capacity, and we would be right to look for a certain degree of consistency of behavior.

"Practice," of course, is a vague term. Although I do not think its limits need be set here, it is important to realize that many skills are related and that practice for one skill may thus serve as practice for another. Hence, on those occasions when it appears that we know how to do something without having practiced it, upon reflection we will discover that we have had practice in a related skill. It is possible, also, for the accidental or lucky occurrence to serve as practice for a skill. For example, if Jones swims to shore although he has never had practice in swimming, this very swimming may provide him with practice.

It is not denied here that we do exhibit some patterns of behavior with consistency although we have not practiced them. Yawning, crying, sneezing are examples. We call these reflexes, not skills, however, and do not speak of "knowing how" to yawn, cry, or sneeze. The exception is the case of the actor who is able to perform these behaviors at will. We might actually say of him that he "knows how" to yawn, cry, or sneeze, but it is clear that he has learned to do so through practice.

It appears, then, that although Hartland-Swann's reduction of "knowing that" to "knowing how" is legitimate for those "knowing that" sentences which are cases of knowing factual propositions, there is still a basic distinction between these sentences and the kinds of "knowing how" sentences which are cases of knowing how to perform an operation. Whether or not it is agreed that the basis for the distinction is practice, I do not think the distinction itself can be denied.

Selected Readings

Peters, R. S. *Ethics and Education*. London: Allen and Unwin, 1965.

This book gives an analytical exploration of such concepts as freedom, authority, equality, and democracy. It sets forth an ethical position with a point of view regarding moral theory.

Peters, R. S., ed. *The Philosophy of Education*. London: Oxford University Press, 1973.

This collection brings together writings of such figures as Paul Hirst, Israel Scheffler, and D. W. Hamlyn. The various contributors analyze and attempt to clarify such important concepts as the aims of education, curriculum planning, and educational relevance.

Scheffler, Israel. *The Language of Education*. Springfield, Ill.: Charles Thomas, 1960.

This work is a major statement by a leading analytic philosopher in the field of education. He examines the uses of language in education and the meanings of various educational concepts.

Soltis, Jonas F. *An Introduction to the Analysis of Educational Concepts*. Reading, Mass.: Addison-Wesley, 1977. Second Edition.

A brief but well-written introduction to analytic philosophy in education. This book is more restricted in scope than some introductory works in the field. It is recommended as an excellent beginning treatise on the uses of analysis.

The preceding chapters explored the contributions of various philosophical systems to educational thought. This chapter will investigate the nature of educational theory, the theoretical positions that have been derived from, or otherwise influenced by, philosophy, and the contributions philosophy can make to the further development of educational theory. In recent years, there have been some fundamental questions raised about the role of philosophical theory in education. There are those who maintain that theory is too unrealistic and remote, having little to do with the actual day-to-day problems of education. As a consequence, they say, what we need is less theory and better practice to deal with educational problems in the real world. There are others, including the authors of this book, who believe that theory can serve to modify and improve educational practice just as practice can modify and improve theory. In this view, theory becomes one of the most important and practical things with which an educator can work. Educational practice conducted without any sense of direction, purpose, understanding, or intent is blind. If there actually were no theories of education, our efforts would be characterized by random, aimless activity that some critics maintain is the actual case in education today. Even those educators who deny the relevance of theory usually have many explanations about why they do things. These explanations generally serve a theoretical function, even if the advocate is unaware of it. For example, it is often said that "experience is the best teacher," and this is usually meant to convey the idea that one learns best by actually undergoing certain experiences or doing certain things in relation to the things to be learned. This view is an essential part of the educational theory of progressivism. The progressives, of course, did not invent the saying "experience is the best teacher," but they made the idea of experience central to their theory and built up educational activities designed to foster "learning by doing" and to emphasize practical life activities every person would need to live successfully in society. While many teachers fail to link this theory with some of the familiar practices in classrooms today, there is a connection. Teaching will be much better informed and aware of itself when conscious connections with theory are made.

There is a definite need for more theoretical understanding, not less, and the intent here is to show how the study of philosophy has influenced theory development and how it may continue to do so. It may be claimed that the final test of any theory is what difference it makes for thoughtful practice and what consequences flow from its use. In the same way, practice informs theory and sets the conditions upon which theory may be altered and strengthened. It is difficult to construct sound educational activities and objectives without some intellectually guiding frame of reference to give them coherence and meaning. Also, it is difficult to construct sound theory without testing it in the crucible of practical educational activity.

PHILOSOPHY AND THEORY OF EDUCATION

The Nature of Educational Theory

Philosophy and the Theory of Education

Some philosophers of education make little distinction between philosophy of education and educational theory. In 1942, for example, John S. Brubacher wrote that "several theories or philosophies" could be used as guides to solutions of educational problems. In this view, philosophy of education is a discipline "peculiarly competent to tell what should be done both now and later on." Philosophy of education, then, has much to offer in the way of theory, even though there may be a great deal of disagreement among philosophers as to what theory or theories to carry out. In Brubacher's view, the need for philosophy becomes apparent when the educator, parent, or learner confronts questions about the proper aims and means of education. If a person tries to establish or select content, or choose a method, he must decide what he is trying to do and what aims or objectives are actually being proposed or assumed in the process. The development of educational aims, however, is complicated and gives rise to numerous philosophical questions: Are there "true" aims? Does the nature of life and the universe itself demand certain aims? Can we know what the "proper" aims of education are? Do aims flow from the practical activities of life and the problems confronting human beings in the course of the every-day world?

In deciding what the aims should be, one is also confronted with deter-mining what kinds of curriculum and techniques will be most adequate or suitable for achieving the aims. Many new questions must then be confronted—philosophical questions concerning the nature of knowledge, learning, teaching, and so on. Brubacher felt that too few educators could formulate or pursue such questions or give adequate responses about why things are done as they are in most schools. He maintained that the study of philosophy of education would help educators build more adequate theoretical bases, and hence, more ade-quate education.

By 1955, Brubacher was attempting to get educators to focus their attention specifically on pressing problems and use philosophical theory in dealing with them. He identified six major issues that revealed widely held assumptions about education to which philosophy of education could address itself: (1) anxiety that education is adrift; (2) concern that educational aims are vague, conflicting, and not conducive to loyalty; (3) beliefs that standards have been seriously relaxed; (4) uncertainty about the role of education in a demo-cratic society; (5) concern that schools give students too much freedom and do not foster respect for authority and control; and (6) fears that schools have become too secular and neglect religion. These problems sound familiar because they are perhaps as significant today as they were when Brubacher wrote about them. His point that philosophy of education could help solve them may not be accepted on a much wider scale today than it was in 1955, but his insistence still seems to be valid that these and other pressing issues cannot be treated satisfactorily without an understanding of philosophical theories that deal with the underlying assumptions about education in our culture.

Brubacher, of course, did not originate the notion that philosophy and educational theory are connected. This connection has a long tradition, but perhaps the most thoroughgoing link between the two was made by John Dewey in *Democracy and Education*, published in 1916. According to Dewey, it could be said that theory of education is a set of "generalizations" and "abstrac-tions" about education. Abstraction has received a bad name in popular speech because it is thought to be remote from practical affairs. It can, however, serve a useful purpose for, as Dewey put it, abstraction is "an indispensable trait in the reflective direction of activity." In this sense, theoretical abstractions or general-ized meanings have a connection with actual, practical affairs. Things are generalized so they may have broader application. A theory of education con-tains generalizations that are applicable to a number of situations. Theory becomes abstract in the remote or abstruse sense when it fails to make refer-ence to practical applications. In the sense of useful theory, however, abstrac-tion broadens it, in a public sense, to include any person or situation in like circumstances, and not just in a narrow sense of a solitary individual.

For example, Dewey observed that a person may know many things that he or she cannot express. Such knowledge remains merely personal and cannot be shared unless it is generalized and abstracted, or to put it another way, expressed in some public language. Then it can be shared and critically analyzed for improvement. In other words, for any one person's thoughts and experiences to be shared, he or she must take conscious account of the experience of others. Not only must experience be shared, but it must be taken back into practice for testing. In this way, practice serves to expand theory and direct it toward new possibilities. Practically everyone has had at least some experience with this because all of us have shared our experience of a particular thing or process with others. We may question friends or acquaintances about how they accomplished something, or we will tell them how we did it and recommend our way to them. Experienced teachers do this quite often. They exchange ideas and methods they have found fruitful in achieving certain educational goals. In this sense, they are theorizing or building theory, even though it may not be very sophisticated. One person tries another's approach, and afterward discusses it. They both find ways to redefine goals and vary, expand, or redirect the approaches for future use. The very "practical" matter of approaches and goals has been generalized to a degree, abstracted if you will. These approaches and goals have been tested and found successful, or they have been altered, improved, or found wanting. In this way theory and practice may build upon each other.

In the more sophisticated meaning of theory, the role of philosophy becomes crucial. In Dewey's view, philosophy deals with aims, ideas, and processes in a certain totality, generality, or ultimateness. It involves an attempt to comprehend varied details of life and the world and to organize them in an inclusive whole. It also involves a philosophical attitude, indicated by endeavors to achieve unified, consistent, and comprehensive outlooks on human experience. This is often what is meant by the definition of philosophy as "the love of wisdom." Completeness and finality in terms of certainty of knowledge are always lacking, however, for philosophy may also be characterized as "the pursuit of wisdom"; that is, it involves a continual search. Thus, terms like "totality" and "ultimateness" refer more to a consistency of attitude than to any final certainty of knowledge. Philosophy, then, is connected with thinking about and seeking what is possible, and not arriving at accomplished knowledge. It does not furnish solutions so much as it defines difficulties and suggests methods for dealing with them or clarifying them.

The philosophical demand for a total attitude, Dewey held, arises out of the need to integrate activities among the conflicting interests of life. It is an effort to discover some comprehensive point of view from which the conflicts may be brought together, and some consistency or continuity restored. This is shown in philosophers' efforts to attack the puzzles of life and bring clarity to confused situations. This kind of effort may involve the struggles of an individual to bring continuity to his own life, but philosophy at its most comprehensive stage seeks to deal with discrepancies and puzzles that affect the community as a whole. When coupled with education, this aspect of philosophy perhaps becomes

clearer because education is one of those inclusive human activities that concerns the whole community. To Dewey, education offers a vantage ground
"from which to penetrate to the human, as distinct from the technical, significance of philosophic discussion." When philosophy is viewed from the standpoint of education, the life-situations it studies are never far from view. As
Dewey put it: "If we are willing to conceive education as the process of forming
fundamental dispositions, intellectual and emotional, toward nature and our
fellow men, philosophy may even be defined *as the general theory of education*."

Some philosophers of education prefer a more inclusive view of educational theory than one only in terms of philosophy of education. For example, in
1971, Richard Pratte maintained that educational theory need not be specifically
philosophical even though it may have philosophical presuppositions. In other
words, educational theory not only uses philosophical tools but also the relevant
findings of psychology, history, sociology, and other disciplines. In this sense,
educational theory is broader than philosophy of education.

Behaviorism is a case in point. While it is not a philosophical system per
se, it has many ramifications for philosophical thinking that pertain to the nature
of freedom, human nature, social control, and individual and communal patterns
of existence. Indeed, many of its basic tenets are anchored on philosophical
assumptions rather than on the findings of social science. Thus, behaviorism has
all the earmarks of an educational theory that can be treated from a philosophical standpoint. Philosophical description and analysis may enlighten us about
the theory, but it does not tell us all there is to know about behaviorism.

According to Pratte, a distinguishing characteristic of theory is that it
consists of a plan and is an instrument for viewing, ordering, and examining ideas
and events systematically. A theory need not be "proven" in the sense of a
scientific fact; rather, it helps us generalize, explain, organize, and predict in at
least a limited way. Pratte gives as an example the postulate that "man is innately
good." This cannot be proven and it does not stand as fact, but it can be used to
enable us to organize educational ideas, aims, and activities in a particular
manner. The postulate serves as a guideline for organizing possibilities for
thought and action. It is not difficult to imagine that one who believes people are
innately good will come out with ideas, plans, actions, and directions far different
from those pursued by someone who believes people are innately evil. The
importance of the theoretical postulate in this case is connected with a fundamental attitude toward people, things, ideas, and so forth, of which Dewey
spoke. In other words, Pratte believes that a theory need not be tied to specific
or definite factual or material phenomena. They may influence it, but it is not
dependent upon them. What theory provides is "order and intelligibility out of a
miscellaneous and unrelated profusion of phenomena."

Take, for example, Darwin's theory of the origin of species. Most of the
central ideas of his theory had been enunciated by others before him. Even his
investigations of flora and fauna during the famous voyage of the *Beagle*, while
uncovering new and novel biological discoveries, did not add much new to the
theory itself. What did occur of major significance for theory was the manner in
which Darwin connected the many disparate elements into a coherent, compre-

hensive, and logical system, Thus, the world gained a renowned theory that has influenced us all.

According to Pratte, *explanation* or *description* is the essence of theory. The aim is to bring order and intelligibility to what appears to be a discordant and unrelated mass of phenomena. The effort is to link these together in some reasonable or intelligible whole by abstracting what is common to all the phenomena under study. Bits and pieces by themselves are unimportant, for they become significant only as they are bound together conceptually into a theory that accounts for them, explains them, and makes them meaningful.

Pratte cautions that educational theory is not the same as scientific theory. Scientific theory seeks to discount or negate nonscientific elements, particularly metaphysical beliefs and value judgments. Furthermore, it is based on the assumption that phenomena are caused by antecedent conditions (the cause and effect relation), and if causal conditions can be determined, then effects can be predicted within certain degrees of exactness. In these terms, the word "theory" is justified only when it is applied to established findings of scientific experiment. Scientific theory, then, is one of the end products of empirical research. The trouble with this version when applied to education is that educational theory does not serve as an end product but as a directive for rational educational practice. In other words, educational theory serves as a background and as a guide to practice. It does not predict *exact* effects; rather, it gives direction to what may or may not be done in a planned, practical educational activity. It serves an instrumental function of guiding practice. Scientific theory seeks to produce knowledge while educational theory seeks to produce practical activity and what is thought to be worthwhile educational outcomes. Educational theory, according to Pratte, "involves description, explanation, interpretation, and direction of the everyday interaction of human beings in an educational setting."

If we examine the basic points thus far discussed, we will see that certain elements stand out. First, there is the assertion that philosophy can enable us to build more adequate educational theory. This is based on several points and among them is philosophy's role in helping us to clarify aims and methods and to analyze underlying cultural assumptions about education critically. More central, however, is the role of philosophy in providing overall perspective and comprehensiveness. This is illustrated by the philosophical attitude of a consistent and continual effort to think about what is possible. The effort is largely dominated by concern for integration and continuity. Philosophy, in this sense, may even be considered to be educational theory in the most general sense. Educational theory may also be considered, however, to include more than philosophy because it uses relevant contributions from a number of fields. Theory serves as a guide to the organization of thought about education and helps to provide order and intelligibility to the process. It serves as a directive to educational practice by helping educators clarify and organize educational practice reflectively. A common element in all of these points is that central to philosophical and theoretical discourse on education is the necessity for reflection and the organization of ideas for eventual practical activity.

Theory and Practice

A common assumption many people make is that *good* theory can be directly applied to practical matters. It can be "plugged" into ongoing practical situations and yield direct results. If the theory does not work, it is obviously not a good theory. This assumption may be the reason that many people show disdain for theory and call it impractical, for there are few, if any, educational theories that can be applied directly to practical conditions in the sense one applies aspirin to a headache. There are those, however, who do attempt such applications of theory and who seldom fail to be disappointed.

Why this is so relates to the characteristics of both theory and practice. The point has been made that theory and practice must be connected and that each can inform and expand the other. To affirm a connection, however, is far from saying that there is a direct or one-to-one relationship between theory and practice. Dewey, who said philosophy is the general theory of education, also said, "It is an idea of what is possible, not a record of accomplished fact. Hence, it is hypothetical, like all thinking." Pratte characterized educational theory as a directive for practice, but, in addition, he wrote ". . . a theory is an instrument, a guide to thought, not necessarily a guide to direct practice."

Yet, theory serves a practical function in many ways, and if the "plug in" approach is usually doomed to failure, it is often not so much the fault of any given theory as it is its application. One practical feature of theory is its *general* nature. It contains ideas and propositions that allow for comparison, contrast, readjustment, and criticism from a variety of sources because they are stated in a public sense and are not locked only into the subjective thoughts of private individuals. Theoretical discourse invites argument and counterargument, for otherwise it ceases to be theoretical and passes into dogma or accepted "fact." Theory also is an aid in providing us with a more comprehensive perspective. It helps us evaluate or place in perspective what it is we are doing or could be doing. It helps us locate ourselves in relation to an overall or larger perspective. In addition, theory invites an attitude of seeking out possibilities, an attitude that constantly seeks a new or better way. Finally, theory aids in defining difficulties, clarifying confusions in thought and language, and sorting out and organizing plans for action. It provides rationale and gives direction to practical activity.

Practice, on the other hand, provides both raw materials and testing grounds for theory. The value of a theory may well reside in what difference it makes in the practical world by helping us in our approach to everyday educa-tional endeavor. William James was fond of quoting the Biblical passage, "By their fruits shall ye know them," and it is this character of consequences or outcomes that helps determine the validity of any theory. If a theory does not help us communicate in a better or more advantageous way, criticize our assumptions and actions, gain perspective, seek out new possibilities, order and direct practice, then we had better let it go or revise it in new directions. It has lost its connection with practice, and the fruitful interchange has ceased.

These, then, are some of the practical aspects of theory. Prescription of detailed classroom activities, however, is seldom one of the practical applications. The reasons for this are obvious enough if we examine the characteristics of theory. A major characteristic is that theory suggests possibilities; however, this does not mean that any theory could foresee all the possible practical situations confronting an educator in the fluid world of ongoing activity. Conditions change, people come and go, and even individual persons change and develop, so it is virtually impossible to establish preexisting rubrics that will always be applicable. The suggestion of possibilities aids us in organizing and directing our thinking about educational activity: it does not dictate the activity.

Basically, then, what theory accomplishes is that it helps us organize specific practices or practical activities with a sense of direction, purpose, and coherence. It gives administration, curriculum, and our daily plans order and organization, and it aids us in constructing, for example, specific teaching and learning objectives and accompanying methods and techniques. This is the practical connection of educational theory to educational practice, and in this sense educational theory can be applied to educational practice.

Theories of Education

Many of the different contemporary educational theories are generally outgrowths of more traditional philosophies or have their roots in those traditions. In preceding chapters, we examined some of those roots and traced the historical and contemporary development of each philosophy, showing some of its major influences on education. What follows will look at some of the contemporary educational theories that have evolved and show their connection to various philosophical traditions. The intent is not to trace all the elements of a given theory since a theory of education may draw upon several disciplines in addition to philosophy; rather, the focus is on the leading philosophical assumptions of the theories and their connections to philosophy. It will be noted that some theories are little different from their parent philosophies, while others are unique developments showing links with several philosophic approaches.

Perennialism

Although perennialism is a relatively recent term in educational thought, its roots can be traced back to classical antiquity. Though there are a variety of perennialists, all with their own special idea of what perennialism is and how it can be used in education, their basic motif is usually identified either with idealism or classical realism—sometimes a combination of the two. Most perennialists hark back to classical forms of idealism and find great affinity with the works of Plato. It was Plato who stressed the importance of ideas as the only true reality, and some perennialists say this is still true today. Others, while perhaps accepting some aspects of a material universe, even perhaps accepting it *in toto*, still stress the superiority of mind over matter. For that reason perennialists promote a cognitive approach to education—one that stresses thinking, and particularly philosophical thinking as its primary goal.

Essentialism

Probably, there are more varieties of essentialism than any other educational theory. The kind of educational philosophy espoused by the majority of essentialists is, however, of an empirical nature. When Aristotle declared the reality of matter as independent of the thinking process, he inaugurated a philosophical tradition that has led many essentialists to deemphasize a strictly rational approach to knowledge. They favored one that emphasized observational or empirical data as equal to, or superior to, rational thought. Although Aristotle believed that the philosophical and scientific ways of looking at things complemented each other, many scientists or technicians had difficulty in understanding the complementarity between science and philosophy. The predominantly rational approach permeated philosophy for so long, particularly in its religious emphasis, that it led many essentialists to revolt and put primary emphasis on an examination of physical phenomena. Thus, essentialist educational theory has tended to stress factual, observable data as predominant over a purely rational approach. In terms of actual practice, this theory dominates a great many schools today.

Thomism

Thomism is a theory based on the writings of Thomas Aquinas. It has been the leading philosophical system in the Catholic Church for a long time and exerts influence in Catholic schools today. It has also been strongly felt in many other religious organizations and institutions. Thomistic thinking begins with a realist orientation toward man and the physical universe, but its basic view is that the real purpose of life is to try and understand man's relationship with God.

Thomistic education places great emphasis upon exploring a material universe but believes that we must transcend purely physical phenomena in order to attain the universal principles or essences that underlie them. Thomism encourages us to see ourselves as part of a rational universe that we can understand in large part through a logical process of thought. Education must deal with both the temporal and spiritual sides of life, and Thomists believe that any worthwhile educational activity is one where we are led closer to the divine meaning of life.

Progressivism

The progressivist approach to education is to some extent an outgrowth of the pragmatic philosophy developed by Peirce, James, and Dewey. Like pragmatism, progressivism is a theory that extols the practical features of life, and one of the most practical and useful forms of social life is education.

What progressivists have emphasized more than anything else in education is problem solving. They feel that this is a learned activity and that a good problem solver is the one best equipped to face life's problems, whatever they may be. Like the pragmatist, the progressivist emphasizes workability. By learning the techniques of problem solving, we will be in the best position to find those things that work to make our lives more fulfilled.

Progressivists promote an interdisciplinary approach in education. They also emphasize the role of the learner in the learning process, and "learn by doing" has become a slogan identified with progressive education. Progressivists think learning should involve a cooperative interchange between school and society. They promote a democratic approach to learning and maintain that this affords the best approach for changing society in an intelligent and humane way.

Existentialism

Existentialist educational theory is an outgrowth of contemporary existential philosophy and focuses upon human existence in an "absurd" world. What the existentialists stress most is individuality, that is, the role of the individual as a choosing and commitment-making being. Existentialist theory opposes any single mode of education, but existentialists do feel that whatever we do in the name of education should allow the individual to pursue his or her own choices in a free environment. Existentialists are, as a rule, quite critical of modern education that they feel is largely propaganda stuffed into the minds of a captive audience. Modern education, they charge, does not provide enough room for individual thinking and for criticism.

Existentialists promote a neohumanistic, "inner-directed" approach to education. They feel that the learner should be allowed freedom of choice in terms of curriculum and educational outcome. They oppose treating the student as an object and believe that the best kind of education exists where the teacher and learner are equal partners in the learning process.

Humanism

Although all educational philosophies stress some kind of humanism, it has become a theory of its own without its adherents necessarily following any particular philosophical or psychological system. Basically, humanists believe that the focal point of any study is the human being. They are opposed to philosophical and religious systems that either ignore human problems, or relegate them to a lesser category. Historically, humanists claim, there has been a gradual freeing of humanity from fear, superstition, and authority. This has not been easy since many agencies such as schools, churches, businesses, and political systems have used people for their own ends. Man, the humanists cry, is an end in himself and should be treated so.

Humanists have strongly endorsed a humanistic curriculum in education. These studies, they say, focus upon interests, concerns, and problems germane to all people. Although such works may deal with powerful institutions, they show what man can do in the face of such power. Humanists believe that education should be more human centered in its scope. It should use the great ideas of both the past and the present to shed light on the human predicament.

Reconstructionism

It is not enough to say that reconstructionism as an educational theory is an outgrowth of pragmatic or progressive education because reconstructionism has a history as old as mankind. It might be said that if people had not developed reconstructed or utopian views toward change, we would still be living in caves. Reconstructionists feel that the seriousness of today's problems cannot wait for long-term solutions. They argue that education in its present form often adds to the problems of society rather than solves them. The kind of education they promote is one that is international in scope, contains a great deal of practical experience, and leads to social change.

Whereas progressivism provides a more liberal approach to social and political change, reconstructionism is more radical in nature. Progressivists believe that social change can be undertaken as a cooperative venture with various factions. Reconstructionists, however, promote immediate social change, even if existing social institutions must be changed or overthrown.

Marxism

Marxism is a comprehensive political system developed originally from the writings of Karl Marx. Marx believed that educators could make people realize how they are being exploited and give them the power to make changes in society. Marx felt that basically everything is a result of various economic forces that operate in a dialectical way. Education is also shaped by economic change and in turn helps to create new changes. Marxists argue that much of what passes for present education is really indoctrination to enslave the masses to existing economic, political, and social systems. The "hidden curriculum" teaches docility and subservience to the present system. They believe that such education must be eradicated if we are to prevent exploitation and move toward a world of economic and social justice. In order to do this, students must be exposed to new and radical points of view and encouraged to become agents for change in building a better society.

Behavioral Engineering

Behavioral engineering techniques are widely used in education today. While this approach may not be a theory drawn from a comprehensive educational philosophy like perennialism or essentialism, it still has many overtones for philosophical thought. Basically, behavioral engineering as developed from behaviorist psychological theory utilizes the techniques of operant conditioning. It advocates the use of immediate reinforcement (that is, reward and punishment) as the best method for obtaining specific educational goals.

Behavioral engineers agree that education and life are a process of formal and informal conditioning; thus, the argument should not be to condition or not to condition, but what kind of conditioning is best to achieve desired educational and societal goals. They point out that society has long supported the idea of developing individuals who are honest, truthful, loyal, and humane, and conditioning affords the best method for achieving such aims.

Behavioral engineers think of schools and other social institutions as total conditioning units. Through behavioral engineering we may initiate the kinds of changes necessary to create a new and better world.

Linguistic Analysis

Language analysis is an integral part of the analytic movement that has been of great importance in education in recent years. Although a concern for an analysis of ideas and concepts is as old as philosophy itself, it was not seen as an integral theoretical approach in education until recently. Today, there are some educational philosophers who argue that analyzing language should be a major focal point in educational theory. They maintain that what we need in education is to become aware of how language can be used to influence both thinking and action. Analysts are concerned that too many people accept educational ideas without seriously studying them. In many cases, this occurs because their education did not provide them with the necessary tools.

At one time in American educational institutions, particularly in institutions of higher education, logic was taught as the *sine qua non* of correct thinking. Today students rarely encounter the subject unless they are majoring in philosophy. Perhaps this explains in part why so many people are unduly influenced by sloganeering, advertising, and utterances from the political arena.

Some analysts would like to see a major emphasis on analysis and semantics in educational theory. They contend that not only educational problems, but the social, economic, and political problems of today could be solved or at least abrogated by a more precise and informed use of language. While language analysis has been most evident in university level teacher education, it has also had some impact on curriculum theory and educational policy studies. Its emphasis has not been so much on broad views of education or day-to-day classroom and school activities as it has been on how educational activities and problems are described and clarified.

Philosophy, Educational Theory, and Practice Reconsidered

The Question of Implications

In the recent past, a growing development in philosophy of education has served to split the field into two large factions. On the one hand are those who look to philosophical study as a means of developing a broad understanding of education. These people adhere more or less to a speculative approach, the "established" theories of education, or broad philosophical approaches. In most respects, members of this group maintain that philosophy of education should be a "normative" study or pursuit; that is, it should seek to find, study, or develop broad, general principles and explanations to aid in the development of educational practice. In still other respects, advocates believe that philosophy of education should be concerned primarily with a normative approach focusing on social philosophy and the moral nature of education. The second group maintains that speculation, traditional approaches, and normative philosophy have little to offer education. The proper course is to clarify the language of education, develop logical critiques of educational propositions, and concentrate on small-scale but pressing problems. This sector is most prominently influenced by a concern with philosophical method rather than with the construction of normative principles on a broad scale. Basically, this group is in general agreement and identifies with the "spirit" of the analytic approach to philosophy.

It is always somewhat artificial to divide a field of such diversity as philosophy of education into camps or groups, and the split is much more complex than can be shown by reference to two large factions. If the caution about complexity is kept in mind, however, it seems reasonable to try to explain the split or division between the broad approach and the more narrow, piecemeal approach. For purposes of discussion, the first grouping is called the "normative" approach, and the second the "analytic" approach. The complexity of the situation is further heightened because the split does not revolve about a single issue but swirls around a fundamental question: What is the role of philosophy of education in the development of educational theory and practice?

This question is clearly involved with the issue of whether a formal philosophy has logical implications for educational practice. In other words, can we logically develop educational practice from formal philosophy? Does what a Plato or a Dewey say have any direct logical bearing on educational practice?

It can readily be seen that questions of this nature strike directly at the heart of philosophy of education. If the answer is a clear, generally agreed upon, and demonstrated *no*, then a great deal of the body of philosophy of education is thrown into question, and the validity of many traditional and contemporary theories of education is called into question. A clear, general, and consistent negative response has not been forthcoming, however, and this lack of agreement is basic to the dissension in philosophy of education today.

In 1958, Joe R. Burnette explored the issue of logical implications and distinguished three conceptions. The first is what he calls the "lay view." The lay view assumes that formal philosophy is rich with implications for specific educational practices. It believes that formal philosophical principles can, by logical extension, provide statements about factual conditions, even those existing after the principles were constructed. This view, according to Burnette, is nonsense. A formal philosophical theory ordinarily has nothing to say about a specific matter of fact until that fact has been denoted and connected with the formal theory. This is akin to saying that since Plato recommended certain things about education based on his philosophical principles, we should follow those recommendations in a specific educational circumstance today. Plato could hardly have foreseen a specific or factual situation today, such as the role of nuclear power in modern life. He would have had a marvelous prescience in order to do so. Thus, the lay view of logical implication is unsuitable.

Second, there is the "formal" view that looks to valid form within a philosophy and logically deduces descriptions and prescriptions for educational practice without due regard for matters of fact in specific educational situations. This view is clearly wrong, Burnette maintains, if it concerns itself *only* with the philosophical position and not the practical educational conditions.

Finally, there is what Burnette calls the "situational" view. This is where people come to philosophy with experiences, outlooks about practical conditions, and other background knowledge. They come to the theory with practical contexts firmly in mind. When experiences with and knowledge of the contextual situation is given symbolic expression that can be connected with the philosophy, then the grounds are laid for drawing logical implications from the philosophy to develop theoretical and practical formulations in education. In other words, the logical connection of philosophical principles with practical contexts must go through a valid process. This is not totally a logical process, however, for the successful use of logical implications also involves connections of imagination and insight into the practical context, with a thorough understanding of the philosophy.

Hobart Burns countered this argument in 1962. He claimed that if there is any connection between a formal philosophy and educational practice, the connection is *psychological* and not logical, or put another way, the implications are "pragmatic" and not logical. Those who claim a direct logical connection are using the term "logical" too loosely. A logical implication is a *necessary* one, and claimants have not shown that the connection between a philosophy and prescribed educational practice is necessary because people can arrive at a very different prescription when starting from the same philosophical principle. Thus, the connections claimed to be logical are something else. Primarily, they are based on beliefs about the nature of education or human beings, and the implications or connections are more *psychological* than logical. A person follows some set of educational procedures because of his philosophic presuppositions. This does not mean that educational implications cannot be drawn from formal philosophy, but it does point to the need to be clear on the nature of the implication, a clarity that has not been fully explored and remains vague and ill defined.

The lines of dissension in philosophy of education today have more or less drawn around these kinds of positions and similar arguments on related issues. One faction has continued to pursue an "implications" approach to philosophy of education, and the other has moved toward a philosophical analysis of language problems in education. The divisive nature of these approaches is explored in more depth in the Epilogue. It is enough to say at this point, however, that neither faction has provided an entirely satisfactory resolution to the problem of philosophical implications.

In 1974, Clive Beck suggested that the controversy over implications swirls around a misunderstanding of the nature of implication. A philosophical theory or principle normally yields implications only in conjunction with other theories and principles. Thus, it is not necessarily illogical to find people who agree on *some* theoretical principles arriving at differing conclusions. Simply because two people embrace the same theory does not mean they agree on everything dealing with education. At the same time, two people who disagree on theory may also arrive at similar conclusions. According to Beck, the main reason for the breakdown between theory and practice is primarily the inade- quacy of the theories. Some theories are presented as if they have *all* the answers, and the limitations have not been adequately recognized. Other theo- ries deal only with specific aspects of the educational situation and thus fail to develop comprehensiveness and integration. The task is to recognize limita- tions, work out shortcomings, and articulate the various branches of theory into a coherent whole. However, theory must not become too general and abstract; if it is to have any influence, it must also be supplemented with a less abstract and general theory so that specific educational problems can be worked out. In addition, theory must be expressed in a language that is psychologically effective in guiding action. In other words, it must contain elements that stimulate and inspire on a comprehensive basis, and elements that give guidance to specific educational contexts.

This book has presented a number of philosophical positions in a "schools" or "systems" approach. The authors are well aware that there are drawbacks to this approach, for readers may fail to see how the philosophies are interrelated and connected, or how they may relate to contemporary educa- tional problems not specifically mentioned. However, in terms of an organiza- tional technique for introductory study, the approach has some advantages in that philosophical developments are presented in an organized and orderly fashion. This enables the reader to grasp the essential elements and basic principles of each philosophy and to see how they have influenced educational theory and practice.

Philosophers have recognized the difficulties of a "systems" approach to philosophy. John Dewey argued for the "reconstruction" of philosophy early in the twentieth century. He held that the concentration on "received" systems made philosophy a very conservative discipline, and the teaching of philosophy inevitably magnified the history of past thought. The problem is that philoso- phy's attention is drawn away from contemporary difficulties whose solution must then depend solely on other disciplines. Dewey, however, cautioned against turning abruptly away from all traditional issues. It would not only be impossible but it would be the undoing of those who attempted it. The ideas of philosophy are embedded in Western civilization and are a part of the thought patterns of most people. The task is to relate or translate newer movements, issues, or problems in terms of general ideas to assist in the clarification and redirection of thought for today.

We agree with Dewey and Beck that students of education need a comprehensive approach that includes the traditional with the nontraditional. Educators must have a variety of sources and directions to consider when facing the troublesome educational problems of today and tomorrow. There is no perfect system, method, or approach, and it is unlikely that there ever will be. We no sooner come to grips with one problem than the movement of events rushes us on to the next.

The material presented here can be used in a variety of ways, depending upon the previous background and knowledge of the reader, his or her motivations and interests, and the reciprocal relationship that exists between teacher and student. It is introductory, however, and the development of a mature grasp of philosophy of education requires both practical experience and concentrated study.

Developing a Philosophy of Education

Unless educators can see that philosophy of education makes a difference in their outlook or activity, they may fail to use it, or even ignore it altogether. Thus, they must translate philosophical ideas and thought patterns in ways that can lead to more consciously directed activity. This does not mean an uncritical acceptance of this or that principle or this or that system; rather, it means a responsible examination of philosophy of education in light of existing societal and educational conditions. As conditions change, there may be the need to reexamine perspective and outlook. Philosophy of education cannot be viewed in a vacuum but must be seen in the interplay with other forces.

Charles D. Marler has suggested a "responsible eclecticism" in building a personal philosophy of education. In suggesting this approach, he points out that no two people are at the same level in their intellectual and psychological development; therefore, perhaps no single educational philosophy may be suitable at any particular moment. This does not mean, however, that one should not consider various thought systems in relation to educational problems. We do need to be responsive to how philosophy of education can be used to help clarify and expand educational thought and practice.

Anyone who ventures through the typical American school of today can see how a variety of educational philosophies have influenced practice. It is difficult to find a school where only one philosophy of education exists. Even where one philosophy is dominant, it has generally evolved to fit newer demands. Beck distinguishes between an "official" philosophy such as one encounters in professional education courses and curriculum guidebooks, and "actual" philosophy that guides a person's everyday educational activities. Therefore, it is possible for a person to believe he is a progressivist and yet exercise authoritarian control and conduct classes through rote memorization. This has come about because of two reasons: the inadequacy of the philosophy in dealing with actual educational settings, and a lack of understanding of the nature of philosophy on the part of educators. Often, philosophical theories of education have become separated from the real needs of teachers. In addition, the theory is often written in a language so generalized and abstract that educators cannot connect the theory with specific situations. Beck says that the solution to this problem is to encourage educational theorists to present ideas in language that is psychologically palatable to the practitioner, that is, written in a way that the educator can connect theory with practice. While this may be difficult to do, the first step is to provide a comprehensive background that gives the teacher a framework on which to build his or her own teaching activities. This involves not only seeing theory and practice as related in the present context, but to see them as a part of an ongoing educational development.

Developing a philosophical perspective on education is not a simple or easy task. It is, however, a necessary one if a person wants to become an effective professional educator. A philosophical perspective helps one see the interaction among students, curriculum, administration, and goals; thus, philosophy becomes very practical. In addition, educators are often required to articulate a philosophical perspective in job applications, as members of curriculum committees, as spokesmen for school programs, in administrative statements on school policies, and even in explaining the purposes of classroom activities and curricular programs to parents and students. Most important, however, educators need a philosophical perspective in order to give depth and breadth of meaning and direction to their personal and professional endeavors. This is not to say that they must have a particular philosophical perspective; instead, educators must think deeply about what they do.

There is no one way to develop a philosophical perspective, yet some observations can be made that may assist in developing a perspective. One approach that could be used is as follows:

1. *Becoming aware of education as more than school or classroom activities.* It is easy for a classroom teacher or school administrator to get bogged down in the day-to-day details of operating schools. There is little time for reflection about what one does if he becomes enmeshed in meaningless details or loses sight of desirable objectives. An educator is often harried, and it is not uncommon to use this as an excuse for not thinking reflectively. For example, the classroom teacher may become convinced that the sum total of education is what happens in his or her classroom. The school principal may believe that the most important thing is an orderly master schedule or the administrative flowchart. However, education is interrelated with the development and direction a society takes, and a teacher must become aware of this. In the broadest sense, education involves at least two things: passing on the cultural heritage from one generation to the next so that at least essential social and cultural continuity exists; and providing the skills, abilities, and understanding to develop new ways of doing things in light of changing conditions. When educators become aware of education in these terms, a necessary ingredient is present for developing a philosophical perspective.

2. *Becoming aware that philosophy provides a comprehensive view of education.* An educator may develop a broad understanding of education, but this may lack a sense of focus and organization. Philosophy as a disciplined study is concerned with developing a coherent, logical, and comprehensive outlook. Philosophy has traditionally involved itself with a wide range of issues and problems, and

education has long been of importance to most philosophers. Thus, there is an extensive body of literature available to the educator to assist in bringing clarity to the awareness of education as a broad-based enterprise. When the educator becomes aware of the comprehensive perspectives and the tools for developing organized and structured views philosophy contains, the basic groundwork for a philosophical perspective on education has been laid.

3. *Studying the historical development of philosophical ideas and their relation to education.* The study of philosophical ideas does not guarantee a person will become an accomplished philosopher or conscious of all of the various forces affecting education. It does provide, however, a chronological and systematic body of knowledge one can use to understand what has happened in educational thought up to the present. It shows how aims, objectives, and practices have evolved and how what we often consider new departures in education are really only restatements of ideas that go back for centuries. It may also help one to develop an appreciation of educational traditions and provide the basis for a more intelligent and critical evaluation of such traditions. Not only does it give us a sense of continuity but provides us with a basis for developing new ideas and gives us a vantage point from which to evaluate new aims and practices.

4. *Studying the philosophical treatment and analysis of specific issues in education.* Philosophically, there is a need for both a broad perspective and one that focuses on particular problems. Problems such as equality of educational opportunity, moral education, human sexuality, religion, and political ideologies, may be looked at from the standpoint of psychology, theology, sociology, and political science. Yet, philosophical analysis has a unique contribution in that it can provide a look at such problems in a critical, holistic, and ethical fashion. It examines the interrelationship of the problem with other aspects of life and connects novel aspects of the problem with familiar traditions. It helps us to organize the various elements of the problem in a clear and concise way so that we can treat it more intelligently. Philosophy helps us to identify and express problems in clear and logical language.

5. *Engaging in continuing personal research, reading, and study in philosophy of education.* For an individual really to appreciate the uses of philosophical thinking, he or she must become personally committed to continuing study. One way this can be accomplished is to become actively involved in "doing" philosophy. Such doing may involve actually creating new outlooks through combining, interrelating, and drawing connections from philosophical ideas. Although the classroom teacher may argue that professional duties do not allow time for such doing, it may be observed that professional and personal growth often depend on independent reading activities

that provide a broader base for understanding educational problems and issues. An educator can also enhance educational perspectives by attending professional meetings where issues are discussed from a philosophical standpoint. Primarily, the educator must see the need for personal involvement and doing in order to develop a philosophical attitude toward educational problems.

6. *Developing a philosophical perspective and internalizing it.* When a person becomes deeply engaged in philosophical activity, there is usually a continuous reassessment and reevaluation of one's value system, social mores, authority constructs, and educational beliefs. It is this internal-external process where personal values and beliefs are held up against other philosophical perspectives that enable us to begin to readjust and modify, or strengthen our ideas. This process internalizes a philosophical perspective to the point where individuals not only think about philosophical ideas, but where such ideas become a part of their mode of professional behavior and outlook on life.

THE QUEST IN PHILOSOPHY OF EDUCATION

When one assesses the role of philosophy of education in today's society, he also assesses the role of philosophy in general. Historically, philosophers and philosophy have not always been in great demand even though the influence they have exerted on society's development has been significant. There are several reasons for this. First, the thinking person has generally been conceived differently from the doing person. This is not to imply that philosophers reject doing, but they have generally extolled reflection ahead of doing and have promoted the cognitive over other kinds of development. Further, the nature of philosophy is such that it encourages a constant reexamination and frequent change of existing ideas and institutions, and thus philosophical ideas have been looked upon as threatening by many people. Finally, we cannot overlook the fact that thinking, particularly philosophical thinking, is hard work. It demands extensive study and the development of a critical attitude. Plato suggested that the dialectic be reserved for those over thirty, and it was his contention that the development of philosophical wisdom is both a painstaking and slow process.

Some practitioners of philosophy of education find it annoying that they are not called upon more frequently by state departments of education, school systems, and other established social agencies to provide input into the educational process. This may be due to a general feeling that what the philosopher has to offer is not as valuable as that of the statistician or the curriculum consultant, or it could be a feeling that philosophers only obfuscate issues and never bring anything new to bear upon them. Some critics of philosophy maintain that contemporary philosophers are ensconced in their ivory towers either unable or unwilling to communicate with ordinary people. Some philosophers of education argue that it is not that they are unwilling or even unable to communicate their ideas; rather, the problems of education as they see them are so complex that their analysis may seem too abstract and complicated. John Dewey is a case in point. Because of the perceptive quality of his work he often ventured into thoughts about education that seemed abstruse and impractical.

In addition, Dewey's style of writing led to many different interpretations and reactions. Although Dewey attempted to write in a style that communicated with a wide and general audience, he faced the problem of trying to deal with extremely complex problems in a language system full of ambiguities. His use of the word "experience," for example, was interpreted by many to refer to a mentalistic kind of experience, whereas others felt it was purely behavioral and objective. He tried to use the word to include elements of both, but this only confused people further.

The dilemma posed by philosophers' desires both to inform and to be informed by participation in practical affairs is particularly acute in philosophy of education today. Part of the difficulty lies in connecting the results of philosophical reflection on education with those areas of practical life where such results may be educationally pertinent; part resides in confusion over the philosophical approaches and directions to be taken in the present and the near future.

The dilemma is not a new one. One may say that Socrates faced it in presenting his theories and trying to put them into effect. He met the ultimate confrontation when he tried to show his fellow Athenians that his ideas were uplifting rather than detrimental to existing society. Today the analytic movement, which has attempted to clarify the language of education, has faced insurmountable problems in making philosophical ideas more relevant to contemporary life. One might argue, however, that the age-old difficulty of joining thought with action is not necessarily bad. It may point to the need for a constant study of ideas on the most rigorous plane possible to improve their impact on human affairs.

The attention given to fixed systems of thought has been one enduring problem of philosophy. The problem with fixity in any area is that it stifles creativity, creates automatic responses to situations, and colors our view of the world. Human existence, however, is not always characterized by fixity, certitude, and systematic living, for old answers do not always speak to present problems. This has been particularly true in education, and there has been a concerted effort to move away from philosophical systems in dealing with educational problems in recent years. Dewey tried to do this by urging that we begin inquiry with actual human problems in order to arrive at solutions rather than to start with old philosophical assumptions. Existentialists have attempted to do this by promoting an antisystems approach and a radical individualism. The effort to avoid the pitfalls in a systems approach to thinking was one of the major factors in the birth of philosophical analysis. Numerous critics in philosophy and philosophy of education point to the difficulties in drawing implications from formal philosophies and applying them to the problems of education. They say it is an artificial approach that leads to answers that are both abstract and unworkable. The contemporary effort must go beyond such an approach.

A partial explanation for this divergent character of philosophy of education can be found in briefly tracing the development of the role of philosophy in American teacher education. As the public school movement gained momentum in the latter part of the nineteenth and the early twentieth centuries, pressures increased to provide more adequately for the preparation of teachers.

Where formerly "teacher training" had been left primarily to "normal schools" (often little more than specialized secondary schools), the direction now turned toward training at the college and university levels. One pattern was to include "pedagogical studies" in existing academic departments. In these circumstances, professors of "general pedagogy" held low status, and their presence was barely tolerated. Jonas Soltis sketched the development of philosophy of education in this context along three modes: (1) rare but sometimes rigorous efforts to produce original philosophical thought on education, (2) more frequent attempts to derive educational principles from philosophical schools of thought, and (3) often a "journalistic" or "cracker-barrel" approach to philosophizing about education. John Dewey, one who produced original educational thought at the time, came to dominate philosophical discourse on education in the first half of the twentieth century, and many philosophers of education settled into supporting Dewey or attacking him; deriving educational principles from the philosophical schools of idealism, realism, and so forth; or attempting to develop philosophical views from which to derive educational directives. If these methods proved unsuitable, they could always talk about Plato, Rousseau, Locke, and others. In addition, the glaring inequities in American life divulged by the conditions of the Great Depression in the 1930s led to the development of the social reconstructionist point of view, and educators were challenged to "build a new social order" through the schools. The attention of a number of philosophers of education thus came to focus not so much on abstract philosophical issues as on active participation in solving pressing social problems. Concern for rigorous philosophical investigation was not perceived to be an important priority. In short, by the 1950s, the situation had become very mixed and confused.

To many persons involved in the field at the time, the situation seemed to be deadlocked in an internecine feud among advocates of various "isms" over whose position was correct. There was also the tendency in many quarters to concentrate on educational issues without sufficiently grounding observations from the standpoint of philosophical methodology, even to the point of further separating philosophy of education from academic philosophy and the works being generated by professional philosophers of the day.

James McClellan discussed his experience as a graduate student in the 1950s. Dissatisfied with the state of philosophy of education, many young persons turned to what was called "the revolution in philosophy" afforded by the analytic approach as it developed in England and gradually came to be accepted in American philosophy. Although "revolution" may be too strong a word to describe what was happening, the changes certainly were to have important consequences. Students taken with the new approach chafed under the old rubrics, and although there was still fertile ground to be plowed there, they wanted to stake out their own territory and inquire into philosophy of education in the new directions charted by analysis.

Jonas Soltis described the movement as an effort, in part, to make philosophy of education legitimate by grounding it firmly in professional philosophy. It was an attempt to make philosophers first and educators second rather

than the other way around and to make philosophy of education more philosophical in the academic sense. Richard Pratte characterized the movement as a
reaction to a philosophical approach to education that denied the importance of
methodology. It moved away from a prescriptive or systems approach toward a
concern with clarifying philosophical and educational problems through a more
rigorous attention to method.

    Despite the efforts in some quarters to obliterate the systems approach
in philosophy of education as well as in philosophy itself, this approach is still
used and exerts influence. It is a rather simple way to organize philosophical
subject matter and lends itself to a chronological development. Many people are
predisposed to think in categories or frames of reference, and while this kind of
thinking has its problems, it is a condition to be built upon in order to arrive at
reconstructed thought or an "issues" approach to philosophy of education. The
systems approach may vary in organization, for in some instances there may be
a preference for organizing a system of thought around particular personalities
while others may prefer particular themes. The systems approach can be seen
even in the organizational scheme of historical eras of thought such as the Age of
Belief or the Age of Reason. Some of those who claim to reject the systems
approach unconsciously use it in the kinds of materials they select and in the
issues or meanings they seek to analyze. Even the eclectic approach reflects
"system" by selecting bits and pieces from other systems.

    The organizational approach used in this book is not meant to foster
slavish emulation of any one school, combinations of schools, or even a "schools
approach." The validity of the approach lies in showing how past philosophy
developed, how it has been organized systematically, and how it has been used
to help devise educational policy. Perhaps, after all, the major role of philosophy
in education is not to formulate some system or school of thought, but to help
develop the educator's thinking capacities. As each chapter tries to show, it was
the creative genius of individuals combined with particular cultural developments that eventually ended in a system or systems of philosophy. Individual
philosophers have seldom set out to construct just another system, and many of
them have vehemently rejected being placed or identified with any system or
school of thought. Thus, there is ample reason to say that the cutting edge of
philosophy is not necessarily a finished system, but rather the free and wide-
ranging process of thought in grappling with human problems. Perhaps the test
of any era of human history is not whether it built systems of thought that bound
together what so often appear to be irreconcilable conflicts, but how it went
about or enabled syntheses to occur. Every age accomplishes some kind of
synthesis, "world view," or consensus of thought that provides some basis of
agreement or common ground of varying degrees of satisfactoriness. However,
each age also must write its own "philosophy" or consensus anew. This does not
imply that old ideas are rejected, but rather that thinking goes on, that due
consideration of issues and problems is made, and that some common grounds
are agreed upon.

    An era of transition from an old order to a new one seems to be appearing
today. Some observers say we are leaving the Age of Machines and are entering

the Postindustrial Era. Others say we are suffering so much from the impact of rapid technological development that we are stumbling blindly from "future shock," unable to deal with our problems. Still others say we have entered into an age of experimentation where old values are being reassessed and altered in various life-styles as well as in our views of education. Perhaps every age faces similar difficulties of transition. Whatever the case, there is a great deal of confusion at present, and a new synthesis has not yet been achieved as far as we can tell. It often seems that negativeness, even disillusionment, is the rule rather than the exception.

This confusion is reflected in philosophy of education. Today we find those who have most persistently attacked philosophical synthesis are themselves unsure of their tactics. Perhaps the analytic and existentialist adherents were most vocal in the initial attack, but now some analysts say that we must go beyond the older analytic paradigm, while some adherents of existentialism quarrel back and forth about who is authentic and who is a "pseudoexistentialist" in philosophy of education. Both analytic philosophy and existentialism stand as primary examples of claims to an antisystems approach. Philosophy of education is perceived by some leaders in the field as split into two broad factions or going in two general directions. In 1972, Abraham Edel characterized it as being "at the crossroads." In 1979, Harry Broudy called it "Janus-like," facing two ways at once, and Richard Pratte's analogy was "a two-headed hydra" going in opposite directions.

There has been growing awareness on the part of some philosophers of education that the analytic approach has some serious shortcomings in dealing with educational problems. In 1970, Wolfe Mays examined the analytic "revolution" in philosophy and its impact on philosophy of education. He explored the claims of linguistic analysts that what they teach and the techniques they use are neutral with respect to the religious, ethical, and social beliefs they hold. Mays questioned whether it was possible or even desirable to be neutral on the issues of education. He charged further that the "therapeutic" philosophy practiced by some analytic philosophers is far from neutral, especially in the assumption that speculative philosophy is pathological and needs to be eradicated. Finally, Mays concluded that linguistic philosophy, with its emphasis on therapy, skills, language, and logic, is as much a product of contemporary times as older systematic philosophies were in their own time. Its claim to be neutral has often resulted in a negative stance of showing that philosophers can only concern themselves with the form and logic of argument, and never with the direction an argument should take.

Jonas Soltis, although an analytic philosopher by training and persuasion, has found what he considers to be "anomalies" that give "good reason to doubt the efficacy of the analytic approach" in dealing with certain educational problems. In a paper in 1971, Soltis described how analytic philosophers hoped to provide clarity without themselves making prescriptive recommendations. This "revolution" in philosophy soon spread into the area of education, winning converts and disciples. There was the hope of connecting general philosophy with philosophy of education better, thereby providing education with new tools it could use. Thus, there was the development of a new "paradigm" so successful in its thrust that it is now accepted as a major sector in the field of philosophy of education. Yet, Soltis voiced concern for two troubling problems, one internal and the other external to the analytic paradigm. In the first instance, he maintained that internally the analytic approach has not delivered on its promise to make fuzzy concepts clear and precise, particularly the concept of learning. The second problem is external to analysis and refers to persistent problems in education dealing with values and social issues, matters with which the analytic paradigm is apparently incapable of dealing in its present form.

Soltis used the ideas of Helmut Kuhn to illustrate what may be happening. Kuhn, in *The Structure of Scientific Revolutions*, tried to show how major shifts had occurred in the development of the natural sciences. Such shifts supposedly happened whenever an existing scientific paradigm failed to address itself to pressing problems. Soltis maintained that such a state of affairs may now exist in philosophy of education where the analytic paradigm is failing to provide promised clarity or to deal effectively with social and value issues. A shift may occur if the analytic paradigm does not meet both the internal and external demands placed upon it. Soltis did not venture to say whether such a shift will happen, but he did state that the demands in the areas of learning theory and social and value issues must be met in some fashion by philosophy, whether analytic or some new paradigm. This, he predicted, is the major challenge of the future in philosophy of education.

What is important for present purposes is not so much the fate of analysis as it is the need for a shift or change of direction. However, even if one keeps the example of analysis, there are those who recommend that it cease being neutral and proceed forthwith to deal more effectively with the pressing issues on the contemporary scene. For example, in 1972, Abraham Edel recommended that a more thoroughgoing integration of experimental, normative, and sociocultural concerns be made within the analytic paradigm rather than outside it because the weakness lies within the analytic method as it is now established and not with the general approach. To be effective, however, it must expand not through addition but through integration. In effect, Edel called for major changes in philosophy of education to meet pressing problems, and while he saw analysis as a viable movement to make such changes, he felt it would have to include ethical and social considerations as integral parts rather than ignore them as is now largely the case. While Edel's proposals are not quite so drastic as what Soltis has implied the future may hold, the call is still there for a change that is, to say the least, substantial.

In 1979, Richard Pratte recognized some of these criticisms and responded to them. The brunt of the criticism has focused on the alleged inadequacy of analytic methodology, he held, and it has been charged that analysis has retired from the traditional philosophical approach in education in dealing with meaningful problems; instead, it opts for piecemeal, small-scale tasks of "clarifying meaning, noting distinctions, detecting presuppositions, and so on." In effect, critics are asking analysis to be more than a methodology and become a systematic philosophy, the avoidance of which has been a hallmark of the analytic mode of philosophizing. As Pratte pointed out, analysis makes a major contribution in examining the logic of claims made about education and in clarifying the concepts central to the theory and practice of education. If Pratte rejected efforts to make analysis "systematic" and took issue with the "broad issues" approach, he also recognized that more traditional approaches and analytic approaches can enrich each other and need not be incompatible.

Thus, more recently, the need for a coming together has been recognized, not so much along lines that one side or the other of the "Janus-like" or "two-headed hydra" character of philosophy of education must change, but rather that joining in a common cause to develop philosophy of education itself must occur.

The point is that the philosophical task is still, in spite of contemporary movements to be antisystems, a task involved in the search for wisdom that, if not a "grand manner" approach as in the old days, is still at least an inclusive search.

Existentialism is another philosophy clearly in opposition to a systems approach. Jean-Paul Sartre and Albert Camus once complained that they were categorized under the all-inclusive label of "existentialists." The objections of these two philosophers are acutely pertinent when one realizes that their particular positions on the meaning and role of existentialism created a rift that has never healed.

Existentialism began as a philosophy of protest, clearly seen in the writings of Kierkegaard. He protested not only the social conventions and mores of his time but traditional attitudes in philosophy as well. Contemporary critics such as Brian Hill have maintained that many writers on existential educational theory have done a great disservice by presenting it as another "ism." He has been particularly critical of writers who portray existentialism as one would idealism or realism. Kierkegaard stated that "an existential system cannot be formulated," for the existential way of looking at things is an alternative viewpoint leading to any number of possibilities. Kierkegaard strongly attacked the "ismatics" of Hegel that he felt were both objectionable and unwarranted. Yet, as Hill has pointed out, those analysts who believe they have found an ally in existentialism are sorely mistaken. Their criticism is based on the need for logical or experimental verification, whereas existentialists maintain that rational categories do not accommodate the individual, and analytic methods are just as seriously at fault here as are other philosophical approaches. Existentialists reject the view that clarity is the surest way toward advancing the fulfillment of human potential. They have advanced an awareness of the human as a being not always or even primarily in objective reflection but in subjective decision making.

This idea of subjective decision making is paramount in existentialist philosophy, but many critics have pointed out that it has its dangers in possibly leading toward solipcism or nihilism. The student movement of the 1960s with the cry of "doing one's own thing" led some young people to reject all established values and institutions including all philosophical and religious systems. Sartre argued against such views by his attempt to relate existential philosophy to

Marxism, and he pointed to the fact that one does not have to ignore all organization and structure to retain one's authenticity. Other existentialists such as Marcel, Tillich, and Buber saw their philosophy not in opposition to all formalized systems of thought, particularly religious thought, but as integral and challenging elements of such systems.

In 1979, Donald Vandenburg traced the development of existentialism and phenomenology in philosophy of education since 1950. His observations may be drawn along three broad developments: an initial fascination with existentialism, a move toward phenomenology in the effort to develop a suitable methodology, and finally, the effort to develop a "hermeneutics" approach to philosophical problems in education. Existentialism first attracted attention in American educational circles in the 1950s and gained a fairly substantial follow-ing in the 1960s and into the early 1970s. Its nihilistic features, that is, its focus on meaninglessness, powerlessness, and homelessness seemed to speak to exist-ing personal and social conditions at that time. Adherents also found another side of existentialism, however, and this is its emphasis on working through the absurdities of the world by what Vandenburg has called "enthusiastic engage-ment" to find authenticity and to become self-consciously aware of one's own existence. Many adherents found difficulties with existentialism when they became aware that engagement and authenticity were invariably intertwined with conscious awareness of the world. Phenomenology seemed to provide a methodology to describe the evolution of conscious awareness of the world, especially from the standpoint of the child or learner. Efforts to develop phe-nomenological descriptions of education as it occurs within an individual's life occupied some philosophers of education in the late 1960s and early 1970s.

Vandenburg argued, however, that we must move beyond phenomenol-ogy to "hermeneutics," or to an interpretation of educational phenomena. Hermeneutics is based on the idea that the chief task of the educational theorist is to establish the conceptual framework of educational phenomena. The "her-meneutic theorist" gives priority to the object of inquiry and allows the method-ology to become "field dependent," that is, determined by the particular circum-stances of the inquiry. Thus, several methods may be called for including logical, phenomenological, and analytic methods. The suggestion is that a hermeneutic approach calls for a collaborative or "neutral" philosophical study of education. This gets us away from warring ideological "isms," schools of thought, or methodological camps. Whether such a development will grow from hermeneu-tics, however, remains to be seen.

The problem of viewing education in terms of systems, categories, or "isms" has not been solely the problem of philosophy of education, but a problem of philosophy in general. Plato's monumental treatise the *Republic*, which many commentators consider more a treatise on education than politics, shows system building at its zenith. Plato, due probably in some measure to his love for mathematics, attempted to put forth the ideally perfect and logical system. From Plato down through history there have been attempts to see mankind's development in some understandable, coherent, and orderly fashion. Descartes believed that he was beginning anew to construct an orderly way of thinking that would be uncontestable. This same attitude is found in Kant, Hegel, and even some contemporary philosophers. Today, the feeling for such philosophical order and categorization has either vanished or has been seriously modified. Dewey talked about facts and propositions but couched them in the rhetoric of "warranted assertibility." Reconstructionists talk about goals but with the realization that they may have to be changed on short notice. Both pragmatists and reconstructionists agree that things are too ever shifting and fortuitous for final statements to be made on anything. Even some modern idealists have lost their desire for championing authoritative statements either about man or the universe. Everything is subject to flux and change, and old absolutes are deposed by new uncertainties.

The current mood in philosophy of education today is generally toward understanding and dealing with problems and issues in a contextual sense rather than a return to the idea that individual, society, and education can be understood in an overriding system of thought. The conviction that a set of categories or systems can explain the multitude of variables that pervade actual conceptual, social, and individual relationships in education is gone. There is also an increased awareness of the danger that system building can itself lead to circumstances where we explain actions and events in terms of great and overriding principles, whether they be Kant's categorical imperatives or Descartes's "clear and distinct ideas," rather than in terms of the actual contexts of activities and events.

Thus, philosophical thinking in education has moved into a new arena. The emphasis is not on categorical development but rather on human puzzles and predicaments in specific contexts. Analysts and existentialists have recognized the problem, but it is not altogether clear that they have made the situation any more palatable. In their own zeal for clarity or authenticity, they have unwittingly erected programs of thought that often obscure the very issues with which they were initially concerned, be they linguistic clarity or the potentiality of the human individual. As a result, too many educators talk about aims without any understanding of the relation to the means used to obtain them. Behavioral engineers, for example, discuss education in terms of individual and social control, with a benign sense of the problems and dangers of control and the ensuing ramifications of wide-scale conditioning.

If philosophers no longer seek to provide general explanations and descriptions of the overriding scheme of things, a reasonable query may be "Who will?" Harry S. Broudy recently observed that many people will continue to identify philosophy with the search for wisdom, and they will look to philosophy of education for more than "logical purity and wholesome skepticism." They are not and do not want educators and educational institutions to be neutral about their children's futures. This expectation for philosophical educational guidance may be unwarranted, as recent developments in philosophy of education seem to declare, but as Broudy put it, people are " . . . incurably metaphysical, and if the philosophy of education ignores or merely makes fun of this need, it will be satisfied by nonphilosophical sources."

In Broudy's view, the turn away from overriding substantive philosophical concerns occurred in higher education and has had relatively little effect on educators in elementary and high schools. It was his opinion, however, that we have entered into an era where larger, more substantive issues have gained importance, such as concerns for social justice, the environment, world peace, individuality and the common good, the third world, and personhood in mass society. Humanism and the problems of humanity may once again be in the forefront of scholarly attention.

For educators—teachers, counselors, administrators, and others—the practical problems of aims, curriculum, organization, methods, and teaching and learning continue to demand attention. Broudy emphasized certain things that educators have a right to expect from philosophy of education. These include attention to the problems of education in general and schooling in particular, clarification of educational concepts and issues, critical analysis of proposals and policies, and the advocacy of rational discourse and freedom in inquiry. Educators also have the right to expect at least some attention to be paid to systematic and coherent argument and inquiry into the educational enterprise as a whole. Finally, educators should expect "an interest and standard from which reliable beliefs can spring" from philosophy of education.

Despite the difficulties presented by the current state of philosophy of education, it is still true that the philosophical approach is one of constant probing and inquiry. It is participation in the questioning and challenging attitude of philosophy that this book hopes to encourage among educators.

It can be said that this inquisitive restlessness makes philosophy an enduring human enterprise, one that is never quite completed but is always in the making. In the final analysis, the search for wisdom may simply be an intensive search for better ways of thinking about human predicaments. This search involves education no less than other human concerns. Philosophy, when undertaken in this vein, is not a separate and exclusive search, but is part of human life and education.

SELECTED BIBLIOGRAPHY

Adler, Mortimer, and Milton Mayer. *The Revolution in Education*. Chicago: University of Chicago Press, 1958.

Alcott, Amos Bronson. *Journals*. Boston: Little, Brown, 1938.

Alinsky, Saul. *Rules for Radicals*. New York: Random House, 1971.

Aquinas, St. Thomas. *Basic Writings*. New York: Random House, 1905.

_____. *Summa Theologica*. Translated by Fathers of the English Dominican Province. 3 vols. New York: Bengiger Brothers, 1947.

_____. *The Teacher—The Mind*. Chicago: Henry Regnery, 1953.

Aristotle. *The Nicomachean Ethics of Aristotle*. Translated by David Ross. London: Oxford University Press, 1975.

_____. *Politics*. Translated by Benjamin Jowett. New York: Colonial Press, 1899.

Augustine, St. Aurelius. *Concerning the Teacher*. Translated by George G. Leckie. New York: Appleton-Century-Crofts, 1938.

_____. *Confessions*. Translated by Edward B. Pusey. New York: Modern Library, 1949.

Aurelius, Marcus. *Meditations*. Translated by Maxwell Staniforth. Baltimore: Penguin, 1964.

Ayer, Alfred Jules. *Language, Truth and Logic*. New York: Dover, 1952.

_____. *Russell and Moore*. Cambridge, Mass.: Harvard University Press, 1971.

Bacon, Francis. *Advancement of Learning and Novum Organum*. New York: Colonial, 1889.

Bayles, Ernest. *Pragmatism and Education*. New York: Harper and Row, 1966.

Beck, Clive. *Educational Philosophy and Theory: An Introduction*. Boston: Little, Brown, 1974.

Bell, Daniel. *The End of Ideology: On the Exhaustion of Political Ideas in the Fifties*. New York: The Free Press, 1960.

Bereiter, Carl, and S. Engleman. *Teaching Disadvantaged Children in the Pre-School*. Englewood Cliffs, New Jersey: Prentice Hall, 1966.

Bergson, Henri. *Creative Evolution*. Translated by Arthur Mitchell. New York: Modern Library, 1944.

Berkeley, George. *Principles of Human Knowledge*. New York: E. P. Dutton, 1910.

Bode, Boyd. *Progressive Education at the Crossroads*. New York: Newson, 1938.

Brameld, Theodore. *Education as Power*. New York: Holt, Rinehart and Winston, 1965.

_____. *Patterns of Educational Philosophy*. New York: Holt, Rinehart and Winston, 1971.

_____. *Toward a Reconstructed Philosophy of Education*. New York: Dryden, 1956.

Broudy, Harry S. *Building a Philosophy of Education*. Englewood Cliffs, New Jersey: Prentice Hall, 1961.

_____. "Philosophy of Education between Yearbooks." *Teachers College Record* 81 (1979): 130-44.

_____. *The Real World of the Public Schools*. New York: Harcourt, Brace, Javonovich, 1972.

Brubacher, John S. "The Challenge to Philosophize about Education." In *Modern Philosophies and Education*. The Fifty-fourth Yearbook of the National Society for the Study of Education, pt. I, chap. VII. Chicago: National Society for the Study of Education, 1942, pp. 289-322.

_____. *Modern Philosophies of Education*. New York: McGraw-Hill, 1939.

Buber, Martin. *I and Thou*. Translated by Ronald G. Smith. New York: Charles Scribner's, 1958.

Burnette, Joe R. "Some Observations on the Logical Implications of Philosophic Theory for Educational Theory and Practice." In *Philosophy of Education, 1958*. Proceedings of the Fourteenth Annual Meeting of the Philosophy of Education Society. Edwardsville, Ill.: The Philosophy of Education Society, 1958.

Burns, Hobart W. "The Logic of the 'Educational Implication.'" *Educational Theory* 12 (1962): 53-63.

Butler, J. Donald. *Four Philosophies*. New York: Harper, 1951.

_____. *Idealism in Education*. New York: Harper and Row, 1966.

Camus, Albert. *The Myth of Sisyphus*. Translated by Justin O'Brien. New York: Alfred A. Knopf, 1955.

_____. *The Rebel*. Translated by Anthony Bower. New York: Alfred A. Knopf, 1978.

Childs, John Lawrence. *American Pragmatism and Education*. New York: Holt, Rinehart and Winston, 1956.

_____. *Education and the Philosophy of Experimentalism*. New York: Appleton-Century, 1931.

Comte, Auguste. *A General View of Positivism*. Translated by J. H. Bridges. New York: R. Speller, 1957.

Conant, James. *Education and Liberty*. Cambridge, Mass.: Harvard University Press, 1953.

Counts, George S. *Dare the School Build a New Social Order?* New York: Arno Press, 1969.

Darwin, Charles R. *The Origin of Species by Means of Natural Selection*. London, England: Oxford University Press, 1958.

Descartes, René. *A Discourse on Method and Meditations*. Translated by Laurence J. Lofleur. Indianapolis: Bobbs-Merrill, 1960.

Dewey, John. *Art as Experience*. New York: Capricorn, 1959.

_____. *Democracy and Education*. New York: Macmillan, 1916.

_____. *Essays in Experimental Logic*. New York: Dover, 1953.

_____. *Experience and Education*. New York: Macmillan, 1938.

_____. *Experience and Nature*. La Salle, Ill.: Open Court, 1929.

_____. *How We Think*. Boston: D. C. Heath, 1933.

_____. *The Influence of Darwin on Philosophy and Other Essays in Contemporary Thought*. New York: Henry Holt, 1910.

_____. "The Need for a Recovery in Philosophy." In *On Experience, Nature, and Freedom: Representative Selections*. Edited with an Introduction by Richard J. Bernstein. New York: The Library of Liberal Arts, Bobbs-Merrill, 1960, pp. 16-69.

_____. *The School and Society*. Chicago: University of Chicago Press, 1915.

Durkheim, Emile. *Socialism and Saint Simon*. Edited by Alvin W. Gouldner and translated by Charlotte Satler. Yellow Springs, Ohio: Antioch Press, 1958.

Eastwood, Gordon. "Paradigms, Anomalies, and Analysis: Response to Jonas Soltis." In *Philosophy of Education, 1971*. Proceedings of the Twenty-seventh Annual Meeting. Edwardsville, Ill.: Philosophy of Education Society, 1971, pp. 47-54.

Edel, Abraham. "Analytic Philosophy of Education at the Crossroads." *Educational Theory* 22 (1972): 131-53.

Emerson, Ralph Waldo. *Essays*. New York: Houghton Mifflin, 1883.

Friere, Paolo. *Pedagogy of the Oppressed*. New York: The Seabury Press, 1970.

Freud, Sigmund. *Civilization and Its Discontents*. Translated by James Strachey. New York: W. W. Norton, 1962.

Froebel, Friedrich. *The Education of Man*. Translated by W. N. Hailman. New York: A. M. Kelley, 1974.

Gentile, G. *The Reform of Education*. New York: Harcourt, Brace, 1922.

Gibson, Etienne. *The Spirit of Medieval Philosophy*. New York: Charles Scribner's, 1940.

Greene, Maxine. *Landscapes of Learning*. New York: Teachers College Press, 1978.

_____. *Teacher as Stranger: Educational Philosophy for the Modern Age*. Belmont, Calif.: Wadsworth, 1973.

Hamm, Russell L. *Philosophy and Education: Alternatives in Theory and Practice*. Danville, Ill.: Interstate, 1974.

Harris, William Torrey. "Moral Education in the Common Schools." *Modern Philosophies of Education*. New York: Random House, 1971.

Hegel, Georg Wilhelm Friedrich. *The Phenomenology of Mind*. Translated by J. B. Baillie. London: Allen Unwin, 1949.

_____. *Philosophy of Right*. Translated by T. M. Knox. Oxford, England: Clarendon, 1957.

Heidegger, Martin. *Existence and Being*. Translated by Werner Brock. Chicago: Henry Regnery, 1968.

Herndon, James. *How to Survive in Your Native Land*. New York: Bantam Books, 1971.

Hobbes, Thomas. *Selections*. Edited by Frederick J. E. Woodbridge. New York: Charles Scribner's, 1930.

Horne, Harold H. *The Democratic Philosophy of Education*. New York: Macmillan, 1935.

Hume, David. *Treatise upon Human Nature*. London: Oxford University Press, 1941.

Hutchins, Robert Maynard. *Great Books, The Foundations of a Liberal Education*. New York: Simon and Schuster, 1954.

Huxley, Aldous. *Brave New World*. New York: Bantam, 1932.

_____. *Tomorrow and Tomorrow and Tomorrow*. New York: Harper, 1956.

Illich, Ivan. *Deschooling Society*. New York: Harper and Row, 1970.

James, William. *Pragmatism, a New Name for Some Old Ways of Thinking*. New York: Longmans, Green, 1931.

_____. *Talks to Teachers*. New York: Holt, Rinehart and Winston, 1899.

Jaspers, Karl. *Philosophy of Existence*. Translated by Richard F. Grabau. Philadelphia: University of Pennsylvania Press, 1971.

Jencks, Christopher. *Inequality: A Reassessment of the Effect of Family and Schooling in America*. New York: Basic Books, 1972.

Kant, Immanuel. *Critique of Practical Reason*. Translated by Lewis White Beck. New York: Liberal Arts Press, 1956.

———. *Critique of Pure Reason*. Chicago: University of Chicago Press, 1949.

———. *Education*. Translated by Annette Churton. Ann Arbor: University of Michigan Press, 1960.

Kierkegaard, Søren Aabye. *Fear and Trembling, and the Sickness unto Death*. Translated by Walter Lowrie. Princeton, N. J.: Princeton University Press, 1954.

Kilpatrick, William Heard. *Education for a Changing Civilization*. New York: Macmillan, 1927.

Kneller, George F. *Existentialism and Education*. New York: John Wiley, 1958.

———. *Introduction to Philosophy of Education*. New York: John Wiley & Sons, 1971.

Locke, John. *An Essay Concerning Human Understanding*. New York: E. P. Dutton, 1961.

———. *John Locke on Education*. Edited by Peter Gay. New York: Teacher's College Press, 1964.

Lodge, R. C. *Philosophy of Education*. New York: Harper, 1937.

Marcel, Gabriel. *The Philosophy of Existentialism*. Translated by Manya Harari. New York: The Citadel Press, 1968.

Maritain, Jacques. *Education at the Crossroads*. New Haven, Conn.: Yale University Press, 1943.

Marler, Charles D. *Philosophy and Schooling*. Boston: Allyn and Bacon, 1975.

Marx, Karl. *Capital*. Translated by S. Moore and E. Aveling, Moscow: Progress Publishers, 1965-1967.

———. *The Communist Manifesto*. Translated by Samuel Moore. London: Penguin, 1967.

———. *Writings of the Young Marx on Philosophy and Science*. Translated and edited by Lloyd D. Easton and Kurt Guddat. Garden City, N. Y.: Anchor Books Edition, 1967.

Maurer, Armand. *Medieval Philosophy*. New York: Random House, 1962.

May, Rollo. *Existence: A New Dimension in Psychiatry and Psychology*. New York: Basic Books, 1958.

Mays, Wolfe, "Linguistic Analysis and the Philosophy of Education." *Educational Theory* 20 (1970): 269–83.

McClellan, James E. "In Reply to Professor Soltis." In *Philosophy of Education, 1971*. Proceedings of the Twenty-seventh Annual Meeting of the Philosophy of Education Society. Edwardsville, Ill.: Philosophy of Education Society, 1971, pp. 55-59.

Meadows, Donella H. et al. *The Limits of Growth*. New York: Universe Books, 1972.

Modern Philosophies of Education. The Fifty-fourth Yearbook of the National Society for the Study of Education. Edited by Nelson B. Henry. Chicago: National Society for the Study of Education, 1955.

Montessori, Maria. *The Secret of Childhood*. Translated by Barbara Barclay Carter. New York: Longmans, Green, 1936.

Moore, George E. *Philosophical Papers*. New York: Allen and Unwin, 1959.

Morris, Van Cleve. *Existentialism in Education*. New York: Harper and Row, 1966.

_____, and Young Pai. *Philosophy and the American School*. 2d ed. Boston: Houghton Mifflin, 1976.

Neill, A. S. *Summerhill*. New York: Hart, 1960.

Nietzsche, Friedrich. *Thus Spake Zarathustra*. Translated by A. Tille. New York: E. P. Dutton, 1958.

Orwell, George. *1984*. New York: Harcourt, Brace, 1949.

Ozmon, Howard. *Contemporary Critics of Education*. Danville, Ill.: Interstate, 1970.

_____. *Dialogue in Philosophy of Education*. Columbus, Ohio: Charles E. Merrill, 1972.

_____. *Utopias and Education*. Minneapolis, Minn.: Burgess, 1969.

Pavlov, Ivan Petrovich. *Conditioned Reflexes*. Translated by G. V. Anrap. New York: Dover Press, 1960.

Peddiwell, J. Abner (pseud.). *The Saber Tooth Curriculum*. New York: McGraw-Hill, 1939.

Peirce, Charles S. *Philosophy and Human Nature*. New York: New York University Press, 1971.

Perkinson, Henry J. *The Possibilities of Error: An Approach to Education*. New York: David McKay, 1971.

Pestalozzi, Johann H. *How Gertrude Teaches Her Children*. Translated by Lucy E. Holland and Francis C. Turner. Syracuse, N.Y.: George Allen and Unwin, 1894.

Peters, R. S. *Ethics and Education*. London: Allen and Unwin, 1965.

_____. *The Philosophy of Education*. London: Oxford University Press, 1973.

Philosophies of Education. The Forty-first Yearbook of the National Society for the Study of Education, pt. I. Edited by Nelson B. Henry. Chicago: The National Society for the Study of Education, 1942.

Plato. *Republic*. Translated by B. Jowett. New York: Modern Library, 1941.

_____. *The Laws*. Translated by R. G. Bury. 2 vols. (Loeb Classical Library). New York: G. P. Putnam's, 1926.

Plotinus. *The Enneads*. Translated by Stephen Mackenna. London: Faber and Faber, 1962.

Popp, Jerome A. "Philosophy of Education and the Education of Teachers." In *Philosophy of Education, 1972*. Proceedings of the Twenty-eighth Annual Meeting of the Philosophy of Education Society. Edwardsville, Ill.: Philosophy of Education Society, 1972, pp. 222-29.

Popper, Karl. *The Open Society and Its Enemies*. Princeton, N. J.: Princeton University Press, 1966.

Pratte, Richard. "Analytic Philosophy of Education: A Historical Perspective." *Teachers College Record* 81 (1979): 145-65.

_____. *Contemporary Theories of Education*. Scranton, Pennsylvania: International Textbook, 1971.

_____. *Ideology and Education*. New York: David McKay, 1977.

Quintilian, Marcus F. *Institute of Oratory*. Translated by H. E. Butler. London, England: W. Heinemann, 1921.

Rafferty, Max. *What Are They Doing to Your Children?* New York: New American Library, 1963.

Reich, Charles. *The Greening of America.* New York: Random House, 1970.

Rickover, Hyman G. *Education and Freedom.* New York: New American Library, 1963.

Rogers, Carl. *Freedom to Learn.* Columbus, Ohio: Charles E. Merrill, 1969.

Roszak, Theodore. *Making of a Counter Culture.* New York: Doubleday, 1969.

Rousseau, Jean Jacques. *Emile.* Translated by Alan Bloom. New York: Basic Books, 1979.

Royce, Josiah. *Lecture on Modern Idealism.* New Haven, Conn.: Yale University Press, 1964.

Rugg, Harold O. *The Great Technology.* New York: John Day, 1933.

Russell, Bertrand. *Education and the Modern World.* New York: W. W. Norton, 1932.

————. *Education and the Social Order.* London, England: Allen and Unwin, 1932.

————. *Our Knowledge of the External World as a Field for Scientific Method in Philosophy.* London, England: G. Allen and Unwin, 1926.

————. *Principles of Social Reconstruction.* London: Allen and Unwin, 1916.

————. *Religion and Science.* Oxford, England: University Press, 1935.

Ryle, Gilbert. *Collected Papers.* 2 vols. New York: Barnes and Noble, 1971.

————. *Concept of Mind.* New York: Barnes and Noble, 1949.

Sartre, Jean-Paul. *Being and Nothingness.* Translated by Hazel Barnes. New York: Philosophical Library, 1956.

————. *Critique of Dialectical Reason.* Translated by Alan Sheridan-Smith. New York: Schocken Books, 1976.

————. *Existentialism and Human Emotions.* Translated by Hazel Barnes. New York: Philosophical Library, 1947.

————. *Search for a Method.* Translated by Hazel Barnes. New York: Random House, 1968.

Sarap, Madan. *Marxism and Education.* London: Routledge, Kegan Paul, 1978.

Schaff, Adam. *Marxism and the Human Individual.* Edited by Robert Cohen and translated by Olgierd Wojtasiewicz. New York: McGraw-Hill, 1970.

Scheffler, Israel. *Conditions of Knowledge: An Introduction to Epistemology and Education.* Glenview, Ill.: Scott-Foresman, 1965.

————. *The Language of Education.* Springfield, Ill.: Charles Thomas, 1960.

Shimahara, Nobuo, ed. *Educational Reconstruction: Promise and Challenge.* Columbus, Ohio: Charles E. Merrill, 1973.

Skinner, B. F. *Beyond Freedom and Dignity.* New York: Alfred A. Knopf, 1971.

————. *Walden Two.* New York: Macmillan, 1948.

Soltis, Jonas F. "Analysis and Anomalies in Philosophy of Education," *Philosophy of Education, 1971.* Proceedings of the Twenty-seventh Annual Meeting of the Philosophy of Education Society. Edwardsville, Ill.: Philosophy of Education Society, 1971, pp. 28-46.

————. *An Introduction to the Analysis of Educational Concepts.* 2d ed. Reading, Massachusetts: Addison-Wesley, 1977.

_____. "Philosophy of Education for Educators: The Eightieth NSSE Yearbook." *Teachers College Record* 81 (1979): 225- 47.

_____. "Philosophy of Education: Retrospect and Prospect" In *Philosophy of Education, 1975.* Proceedings of the Thirty-first Annual Meeting of the Philosophy of Education Society. San Jose, Calif.: Philosophy of Education Society, 1975, pp. 7-24.

_____. "Philosophy of Education Since Mid-Century." *Teachers College Record* 81 (1979): 127-29.

Strain, John Paul. "Idealism: A Clarification of an Educational Philosophy." *Educational Theory* 25 (1975): 263-71.

Thoreau, Henry David. *Walden and Civil Disobedience.* New York: Norton, 1966.

Thorensen, Carl E., editor. *Behavior Modification in Education.* The Seventy-second Yearbook of the National Society for the Study of Education, pt. I. Chicago: National Society for the Study of Education, 1973.

Tillich, Paul. *The Courage To Be.* New Haven: Yale University Press, 1952.

Toffler, Alvin. *Future Shock.* New York: Random House, 1970.

_____. *Learning for Tomorrow: The Role of the Future in Education.* New York: Vintage Books, 1974.

Troutner, Lee. "Making Sense out of 'Existential Thought and Education:' A Search for the Interface." In *Philosophy of Education, 1975.* Proceedings of the Thirty-first Annual Meeting of the Philosophy of Education Society. San Jose, Calif.: Philosophy of Education Society, 1975, pp. 185-99.

Vandenburg, Donald. *Being and Education: An Essay in Existential Phenomenology.* Englewood Cliffs, N. J.: Prentice Hall, 1971.

_____. "Existential and Phenomenological Influence in Education." *Teachers College Record* 81 (1979): 166-91.

Watson, John Broadus. *Behaviorism.* Chicago: University of Chicago Press, 1957.

Whitehead, Alfred North. *The Aims of Education and Other Essays.* New York: Macmillan, 1929.

_____. *Science and the Modern World.* New York: Macmillan, 1967.

Whitehead, Alfred North, and Bertrand Russell. *Principia Mathematica.* Cambridge, England: University Press, 1968.

Wittgenstein, Ludwig. *Blue and Brown Books.* New York: Barnes and Noble, 1969.

_____. *Philosophical Investigations.* Translated by G. E. M. Anscombe. New York: Macmillan, 1968.

_____. *Tractatus Logico-Philosophicus.* Translated by D. F. Pears and B. F. McGuinness. New York: Humanities Press, 1961.

Zeldin, David. *The Educational Ideas of Charles Fourier.* New York: A. M. Kelley, 1969.

Howard Ozmon is professor of education in the Division of Educational Studies at Virginia Commonwealth University. He received his doctorate from Teachers College, Columbia University. Dr. Ozmon has taught in elementary and secondary schools as well as at several colleges and universities. He has published numerous books and articles dealing with education and presently teaches courses in philosophy of education and futuristics.

Samuel M. Craver is associate professor in the Division of Educational Studies at Virginia Commonwealth University. He received his doctorate from the University of North Carolina at Chapel Hill. Dr. Craver has taught at both the secondary and university level. He is the author of several articles, papers, and books on philosophical issues in education, and his present interest is in ethics education.

NAME INDEX

Abelard, Peter, 22
Adeodatus, 7
Albee, Edward, 168
Alexander the Great, 6
Alinsky, Saul, 128, 141
Andreae, Johann Valentin, 122
Aquinas, Thomas, 46–48, 51, 53, 54, 64, 266
Aristotle, 41–47, 49, 51, 53, 64, 66, 81, 82, 89, 189, 190, 222, 233, 260
Augustine, 6, 7, 15–20, 22, 27, 46, 47, 121
Aurelius, Marcus, 121
Ayer, A. J., 220, 224, 225, 227, 228, 233

Babeuf, Francois, 122
Bacon, Francis, 45, 47–49, 53, 54, 55, 81, 82, 87, 96, 190, 233
Barnard, Henry, 123
Beck, Clive, 265, 266, 267
Beckett, Samuel, 168
Bellamy, Edward, 122
Bereiter, Carl, 207
Bergson, Henri, 42
Berkeley, George, 8–10, 16, 18, 84
    atheism, 10
Bestor, Arthur, 105
Bode, Boyd, 104
Bradley, Francis Herbert, 15
Brahe, Tycho, 48
Brameld, Theodore, 122, 125, 126–27, 128, 129, 139, 140
Broudy, Harry, 58, 275, 279, 280
Brubacher, John S., 253, 254
Buber, Martin, 157, 158, 166, 171, 278
Burnette, Joe, R., 264, 265
Burns, Hobart, 265
Butler, J. Donald, 15, 18, 21, 23, 28

Campanella, Thomas, 122
Camus, Albert, 277
Carlyle, Thomas, 15
Carnap, Rudolf, 194, 224
Childs, John, 104
Clark, Kenneth, 134
Coleman, James, 142
Coleridge, Samuel T., 15
Comenius, John Amos, 62, 65
Comte, August, 87, 193
Conant, James Bryant, 59, 65, 105
Cooper, James Fenimore, 85
Copernicus, Nicolaus, 48
Counts, George S., 125–26, 129, 130, 133, 137, 138, 142
Crusoe, Robinson, 85

Darwin, Charles, 87–88, 90, 256
Descartes, René, 8–9, 13, 18, 87, 191, 231, 232, 233, 278
Dewey, John, 55, 64, 82–84, 86–107, 123, 124, 125, 130, 142, 174, 233–34, 239, 245, 254–56, 258, 260, 264, 266, 271–73, 279
    aesthetic experience, 95
    consummatory experience, 95
    individuality and social relations, 93
    life adjustment, 85
    religious and moral development, 94
    scientific thinking, 83
Dickens, Charles, 58
Dionysius II, 6

Eastwood, Gordon, 241, 242
Edel, Abraham, 275, 276
Einstein, Albert, 26, 99
Emerson, Ralph Waldo, 15, 54
Engelmann, Siegfried, 207

Faulkner, William, 22
Feigl, Herbert, 194, 224
Fourier, Charles, 122
Freud, Sigmund, 192
Friere, Paolo, 137
Froebel, Friedrich, 62, 63, 86
Fuller, Buckminster, 128

Galileo, Galilei, 48, 67, 191, 231
Gardner, John, 128
Gentile, Giovanni, 15, 16, 18, 19, 21, 28
Goodman, Paul, 134
Gott, Samuel, 122
Green, Thomas Hill, 15
Greer, Colin, 142

Hall, G. Stanley, 86, 104
Hamm, Russell, 60
Harris, William Torey, 15–16, 19, 28, 123
    curriculum plan, 25
Hegel, Georg W. F., 8, 13–16, 18, 20, 21, 26, 28, 85, 90, 122, 156, 220, 277, 279
Heidegger, Martin, 158–60, 175
Hemingway, Ernest, 22
Herbart, Johann F., 58–60, 63
Herndon, James, 129
Hill, Brian, 277
Hirst, Paul, 242–45
Hobbes, Thomas, 189, 191
Hocking, William, 15
Hook, Sidney, 86, 98
Horne, Herman, 15, 16, 18, 19, 21, 25

SUBJECT INDEX